EURASIAN CROSSROADS

JAMES A. MILLWARD

Eurasian Crossroads
A History of Xinjiang

COLUMBIA UNIVERSITY PRESS
NEW YORK

Columbia University Press
Publishers Since 1893
New York
© 2007 James A. Millward
All rights reserved

First published in the United Kingdom by
C. Hurst & Co. (Publishers) Ltd.

Library of Congress Cataloging-in-Publication Data

A complete CIP record is available from the Library of Congress

ISBN 978-0-231-13924-3 (cloth : alk. paper) —

ISBN 978-0-231-13925-0 (pbk. : alk. paper)

∞

c 10 9 8 7 6 5 4 3

p 10 9 8 7 6 5 4 3 2 1

Contents

Illustrations

Maps

Figures

Preface and Acknowledgements

This book is a survey history of a region at the centre of Eurasia. Now known as Xinjiang (pronounced 'Hsin-jeeang'), this area has been known by many names in the past. One of those old names, 'Chinese Turkestan', might well have served as this book's title. 'Turkestan' was a term medieval Islamic writers applied to the northern and eastern parts of Central Asia—the lands of the Turkic speaking nomads, as opposed to the Persian-speaking dwellers in the oases. Marco Polo also used this name. When Tsarist forces conquered Central Asia in the nineteenth century they followed suit, calling their new imperial acquisition 'Turkestan'. Logically enough, European writers around the same time began to refer to those parts of Central Asia further east, those under the control of the Qing dynasty, as 'Chinese Turkestan', distinguishing it from Russian Turkestan.

Though old, the term 'Chinese Turkestan' retains a certain relevance. Xinjiang has for a millenium and a half been a land of Turkic-speaking peoples, now represented by Kazaks, Kirghiz and mainly the Uyghurs, who comprise the bulk of the non-Han Chinese population in the region. On the other hand, Xinjiang—as opposed to parts of Central Eurasia lying west of the Pamirs—has also long had close contacts with China, and for most of the time since the mid-eighteenth century it has lain under the control of Beijing. In this way, Xinjiang is indeed both Turkic and Chinese.

However, the term 'Chinese Turkestan' is controversial. Although the People's Republic of China (PRC) frequently refers to 'China's Tibet'—and even publishes an English-language propaganda magazine under that title—any reference to 'Turkestan' evokes the two short-lived 'Eastern Turkestan Republics' of the 1930s and 1940s, as well as the names of more recent Uyghur separatist groups. Since the PRC officially maintains that Xinjiang has been part of China since the first century CE, any allusion to the region's other past political and ethnic identities is unwelcome. It is the eighteenth-century term 'Xinjiang' by which the PRC and the rest of the world now refers to the area; the term 'Turkestan' only appears in China if carefully quarantined in quotation marks and attributed to Western colonialists or contemporary terrorists.

On the other hand, Uyghur nationalists, who consider the Xinjiang region their own homeland unjustly invaded and conquered by China, likewise have little use for the label 'Chinese Turkestan', though for opposite reasons: the term codifies the region's modern Chineseness.

The name 'Chinese Turkestan' thus reflects a key characteristic of the region's history—its ethnic diversity and situation at the overlap of cultural realms—and crystallises the problem of reconciling ethnic and political identities, a problem that has troubled this continental crossroads for most of the past century.

I am neither a Chinese nationalist nor a Turkic nationalist (rather, I like to consider myself a friend of both Han and Uyghur peoples and, more generally, of China). Still, no student of the region's history can escape the politics that suffuses Xinjiang studies today. It pervades the secondary literature, be it PRC publications or Uyghur websites. Scrutiny from Beijing forces even non-Chinese scholars to think and rethink what they write and say in public settings. (The draft of a recent volume of collected articles about Xinjiang by Western scholars was smuggled to China, translated, circulated and rebutted internally in the PRC before it had even been published in the United States.) US military expansion into Central Asia, the casting of Xinjiang tensions as part of the 'global war on terror', and the incarceration of Uyghurs in the US prison camp and off-the-books legal purgatory at Guantanamo means that Washington too has a growing interest in the Uyghurs and Xinjiang—an interest that makes the PRC in turn suspicious. Any effort to sort out the history of the Xinjiang region is complicated by these political concerns. Moreover, besides the rival primordialist claims on the region—is the region 'Chinese' since ancient times, 'Uyghur' since ancient times, or something else?—there are other issues with contemporary implications. What has been the role and nature of Islam in the area? What are the benefits and drawbacks of Xinjiang's twentieth-century development and globalisation? How have Uyghurs and other minority peoples in the PRC fared under the policies of the Chinese Communist Party? Is Uyghur dissent tied to international Islamist terror networks?

Although I address these and similar fraught questions in the follow-ing pages, the goal of this book is not to weigh in on the political issues besetting Xinjiang today. Rather, I hope to provide an overview to the history of a region that has played an important role in world history, but for which there is no good introduction in English. Xinjiang, as the hub of the Silk Road and point of contact of various Eurasian peoples and cultures, has long fascinated readers for its diversity and exoticism. But for precisely these reasons, the sources for the study of the region's history are challenging, requiring specialised knowledge and access to materials ranging from artefacts unearthed in the desert and paintings daubed on the walls of caves, to texts in Tokharian, Türk, Soghdian, Ti-betan, Mongolian, Manchu, classical Chinese, Chaghatai and Persian, not to mention important secondary works in Chinese, Russian, Japanese, French, Turkish, German and other modern languages. These materi-als are scattered in libraries and museums across the globe. Moreover, Xinjiang has in one way or another been part of the histories of the Tibetan, Arab, Turkic, Mongol, Russian as well as Chinese empires, so its historiography involves place names and personal names in multiple languages. Specialists in one of these historiographies may well struggle with terms from another.

Although there are important specialised works in English on Xinjiang history, for the non-specialist reader these have been somewhat hard to find and hard to grasp without considerable background knowledge. One great challenge has been precisely the lack of a general history to provide that background—I encountered this problem myself some years ago when I first began my study of the Qing empire in Xinjiang. This book, then, is an attempt to fill that gap with a synthetic survey of the history of the Xinjiang region from earliest times to the present—from Tienshanosaurus to the twenty-first century, one might say. Obviously, I have had to be selective, and my coverage is more detailed for more recent periods, with the twentieth century receiving the closest atten-tion. I have written this book for a general audience including students, travellers, journalists, politicians and policy-makers, as well as specialists in the history of China or Central Asia who wish to know more about Xinjiang. I believe, moreover, that even Xinjiang specialists will find something new in these pages: I have, for example, written the first at-tempt at a general history of the region since 1978. I do not pretend to have scoured every possible source or to be an expert on all aspects of

Xinjiang history; still, I have tried to base my survey on the most recent scholarship. The notes and bibliography should lead anyone who wishes into the specialised literature on particular periods and topics.

Although this book is intended primarily as a straightforward source of information, in the course of writing it I have identified certain themes that run through Xinjiang's history. These, I hope, lend the subject matter a certain unity despite the long time span and variety of peoples and regimes covered. For example, as mentioned above, the term 'Chinese Turkestan' encapsulates the cultural and political multiplicity of this region, its quality of overlap rather than exclusivity. As the crossroads of the Silk Road, Xinjiang lay astride routes linking the Mediterranean Basin, Persia, India, Russia and China. Xinjiang was thus both conduit and melting pot for the transfer of arts, technologies, ideologies and trade items across Eurasia. Palaeolithic hunter-gatherers crossed Xinjiang, as did early Eurasian farmers and nomads after them. Monks, missionaries, traders, soldiers, settlers and tourists followed thereafter. Xinjiang was also a meeting point for nomadic and sedentary societies, for the pastoralist Hunic, Turkic and Mongol peoples from the steppes and the farmers of the Tarim Basin oases.

Each of these peoples, ideas and products has been part of the region's history. Many peoples and cultures met in this region; extant artefacts and indeed the very faces of the region's inhabitants bear the stamp of those encounters. Although for much of the twentieth century Xinjiang has seemed a backwater, more recently its global linkages have expanded quickly and the region is now firmly enmeshed in global as well as pan-Eurasian networks. One main theme to be traced below, then, is Xinjiang's intermediate position, its role as a conduit, and its linkages to other places.

Any visitor to Xinjiang is struck by its geography. In an arid, wide-open region not only are geographic features—vast deserts, high mountains, broad steppes, snow-fed rivers—more visible, they also exercise more perceptible historical effects. Certain patterns of Xinjiang's past, notably the tendency of nomads based in the north (where one could raise horses) to control and tax the oases of the south (where one could raise grain), arise from its geography. As discussed in detail in Chapter 1, this feature of Xinjiang's geography also embroiled it in the enduring rivalry between nomadic powers based in Mongolia (which communicates easily with northern Xinjiang) and states based in north China.

Likewise central to the area's history is the role of water in supporting and limiting agriculture, settlement and urbanisation. Developments in the eighteenth century led to a rupture with past geopolitical patterns, a decline of nomad power, easier control of Xinjiang from north China, and increased Chinese settlement in the area. Nevertheless, efforts to integrate Xinjiang more closely to China still depend upon water supplies, which in turn remain dependent on the region's basin and range geography. Global warming, moreover, now threatens the future of those water sources. The role of geography and the environment, then, is a second theme arising at various points in this book.

As mentioned above, much of the writing of Xinjiang history in recent times has been shaped by contemporary nationalistic agendas. From a dispassionate point of view, however, any attempt to use history to claim the Xinjiang region as more 'Chinese' or more 'Uyghur' or even as a home for 'Europeans' (an assertion inspired by mummies from the Tarim Basin) is off the mark. The continental, racial and national categories with which we are accustomed today do not readily apply to earlier historical eras. The names which we ascribe to peoples in Xinjiang through history derive more from historiographical convention than from genetics. Throughout most of their history the population centres in southern Xinjiang have been ruled either by tribal powers based in northern Xinjiang, Semirech'e or Mongolia; by dynasties based in north China, sometimes comprised of Han Chinese, sometimes of Inner Asian élites; or by local ruling families made up of Mongol imperial descendents or orders of Islamic shaykhs claiming descent from the prophet Muhammad. Conventionally for those periods we write the name of the ruling power (Han, Hephthalite, Western Turk, Qarakhanid, Qara Khitay, Uyghur, Yarkand khanate, Zunghar, Qing) over the space Xinjiang occupies on the map. However, the subject population did not change with each new conquering élite, though the new rulers augmented the local population and cultural characteristics that had evolved over time. Religions came and went (Buddhism flourished then gave way to Islam), and languages of majority populations shifted (from Indo-European to Turkic to Sinic). The modes of social organisation and identity in this context, then, are themselves interesting subjects of analysis, as are the ways in which ruling powers accommodated ethno-linguistic, religious and socio-economic diversity among subject peoples in a diverse and fluid area. To assert a simplistic national identity upon this rich and fluid

past is a meaningless and ill-advised endeavour, particularly when the
contenders are such hard-to-define, historically-evolving notions as
'Uyghur' and 'Chinese.' The history of Xinjiang is the history of many
interacting peoples, cultures and polities, not of a single nation.

Thus a third theme runs through the narrative that follows: the variety of ways in which people in the Xinjiang region were organised
and organised themselves. We do not have the right kind of sources to
discuss 'identity' of Xinjiang peoples in detail for any time before the
twentieth century. However, as we trace the region's political-military
vicissitudes and the ebb and flow of various cultural influences, we may
strive to understand how political life and social identity were structured
in a place and time with no single prevailing national identity. Though
local oasis identities were no doubt strong, for many of Xinjiang's inhabitants broader associations were also possible. These included affinities
based on language (Tokharian, Turkic, Chinese, Soghdian); on religion
(Mahayana or Theravada Buddhism, Zoroastrianism, Nestorianism, Islam and various Sufi orders or particular holy men and their shrines); on
tribal lineages (Qarakhanid, Chinggisid Mongol, Zunghar, Kazak); on
loyalties to distant dynasties and their imperial metropoles (Chang'an,
Lhasa, Balasaghun, Moscow, Beijing); or to far-flung commercial and
familial networks (the Soghdians, Chinese merchant guilds). Xinjiang's
history provides examples of many kinds of overlapping political and
social groupings before the racial or national categories of 'Turkic',
'Uyghur' and 'Chinese' became current in the twentieth century.

Because over the past two millennia Xinjiang has fallen under many
empires and been entered into many historiographies, the places of the
region have many names. The city of Turfan—or cities very near its current site—for example, has been known at various times and in various
languages as Jushi, Gaochang, Qocho, Qarakhoja, Turpan and Tulufan.
Southern Xinjiang is referred to in the literature as Kashgaria, Altishahr,
Huibu, Nanbu, Little Bukharia, the Tarim Basin and Eastern Turkestan.
Even today many cities have two names and more than two spellings:
Ghulja, Kuldja, Kulja, I-ning and Yining are all the same place: a large
city in north-western Xinjiang.

There is no simple solution to the challenges of Xinjiang place names.
One cannot simply pick a standard form and stick with it, because for

historical, linguistic and political reasons there is no universally accepted standard. Were I in this book to call the main city in south-western Xinjiang by the Chinese name commonly appearing on today's maps, for example, it would be 'Kashi'. Would readers then recognise this as the same city that Marco Polo, the *New York Times* and most of the historical literature calls 'Kashgar'? Even the modern Uyghur spelling in modified Arabic script, 'Käshgär', differs from that in older texts written in Arabic scripts.

I have chosen, therefore, the following compromise. My main goal is not to be consistent, but to guide non-specialist readers through the onomastic thicket of Xinjiang history. Thus I generally use the place name most appropriate or recognisable for a given time period; this is usually the name most commonly used in the secondary literature about that period. In the index and at first appearance in each chapter, however, I gloss that name with other names for the same place, especially where both Turko-Mongolian and Chinese names are current for a single city. Where possible I use linguistically accurate transcriptions, but I avoid most diacriticals and do not value technical accuracy above easy recognition and pronunciation by the reader. Although some people still use them, I eschew old spellings based on the romanisation system introduced for Uyghur in the 1960s in the PRC (*yengi yäziq*). This system had many problems and has now been officially abandoned.

Many of these same concerns apply to personal names, the spellings of which are if anything even more varied in the literature than those of place names. Here too I have adopted user-friendliness as my main principle. Where I have been able to ascertain their standard spelling in modern Uyghur, however, I have attempted to transcribe modern Uyghur names consistently in Uyghur, rather than in either Arabic or Chinese form.

In the course of writing this book I have received help from many institutions and individuals. I am thankful for summer and sabbatical support from the Edmund A. Walsh School of Foreign Service and the Graduate School of Georgetown University. In addition, Georgetown's National Resource Center for Eurasian, Russian and East European Studies (CERES) has on two occasions funded my research for this project through its Title VI grant from the Department of Education.

A Woodrow Wilson Center/George Washington University Asian Policy Fellowship in 2001–2 provided me with a year's leave from teaching, during which time I was able to write four chapters of this book (and finish editing another book). For the half of that year that I spent at the Woodrow Wilson Center, Janet Spikes helped track down old books and articles from the Library of Congress, and my intern, Frew Hailou, helped gather other materials. During the second half of that year I enjoyed the collegial atmosphere of George Washington's Sigur Center for Asian Studies, where Bruce Dickson, Mike Mochizuki and David Shambaugh engaged me in thoughtful discussions and Debbie Toy and Ikuko Turner were unfailingly friendly and helpful. Both the Wilson and Sigur Centers furnished me with opportunities to present my work to interested audiences.

During that same year Yves Chevrier invited me to give a seminar at EHESS in Paris, where I was pleased to meet a group of scholars engaged in research on China's frontiers, including Paola Calanca, an old classmate from Renda, whose hospitality I enjoyed. The staff at the photo-archive at the Musèe Guimet graciously allowed me to preview a large collection of photos from the Pelliot collection before they were fully ready for posting on the web.

Hakan Wahlquist, Stefan Rosen and 'Uncle Sven' were my hosts in Sweden, where I had the chance to speak at the Institute for Oriental Languages at Stockholm University and visit Gunnar Jarring's collection of books on Central Asia and the Hedin Collection at the Ethnografiska Museet Library. The staff at the Riksarkivet in Stockholm efficiently guided me through the photo archive of the Swedish mission in Kashgar. The archive generously permitted me to reproduce several of the photos from the Samuel Fränne Östturkestan Samling free of charge in this book. Margareta Höök, who was born in Kashgar but later evacuated to Kashmir in a cradle slung from the back of a yak, treated me to a curry and her fabulous transparencies taken by the mission in Xinjiang. Later, Eric Nicander of the Lund University Library helped me locate a reference and facilitated my obtaining another illustration used below. The photo of Adil Hoshur, which appears in the conclusion, is reproduced courtesy of Deborah Statman, who also explained to me a good deal about her times with the Uyghur diwaz artists.

Other trips and other colleagues have likewise helped make this book possible. Miao Pusheng, Xue Zongzheng and other scholars at the Xinjiang Academy of Social Sciences in Urumchi organised a seminar on short notice for my benefit; I filled a notebook with their suggestions for sources I should read. I'd particularly like to thank Pan Zhiping for his comments on my work. The Xinjiang Regional Archive allowed me to consult their holdings on two separate occasions. While in Beijing I have often met with Ma Dazheng and Li Sheng of the Frontier History and Geography Research Center and Xinjiang Studies Institute, and have benefited greatly from their own and other publications by members of their units.

I am grateful to Mrs Krishna Dey, Mrs Jaya Ravindran and Mr P.K. Roy for their help at the National Archives of India, where I learned something of the situation in Kashgar after the British consulate became the Indian and Pakistan consulates. During my stay in New Delhi Gudi and Om Malhotra made their home my own and fed me grandly. Savita brought me my morning bed-tea, and Sachen Malhotra introduced me to the dangerous pleasures of *car me bar* in flooded streets of Lajput Nagar after a downpour.

My thanks to Professors Nakami Tatsuo and Shinmen Yasushi for bringing me back to Japan in 2004 and 2005 and providing me with opportunities to present my work to Japanese colleagues and benefit from the deep and broad scholarship on Xinjiang being carried out in Japan. Anyone who hopes to work in the field of Xinjiang history really must consult the Japanese scholarship—ideally, more than I have here. Sugawara Jun continues to amaze and educate me with his knowledge of modern Xinjiang and the new historical sources he discovers. Who knew that one could still buy old documents wholesale in Kashgar bazaars in the 2000s? My thanks for Professor Kusunoki Yoshimichi's invitation to participate in the 42nd annual *quriltay* of the Japanese Altaic Studies Society, an enriching and enjoyable time on the quiet shores of Nojiriko, and to Seo Tatsuhiko for allowing me to present my work in his symposium on cities and the environment at Chuo University. Steve Tong and Anne Campbell generously shared their home in Tokyo with my family for a summer, letting my wife and I convert their dining table into a desk. While we tapped away on laptops, they served us the best cappuccino east of the Pamirs. We are extremely grateful for their hospitality and friendship over the years.

Back in Washington, Mi-chü Wiens and the staff of the Asian Reading Room are always helpful during my visits to the Library of Congress.

Nor could I have consulted on-line resources so easily without the assistance of the reference librarians at Georgetown's Lauinger Library. At Georgetown's University Information Services a former student of mine, Ryan Norton, has exorcised my trickiest computer gremlins. (He's better than many other techies because, as a historian at heart, he solves problems by *doing research*.) Jim Clark and his informative website taught me a bit about Xinjiang palaeontology. Doug Eagles, Steve Hannum, Sara Fisher and Steven Singer of Georgetown's Biology and Chemistry departments responded to an odd question from a historian colleague with a spirited email discussion of the comparative salinity of desert groundwater, blood and camel urine, a conversation on which I was privileged to eavesdrop.

Gardner Bovingdon, Jay Dautcher, Al Dien, Ruth Dunnell, Turdi Ghoja, Ablet Kamalov, John McNeill, John Olson, Matthew Oresman, Alexander Papas, Peter Perdue, Sean Roberts, Stan Toops, Nury Turkel, John Witek and Thierry Zarcone have provided me with references or answered questions on many occasions. My neighbour and friend Judy Shapiro delivered to me her stack of neatly-sorted research on contemporary Xinjiang and Chinese Muslims in return for a rickety old bookcase. Ildikó Béller-Hann and Rachel Harris invited me to an informative symposium of new historical and anthropological work on Xinjiang held at SOAS in London in the autumn of 2004. My gratitude to them all. I would also like to thank Jan Berris and Steve Orlins of the National Committee on United States-China Relations for their help.

Hua Li has been teaching me about Qing history and Xinjiang for years, whether in China, Japan or the United States. I am grateful for all her help and for our friendship. Likewise I have learned much from my friend Nabijan Tursun, especially in regard to Uyghur- and Russian-language historiography. He is without doubt the most knowledgeable scholar of early-twentieth-century Xinjiang living in the United States today.

Al Dien and Laura Newby read and commented on early chapters of this book, and Carol Benedict, Andrea Goldman, Kang Xiaofei, Ed McCord, Tobie Meyer-Fong, Mary Rankin and Keith Schoppa gamely read a not-quite-complete manuscript. Their comments, like the suggestions and tips I've garnered from all my colleagues, were extremely welcome and have made this a better book.

Michael Dwyer of Hurst & Co. first approached me about this project several years ago; I appreciate his patience over the years it has taken to complete. Anne Routon at Columbia University Press has likewise been unfailingly encouraging. My thanks, too, to Sebastian Ballard for producing clear maps from my complex instructions and long lists of placenames. Jonathan Hoare copy-edited the manuscript with great patience and skill. The usual mistakes remain for which I alone am to blame.

I finished a previous book on my wedding anniversary, and have done so again this time. Though Madhulika no doubt suspects that I undertake these books mainly as an excuse for a host of ineptitudes, much credit is due to her for both the growing number of books and for the (rather more quickly) growing number of anniversaries.

My daughters, Maya and Priya, have likewise done all they can to hasten this book along: patiently waiting to go on bike rides, have dinner or hear a story until I finished yet another page; never shouting, fighting or doing anything else that might disturb me while I am working; changing their clothes, brushing their teeth, getting ready for school, doing their homework and practising the piano without being reminded; and even volunteering to relieve me of such tiresome chores as filing, photocopying and dusting the knick-knacks in my study. Or, as they would say, 'Psych!'

J.A.M.
Tokyo, July 2005

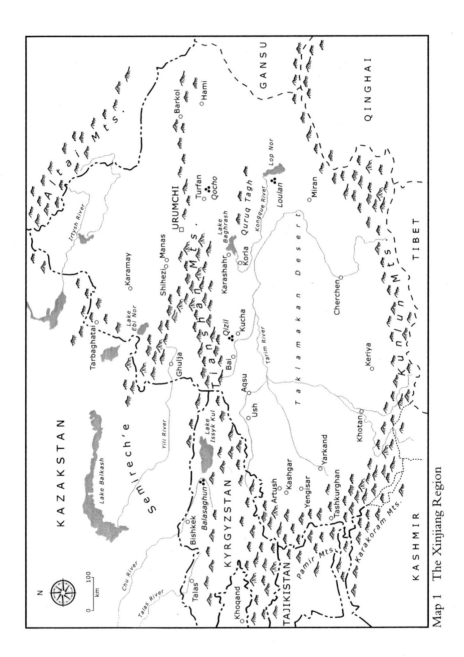

Map 1   The Xinjiang Region

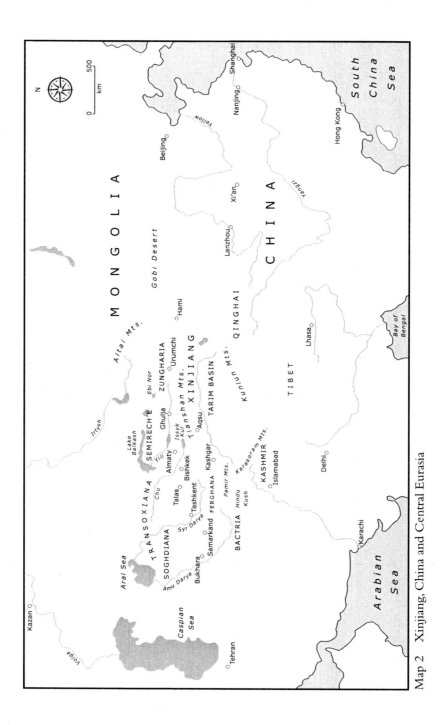

Map 2   Xinjiang, China and Central Eurasia

1. Ancient Encounters

(earliest times–8th century)

Writers have attached a number of metaphors to Xinjiang. It is the hub of the Silk Road, the crossroads of Asia, the heart of the continent. Owen Lattimore—caravaneer, Inner Asianist and, according to Senator Joseph McCarthy, 'the top Soviet espionage agent in the United States'—called Xinjiang the 'pivot of Asia'.[1] Some might question Lattimore's assessment of the region's geopolitical significance in the mid-twentieth century. Nevertheless, when viewed broadly, the idea behind all these labels is clear enough: Xinjiang's centrality and intermediate position in Eurasia. This book is devoted to examining the region's 'betweenness' over a long chronological perspective. A good place to begin is from another sort of long perspective, from a satellite above the earth at the beginning of the twenty-first century.

A glance at a satellite image or topographical map of Eurasia reveals the dense knot of mountains at the continent's core. These mountains define Xinjiang as we know it: the region is a rough triangle consisting of three basins, the Tarim to the south, Turfan (Turpan) to the south-east, and Zungharian to the north. The Kunlun range and its eastern offshoot, the Altyn Tagh, form the southern boundary of the Tarim Basin, and the Tianshan forms its northern edge, dividing the Tarim Basin from Zungharia. The Altai range divides Zungharia from Mongolia on the north-east. To the south-east, the Quruq Tagh, a spur of the Tianshan, separates the Tarim and Turfan Basins.

Xinjiang thus defined by mountain ranges is a relatively recent geo-logical creation. It is not, for example, the Xinjiang known by Tienshano-saurus or other dinosaur species from the Jurassic and early Cretaceous

---

[1] Lattimore 1950. For Macarthy and the witch-hunt against Lattimore, see Newman 1992.

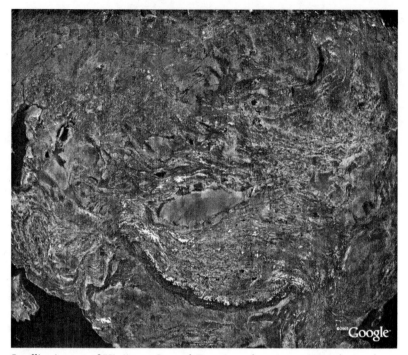

Satellite image of Xinjiang, Central Eurasia and environs (Google Earth, published with permission)

whose remains have been found there.[2] In fact, what most dramatically distinguishes Tienshanosaurus' home some 160 million years ago from the Xinjiang we know are precisely those mountain ranges, the high ground at the centre of Asia. The Qinghai–Tibetan plateau, the world's highest place, and the landform which, along with Antarctica and the Arctic, exercises the most climatic influence on earth, began to rise some 100 million years ago with the subduction of the Indian plate under Eurasia and the breaking away of the Indian continent from Gondwana-land. India sped north and collided at high-speed (up to 15 cm per year) some 60 million years ago with continental Asia, there joining South China and North China, which had themselves only relatively recently met and taken their place at the Eurasian table. The Indian collision lifted

2 Scientists on Sven Hedin's expedition discovered the first fossils and named Tienshanosaurus. James Clark and Xu Xing, 'Dinosaurs from Xinjiang, China', 2001 at <http://www.gwu.edu/~clade/faculty/clark/china.html> (accessed 5 May 2005).

the Qiangtang plateau of northern Tibet and raised mountain ranges in a series of folds across the centre of Eurasia.

The uplift continued, by twenty-two to fifteen million years ago reaching a threshold height that created the Asian monsoon weather pattern. In this weather cycle, warm and moist air from the Indian and Pacific oceans is drawn in the spring and summer into the Indian sub-continent and East Asia by rising air masses over Tibet and Mongolia, bringing the monsoon rains. In the autumn and winter, cool high pressure zones centred on the high Inner Asian regions block warmer, moister air from the sea, causing relatively dry winters in Asia. The mountains and the monsoon climate they produced have profoundly affected the history of Asia, influencing everything from agriculture to navigation in the Indian Ocean and South China Sea to, arguably, social and political structures in eastern and southern Asia.

We may thus add another metaphor: if Tibet is the roof of the world, Xinjiang lies in its eaves. This tectonic and orographic history has also shaped Xinjiang's history, albeit in a fashion diametrically opposed to that of areas lying closer to the sea: The mountains ringing Xinjiang and lower ranges further east create a barrier effect, shielding the Tarim Basin from south-easterly winds and the influence of the monsoons that determine China's and India's climate. Moreover, whereas long-term shifts to warmer temperatures have increased precipitation in the rest of China, such climatological changes have increased aridity and desertification in Xinjiang. Conversely, climatic cooling produces aridity in eastern China but increases precipitation and glaciation in Xinjiang's highlands. The mountains, then, separate the Xinjiang region from the climatic regime of eastern and southern Asia.[3]

In fact, Xinjiang lies at the midpoint of two climatic belts extending across Eurasia's midriff. A climatic map of Eurasia reveals a series of horizontal bands. Furthest north lies the arctic tundra; below that, a strip of coniferous forests, or taiga, comprising most of Siberia. The next band, a belt of steppe grasslands reaching from northern Mongolia in the east to Hungary in the west, crosses northern Xinjiang. South of that lies the band of deserts running from the Gobi to the shores of the Caspian and contiguous with the Arabian peninsula, north Africa and the Sahara. This band, of course, runs through southern Xinjiang.

3 Zhao and Xia 1984: 311; Issar 2003: 63, 105.

The populous societies that have formed the civilisational cores of
world history lie around the rim of the continent. Xinjiang lies between
them, astride the steppe and desert bands, and roughly equidistant from
the population cores of China, India and the Mediterranean basin. I will
make a good deal of these geographic facts underlying Xinjiang's centrality in the narrative that follows, but won't be the first to capitalise on
them: entrepreneurial Chinese geographers have recently determined
that the 'exact' geographical centre of Eurasia lies in a newly developed
theme-park located a convenient distance from the tourist hotels of
Urumchi (Ürümchi).

THE GEOGRAPHIC SETTING

With an area of 1,664,900 square kilometres, Xinjiang is the size of
Great Britain, France, Germany and Spain—or Texas, California, Mon-
tana and Colorado—combined. If it were a country, it would be the
world's sixteenth largest, just smaller than Libya and just larger than Iran.
Xinjiang comprises one sixth of the land area of the PRC (People's
Republic of China), yet in the year 2000 was home to only 1.5 per cent
of China's population.[4] Although official PRC sources claim the region
has been part of China since 60 BCE, its population has only in the past
century become Chinese-speaking, and the region remains, by Chinese
standards, sparsely settled.

The Xinjiang region was not an integrated political unit with its current boundaries until the eighteenth century. Before then control of
the territory was usually divided among many local oasis rulers or warring empires; parts of Xinjiang were often ruled together with lands in
what are now the Central Asian Republics, and parts by China or Tibet.
Nevertheless, there is a geographic, cultural and geopolitical coherence
to the region that makes writing its history over the very long term a
reasonable thing to attempt.

---

4 The 2000 national PRC census reported mainland China's (excluding Hong
Kong and Macao) total population as 1,265,830,000 ('2000 nian diwuci quanguo
renkou pucha zhuyao shuju gongbao, no. 1', downloaded from PRC State Statistical Bureau website <www.p2000.gov.cn> on 23 January, 2002). The same census
arrived at a Xinjiang population of 19.25 million, including 790,000 Xinjiang residents with no permanent place of residence (*Xinjiang Ribao*, 3 April 2001, via FBIS
document CPP20010517000151).

With its snowy mountains and dry basins Xinjiang is home to both the second highest and the second lowest places on earth. To the north-east the Altai range rises to 4,000 metres, forming the border with Mongolia. The Tianshan range running east-west down the middle of the region has peaks of up to 7,000 metres at its higher western end; the landmark Boghda shan (5,445 metres) is visible on rare clear days from Urumchi. The Kunlun range, to the south, divides Xinjiang from the Tibetan plateau and includes the world's second-highest peak, Mt Godwin Austen (Qiaogeli, 8,611 metres). In the south-west, routes over the high Pamir plateau skirt peaks of 7,500 metres en route to Kashmir, Pakistan and Afghanistan.

The Zungharian (Jungharian, Dzungarian) Basin, or Zungharia, making up the Xinjiang region's northern half, is bounded by the Altai and Tianshan ranges. Although parts of this basin are desert, much is prime grassland, and some areas support agriculture, especially the fertile valley of the Yili (Ili) river in the south-west. The Yili drains west into Lake Balkash in what is today Kazakstan. Northern Xinjiang's other major river, the Irtysh, likewise flows west, filling Lake Zaysan and continuing on to the north-west to Semey (Semipalatinsk) and on past Omsk into Russian Siberia. In fact, along much of its western edge the Zungharian Basin opens without obstacle into Kazakstan's Semirech'e (Yettisu, Seven Rivers) region. Zungharian grasslands have through history generally formed a single unit with the watersheds of the Talas, Chu and other Semirech'e rivers; with these rich pastures to keep their herds strong, nomad powers could dominate both southern Xinjiang and the heartland of western Turkestan, a region now divided among Uzbekistan, Tajikistan and Kyrgyzstan.

Several passes through the Tianshan link northern and southern Xinjiang, permitting the passage of merchants and warriors. Towards the east, where the city of Urumchi is located today, a large corridor opens southward into the Turfan Depression, which lies between the main chain of the Tianshan and a south-eastern spur, known as the Quruq (Kuruk) mountains, which divide Turfan and Hami from the rest of southern Xinjiang. Ayding Kol, a salt lake at the bottom of the depression, lies at 154 metres below sea level—only the Dead Sea is lower. Although the desert surrounding Turfan is unforgiving and summer temperatures in the region can approach 50 degrees Celsius, ample water made the Turfan and surrounding oases a rich agricultural area, one which nomadic powers to the north coveted for the produce and tribute they could exact. For centuries farmers in the Turfan area dug and maintained underground canals called *karez* to tap underground reservoirs filled by mountain run-off and to water their fields with a minimum of evaporation. From Turfan a long desert road leads to the Gansu corridor and thence to the interior provinces of China. Some Chinese dynasties established fortifications along this corridor: Jiayuguan, some 700 kilometres east of Turfan, marks the westernmost extent of the Ming dynasty great wall. Other dynasties, notably the Han and Tang, made the Turfan Depression itself a base of operations.

West of Turfan and the low Quruq Tagh range is the Tarim Basin, also known as Altishahr. This southern half of Xinjiang is dominated by the vast Taklamakan Desert (327,000 sq km), a sand-trap surrounded by mountain ranges that cast an almost total rain shadow from north, west and south. The shifting sand dunes of the Taklamakan can reach 100 metres in height. Encroaching sands have buried towns, and seasonal sandstorms, called *qara buran*, 'black winds', have asphyxiated travellers caught without shelter. But the mountains that starve the Tarim Basin of precipitation also provide the snow and glacial run-off that it lives on. The Khotan, Yarkand, Kashgar, Aksu and many smaller rivers feed into the Tarim River, which drains the west and north of the basin in a clockwise direction before emptying south-east into the desert. Around the Tarim Basin stretch a chain of oases, some spring-fed, others supported by mountain run-off. These oases have provided the grain and other products needed by nomads from the north, as well as tribute to military conquerors. They also facilitated trade: the caravan routes running through the ancient cities along the southern and northern rims of the Tarim Basin comprise the central stretches of the Silk Road. Passes through the Pamir and Karakoram ranges allowed communication between the Tarim Basin and Afghanistan, India and Pakistan as well as with what are now collectively referred to as the former Soviet Central Asian Republics, especially Kyrgyzstan, Kazakstan, Uzbekistan and Tajikistan. Historically, both classical Greco-Roman and Arab sources referred to the heartland of these 'stans' as 'the land beyond the river', referring to the Oxus or Amu river. For convenience below I use the English version of this term, Transoxiana, to refer to the region between the Amu Darya and Syr Darya (*darya* means 'river'), an area that includes the Ferghana Valley as well as the cities of Tashkent, Samarkand and Bukhara.

The Taklamakan Desert at Mazartagh (photo: J. Millward, 1992)

With only 20–150 mm of annual precipitation, the Tarim Basin today supports agriculture only in the piedmont zone, where extensive irrigation can harness the glacier- and snow-melt from the Kunlun, Pamir and Tianshan mountains. Though run-off levels are currently stable, they have fluctuated in the past, with dramatic effects on human habitation in the southern Tarim. Remains of Niya, Dandan-oilik, Endere and other sites deep in the Taklamakan are evidence of times when greater volumes of water brought the rivers flowing out of the Kunlun well north of their current termini. Climatic changes in the late third and late eighth centuries led to the abandonment of these cities to the desert. The desiccated city of Loulan (Kroraina, Krorän) in the south-east of the Taklamakan, once capital of the Shanshan kingdom and a vigorous trade *entrepôt*, is further testimony to the vagaries of water in southern Xinjiang. When the Tarim and Kongque River system shifted course to the south-east around 330 CE, its terminal lake, Lop Nor, disappeared, leaving Loulan high and dry. Abandoned by its people, Loulan settled into the shifting sands until rediscovered at the turn of the twentieth century.[5]

5   Zhao and Xia 1984: 320. Scholars date the abandonment of Loulan to between the fourth and the beginning of the fifth century (De La Vaissière 2004: 113–14).

Since the eighteenth century Qing and subsequent Chinese authorities have expanded the agricultural capacity of the Tarim Basin through vigorous development of hydraulic works. This process accelerated after 1949. But as the Tarim is an ancient sea and an entirely inland drainage, salinisation and alkalisation plague up to a third of arable land—its telltale white residue looks like frost on the surface of many farms. In desert areas groundwater can be saltier than blood.[6] As humankind exploits ever larger areas of land and volumes of river water, natural vegetation, too, suffers, leading to desertification in many areas abutting the desert. From the 1970s to 2000 upstream uses exhausted the Tarim River, leaving little or no water to flow into the desert. The wilderness of salt flats where the river once emptied are now home only to the last surviving wild camels, who have somehow adapted to drinking briny water and dodged the nuclear tests conducted in the Lop Nor region.[7]

XINJIANG IN PREHISTORY

The mountains and basins, steppes and oases that characterise Xinjiang's geography, and the imperatives of water and land that govern its settlement have exercised an important influence on the region's history. Despite the massive mountain chains impeding communication, the Xinjiang region is centrally situated, and since prehistoric times has indeed been a crossroads where influences from the four compass-points meet. Its position as a conduit for west-east communication is especially noteworthy. Readers new to the study of the region are surprised to learn that Europoid people lived in Xinjiang from pre-historic times. Along another axis too the region's geography has shaped historical developments in the region. The agricultural oases of the Tarim and Turfan Basins have attracted pastoralists based in the steppes of Semirech'e and Zungharia and the mountain slopes of the Tianshan. This has led

6 In some areas, salt levels in underground water exceeds 4 grams per litre. Blood is about 1.6 g/l, and seawater about 30 g/l. Zhou Hongfei *et al.* 1999: 131, 135. My thanks to Doug Eagles, Steve Hannum, Sara Fisher and Steven Singer in the Biology and Chemistry departments at Georgetown for help with the comparative salinity of various liquids, including camel urine.
7 On the wild camels, see Hare 1998. The Wild Camel Protection Foundation, based in England, has been working with Chinese and international environmental groups to establish a Lop Nor Nature Sanctuary for the protection of the camels, which are genetically distinct from domesticated camels.

to frequent north-south contacts, including trade, raids and conquest. Furthermore, the role of this north-south axis in Xinjiang's history has mostly been to encourage direct or indirect control of the oases of the Tarim and Turfan Basins by outside powers, particularly nomadic peoples based north of the Tianshan.

Stone Age

Although archaeological exploration of one sort or another began in Xinjiang over a century ago, our knowledge of the lives of the region's earliest human inhabitants remains sketchy. Siberia and other parts of Inner and Central Asia have all yielded evidence of Palaeolithic human cultures, but in Xinjiang only a few sites show possible Palaeolithic cores, flakes and evidence of fire use.[8] There is more evidence of humans in Xinjiang dating from the time of the last glacial maximum some 20,000 to 15,000 years ago, when the southern Tarim Basin was less arid than it is today and more snow in the mountains provided more run-off in the deserts. Pebble choppers and other simply chipped tools found south of Khotan testify to the presence of hunter-gatherers exploiting the abundant animal and plant life in the piedmont region. Other, possibly Mesolithic, sites near Khotan, Hami, Musang and Shanshan show a full complement of arrowheads, blades, scrapers and other well-made stone tools from around 10,000 years ago. Many surface artefacts dating possibly to the Neolithic (roughly 10,000 to 4,000 years ago) have been found in sites scattered throughout northern and southern Xinjiang, where there is also evidence of fixed habitations, coloured pottery and a wide variety of microliths and larger chopped and ground stone implements, including mortars and pestles. In these Neolithic settlements, then, people cultivated food-crops and processed grains, probably to supplement continued hunting and gathering. However, in this period there is not yet any indication of animal husbandry, nor can we ascertain much about possible linkages with better-researched Neolithic cultures in western Central Asia, Mongolia or the Gansu-Qinghai area of China.[9]

8 A.P. Okladnikov, 'Inner Asia at the Dawn of History' in Sinor 1990; Yu Taishan 1996: 3–4.
9 Chen Ge in Yu Taishan 1996: 4–9; Olsen 1992.

Bronze and Iron Ages

Archaeologists have not yet found evidence of indigenous development from Stone Age to Bronze Age cultures in Xinjiang. Nevertheless, work on the second and first millennia BCE in Xinjiang has yielded exciting finds. Excavation has begun on a good many sites in both southern and northern Xinjiang, especially tombs, and many artefacts and human remains have been recovered. Although associations between the findings from different Xinjiang sites or with developments in regions outside Xinjiang remain tentative, Xinjiang archaeologists have in recent years succeeded in separating the archaeology of the region from the periodisations and other assumptions of Chinese archaeology. Silk, lacquer and cowrie shells from China show up in some tombs; likewise jade from Khotan was common in ancient China. Nevertheless, analysis of the archaeological record in Xinjiang demonstrates that despite these early contacts, the main story of the Bronze Age in Zungharia, the Tarim Basin and the Turfan Basin involved migrations of peoples from western Central Asia and Siberia. Bronze metallurgy in Xinjiang, beginning in the early second millennium BCE, likely preceded that of Central China: cut-marks on logs found in an ancient cemetery site in Xinjiang from that time are too deep and well-defined to have been made by a stone tool.[10]

The Bronze Age in Central Eurasia is characterised by the emergence of mobile peoples, who applied bronze metallurgy to all aspects of their lives, and from the third millennium BCE employed wheeled vehicles, first heavy carts and ultimately the light war chariot.[11] Xinjiang's Bronze Age is attested by sites in Tashkurgan (in the Pamirs), Loulan, Alagou (Turfan county) and in the Altai and Tianshan mountains. These sites, representing different cultures and different burial types, have yielded a variety of woven materials, ceramics, jewellery, ornaments and figurines, as well as farming tools, grains and animal bones. Interestingly, though there are many small bronze objects in these sites (not large bronzes as in China), agricultural tools from this epoch are still made of stone. Bones of sheep, oxen and horses, hides, woven woollens and felts in many sites demonstrate that animal husbandry had by the beginning of the second millennium BCE become an important component of people's livelihoods, if not yet an independent economic strategy. Xinjiang

10   Wang Binghua 1996, cited in Di Cosmo 2002: 47 n. 11.
11   Di Cosmo 2002: 27–8.

peoples were in contact with the Andronovo culture which spread across Central Eurasia from the Urals to South Siberia during the Bronze Age. These contacts may have been the conduit by which the chariot was introduced to China by around the thirteenth century BCE.[12]

Iron items begin appearing in Xinjiang by around 1200 BCE; this is earlier than anywhere else within China's present borders, but in line with the beginning of the Iron Age further west. Although there are mines and evidence of local smelting in Xinjiang, the advances in metallurgy may be connected with migrations of pastoral nomadic peoples across the Eurasian steppes. The Iron Age across Central Eurasia is associated with the rise of pastoral nomadism—as opposed to sedentary or semi-sedentary herding, and more militarised and socially stratified society on the steppe that was able to intrude upon agricultural areas. This 'Scythian' type culture is distinguished by dynamic representations of animals in metalwork and other media. Some of the ornaments found in Xinjiang display the 'animal style' found across the Eurasian steppe in this period, such as the bronze belt plaques found in the Xiangbaobao cemetery in Tashkurgan or the silver and gold plaques from Alagou, fashioned into energetically posed tigers and lions. Sites in Zungharia and the Turfan-Hami area in particular show signs of independent nomadic pastoralism, as opposed to stock-breeding supplementary to farming— again, in keeping with general Central Eurasian trends. However, the line between nomadic pastoral and sedentary agrarian societies should not be drawn too sharply, and the prehistorical evidence from Xinjiang shows a relationship characterised by complex interactions of herders and farmers and mixed agricultural and pastoral land use.[13]

Consider the woman buried in Qäwrighul near Loulan around 1800 BCE (more conservative estimates date her to the first millennium BCE) whose well-preserved remains have gained her acclaim as the 'Beauty of Loulan'.[14] She was wrapped in a shawl of woven sheep's wool, and the cemetery in which she and others are buried has no agricultural tools, suggesting that the inhabitants of this sandy region were not farmers, but

---

12   Di Cosmo 2002: 29.
13   Di Cosmo 2002: 71; Di Cosmo 1996: 96–8.
14   Mallory and Mair (2000: 140) date the mummies of the Qäwrighul cemetery, of which the Beauty is one of the oldest, to between 1800 BCE and the first centuries BCE; Ma Yong and Wang Binghua (1994: 211–12) date the complex from the seventh to the early centuries BCE.

rather herders, hunters and anglers. Yet she was interred with a winnowing basket and grains of wheat, a testimony to the symbolic importance of agriculture to these people and to possible close interactions with agriculturalists. Likewise, in major archaeological sites throughout western Gansu and southern Xinjiang dating from *c.* 1000 to 400 BCE, stone and metal agricultural implements have been found in association with bronze items in the style usually favoured by nomads.[15]

Given the relatively early stages of archaeological work in Xinjiang, the region's prehistory remains beset with puzzles. Data from material artefacts, human remains and even historical linguistics must be accounted for. One scholar who has attempted to synthesise this complex picture is Victor Mair, the impresario of Tarim mummy studies in the West—and a man who himself bears a striking resemblance to the best-looking male mummy, 'Chärchän Man'. Working together with J.P. Mallory, a specialist on the ancient Indo-Europeans, Mair theorises that from the beginning of the Bronze age (*c.* 2000 BCE), waves of migrants entered the Xinjiang region. The earliest of these, Mair believes, were probably speakers of Tokharian, an Indo-European language attested only in two dialects in the northern Tarim Basin in materials dating from the first millennium CE, but which was probably spoken much earlier in the region (historical linguists believe that Tokharian was among the earliest Indo-European languages to diverge from the main Indo-European linguistic stock then probably located on the Russian steppes north of the Black Sea). Through the second millennium BCE, later migrations brought other peoples from the west and north-west into Xinjiang; they were probably speakers of various Iranian languages (at that time Iranian was common across Eurasia, and was only just becoming the language of Persia). These migrants were mobile peoples, mostly animal herders, and the last waves, corresponding to the Iron Age discussed above, included true nomadic pastoralists.

These or other migrants also brought agrarian technologies and aspects of the ritual culture of sedentarists to the Tarim Basin, possibly from the band of Central Asian agricultural lands from northern Afghanistan to the Aral sea (a region known as Bactria and Margiana). One indication of such an imported origin for the Bronze Age in Xinjiang lies in the fact that both the grain crops (barley and wheat) and domesticated

15 Di Cosmo 1996; Chen Ge in Yu Taishan 1996: 10–31; Ma Yong and Wang Binghua 1994; Barber 1999: Chapter 4.

sheep come from the west. Moreover, in some Xinjiang Bronze Age sites archaeologists have found ephedra, a medicinal herb also used in that period in ceremonies in Bactria, India and Iran. Furthermore, as seen above, there are indications that textile and metallurgical technologies attested in Xinjiang also entered from the west.[16]

According to these theories, then, Xinjiang's Bronze Age culture was not an indigenous development from Neolithic roots, but rather derived from an influx of Indo-European peoples and technologies from the northern steppes and over the Pamirs. By the late first millennium BCE some of these Indo-European-speaking peoples in Xinjiang's archaeo-logical record can be associated with particular peoples known from historical or numismatic evidence. However, as it is difficult to reconcile the names in Chinese histories with those in Greek and other Western sources, such associations are often speculative, even controversial.

One group of Indo-European speakers that makes an early appear-ance on the Xinjiang stage is the Saka (Ch. Sai). Saka is more a generic term than a name for a specific state or ethnic group; Saka tribes were part of a cultural continuum of early nomads across Siberia and the Central Eurasian steppe lands from Xinjiang to the Black Sea. Like the Scythians whom Herodotus describes in book four of his *History* (*Saka* is an Iranian word equivalent to the Greek *Skythos*, and many scholars refer to them together as Saka-Scythian), Sakas were Iranian-speaking horse nomads who deployed chariots in battle, sacrificed horses, and buried their dead in barrows or mound tombs called *kurgans*. Royal burials in-cluded rich inventories of metal objects, often decorated in 'animal style' motifs—one famous example is the trove that yielded the gold fittings known as 'Golden Man', of which a reproduction now stands on a pillar in downtown Almaty. There are Saka sites across Central Eurasia. In Xin-jiang sites with Saka artefacts and Europoid remains have been identified dating from *c.* 650 BCE through the latter half of the first millennium BCE in Tashkurgan (west of Kashgar, in the Pamirs), in Yili, and even near Toqsun, south of the Tianshan. This latter site, dated to between the fifth and second centuries BCE, yielded a statuette of a kneeling warrior wearing a tall conical hat coming to a curved point—headwear associ-ated in Persian sources with the Sakas, and well known in classical Greek and Roman writings as a 'Phrygian cap', after another group of steppe

16   Mallory and Mair 2000: 268–9, 294, 317–81. See also Barber 1999.

invaders who sported it. An identical hat, fashioned from felt, was found in a tomb near Cherchen in the southern Tarim, dating to *c.* 1000 BCE, and on the heads of three women buried in Subashi in the Turfan Basin in the fourth or third century BCE. Very similar hats would centuries later adorn the heads of Soghdians in Tang depictions of these Central Asian, Iranian-speaking merchants.[17]

Another group of early Xinjiang inhabitants appears in Chinese sources of the second century BCE as the Yuezhi (Yueh-chih). The identity and movements of this group have posed one of the great questions of ancient Central Asian history: who were the Yuezhi originally, and what eventually became of them? Many scholars believe the Yuezhi and the Tokharians may be one and the same people.[18] Mallory and Mair argue that the ancestors of the Yuezhi lived first in the region of the Altai mountains and Yenesei River basin, where they formed what is known as the Afansevo slab-grave culture, before migrating south to Gansu and Xinjiang; A.K. Narain, on the other hand, suggests that the Yuezhi may have been indigenous inhabitants of the region around Dunhuang and the Qilian (Ch'i-lien) Mountains[19] of Gansu long before they enter historical accounts—there is a continuous cultural tradition in this area east of the Chinese central plains from as early as can be ascertained archaeologically. In any case, the earliest of the Tarim mummies—that is, the Bronze and Iron Age inhabitants of southern Xinjiang—may have been the ancestral or proto-Yuezhi.

We know from Chinese records of the Han period that in the second century BCE the Xiongnu (Hsiung-nu), then the ascendant nomadic power in Mongolia, attacked and dispersed the Yuezhi from their homelands. While some Yuezhi moved into Qinghai (Kokonor, Amdo) and others may have trickled into the Tarim, the main branch of their ruling clan migrated first to the upper Yili valley (where they encountered another people, the Wusun, who had themselves displaced or somehow

17   Di Cosmo 1999a: 941–4; Barber 1999: 33–4; Mallory and Mair 2000: 220.
18   Tokharian is attested in two widely divergent dialects, A and B, in an Indian script known as Brahmi. The texts date from the latter half of the first millennium CE. Scholars disagree on whether the Yuezhi were Tokharian-speakers or not; For example, Mallory and Mair (2000) and Narain (1990) support the association, while Enoki *et al.* (1994) believe the Yuezhi were Iranian-speaking Sakas (Scythians).
19   Although the term Qilian now refers to a mountain range defining the Gansu corridor on the south, the ancient term may have indicated the Tianshan (Golden 1992: 50), suggesting a somewhat more northern extent of Yuezhi lands.

merged with Sakas in the area). When attacked again, the Yuezhi moved to the Amu (Oxus) river, today the border of Afghanistan and Uzbekistan, where they took control of the Hellenic states of Bactria, the legacy of Alexander's eastern conquests. The Yuezhi divided into five subgroups, each under its own chief (*yabghu*), but one of these divisions seized control of the others. Chinese sources called this new empire Guishang, though some still used 'Yuezhi'. Greek sources, on the other hand, refer to this poeple as 'Tokharoi'.[20] This empire is now known as Kushan.

In the first century CE Kushan exercised military and political influence over the western oases of the Tarim Basin. The exact nature and extent of the Tokharian element in Xinjiang's early linguistic, demographic and political history has not been determined, but Tokharian dialects were employed in the Tarim and Turfan Basins through the first millennium CE, either because a Tokharian-speaking population was continuously settled in southern Xinjiang from prehistoric times, or because Yuezhi took refuge there at the time of the Xiongnu attack, or because of the later influence of the Kushan empire—or due to some combination of the three possibilities.[21] In any case, most important for our purposes here, the Yuezhi/Tokharians/Kushans demonstrate an early case of a phenomenon displayed over and over in Xinjiang's history: a nomadic royal house and its followers forging a confederation and establishing imperial control over sedentary populations.

The oldest surviving Taklamakanians

Finally, a word about the mummies. In recent years popularisations of Xinjiang archaeology, as well as magazine and television specials, have

20 Although many scholars believe the Yuezhi formed the principal ethnic element in Kushan, this question too awaits resolution. In any case, the administrative language of the Kushan empire was not Tokharian, but Eastern Iranian, generally written in Greek script (Golden 1992: 55–6).

21 Narain 1990. An extensive discussion of the Tarim mummy/Yuezhi/Tokharian/Kushan connection and related questions may be found in both Barber 1999 and Mallory and Mair 2000. Documents in Tokharian A have been found in religious sites from Turfan to Karashahr; Tokharian B had a broader range, from the Turfan Basin westward to Aqsu and beyond. Some linguists have posited that a third language, Tokharian C, was spoken along the southern rim of the Tarim Basin from Loulan to Niya, but this is based on only occasional Tokharian loan-words found in documents written in Kharoshti, an Indic language.

made much of the 'discovery' of 'European' mummies in Taklamakan
sites. Some, including an eminent geneticist, have gone so far as to call
them blonde and blue-eyed.[22] (Do mummies still have eyeballs?)

Though understandable as a means of selling magazines and garnering
research funding, the hype is misleading for two reasons. First, European
and Chinese scholars have known about the Europoid mummies for a
century, so the novelty of the 'discovery' is relative. Secondly, these people
were not 'Europeans'! The popular idea that the mummies are European
derives mainly from two factors: their appearance (they are not Mongoloid), and the body of evidence that suggests the Yuezhi or some other
early group in the region spoke Tokharian, an Indo-European language.
But neither of these factors amounts to real evidence that any of the
mummies or any of their ancestors had ever been anywhere near what
is usually understood as 'Europe'—that is, Eurasia west of the Bosporus.
The original speakers of Indo-European languages probably lived on the
steppes north of the Black Sea; from there branches migrated both east
to Central Asia, India and Iran, south to Anatolia and west to Europe.
Judging from calculations based on differences in different branches of
the Indo-European family and rates of linguistic change, the Tokharian
and Saka (Iranian) speakers were among the earliest to take their leave of
the ur-Indo-European population. If they were indeed Tokharian speakers, therefore, the Yuezhi must have come east very early indeed—well
before the inhabitants of Europe themselves spoke Indo-European.[23] As

22 A print advertisement running in 1999 for a Discovery Channel special entitled 'The Riddle of the Desert Mummies' showed the face of a mummy known
as 'Cherchen Man' rising out of the desert sand as in the climatic scene of the
Hollywood film *The Mummy*. The ad caption read, 'How will this face change
history?' Luigi Cavalli-Sforza (2000: 100) wrote that some Taklamakan mummies
have 'unmistakably blue eyes and brown hair'. However, all those that I have seen
in photos and in the desiccated flesh, have had hair too dark to be called blonde in
English—though the Chinese word *huang* covers a range of colours from brown to
yellow and would apply to the mummies' hair. Likewise, though I am no forensic
anthropologist, I doubt that any mummy has blue eyes, as the soft tissue of the
eyeball is not preserved, and the eyes are in any case shut. One certainly cannot
determine eye-colour from photos of the most famous Taklamakan mummies—including the 'Beauty of Loulan'. One would think that if there were mummies out
there with gorgeous baby-blues, their pictures would have been published.
23 The first Indo-Europeans arrived in Greece *c.* 2000 BCE, but the Tokharians,
be they the Afanasevo culture or Neolithic inhabitants of east China, would have
come east from Central Asia earlier than that (Narain 1990: 154). The same scholars

speakers of an Indo-European tongue, ancient Tarimites may well share a common ancestor with later Europeans, and this would explain the linguistic relationship and even the technical similarities that Elizabeth Barber has identified between woven goods in the Taklamakan and some ancient textiles preserved in central European salt mines. But to call the denizens of the ancient Tarim 'Europeans' is equivalent to calling Americans of British heritage 'Australians'. Or, to put it another way, if we describe the ancient Tarimites as 'European', then we should call Iranians and Indians 'European' as well—but we generally don't. Anyone familiar with the history of the distribution of the Indo-European peoples across Eurasia should not be overly surprised to find brown-haired, high-nosed mummies—or living Europoid people—in Xinjiang. But if one remains impressed by the apparent racial incongruity of finding these mummies in what is now part of China, then one should simply call them Europoid or Caucasoid and not confuse the picture by associating them with the western extreme of the Eurasian continent.

Eurocentric sensationalism aside, the mummies do provide valuable evidence about the history of the Xinjiang region. Preliminary mitochondrial DNA data has supported claims of a possible western Eurasian origin for some of the ancient Tarimites. But craniometrical comparisons point to additional complexities, with some earlier mummies displaying similarities to peoples in the Indus valley and later ones showing more affinity to populations in the Oxus (Amu) River valley. Earlier and later mummy groups, moreover, were quite different from one another. Though this complicates the story, it shows that Xinjiang was a Eurasian crossroads with a diverse population already in the second millennium BCE.[24]

THE CLASSICAL PERIOD

In the early twentieth century, after the fall of the Qing dynasty, the new Chinese republic changed many of the Turko-Mongolian place names on their maps of Xinjiang, and replaced them with old Chinese names

---

who like to think of the earliest Taklamakan mummies as 'northern Europeans' date them from c. 3800 years ago—before most of Europe spoke Indo-European languages.

24 Schurr 2001. Schurr cites craniological research by Brian E. Hemphill.

taken from Chinese histories written 2,000 years earlier.[25] The PRC switched most of the names back, but this attempt at onomastic imperialism reflects the abiding pull of the Han period (Western Han 206 BCE–8 CE, Eastern Han 26–220 CE) on China's imagination of Xinjiang. From a traditional culturalist point of view, the Han pushed back the frontiers of barbarism; from a modern nationalist perspective, the Han 'unified' the empire that is China, or a good deal of it at any rate.

Those same histories provide our first detailed information about the societies and military-political vicissitudes of the Tarim Basin and Zungharia. Moreover, besides the rich textual sources, the Han dynasty's penetration of the Tarim region is materially evident in the artefacts unearthed since the late nineteenth century from sites in the Taklamakan Desert, as well as in trade items found from the period across Eurasia. These not only show the presence of Han settlements and cultural influence in southern and eastern Xinjiang, but demonstrate the exchange of luxury goods and artistic motifs from the ends of the Eurasian continent. 'Roman' glass,[26] Chinese silks, Indian Buddhism—these summarise the types of exchanges that have led the Xinjiang region to be considered the hub of the Silk Road. This period from the second century BCE to around the third century CE comprises the first fluorescence of the land and sea bridges indirectly linking the ends of Eurasia. The narrative here, however, will focus on another feature of the Xinjiang region during this period: its role in the strategic relationship between China-based, and Mongolia-based, powers.

The Han and the Xiongnu

The relationship between nomadic pastoralist and sedentary agrarian societies in Xinjiang took its classic form after a confederation of tribes known as the Xiongnu (Hsiung-nu, possibly related indirectly to the peoples known as Huns in Europe) formed an empire encompassing Mongolia, north-west China and Zungharia. Unlike the Indo-European groups discussed above, most Xiongnu probably spoke an early form of

25   Millward 1999.
26   An Jiayao 2004. But see Liu Xinru 1988: 18–22 *passim* for an argument that the much vaunted linkages between Rome and Han lack hard evidence, and that most contacts between the Mediterranean and China were by sea first to India, then overland to Xinjiang and China.

Turkic.[27] The *Records of the Grand Historian* (*Shiji*) by Sima Qian (Ssu-ma Ch'ien), China's 'father of history', contains a long ethnographic description of the Xiongnu as pure nomads 'chasing grass and water', a phrase that became the stock description of northern nomads in later Chinese sources. Sima Qian tells us of a people all but born in the saddle: children first learned to ride on sheep, shooting bows and arrows at rats and birds before graduating to larger mounts and game. But archaeologists have discovered Xiongnu houses and fortifications and evidence of agriculture along river valleys from Manchuria to Zungharia. The picture of pure nomads living entirely on the hoof is much overdrawn.[28]

From *c.* 500 BC, as we know from both Han Dynasty historical sources and frozen tombs in the Altai mountain site of Pazyryk, the small city-states of the Turfan and Taklamakan areas had traded with and paid tribute to nomad overlords based north of the Tianshan—Xiongnu or their predecessors.[29] Dominance by Xiongnu over south-eastern Xinjiang was politically institutionalised in the first half of the second century BCE, when Xiongnu defeated the Yuezhi and drove them from the Gansu corridor (175 BCE), and then attacked them in what is now northern Xinjiang (162 BCE). By 130 BCE the Yuezhi had made their migration south-west to the Amu river, yielding the rich valleys of the Yili and Chu rivers back to the Wusun. The Xiongnu established a commandery south of the Tianshan, in the region of Lake Baghrash (Bohu or Bositeng), to

27   Golden 1992: 57.
28   In his masterly study of the relations of early northern peoples with Chinese states and the historiography of Sima Qian, Nicola Di Cosmo argues that the Xiongnu confederation arose out of the crisis caused by the northward expansion of Chinese states (Yan, Zhao and Qin). The first long walls were built not to protect Chinese farmers from nomad depredations, but to secure territory newly conquered by the Chinese states as they expanded and strengthened. Chinese states, including the post-unification Qin empire, expanded northward to gain pastureland on which to raise horses, which were essential not only to pull chariots but increasingly to field cavalry, then becoming an essential component of Chinese military forces. But these same lands had served as an agricultural base for northern peoples, who, contrary to stereotype, had engaged in a mixed agrarian and pastoralist economy, much like the Scythians Herodotus describes north of the Black Sea. Loss of those lands engendered a crisis which Maodun exploited to meld his powerful coalition out of the various tribes. Northward Chinese expansion and wall-building, then, was not designed to defend against an existing nomad menace; however, it did contribute to the creation of the Xiongnu threat (Di Cosmo 2002).
29   Di Cosmo 1996: 96.

control the Tarim Basin. From this office (referred to in the Chinese sources as 'Commandant of Slaves') the Xiongnu levied taxes and conscripted labour from Loulan and other Tarim Basin cities.

Meanwhile, further east, the Han dynasty had its own problems with the Xiongnu. From 198 BCE the Han court entered into a pragmatic if somewhat degrading relationship with the powerful northern nomads: known as *heqin*, it entailed recognising the Xiongnu rulers, or *chanyus* (sometimes spelled *shanyu*) as equals to Chinese emperors, letting them marry Han emperors' daughters, and paying tribute to the nomads to keep them at bay. However, the cost of the tributes kept rising, and both Han generals who had defected to the Xiongnu and Xiongnu generals continued to raid Han territory anyway.[30] After some sixty years of dispatching silk, wine, grain and princesses off to the barbarians without securing peace, the Han turned to a more aggressive approach under a new emperor, Wudi. Wudi first attempted to eliminate the Xiongnu ruler and his core force with a trick. The ambush failed dismally and open war soon broke out, in which one Han strategic objective was to 'cut off the right arm of the Xiongnu' by driving them from the Turfan and Tarim Basins.

Xiongnu prisoners reported that the Xiongnu *chanyu*, upon driving the Yuezhi from Gansu, had killed the Yuezhi monarch and fashioned his skull into a drinking cup. Wudi's court concluded, not unreasonably, that the Yuezhi might be amenable to an alliance with Han against the Xiongnu. Wudi thus decided to dispatch an envoy to discuss the idea with the Yuezhi. Zhang Qian, a former palace attendant, volunteered for the job and left Han in 139 BCE with an escort of over a hundred men, heading across the heart of Xiongnu territory toward the Yuezhi in the Yili valley. The party was promptly captured by the Xiongnu, who held Zhang Qian prisoner at the *chanyu's* court north of the Gobi, but gave him a Xiongnu wife with whom he had a son. A decade later Zhang Qian escaped with his wife and some of his men and made his way west. By this time the Yuezhi had already decamped from the Yili and Chu valleys, so Zhang Qian journeyed on to Ferghana (Dayuan), Soghdiana (Kangju) and Bactria (Daxia), where he finally found the Yuezhi on the north bank of the Amu River. By then, of course, the Yuezhi had left the Xiongnu and dreams of vengeance far behind them. Zhang Qian

---

30   See the discussion in Di Cosmo 2002: 193–5, 210–17.

thus returned east via the southern Tarim, and after another year-long Xiongnu detention returned to the Han court, where he became Han's pre-eminent 'Western Regions' specialist. Though he had not secured a military alliance with the Yuezhi (and would not with the Wusun either during a later mission in 116 BCE), the intelligence Zhang Qian gathered on his journeys formed the core of Han geographic, strategic and ethnographic knowledge of lands to the west.[31]

A series of victories against the Xiongnu allowed the Han to penetrate the Gansu corridor as far as Lop Nor by around 120 BCE. For the next sixty years Xiongnu and Han forces engaged in a tug of war over the Tarim Basin. The region's many small city-states did what they could to weather the geopolitical storm, with much pragmatic shifting of allegiance. For example, the important trade city of Loulan, near Lop Nor, sent hostages to both Han and Xiongnu courts. Jushi, straddling a pass through the easternmost spur of the Tianshan (between modern Turfan and Jimsar [Jimsa]) was the scene of many Xiongnu-Han battles, until the Han relocated the city's population wholesale.

The Tarim and Turfan Basin oases, especially Jushi, were essential to the Xiongnu as sources of agricultural products, man-power and tribute revenue. The Han, on the other hand, was fighting for strategic position, not economic gain. This Han campaign is best characterised by the scholars Hulsewé and Loewe:

[From c. 115] ... up to 60 BCE the governments of Western Han were ready to take drastic and violent action to secure or promote their interests. We know of two military expeditions designed to force the submission of other peoples and their acceptance of kings favoured by Han (Dayuan and Qiuzi); of five occasions in which Han officials staged or were implicated in plots to murder a local king (Suoju, Yucheng, Wusun, Jibin and Loulan); of one case when the local inhabitants were all put to the sword as a reprisal for resistance (Luntai); of one instance in which a puppet king was set up and the inhabitants displaced from their lands, which were then made over to the Xiongnu (Jushi); and one case in which the authority of a state and control of its population was divided between two local leaders (Wusun).[32]

---

31   Yu Taishan (1996: 49–51) argues that Zhang Qian crossed the Altai, followed the Irtysh River west, and skirted south of Lake Balkash to Ferghana. The main sources on Zhang Qian's journey are the 'Dayuan zhuan' of the *Shiji* and 'Xiyu zhuan' of the *Hanshu*.

32   Hulsewé and Loewe 1979: 49, transliterations changed to Pinyin.

Both traditional and modern Chinese historiographic propaganda have played down the military character of Chinese penetration of Central Asia. In a curious hybrid of the two, the Nationalist Chinese leader Chiang Kai-shek (Jiang Jieshi) described the above events as 'the Han Dynasty's direct contact with the "Western Region"'. The 'various stocks' of China, he asserted, including that 'east of the Pamirs' came to be 'amalgamated' because of cultural attraction (*wangdao*—the way of the prince) and not force (*badao*—the way of the hegemon): '... they have now become integral parts of one nation. In this process, culture and not military might has been the actuating force; the method of assimilation has been by a stretching forth of a helping hand, and not by conquest.'[33]

After 60 BCE the Han stretched its hand further into the Tarim Basin, replacing the Xiongnu 'Commandant of Slaves' with its own 'Protector General' (*duhu*). By splitting the nomad confederation into northern and southern factions, moreover, the Han temporarily relieved pressure from the Xiongnu. The Han also began to establish military agricultural colonies, or *tuntian*, an institution that Chinese regimes right up to the present PRC government would use, with minor variations, to resolve logistical problems and enhance frontier security, especially in Xinjiang.

Tuntian colonies were state farms worked by Han soldiers. They allowed the Han to station loyal troops in places too far to supply from the Chinese interior, without imposing upon local populations for food. Even before 60 BCE, the Han founded *tuntian* colonies in Luntai and Quli (between modern Kucha and Korla); later, groups of a few hundred soldiers irrigated and farmed lands in the Turfan-Hami region, near Lop Nor, and in the eastern part of the southern Tarim Basin. At the height of Han Central Asian power, in the mid-first century BCE, there was even a *tuntian* near Issyk Kul in Kyrgyzstan, but during the latter half of the Han period (Eastern Han, 25–220 CE) the dynasty maintained a military farm only in Yiwu, near present-day Hami.[34]

The Han was forced to leave the cities of the Tarim pretty much to themselves during a civil war in the Han heartland (Wang Mang's usurpation of the imperial throne, 8–25 CE). When the Han dynasty was

33   Chiang Kai-shek 1947: 11, 4. The translator notes that this passage regarding amalgamation is revised from an earlier edition; the original makes the same point, though the phrases are ordered differently.
34   Ma Yong and Sun Yutang, 1994: 240. See also Fang Yingkai 1989 and Zhao Yuzheng 1991.

restored (as the Later or Eastern Han, 25–220) it initially had little to do with the Western Regions, and the oases' city-states took to warring among themselves for supremacy. The Northern Xiongnu exploited the power vacuum and re-established nomad overlordship over the lands south of the Tianshan. Finally, in the 70s–90s CE renewed Han military offensives and the emergence of other nomad powers in Mongolia drove the Northern Xiongnu to Zungharia, while the Han general Ban Chao re-established military colonies and bullied the Tarim city-states into renewing their vows of allegiance to Han and sending token tributes east to the Han capital. Although his biography notes thousands of Western Regions heads lopped off, Ban Chao is famous for achieving the reconquest of the Tarim more by boldness and guile than by superior force. In one celebrated incident the rebellious King Zhong of Kashgar (Shule) was promising to renew his loyalty to the Han while in fact conspiring with Kucha (Qiuci) and to kill Ban Chao in a surprise attack. Ban Chao pretended to be fooled and invited Zhong and his men to a banquet. When wine had been served, Ban Chao shouted an order and Zhong was bound and beheaded. Han troops then killed 700 of Zhong's men, and the southern route through the Tarim was pacified.[35]

However, after Ban Chao's return east in 102 CE the Han again retrenched, once more ceding the Tarim to the Northern Xiongnu from 107 to 125. Ban Chao's son, Ban Yong, then embarked on a new series of campaigns and the Han re-established a measure of control over the Tarim from 127 to c. 150.[36]

After that the Yuezhi—through their Kushan descendents—reclaimed the stage. From the latter half of the first century CE to the late third century Kushan seems to have enjoyed political sway in the southern Tarim Basin equivalent to that once enjoyed by Han. Administrative documents in the Indic dialect and script used by the Kushan empire (Kharoshthi) have been found in Loulan, Khotan and Niya; there are also bilingual Kharoshthi-Chinese coins.[37]

---

35 *Hou Han Shu*, 77 (*liezhuan*, 37), 'Ban Chao'. Fan Hua 1961: 2: 317. Grousset 1997: 45, citing Chavannes' translation of the *Hou Han Shu* biography of Ban Chao, in 'Trois généraux chinois de la dynastie des Han', *T'oung Pao* (1906).
36 All accounts of the Han struggle with the Xiongnu are based on the *Hanshu*, *Hou Han Shu* and *Shiji*; I have substantially followed secondary narratives based on these sources by Yü Ying-shih 1986, Hulsewé and Loewe 1979, and Samolin 1964.
37 Burrow 1940; Ma Yong and Sun Yutang 1994: 234–5.

Han imperial policing of the 'Western Regions' had encouraged the exchange of local goods and luxuries from west and east along what would later be named 'the Silk Road.' After the Han retreat Kushan, from its position in Bactria astride trade routes linking China, India and Rome, likewise maintained and was enriched by this trade. Kushan also played a part in the introduction of Buddhism to southern Xinjiang and China, as well as in the translation of Buddhist texts into Chinese and other languages.[38]

Assessing the Han and Xiongnu record in Xinjiang

At this point, since the Han period is officially cited as the beginning of Chinese rule in Xinjiang, it is worth pausing to take stock. Between 162 BCE (when the Xiongnu established their commandery south of the Tianshan) and 150 AD (after which neither Han nor Xiongnu enjoyed any influence in the south) the Xiongnu managed some seventy years of definitive control over the Turfan and Tarim Basin oases together, and the Han some 125 years. The rest of this 310-year-period of engagement with the region may be characterised as partial control and tug-of-war, the waxing and waning of one power or another. There were, to be sure, spectacular temporary Han military successes, such as Li Guangli's punch through to Ferghana to obtain 'blood-sweating horses' (102 BCE) and Ban Chao's oasis-hopping juggernaut (73–102 CE). The Han partly set-tled or at least garrisoned the Tarim Basin with military colonies; but the Xiongnu had maintained an administrative centre in southern Xinjiang continuously for a century (longer than the Han Protectorate General that displaced it). Moreover, the Han never had a foothold in Zungharia (northern Xinjiang), which the Xiongnu and the Wusun dominated for this whole period. The impression that all Xinjiang was Chinese ter-ritory throughout the Han Dynasty is a distortion arising from later historians' emphasis on certain aspects of this mixed record. In this case, the historians have proven more powerful than armies.

More important for us, however, are the two dynamics underlined by the Han-Xiongnu struggle: first, a nomad power in Mongolia and Zungharia exploited the Tarim and Turfan Basin oases for foodstuffs and revenue. Second, in its war against the northerners, a China-based power

38 Silk Road trade and Buddhism have been the subject of much research and several recent accessible books. See, for example, Foltz 1999 and Wood 2002.

campaigned west to Xinjiang in order to undermine its nomad adversary's resource base and thus reduce its ability to harass north China. Han expansion into the 'Western Regions', in other words, arose from its long rivalry with the Xiongnu and was motivated by security concerns, not desire to secure trade routes or new land.[39] This is a pattern we will see again.

MEASURED AUTONOMY AND CONTINUED CONNECTIONS, 3RD–6TH CENTURIES

The situation in Xinjiang during the three hundred years following the decline of the Xiongnu and fall of the Han is poorly documented historically. Due to political and military chaos in China, north-China-based states managed only limited and sporadic involvement in the Tarim Basin. But although this period is often treated as a kind of dark age in China, trade, diplomatic and religious communications remained vibrant in the Tarim Basin and even continued to link north-western China with India and Soghdiana. Indeed, during these centuries Soghdian commercial networks expanded across the Tarim Basin and Gansu Corridor, and Buddhism developed, nourished largely by these same lines of communication.[40]

Chinese links with the Tarim Basin were attenuated but not cut off after the fall of the Han. The Chinese annals register occasional diplomatic visits by emissaries both from Xinjiang city-states and further west. Twice in this period (324 and 382 CE), rulers in the Gansu region dispatched armies to subdue Karashahr (Qarashahr, Yanqi) and Kucha (Qiuci, Qucha) and awe the other petty principalities of the Turfan and Tarim Basins into pledging allegiance and sending tribute. The general in charge of the second invasion, Lü Guang, needed 20,000 camels to bring his plunder back when he returned east two years later. Gaochang (Qocho, Karakhoja), near Turfan, while enjoying political autonomy, retained Chinese language for official documentary use. In parts of the Tarim Basin further west and south, the archaeological record suggests the rising influence of the Kushan empire, which was based in Bactria (present-day northern Afghanistan and southern Uzbekistan), but there

---

39   Di Cosmo discusses the reasons for the shift 'from peace to war' between the Han and the Xiongnu, particularly as reflected in the *Shiji* (2002: Chapter 6).
40   De La Vaissière 2004: 65–7.

remained some continued Chinese presence or at least Chinese-style agricultural settlements at Niya, and Chinese official documents found in the Lop Nor region dating to the Wei (220–65) and especially Western Jin (265–316) testify to the presence of Chinese outposts from these courts in the Shanshan kingdom, of which Loulan (Kroraina) was the capital. Chinese merchants dealt in silk and precious stones throughout the Shanshan kingdom's five main provinces in the south-eastern Tarim and Lop Nor area.

When the travelling monk Faxian (Fa-hsien) passed through Shanshan in 399, however, he noted no Chinese there. Moreover, he described the landscape he had crossed on his way from Dunhuang in the following famous terms:

Amidst these rivers of sand are evil spirits and hot winds—all who encounter them perish. No birds fly above; no beasts walk below. One gazes all around as far as the eye can see, hoping to find a place to cross, but can chose none. The bleached bones of the dead provide the only sign.[41]

Yet Loulan could hardly have become a thriving *entrepôt* between Dunhuang and Khotan and a Silk Road hub if the route had always been so treacherous. In fact, conditions had worsened since the first century. From roughly 50 CE the climate grew increasingly warm and dry, resulting in less precipitation in the mountains and therefore less run-off. Several cities on the southern rim of the Tarim Basin, including Karadong and ancient Niya, were abandoned around the end of the third century, probably because the rivers flowing northward out of the Kunlun mountains, on which these cities relied, penetrated less far into the desert.[42] As noted above, the Tarim and Kongque system changed course in the early fourth century, and the ancient Lop Nor, which these rivers fed and which supported the city of Loulan, 'moved' with them. During the fourth or early fifth century Loulan's inhabitants abandoned the site entirely. While other cities in the Shanshan area survived and new ones were founded, from this time on the main east-west trade route began to shift to Kucha and Aqsu along the northern rim of the Tarim Basin.[43] The Chinese presence in the south-eastern Tarim Basin in the post-Han

41   Faxian, *Foguo ji* (Record of Buddhistic Kingdoms), translation by Millward. For English edition, see Giles 1981.
42   Hoyanagi 1975: 95–6; Issar 2003: 68; Zhong Wei *et al.* 2001: 3–5.
43   De La Vaissière 2004: 112.

period apparently did not survive climatic and hydrological changes and the geographic realignment of trade routes which resulted.

Even before these developments, and despite the Chinese garrison in Loulan and occasional Chinese intervention on the northern Tarim route, the larger principalities of the Tarim and the Shanshan area were in the third and fourth centuries mostly governed independently by local rulers. The Prakrit-language documents written in Kharoshthi script found in Loulan and Cadh'ota, a site in the desert north of Minfeng, indicate a feudal, agrarian kingdom carrying on its business with little reference to either Kushan or China except in matters of luxury trade. An élite of officials presided, while serfs and slaves raised sheep and goats and worked the land, growing primarily grain (wheat, millet and barley) and grapes (for wine). Women could own property, but were also bought and sold, both as slaves and adoptees, in higher numbers than men. Provincial governors and county officials adjudicated disputes, applying a sophisticated legal code, and collected taxes. Among the most burdensome tax levies was the *corvée*, which consisted mainly of watching camel herds. Buddhism, both Hinayana and Mahayana, thrived in the kingdom, but the monks lived not in monasteries but dispersed among the community, and could own private property, marry and have children.[44]

Further west the kingdom of Khotan displayed its intense devotion to Mahayana Buddhism with pagodas in front of each house, fourteen large monasteries and countless smaller ones. Faxian describes a great procession of the image of the Buddha, with attendant bodhisattvas and devas, in a carriage decorated with precious metals, gemstones and silk pennants and canopies.

When the images are one hundred paces from the city gate, the king takes off his cap of State and puts on new clothes; walking barefoot and holding flowers and incense in his hands, with attendants on each side, he proceeds out of the gate. On meeting the images, he bows his head down to the ground, scatters the flowers and burns the incense. When the images enter the city, the queen and Court ladies who are on top of the gate scatter far and wide all kinds of flowers which flutter down and thus the splendour of decorations is offered up complete.[45]

---

44 Atwood 1991.
45 Faxian, *Foguo ji*, j. 3. Translation Giles (1981: 5–6).

Kucha was another great Buddhist city in the third and fourth centuries. We know that the Kucheans

[had] a walled city and suburbs. The walls are threefold. Within are Buddhist temples and stupas numbering a thousand. The people are engaged in agriculture and husbandry. The men and women cut their hair and wear it at the neck. The prince's palace is grand and imposing, glittering like an abode of the gods.[46]

Kucha was one of the most important Buddhist centres in Central Asia, and the birthplace of Kumarajiva (Ch. Jiumoluoshi; 343?–413 CE), a celebrated Buddhist monk born of an Indian father and Kuchean mother. When his mother decided to become a Buddhist nun, the nine-year-old Kumarajiva accompanied her to Kashmir, where he studied several schools of Hinayana Buddhism. A few years later mother and son left Kashmir and returned to Kucha by way of other Central Asian Buddhist monastic centres, including Yarkand, where Kumarajiva encountered and embraced Mahayana Buddhism. By the time they returned home Kumarajiva enjoyed an international reputation as Buddhist scholar and polyglot. He was famous even in north China, and General Lü Guang brought him back east in 384 after conquering Kucha. Kumarajiva then set to work training disciples and translating Buddhist sutras into Chinese. His knowledge of Chinese, Sanskrit and various Buddhist schools made him an apt interpreter of Buddhism into a Chinese idiom, and his work left a deep impact upon Buddhism in China. In the proud words of a modern Indian scholar, 'Kumarajiva symbolises the spirit of cultural collaboration between Central Asia and India and the joint effort made by the Buddhist scholars of these countries for the dissemination of Indian culture in China.'[47]

Near Kucha were many Buddhist monasteries and sanctuaries, including the rock-cut caves at Qizil (Kizil). Qizil represents the extension to Central Asia of the Indian tradition of excavating and painting caves as sanctuaries; other examples of this temple form include caves at Bamiyan (Afghanistan), Bezeklik (near Turfan), Dunhuang (Gansu), Binglingsi (near Lanzhou) and Longmen (in Henan province). From at least the third century CE until around the time of the Tang conquest

46 *Jinshu* 97: 8a, cited and translated in Samolin 1964: 50, last sentence translated by Millward.
47 Hambis 1977: 91; Bagchi 1981: 42–5.

in the seventh century, local aristocracy and wealthy merchants sponsored the decoration of caves at Qizil and other sites in the Kucha area
with three-dimensional Buddha images, frescos of the life of the Buddha
and other scriptural scenes, drawing on diverse influences from Soghdia,
Gandhara, India and Iran. The striking green and blue palate of the Qizil
frescos, however, is uniquely Kuchean.[48]

During these centuries, and indeed through at least the eighth century,
Silk Road commerce was mostly in the hands of Soghdian merchants.
There were Soghdian communities in most major cities along a belt
running from Soghdia (Transoxiana) across Xinjiang and the Gansu corridor, and, by Tang times, across northern China. The term 'Silk Road'
is in fact almost a misnomer: silk was only one of many products exchanged, of which the Western imports to China were as important as
Chinese exports. And there was not a single but rather multiple routes.
'The Soghdian network' would perhaps be a better, if less romantic,
term, for these Iranian speaking merchants dominated east-west trade
from communities scattered across Semirech'e, Bactria and the Upper
Indus Valley as well as Xinjiang and western and northern China. Ultimately they even opened trade links with Byzantium. Soghdian became
the Silk Road *lingua franca*, and not just in commercial settings. In larger
communities like Gaochang there were communities of Soghdian farmers and artisans as well as merchants by the early seventh century. Of
the thirty-five commercial transactions listed in a tax document from
Gaochang in the 620s, twenty-nine involved a Soghdian.[49] After climate
changes forced the abandonment of Loulan, it was élites with Soghdian
names who established new cities in the Shanshan region. Besides engaging in commerce, Soghdians served as diplomatic envoys, and their
caravans often provided passage for pilgrims and monks. Though most
Soghdians were Zoroastrians, some adopted Buddhism and joined the
cadre of translators rendering Buddhist scripture and commentaries into
Chinese and other languages.

The Soghdian network was already in place across the Tarim Basin
and Gansu corridor in the early fourth century. We know this because of

48 Summarised from the gallery guide, 'The Cave as Canvas: Hidden Images of
Worship along the Silk Road', exhibition at the Arthur M. Sackler Gallery, Smithsonian Museum, 9 September 2001–7 July 2002. See also Zhu Yingrong and Han
Xiang 1990.
49 De La Vaissière 2003: 25.

a remarkable set of letters dating to 313 CE found in a watchtower near the Jade Gate, 90 km west of Dunhuang. The letters, written in Soghdian, discuss chaotic events in China, including the sacking of Luoyang by the *Xwn* ('Hun', i.e. Xiongnu), and also commercial matters. One letter is a business communication from a merchant based in Gansu to his 'home office' in Samarkand. Among the trade goods mentioned in the letters are silver, gold, wine, pepper, camphor, Tibetan musk and a white powder, possibly lead used for cosmetics. Two other letters are private correspondence written by a woman to her mother and her husband. All the letters are addressed and wrapped in a standardised fashion, indicating that the Soghdians in Samarkand, Khotan, Loulan and Dunhuang and elsewhere could communicate by means of an established postal system.[50] Soghdians would become still more important players in Xinjiang and north China between the fifth and the eighth centuries.

TANG, TÜRKS AND TIBET

During what I have called the classical period the rivalry between powerful states in north China and Mongolia ultimately spread to Xinjiang. The same thing happened from the seventh through eighth centuries, another high-point of Chinese historical involvement in the region. This time, however, other surrounding powers joined in the struggle for control and influence in the Tarim Basin.

From the mid-fourth century CE a new nomad confederation, the Ruanruan, arose in Mongolia from the ruins of the vast Xiongnu empire, eventually occupying Zungharia and collecting heavy tributes from the oases cities south of the Tianshan. A century later, under assault from the Wei Dynasty based in north China, the Ruanruan allowed control of the Tarim to fall to the Hephthalites, a nomad empire of obscure origins that ruled the old Kushan lands from *c.* 450 to 560.[51] From their base in

50 The letters were discovered in 1907 by Aurel Stein. There is a dispute over their actual date, but most scholars agree on 313–14. On the Soghdian network in this period and the letters, see De la Vaissière 2004: 43–67, 117–22 *passim*; new English translations by Nicholas Sims-Williams of four of the Soghdian ancient letters are posted along with translations of other primary texts related to the Silk Road on the Silk Road Seattle website at <http://depts.washington.edu/uwch/silkroad/texts/sogdlet> (accessed 5 May 2005).

51 The Hephthalites appear in Greek and Chinese sources under a variety of different names: Hua, Hyôn (Hun) in addition to Hephthalite and its variants;

Soghdiana and Bactria, the Hephthalites invaded southern Xinjiang as far as Turfan, and by the first years of the sixth century were sending embassies to the Wei dynasty in northern and north-western China. Like their predecessors, they interfered little in the affairs of the Tarim cities after subduing them, contenting themselves with the collection of taxes. The Hephthalites remained overlords of southern Xinjiang until shattered around 560 CE by the newest steppe empire to ride out of Mongolia: the Kök Türk (Ch. Tujue). Meanwhile, powers based in Tibet and in the west, from Arabia to western Turkestan, would enter a new geopolitical struggle that involved both southern and northern Xinjiang.[52]

First, the Türks. The Kök Türks are not to be confused with the Turks of modern Turkey—though the latter point to the former as ancestors. (Though the words are the same, for clarity I will use 'Türk' for the imperial state of the sixth through ninth century, and 'Turk' as a generic term for their offshoots thereafter. Hence, 'Turkey' and 'Turkish' will refer to the modern nation and its language; 'Turkic' will indicate the broader ethnic and linguistic category which includes Turkish, Uyghur, Uzbek, Kazak, Kyrgyz and others.) The Türks were a tribe initially under Ruanruan rulership. They spoke the same languages and probably differed little from the Ruanruan in appearance—that is, they looked Mongoloid. The Türks overthrew the Ruanruan and founded a state; soon thereafter (583) the new empire divided into a western and an eastern khaghanate (*khaghan* is an Altaic word for emperor, roughly equivalent to, though more exclusive than, 'khan'). The eastern khaghanate remained mainly in Mongolia. The Western Türks ruled Zungharia, the Ferghana Valley, the western Tarim Basin and parts of Afghanistan and northern India. They enjoyed diplomatic relations with Byzantium and warred with the Sassanid dynasty of Persia. As we will see, the splintering of the Türk imperial confederation passed on to subsequent Central Eurasian history a plethora of Turkic tribes, whose language, political formation and military force would dominate the region for centuries.

China-based powers were closely involved in Türk politics and with Xinjiang, starting with the reunifying Sui (581–618), which encouraged Türk factionalism and established footholds in Hami (Yiwu) and at

---

some scholars link them with the Var or Avar. They are thought to be composed of Xiongnu fragments (hence they are 'Huns') with some Iranian elements (Sinor 1990: 301).

52   Samolin 1964: 52–8.

Ruoqiang (Shanshan) and Qiemo in the southern Tarim. These policies continued under the Tang dynasty (618–906), which succeeded the Sui. The Tang, following the precedents of other north-China-based dynasties, endeavoured to weaken the nomad empire to its north by both diplomatic and military means. Unlike the Han, however, the royal house of the Tang was closely associated with northern peoples. During the chaotic period that followed the fall of the Han many nomad groups had established dynasties in north China with the result that the medieval Chinese aristocracy, including the Li family founders of the Tang, were intermarried with families of nomadic conquerors. The usual way of reconciling this with the purposes of nationalistic Chinese historiography is to argue that the northerners had thoroughly 'sinicised', but it makes as much sense to say that the Chinese aristocracy was 'Turkicised'. Either way, many members of the Tang court displayed many Central Asian and steppe influences: riding horses, speaking Turkic in preference to Chinese, and playing polo (even women). Tang élites also indulged in a passion for Kuchean music, for Soghdian whirling dance and for the exotic western goods brought by Soghdian merchants. One Tang prince chose to live in a yurt, and would offer guests chunks of roast mutton carved off with his own dagger. Tang music was played on the lutes, viols and percussion instruments of Central Asia and India; Tang poets sang of infatuation with western dancing girls. For these and other reasons the Tang period was one of imperial China's most open and cosmopolitan.

This 'Turkicness' of the Tang may in part explain its success *vis-à-vis* the Türk empire to its north. By 630 the Tang had taken the Eastern Türk Khagan prisoner and subsequently controlled the Eastern Türks for fifty years. The Tang also skilfully employed the politics of recognition and marriage to keep the Western Türk khaghanate off-balance. In order to weaken the Western Türks and maintain control of the Silk Road trade routes, the Tang also expanded westward, mobilising its Eastern Türk allies to conquer the oasis city-states in Turfan and the Tarim Basin. Khotan (Yutian), Kashgar (Sule) and Yarkand (Suoche) accepted Tang suzerainty in the 630s; the Gaochang kingdom (in the Turfan Basin) and Kucha were bloodily subdued in the 640s by massive forces under the command of the general Arshila (A-shi-na) She-er, a Türk prince in Tang service.[53] The Tang ruled the Tarim indirectly, ultimately establish-

53   On the identification of Arshila with A-shi-na, see Beckwith 1987: app. C.

ing a seat of government (the Protectorate-General of Anxi—'Pacified West') first at Turfan, then at Kucha to supervise native rulers in the Tarim Basin city states. Anxi (Kucha) and three other bases at Karashahr, Kashgar and Khotan comprised the Tang's 'Four Western Garrisons'.

Further Tang expansion followed. The Western Türk Khaghan He-lu (r. 651–7) briefly succeeded in reuniting the Western Türks and retaking the Tarim, as well as lands as far as Persia. When Tang forces defeated the Western Türks at Issyk Kul (in modern Kyrgyzstan) in 657, the Tang emperor installed two rival khans to rule the vast Western Türk empire, and scattered Tang protectorates-general and garrisons throughout it. Tang suzerainty thus extended thinly from Talas and Tashkent in the north, over Samarkand, Bukhara, Kabul and Herat, and as far southwest as Zarang in modern Iran. Tang thus abutted the frontiers of the expanding Arab empire. Cartographers tend to choose this moment of the Tang's greatest extent to depict historical maps of the Tang,[54] but five years later, by 662, the western Central Asian regions nominally under Tang protectorates and prefectures were in rebellion, and after only a few years the Western Türks succeeded in overthrowing their puppet khans and restoring their independence throughout their former territories. Although the Tang would regain its sway over western Türk tribes on occasion thereafter and Tang maintained a Zungharian foothold in Beiting (Beshbaliq, north of Jimsar in the vicinity of modern Urumchi),[55] direct Tang influence beyond the Pamirs was momentary.[56]

The Tang position in southern Xinjiang came under threat from a different quarter: the Tibetans, at the time an expansive force in Central Asian affairs. By the early 660s the Tibetans dominated the region around Gilgit and Wakhan, where the Karakoram and Pamir ranges meet, offering them a back door into the Tarim as well as into North India, Bactria and Transoxiana. In alliance with Türk groups, Tibet conquered Kashgar and Khotan. Around the same time Tibet attacked and drove the Tuyuhun (a Mongolian-speaking people) out of the Qinghai region and into Tang protection. From this position of strategic dominance the Tibet-

---

54 For example, Tan Qixiang 1982–7: 5: 32–3; Bentley and Ziegler's popular world history textbook represents the Tang with a map of the same four-year period (2000: 329).

55 On the location of Beiting/Beshbaliq, see Shimazaki 1974. Aurel Stein surveyed the ruined city in 1914 (Stein 1928: 2: 560ff).

56 Beckwith 1987: 38–9; Twitchett 1979: 224–8; 279–80; Samolin 1964: 59–60.

Ruins of a Tibetan fort at Miran, south-eastern Xinjiang (photo: J. Millward, 1992)

ans accepted submission of a large branch of the Western Türks, and in
670 launched an invasion of the Tarim Basin with the aid of Bhutanese
troops. Tang abandoned its Four Western Garrisons and moved the Anxi
Protectorate-General back to the Turfan depression. Chinese chroniclers
attempted to put the best possible spin on this debacle, writing in the
Tang official history (*Jiu Tangshu*): 'When [Tang emperor] Gaozong succeeded to the throne, he did not want extensive territories to trouble the
people, so he ordered the officials concerned to abandon Kucha and the
other of the Four Garrisons, and move the Protectorate-Generalship of
the Pacified West to Xi *zhou*, where it had been of old.'[57] The fact was,
however, that Tang had lost control of the silk route and was in full flight
from its empire in Central Asia.

Not until 693 did Tang defeat the Tibetans and re-enter the Tarim,
when divisions between the Tibetan emperor and generals provided an
opening. Tang then re-established its Four Western Garrisons and moved
the Anxi Protectorate-General back west to Kucha (although Tang did

57 *Jiu Tangshu* 198: 5304, translation in Beckwith 1987: 38 (Wade-Giles changed
to Pinyin); Beckwith 1987: 28–38.

not recover Kashgar until 728).[58] Nevertheless, the Türk and Tibetan threats remained, and continued insecurity in the southern Tarim kept the Tang from intervening meaningfully beyond the Pamirs, where in the early eighth century the Arabs were advancing into Bactria, Ferghana and Soghdiana. Despite a renewed Tang position in the Issyk Kul region and Ferghana in 714–15, the Western Türk confederation was restored under the Türgesh tribe, and a year later was besieging the northern Tarim cities of Aqsu and Uch Turfan in alliance with Tibetan and Arab forces. Despite a flurry of diplomatic activity and bestowal of titles upon small states in North India, the Pamir, Ferghana and Soghdiana, Tang could play no direct role in the Tibetan-Arab-Türk struggles for trans-Pamir Central Asian supremacy in the 710s–20s. Rather, Tang outposts continued to suffer raids from Tibet and the Türgesh, and Tang access to the trade routes over the Pamirs to India was endangered by Tibetan pressure in the 720s and outright conquest of the Pamir region in 736.[59]

Tang was to enjoy one last blaze of glory in Xinjiang and Central Asia. In the 730s it consolidated its position in the Tarim and Zungharia, increasing troop deployments at Kucha and Beiting. It crushed the Türgesh confederation in 744 and once again projected power into the Yili Valley and Issyk Kul area, and thus largely secured the trade routes south and north of the Tianshan, which now became a source of transit tax revenue supporting the Tang garrisons. With the north thus under control, Ko Sŏnji marched to the Pamirs, where in a famous campaign he drove the Tibetans out of the Pamir mountain states. (Ko, or Gao Xianzhi in Chinese, was a Korean serving the Tang as 'Assistant Protector-General of the Pacified West and Four Garrisons Commissioner-General in Charge of Troops and Horses'.)[60] A few years later, when hostilities broke out between Ferghana and Tashkent, the latter allied with remnants of the Türgesh tribes, Ferghana sought aid from the Tang, and with Ko Sŏnji's force behind it, Ferghana prevailed. Ko captured Tashkent, where he accepted the submission of the local ruler but then executed him and allowed Tang troops to loot the city. The son of the unfortunate Tashkent king fled to the Arabs in Samarkand, who fielded

58 Beckwith 1987: 53–5; Samolin 1964: 61–4.
59 Beckwith 1987: 87–8.
60 · The region and campaign has been described by Aurel Stein (1912: 52–72 *passim*) and, most recently, by Whitfield (1999: 'The Soldier's Tale').

an army and marched on his behalf toward Tang territory. Ko Sŏnji mobilised his own forces, reinforced with troops from another Turkic tribe, the Qarluqs (Karluks),[61] to block an Arab attack on the Four Garrisons. Arab and Tang forces with their Turkic auxiliaries met near Talas (Taraz, in today's Kyrgyzstan). The battle went badly for Ko: his Qarluq Turks rebelled and attacked him from the rear.[62]

The Battle of Talas (751) has become a landmark event in history surveys. One significant result was that Chinese captives taken in the battle and held in Samarkand introduced large-scale paper manufacture, and the use of paper thereafter spread (thanks to Soghdian merchants) throughout the Islamic world, replacing papyrus, parchment and other more costly and less convenient media.

The Battle of Talas is mainly remembered, however, as the first and last meeting of Arab and Chinese armies. Yet despite Ko's defeat, this battle in and of itself was not strategically important: the Arabs never advanced into Xinjiang. It was not Ko's exploits that drove the Tang from Central Asia but those of another foreign general in Tang employ, An Lushan, whose rebellion from 755 to 763 tore apart the Tang realm and was suppressed only with the help of the Uyghurs (see below). An Lushan was half-Soghdian and half-Türk (his name, Rokhshan—'luminous'—is the same as that of Alexander the Great's Soghdian wife). His status as a general in the north-eastern reaches of the Tang empire testifies to the importance of Soghdians not only in commerce but in administration across north China during the Tang; indeed, Étienne de la Vaissière refers to northern China under the Tang as a '*milieu turko-sogdien*', and has argued that An Lushan's rebellion was to a hitherto unknown extent a Soghdian movement, supported by Soghdian traders. An Lushan's ceremonial jades bore the Soghdian royal title 'jamuk' beside the Chinese term *huangdi* for emperor.[63]

---

61 The Qarluqs were a tribe formerly under Eastern Türk rule who had joined with Uyghur and Basmil tribes to overthrow the reconstituted Eastern Türk khaghanate. Having done so, they allied with the Uyghurs to wipe out the Basmils. After the Uyghurs established a khaghanate under their own rule in 744, the Qarluqs moved west to Zungharia, into lands made available by the Tang scattering of the Türgesh confederation.

62 Twitchett 1979: 426, 433–5, 443–4; Samolin 1964: 64–7. The actual 'Battle of Talas' took place at Atlakh, a few miles from the city of Talas (Beckwith 1987: 139 n. 188).

63 De la Vaissière 2004: 195–203; De la Vaissière 2003: 26.

The An Lushan rebellion in the Tang homelands necessitated a pull-back from Tang outposts in Xinjiang. By the end of the eighth century Tibet had taken over the southern Tarim and was struggling with the Uyghurs for eastern Xinjiang and Gansu; northern and western Xinjiang fell under Qarluq overlordship. Although the Tang dynasty survived the An Lushan rebellion, it would never again extend power as far west as Xinjiang. In fact, there would not be direct rule over Xinjiang by a China-based state for almost exactly one thousand years.

Assessing the Tang, Türks and Tibetans in Xinjiang

Once again, because of the influence of Chinese sources on the subsequent telling of history, it is worth reconsidering the Tang record in Xinjiang as a whole. From its first active efforts in the region in the 630s to the An Lushan rebellion Tang enjoyed, all in all, some hundred years of relatively firm sovereignty over the Tarim city states, divided into two episodes by a spell of Tibetan rule, and frequently disturbed by Türk and Tibetan attacks. Over this period the Tang also controlled Zungharia for about twenty years—something the Han Dynasty had never achieved. To be sure, for some of the time the Tang could claim 'submission' of Western Türk tribal leaders based north of the Tianshan, and when the chiefs were not actively attacking Tang interests this alliance can be said to have had some military and political substance. But it must be added that except for its easternmost garrisons in the Turfan region,[64] nowhere were large numbers of Tang Chinese settled; to the contrary, Tang rule was indirect, with local élites left in place, and Tang garrisons largely staffed by Turkic soldiers and led by non-Chinese commanders like Arshila She-er and Ko Sŏnji. The merchants carrying out the trade between China, Xinjiang and parts west were mostly Soghdians, who dominated commerce not only in Xinjiang, but across north China up to the Korean border. Chinese merchants, on the other hand, are notable for their 'stunning absence' in Tang sources up to 755.[65]

As noted above, here again the pattern of political control of the Tarim Basin by outside powers is evident. This time Tibet often dominated the

64   Quantities of documents detailing Tang period household census, land registration and labour service have been gathered from the Turfan region by Western, Japanese and Chinese archaeologists. See Yamamoto and Dohi 1984–5.
65   De la Vaissière 2004: 162.

southern Tarim Basin, Turkic nomads controlled Zungharia, and China-based powers held sway over the Turfan region and Gansu corridor. As during the Han-Xiongnu conflict, the political and military fate of Xin-jiang was in this middle period again linked to the quasi-cyclical pattern by which great powers on the plains of north China and in Mongolia have risen almost simultaneously. Many scholars, including Ellsworth Huntington (1919), Owen Lattimore (1940), Joseph Fletcher (1986), Sechin Jagchid (1989), Thomas Barfield (1989) and Nicola Di Cosmo (1999b) have offered explanations for the often parallel emergence and interaction of powerful sedentary and nomadic states across the ecological divide between Mongolia and north China. Environment, strategy, trade, technological change, internal socio-political dynamics, external pressure and historical memory all have played a role in this process. The fourteenth-century Arab 'sociologist' Ibn Khaldun famously analysed the relationship between nomadic and settled people in terms of a waxing and waning cycle of 'group solidarity' (*'asabiyya*) engendered by the hard conditions of the desert.[66] Peter Perdue has recently provided a useful comparison and analysis of all these theories, and reminded us, on the basis of his study of the Zunghars and Manchus, that strong leaders have also played a large part.[67] For our purposes, it is sufficient to note again that the political history of the Xinjiang region has been repeatedly implicated in this relationship across the Sino-Mongolian borderlands: rivalries with Mongolia-based states led powers in China to expand westward in order to cut off the nomad powers' other sources of agrarian supply, commercial revenue and tribute.

The Xinjiang region also fell within other circuits of interstate power relations and economic interchange. Though the peaks of the Pamir and Karakoram are awe-inspiring, below them lie plateaus along which traders and armies moved with relative ease. Kushan, and the Hephthalites after them, projected power into the Tarim Basin. The Arabs came close to doing so. Tibet and Tang warred over control of these very passes because of the importance of the routes to Bactria and Transoxiana running through them. Turkic powers based in Zungharia, the Talas River or Issyk Kul area vied to hold both the western Tarim Basin and Ferghana. To the east, Qinghai-based powers including the Tuyuhun, Tibet and, as we will see in Chapter 2, the Tanguts (Xixia), struggled with China

66   Ibn Khaldun 1969 (1377): Chapter 2.
67   Perdue 2005: 532–6.

over the Gansu corridor, Dunhuang (where the silk route forked north and south) and eastern parts of what is now Xinjiang. The political and military fate of Xinjiang, particularly the Tarim and Turfan Basins, then, was closely linked in this period to struggles along three enduring political and cultural frontiers: the Sino-Mongolian, the Sino-Tibetan and the Pamir/Tianshan belt dividing western from eastern parts of Central Asia. Meanwhile, the Soghdians, who worked with whoever seized power in the Central Asian oases and north China cities, managed commerce and other cultural communication from Ferghana to Manchuria.

2. Central Eurasia Ascendant

(9th–16th centuries)

Long-lived, territorially vast empires are convenient for mapmakers and students of history. One pair of dates and a single name can cover a big chunk of time and is easily represented by a broad monochrome space on the map. By contrast, eras of invasions, migrations and political flux are hard to grasp. Space and time are repeatedly divided and subdivided, and there are the names of multiple ephemeral rulers and dynasties to be recalled. Just compare a historical map of the Roman empire at its greatest extent—an easily legible band of solid colour encircling the Mediterranean—with that of the post-classical Europe and the *Völkerwanderung*, in which a tangle of arrows representing barbarian invasions writhe like serpents across a patchwork quilt.

During the centuries covered in this chapter, nomadic powers in this era enjoyed their greatest advantage over the agrarian states of the Eurasian rimlands. In the east the Uyghur, Tangut, Khitan and Jurched all established large states incorporating agrarian areas; in the west the Qarakhanids, Ghaznavids and Seljuks did the same. Next the Mongols outdid them all with an empire that spanned the continent. Chinggis (Genghis) Khan's successors instituted an enduring pattern of Central Eurasian aristocracies ruling over pastoralist and agrarian areas from Iran to China. Timur (Tamerlane), himself a Turk, temporarily reprised the western Mongol empire.

For all their might, however, Central Eurasian nomad powers were fractious. Their customary acceptance of either lateral (to brothers, uncles or cousins) or patrilineal succession, depending on who won the political and military contest to inherit the khanship, ensured any number of bloody transitions and political fragmentations. Besides internecine struggles, campaigns of conquest and wars between tribal confederations displaced states and ruling élites with relative rapidity. Even states with a long track record, such as that of the Uyghurs based in the region of modern Turfan, shifted through several complex political relationships with the dominant powers in the neighbourhood.

The events covered in this chapter, then, are complex. The names of rulers, dynasties and places flash by bewilderingly. Perhaps for this reason, many accounts of Xinjiang and Central Eurasian history skip or radically abbreviate coverage of this period. I have provided somewhat more detail, however, because this period exemplifies the principal themes of this book: the region's geography made the Tarim Basin a prize over which nomadic powers based in Mongolia, Zungharia or Semirech'e struggled, and from which powers in China hoped to interdict them. The shifts in ruling power were more rapid than changes in underlying demography and culture, but nonetheless left their mark. The Tarim population became linguistically and, arguably, genetically more Turko-Mongolian in this period; it also became Islamic. Though the names of states pass by in quick succession—Qarluq, Qarakhanid, Qara Khitay, Mongol, Chaghatayid, Moghulistan, Yarkand khanate—by the end of this period some more familiar names have mounted the stage: Uyghur, Kazak, Kirghiz, Uzbek. Though these names do not quite signify what they will come to mean in modern times, their emergence does show that it was in the aftermath of the Mongol empire that the seeds of modern religious and national identities began to be sown. (The Appendix is intended as an aid to following the names and chronology in this and other chapters)

The era of the Tibetan, Arab, Tang and Türk rivalry in Central Asia bequeathed a complex legacy to Xinjiang and world history. The Tibetan empire left its mark on frescos in Dunhuang and some architectural artefacts in the southern Tarim, including a fortress on the Khotan River at Mazartagh and ruins at Miran. Although the Arabs did not penetrate Xinjiang in the eighth century, Islam would spread westward from Central Asia into Xinjiang over subsequent centuries. Tang military farms and settlements in the Turfan area and close communications with China during the Tang period left an enduring stamp upon local culture and administration in eastern Xinjiang. Besides the imports to China mentioned above, trade and other exchanges between Tang and Central and Western Eurasia also left cultural traces in Central Asia and the West; just one example would be the famous Tang three colour glaze (*sancai*) of which versions may still be seen in pottery across Eurasia and even as far west as Eastern Europe. Chinese coins continued to circulate extensively in Xinjiang. Although the direct influence of the Tang military garrisons in Zungharia and Transoxiana was short-lived, associations with north Chinese states continued to be a source of prestige even for later Turkic empires. The khans of both the Qarakhanid and Qara Khitay empires (see below) referred to themselves as Chinese emperors—though the terms they used for 'Chinese'—Tabghach and Khitay—were actually names of Inner Asian conquerors who had established states in north China.

The greatest influence of this period was that of the Türks, politically, genetically and linguistically. The Türk empire and its dissolution led to one of history's great *Völkerwanderung*, a movement of Turkic-speaking tribes into Xinjiang and across Central Eurasia. The Tang use of Turkic soldiers likewise sped the westward Turkic migrations. Whereas much of Central Eurasia, including the oases of what is now Xinjiang, had been Indo-European speaking, the seventh century saw the beginnings of a process of linguistic Turkicisation that would ultimately replace Tokharian and Soghdian in the Tarim Basin with Turkic languages and create the modern patchwork of Turkic and Iranic speakers in Transoxiana.[1] Steppe empires after the Kök Türks, even if their élites were not Turkic, were made up largely of Turkic tribes. Much more than was the case with the Xiongnu, the memory of the Türk khaghanate would have a momentum of its own, inspiring subsequent states to emulate it and adopt certain of its symbols of legitimacy. Many peoples and now states across Eurasia have continued to identify themselves as Turks, despite the rise of Islam and of the later Mongol empire, which greatly surpassed the territorial extent of the Türk khaghanate.

THE UYGHUR KINGDOM IN XINJIANG

The Uyghurs, the next major conquering power on the Xinjiang scene, originated, like many of their predecessors, in the Mongolian core lands of the Orkhon river valley (see Map 2). The tribes known by the term Uyghur (and other names, including *Toqquz Oghuz*, 'the nine tribes'),[2]

---

1 Grousset 1997: 100–1; Samolin 1964: 60
2 As is often the case with steppe empires, the details of their makeup and backgrounds of their ruling families are complex and hard to determine with certainty on the basis of existing sources; there are thus several names closely associated with the Uyghur. The Gaoche or Gaoju people, ancestors of the Uyghurs of the

were former components of the Türk khaghanate, spoke and wrote a language virtually identical to that of the Türks before them, and were at first somatically Mongoloid—that is, they resembled other eastern Altaic peoples with epicanthic fold and sparse facial hair, and not the high-nosed, bearded Iranian peoples who were then still the primary inhabitants of the Tarim, and who remain a major component of Xinjiang's historical population. The Uyghur patrons depicted on the walls of temple 9 at Bezeklik near Turfan probably give a good idea of what the Uyghur aristocracy in Xinjiang initially looked like, before centuries of intermarriage with local peoples of eastern Iranian stock. (A twelfth-century Chinese envoy would describe the oasis inhabitants of the Uyghur region with 'curly hair, deep-set eyes, straight and thick brows, many have curly beards'.)[3]

The Uyghurs of the Uyghur khaghanate were primarily nomads, though they also built impressive cities, such as their capital, Ordu Baliq (literally, 'Royal Camp Town'),[4] and some engaged in agriculture. They were not Muslims, but rather Manichaean. Later, the Uyghur state in eastern Xinjiang tolerated Buddhism and Christianity among its urban population—it opposed Islam. The Uyghur aristocracy of the Uyghur khaghanate who migrated to the Turfan Basin, therefore, while certainly

---

Uyghur khaghanate, were part of a confederation of many tribes known by the name Tiele in the Chinese records. The Tiele became 'recalcitrant vassals' of the Türks. The word 'Uyghur' (Ch. Yuanhe, Weihe), the name of the pre-eminent tribe in the Tiele confederation, may have come to serve as an omnibus term for all of them. Chinese sources also called this confederation *jiu xing*, or 'Nine Surnames', which corresponds with the Turkic term 'Toqquz Oghuz' adopted by Muslim sources for 'both the Uyǧur Qaǧanate in Mongolia and the subsequent diasporic Uyǧur states'. There is doubt, however, whether the term 'Toqquz Oghuz' in its original sense included or excluded the ruling Uyghur clans of the khaghanate or the rulers of the Uyghur polity established after 840 in north-eastern Xinjiang (Golden 1992: 156–8). In the eighth-century Orkhon Inscriptions of the Eastern Türk khaghans, 'Toqquz Oghuz' is used in a way that suggests it meant the Turkic people in a tribal sense broader than the political scope of *Kök Türk*—there were Toqquz Oghuz tribes that did not accept the political rule of the Türk khaghans. The Orkhon inscriptions use the term 'Uyghur' separately, for the Uyghur tribes. In Muslim authors before Mahmud Kashghari, 'Toqquz Oghuz' became synonymous with 'Uyghur'. Kashghari, however, used 'Uyghur'. For a long discussion of the problem, see Minorsky 1970: 264–71, and 1978: I: 285–90.

3 Golden 1992: 168, citing Hong Hao's *Songmo jiwen*.
4 Also known, in Mongolian, as Qarabalghasun. Golden 1992: 171 n. 1.

Uyghur princes from a wall painting in the Bezeklik caves, near Turfan
(cave temple 9, 8th–9th century CE; Collection of the Museum für In-
dische Kunst, Berlin, MIK III 6876a)

among the ancestors of today's Uyghur people, are not their only ancestors. They and other Turkic migrants compose some part of modern
Uyghurs' genetic makeup; the Uyghurs from the Uyghur khaghanate
were also some cultural distance away from the sedentary agriculturalist
Muslim Turki of the Tarim oases in the eighteenth and nineteenth centuries who came by the twentieth century to call themselves 'Uyghur'.

   As noted above, the Uyghurs, component tribes of the Türks, joined
the Qarluqs and Basmils in overthrowing the Eastern Türk khaghanate.

The Qarluqs and the Uyghurs then displaced the Basmil khan, and in 744 the Uyghurs drove the Qarluqs west and established their own Uyghur royal house at the head of an empire based in central Mongolia and extending into north-west China, parts of Zungharia and at times as far west as Ferghana. This Uyghur khaghanate provided the military aid that allowed the Tang dynasty to survive the An Lushan rebellion, but exacted a heavy price for it: in the course of fighting An Lushan, the Uyghurs sacked and plundered the Chinese city of Luoyang, even burning the temples in which people sought refuge. Later, for decades they maintained an extortionate trade of horses for Tang silk, exchanging one horse for an average of 38 bolts of silk. An Arab traveller describes the Uyghur king's tent as made of gold and pitched on top of his castle; this monarch, he relates, received annual tribute from China of 500,000 pieces of silk.[5]

The Soghdians were deeply involved in the rise of the Uyghur state. Their commercial networks linked north China, Mongolia and the Xinjiang regions, in all of which the Uyghurs had interests. Moreover, not only did the Soghdians work as middlemen in the silk-horse trade with the Tang, but they provided the Uyghur khaghanate with a cultural and administrative model critical to its transition from tribal power to far-flung empire ruling both nomadic and settled subjects. This cultural package included the Soghdian script (itself ultimately derived from Aramaic), which was adopted for writing the unrelated Uyghur language, along with such loan vocabulary as was necessary to imperial administration over oases and to life at a fixed court. It also included the systematised religion of Manichaeism. In 762 or 763 the Uyghur khaghan Bögü (Ch. Mouyu) converted to this faith after contact with Soghdians in Luoyang. Many Soghdians served the Uyghurs in administrative capacities.[6]

It is interesting that, given the choices available to them, the Uyghurs chose for their cultural and political infrastructure not the Chinese but the Soghdian model, despite (or perhaps because of?) the Uyghur relationship with the Tang as military ally and supplier of horses. The memory of how the Eastern Türks had been co-opted and incorporated by the Tang was no doubt still fresh; indeed the Türk khaghan Kül Tegin had only thirty years earlier carved into his memorial stone in the

5   De la Vaissière 2004: 278–9; Minorsky 1978: I: 283.
6   De la Vaissière 2004: 200–3.

Orkhon valley an explicit caution to the Türk people not to be co-opted by the southerners. Beware the 'sweet words and soft materials' of the Chinese, he wrote. It was a warning the Uyghurs heeded.[7]

In 840 the steppe capital of the Uyghur state was itself destroyed and the tribes scattered by yet another tribal confederation, the Kirghiz (Qirghiz, Kyrgyz), who moved south from the area of today's Tuva and after twenty years of conflict ousted the Uyghurs from the Orkhon River valley. Juvaini, the Persian historian of the Mongol empire, described the Uyghur diaspora in vivid terms:

> The tribes and peoples of the Uighur, when they listened to the neighing of horses, the screaming of camels, the barking and howling of dogs and beasts of prey, the lowing of cattle, the bleating of sheep, the twittering of birds and the whimpering of children, in all this heard the cry of '*köch, köch!*' ['move, move!'] and would move on from their halting-place. And wherever they halted the cry of '*köch, köch!*' would reach their ears. Finally they came to the plain where they afterwards built Besh-Baligh, and here that cry was silenced ....[8]

Some Uyghurs fled south to China; others moved to the Gansu/Qinghai border region with Tibet, where they established a kingdom that survived until absorbed by the Tanguts around 1030. Another group of tribes migrated to north-eastern Xinjiang, establishing a state centred on Beshbaliq as their winter capital (where the nomadic tribesmen remained to pasture their herds all year) and Qocho as their summer capital. Qocho's impressive ruins of houses, palaces and temples may still be seen today (the site of this ancient Uyghur capital near Turfan is also known as Gaochang, Huozhou and Qarakhoja). The domains of the Qocho Uyghur state extended east as far as Hami and west to Kucha.[9]

---

7   The Orkhon Inscriptions are translated in Silay 1996: 1–10. On these inscriptions, see note 17 below.

8   Juvaini 1997: 61.

9   Beckwith 1987: 155–72; Golden 1992: 163–4; MacKerras 1990; Xue Zongzheng *et al.* 1997: 325–6. According to some scholars, the group of Uyghur tribes that eventually became established in Turfan/Beshbaliq/Kucha was not the Uyghur royal clan itself, but the Toqquz Oghuz, tribes from the west who had escaped the Kirghiz assault and later moved south of the Tianshan into the vacuum left by the crumbling of Tibetan power around the same time as the Uyghur diaspora. Although under Uyghur suzerainty the Toqquz Oghuz were distinct from them. According to this view, Muslim sources are thus correct in referring to the rulers of the Turfan-based polity as 'Toqquz Oghuz', while Chinese sources mistakenly call them 'Uyghur'. In any case, the Uyghur period in north-eastern Xinjiang saw the

Ruins of Qocho (Gaochang) (photo: J. Millward, 2004)

Enduring from the ninth to the thirteenth century, the Qocho Uyghur
state was longer-lived than any previous imperial power in the region.
In the 1130s it accepted the Qara Khitay (Western Liao; see below) as
suzerain, sending Uyghur royal family members as hostages to the court
of this new dynasty. In 1209 it submitted promptly to the rising Mongol
empire, thus assuring its own continued local authority until the 1370s,
when it was finally destroyed and incorporated by the Mongols. Even as
vassals, however, the Uyghurs exercised a strong cultural influence upon
Chinggis Khan's empire. By then a firm amalgam of Inner Eurasian oasis
and steppe traditions, the Uyghurs provided the Mongols with a writing
system and officials to employ it—just as the Soghdians had earlier done
for the Uyghur khaghanate. A Uyghur taught Chinggis Khan's sons to
read and write, in the Uyghur script.[10]

---

assimilation of a variety of groups, including Iranian, Tokharian, other non-Uyghur
Turkic, Chinese and perhaps even some Mongolian peoples into the ruling and
subject groups of the region (Golden 1992: 164–5).
10   Barthold [1900] 1968: 387.

The Uyghur state initially resembled the paradigmatic form we have already noted in Xinjiang's history: a Turko-Mongolian nomadic power ruling Indo-European oasis agriculturalists indirectly from across the Tianshan. Yet the Uyghurs reached south far enough to maintain an administrative capital (Qocho) in the Turfan Basin. Over time, moreover, the populations and cultures of nomad ruler and oasis ruled blended; religious, political and cultural influences from Soghdia, India and China were incorporated as well. The Qocho Uyghur rulers dropped the title 'khan' in favour of *idiqut* (*iduqqut*), a term meaning 'sacred majesty'. This state continued to enjoy good relations with China-based dynasties of the Tang, the Five Dynasties-period northern states, the Song, the Liao and the Jin, with whom they and the ubiquitous Soghdian merchants traded a variety of pastoral, agricultural and mineral products. Frescos at Bezeklik (near Qocho) and Qizil (Kucha area), lands under Uyghur control, provide evidence of Uyghur patronage of Manichaeism, Buddhism and Nestorian Christianity. These same paintings reveal, in their variety of religious imagery, dress and hairstyles (including braided queue, coiled bun, bobbed or loose and long styles) a complex and diverse society.[11] Owing to the warm climate and the availability of run-off from the Tianshan, Qocho's agriculture flourished, allowing double-crops of grain, as well as the production of a wide variety of fruits and vegetables. Cotton had been grown in the region for centuries, and as this fibre was not yet prevalent in China, cotton cloth was among the exports to the east. Grapes, then as now, were a local specialty, and wine was bartered and collected by the Qocho government as tax.[12]

A description from a Song (Chinese) envoy who travelled to Qocho in 984 gives a taste of the city's diversity and prosperity:

There is no rain or snow here and it is extremely hot. Each year at the hottest time, the inhabitants dig holes in the ground to live in ....The earth here produces all the five grains except buckwheat. The nobility eat horseflesh, while the rest eat mutton, wild ducks and geese. Their music is largely played on the pipa and harp. They produce sables, fine white cotton cloth, and an embroidered cloth made from flower stamens. By custom they enjoy horseback riding and archery ....They use the [Tang] calendar produced in the seventh year of the Kaiyuan reign (719) .... They fashion pipes of silver or brass and channel

11   See, for example, Hambis 1977, plates 65, 70, 87 (descriptions on pp. 116, 152) and vignette on p. 145 (152) for men's hairstyles.
12   Xue Zongzheng *et al.* 1997: 327–34, 337–40.

flowing water to shoot at each other; or they sprinkle water on each other as a game, which they call pressing out the sun's heat to chase off sickness. They like to take walks, and the strollers always carry a musical instrument with them. There are over fifty Buddhist temples here, the names inscribed over their gates all presented by the Tang court. The temples house copies of the Buddhist scriptures (*da zang jing*) and the dictionaries *Tang yun*, *Yupian* and *Jingyun*. On spring nights the locals pass the time milling about between the temples. There's an 'Imperial Writings Tower' which houses edicts written by the Tang emperor Taizong kept carefully secured. There's also a Manichaean temple, with Persian monks who keep their own religious law and call the Buddhist scriptures the 'foreign Way' .... In this land there are no poor people; anyone short of food is given public aid. People live to an advanced age, generally over one hundred years. No one dies young.[13]

Worth noting in this description, besides what seems a rather pleasant way of life, is the continuing respect for Buddhism and the legacy of Tang-era Chinese rule, even under a nomadic Uyghur élite with its own religion and customs.

A Persian geography from the same period, though confused about some details, gives a similar overall picture of the Uyghur or 'Toghuz-ghuz' (Toqquz Oghuz) kingdom to the west of 'Chinistan' (China). The source, the *Hudud al-'Alam*, describes the Toghuzghuz kings as a warlike people, once rulers of all Turkestan (i.e. roughly the lands of the Türk empire), who lived as nomads on the northern steppes, lands that produce musk, furs and horn. Their capital Qocho, interestingly enough, is here called 'Chinese town'; it is pleasant in winter but terrifically hot in summer (something any summer tourist to Turfan can attest to). The 'Five Villages' (a standard term indicating five principal Uyghur towns) were inhabited by Soghdians, among them Christians, Zoroastrians and heathens—perhaps indicating Buddhists?[14] A variety of Soghdian Christian texts have been discovered in the Turfan Basin.[15]

To the south and east of this Uyghur kingdom the Tibetan empire was crumbling, and by the tenth century the Uyghurs definitively wrested the northern rim of the Tarim Basin and the Tianshan range from their

13 *Songshi* j. 490, 'Gaochang', translation by Millward. The envoy was Wang Yande. An English adaptation of a French translation of this passage is cited in Soucek 2000: 79.
14 Minorsky 1970: 94–5 (n. 12).
15 Sims-Williams 1992. Major secondary works on the Uyghurs include Gabain 1961 and 1973.

influence. By 938 the city-state of Khotan resumed sending its own diplomatic missions to the Chinese court. However, by the 990s the Tangut
(Xixia) state had spread westward from its base in the Ordos oxbow
of the Yellow River, and was asserting itself in the Gansu corridor and
Qinghai. By the 1030s it had absorbed the Gansu Uyghur state, including
perhaps Dunhuang. Although the scanty records of this strongly Buddhist state reveal that Uyghur monks and even princesses were present in
the Tangut lands, this 'Great State of White and High' obstructed Qocho
communication with the China-based courts of Song, Liao and Jin.[16]

THE QARAKHANIDS

To the west of the Qocho Uyghur polity a new confederation emerged
in the ninth century from the welter of Qarluq, Yaghma and other Türkic
tribes driven west by the rise and fall of the Orkhon Uyghur state. These
tribes ultimately formed an empire in Kashgaria, Semirech'e and Transoxiana, and are known to modern scholars as the Qarakhanid dynasty.

To understand the rise of the Qarakhanids one must appreciate the
politico-religious importance of Turkic royal titles, as well as of the imperial heartland territories, particularly the Ötükän forest mentioned in
the Orkhon inscriptions[17] and the Western Türk capital of Balasaghun,
on the Chu River near Issyk Kul. Before they overthrew the Türk state
the Uyghur and Qarluq rulers had styled themselves *yabghu*—a term that
implies descent from the Türk royal clan (Arshila/A-shi-na). The Türk
rulers themselves, on the other hand, were khaghans (khans), a term that
became reserved for those controlling these sacred refuges of the Eastern
or Western Türks. After establishing their own Orkhon-based imperial
rule, the Uyghurs themselves could become khaghans. After the Kirghiz
drove them from the sacred Orkhon heartland, however, the Uyghur
rulers no longer used the khanal title. Nor did the Kirghiz adopt the
term. However, the Qarluqs and their confederated tribes did assume the
status of rightful imperial successors of the Kök Türks, and their rulers
adopted the title khan (khaghan) by virtue of their occupation of the

16   On the Tanguts, see Dunnell 1996.
17   These eighth-century texts carved in a runic Turkic script on stone steles
found in the Orkhon region of Mongolia tell of the rise and fall of the first Turkic
khanate, and of the exploits of the khans who restored the Türk state before it was
overthrown by the Basmil, Uyghur and Qarluqs.

western sacred refuge on the Chu River. When the royal family split into
two branches, one line of khans became the *arslan*, or lion khans, and
the other the *bughra*, or bull camel khans. In Islamic sources their polity
was known as *al-khaqaniyya* (the Khaghanal house), or *al-khaniyya* (the
khanal [kings]).[18] Interestingly, the Qarakhanids also employed the title
'Tamghaj (Tabghach) Khan', meaning 'khan of China'.[19]

As during the previous era, then, the region we now know as Xinjiang was from the ninth through the thirteenth centuries once again
divided into separate spheres, with the Uyghur state in the north-east
ruling Beshbaliq and the northern Tarim cities as far west as Kucha; the
Tanguts controlling the south and south-east; and the Qarakhanids ruling the west.

ISLAMICISATION OF THE TURKS

Through the Qarakhanids the western Tarim became closely linked to
the Islamic world of Transoxiana. While the Uyghur state provided today's Uyghurs with their ethnonym, the Qarakhanids were largely responsible for their religion. A quasi-legendary account from the Kashgar
area attributes the Islamicisation of the Turks to the following event. A
brother of the ruler of the Irano-Islamic Samanid state in Transoxiana
is said to have sought asylum with Oghulchaq, a member of the junior,
Bughra branch of the Qarakhanids ruling in Kashgar. The Bughra Khan
installed this eminent Samanid refugee as Governor of Artush, an important caravan station just outside Kashgar. There the new governor built
a mosque. Somewhat later Oghulchaq's nephew Satuq was inspecting
caravan goods in Artush when he noticed the Muslim merchants stopping all business to pray as soon as they heard the muezzin's call. Satuq,
profoundly moved by this sight, began studying the Qur'an himself. (In
another version, Satuq while out hunting one day encounters a talking

18   Origins of the Qarakhanids are complex and disputed, with Barthold's 'Yaghma
hypothesis' at odds with Pritsak's 'Qarluq theory' (Biran 2001a: 81–2). Component
tribes of the Qarakhanids probably included the Yaghma, Chighil and Tukhsi as
well as remnant Türgesh and the Qarluq. Principal scholarship on the question is
by Barthold (for example, 'History of Semireche' in 1956–62 and his entry 'Karluk'
in *Encyclopaedia of Islam*, first edn, 1913–42) and Pritsak 1951. Here I follow Golden
1992: 214–16 and 1990: 348–51, with reference to Samolin 1964: 76–85.
19   Biran 2001a: 78.

rabbit who turns into a shaykh and induces him to repeat, 'There is no god but God, and Muhammad is his prophet.')

After his conversion Satuq fought and defeated his uncle the Bughra Khan, and then, perhaps with Samanid assistance, took Balasaghun and displaced the senior Arslan khans. Satuq Bughra Khan promoted Islam among his subjects. According to Islamic sources, Islamicisation in Xinjiang achieved a breakthrough in 960, five years after Satuq's death, with the conversion of '200,000 tents of the Turks'. Satuq Bughra Khan remains a revered figure in the Artush and Kashgar area, where his tomb, associated college and shrine, was rebuilt and endowed by Ya'qub Beg (see Chapter 3) and is now again under reconstruction.[20]

This heroic tradition notwithstanding, it is likely that the conversion of the Qarakhanids took place more gradually. A Muslim scholar, Kalimati, in the Qarakhanid court around this time may have played a role; also of likely significance were shaykhs and mystics on the steppes, and the penetration everywhere of Muslim merchants.[21]

The conversion of the Turks to Islam was an event of world-historical significance, for the Qarakhanids went on to destroy the Samanid dynasty (1000) and assume control of firmly Muslim Transoxiana. They would be the first of several Turkic ruling dynasties in the Islamic world. From the perspective of modern Uyghur nationalism, however, the discrete histories of the Qarakhanids and the Uyghur Qocho state present a problem. While the modern Uyghur people take their name from the Uyghur empire and Qocho state (known as Uyghuristan in Islamic sources), it was the Qarakhanids in northern Xinjiang and the western Tarim Basin, including what is today the quintessentially Uyghur city of Kashgar, who adopted Islam.

Many Uyghur and some Han Chinese scholars have embraced an alternative view of the origins of the Qarakhanids and Satuq Bughra Khan. The relationship between the Qarluqs, the Qarakhanid state and its other component tribes is uncertain, but it is known that the Yaghma, one of the Toqquz Oghuz tribes that fled west after the fall of the Uyghur Orkhon state in 840, were in early possession of Kashgar; moreover, Yaghma rulers used the title 'Bughra Khan', which would later be employed by the Kashgar Qarakhanids. As noted, the Toqquz Oghuz tribes

20 Bellew 1875: 308–9.
21 Golden 1992: 214–15; Samolin 1964: 78–80; Barthold [1900] 1968: 254–6; Barthold 1956: I: 20.

are closely associated with the Uyghur. Thus it may be argued, as did the Russian orientalist Elias, that 'the dynasty of *Ilak Khans* [i.e. Qara-khanids] ... were, according to the best authorities, Uighurs', or at least, as Golden puts it, that the Yaghma were a continuation of the Uyghur royal house.[22] Thus both the Qocho Uyghur state *and* the Qarakhanid dynasty are 'Uyghur' in as much as the ancestry of their ruling houses may be traced to the Orkhon khanate of the Uyghurs. Others, disputing the connections between the Yaghma and both Orkhon Uyghurs and Qarakhanids, argue differently.

In either case, underlying the quibbling about the identities of ninth and tenth century Turkic tribes (a heated academic and touchy political issue in the PRC[23]) is the modern nationalist concern over the identity of the Uyghur *minzu* in China today and its historical 'claim' to the Xinjiang region. However, debate on this question seems to me misdi-rected. Both Qocho Uyghur and Qarakhanid regimes were established by outside conquest élites who ruled over and intermarried with a local population with its Tokharian, Iranian, possibly Indian and, in Qocho, Chinese elements. Besides a genetic legacy, such imperial courts left a political, historical and cultural legacy upon the territories and peoples they ruled. All of these have been bequeathed to later inhabitants of this region and together become part of their history, regardless of what name the conquering tribes went by—or in the case of the Qarakhanids, what name later historians ascribed to them. One cannot construct a neat uni-linear narrative of Uyghur history, but that does not mean no narrative is possible or that certain branches must arbitrarily be excluded.

In keeping with this broader conception of the modern Uyghurs' ancestry is the high place occupied by Qarakhanid figures in the pan-theon of Uyghur national and cultural heroes. One of these is Mahmud Kashghari, a well-travelled, well-educated member of the Qarakhanid ruling family who studied in the Halik madrasa (college) in Kashgar. He later moved to the Baghdad court of the Abassid caliph, where in the

22   Mirza Muhammad Haidar, 1895 [1972]: 287, n. 1. See also Barthold ([1900] 1968: 254) who is agnostic on the question and Golden (1992: 196–9, 201), where may be found specific references to the Islamic geographers (including the well known *Hudud*, cited above) who provide the primary evidence for this interpreta-tion. Cf. Hambis 1977: 24, who follows the *Hudud al-'Alam*.
23   For a brief discussion with references to the positions of Wei Liangtao and Liu Yingsheng, see Biran 2001a: 79.

1070s he wrote an Arabic–Turkic dictionary that describes and compares the various Turkic dialects in great detail. His *Compendium of the Turkic Languages* (*Divanu lugat-it-Türk*) brought the sophisticated techniques of Arabic lexicography to the study of what the Islamic world had generally despised as the crude language of barbarians who roamed the steppes and mountains between Anatolia and China. Perhaps the fact that the caliphate had recently become a protectorate of the Turkic Seljuk dynasty has something to do with Kashghari's compiling his dictionary at this time. In any case, Kashghari displays a clearly Turkic sense of self: despite his erudition in Arabic and Persian, he defines Uyghur and Qarakhanid dialects as 'the most elegant' and 'purest' of the Turkic dialects because they had not mixed with Persian. Besides its linguistic value, the terms, verses and proverbs Kashghari cites in his work are a rich store of literary, historical and cultural information and give a vivid sense of Turkic life in the eleventh century.[24]

Yusuf Khass Hajib is another Uyghur literary hero from the Qarakhanid era, likewise a former student at the Halik madrasa. His *Wisdom of Royal Glory* (*Kutadgu Bilig*), completed in Kashgar in 1069, is a guide to statecraft, a mirror for princes, written for the Turkic rulers. The book draws on ideas from the older Islamic-Iranian tradition, as well as the values of Sufism, and sets them in Turkic verse. It consists of a series of dialogues between four allegorically-named characters—a king, a vizier, a sage and an ascetic—who respectively represent the principles of Justice, Fortune, Wisdom and Man's Last End (Religion). The conversations involving the ascetic (named 'Wide Awake'), occupying the latter half of the book, turn on a debate then prevalent in the Islamic world over whether it was better to become actively involved in affairs of the community and state, or to withdraw to the mountains and devote oneself to religious contemplation.[25] As we will see below, Sufis in Xinjiang later found it possible to reconcile spiritual and temporal concerns, to serve both God and king, and did so with a vengeance.

Both Mahmud Kashghari and Yusuf Khass Hajib are celebrated as national heroes in Xinjiang PRC today. Kashghari's tomb has been restored, and a modern shrine built to honour Yusuf—both sites have entered Kashgar tourist itineraries.

---

24   Kashghari, Mahmûd 1072–7. A brief biography of Mahmud Kashghari may be found in Soucek 2000: 87–91.
25   Robert Dankoff, 'Introduction' in Yûsuf 1983: 1–35.

THE CONVERSION OF KHOTAN

The one Tarim city-state still independent of either Qarakhanid or Uyghur control at this point was Khotan, a Buddhist kingdom whose inhabitants, like those of early Kashgar and Yarkand, spoke the Iranian Saka tongue. Khotan's indigenous dynasty (all of whose royal names are Indian in origin) governed a fervently Buddhist city-state boasting some 400 temples in the late ninth/early tenth century—four times the number recorded by Xuan Zang around the year 630. Khotan enjoyed close relations with the Buddhist centre at Dunhuang: the Khotanese royal family intermarried with Dunhuang élites, visited and patronised Dunhuang's Buddhist temple complex, and donated money to have their portraits painted on the walls of the Mogao grottos. Through the tenth century Khotanese royal portraits were painted in association with an increasing number of deities in the caves,[26] suggesting the Khotanese royalty knew they were in trouble.

The trouble, specifically, was the Qarakhanid empire. Satuq's son, Musa, began to put pressure on Khotan in the mid-900s, and sometime before 1006 Yusuf Qadir Khan of Kashgar besieged and took the city. This conquest of Buddhist Khotan by the Muslim Turks—about which there are many colourful legends—marked another watershed in the Islamicisation and Turkicisation of the Tarim Basin, and an end to local autonomy of this southern Tarim city-state. Around the same time, the Qarakhanids destroyed the Samanid dynasty in Transoxiana (or, as the region was now called in Arabic and Persian sources, Mawarannahr, 'land beyond the [Amu] river'). The Qarakhanids thus became the first Turkic dynasty to rule in Islamic Central Asia, and they did so with the support of the Islamic *'ulama*. (The Qarakhanids went on to struggle with the Ghaznavids and Seljuks, likewise Turkic Central Asian powers.) The complete Qarakhanid conquest of the western Tarim and western Zungharia, together with Transoxiana, inaugurates a period in which powers based in Semirech'e controlled Xinjiang, especially the western

---

26 Xue Zongzheng *et al.* 1997: 373, citing Zhang Guangda and Rong Xinjiang, 'Dunhuang "Ruixiang ji", ruixiangtu ji qi fanying de Yutian' ['Record of Auspicious Likenesses', auspicious likeness paintings, and their reflections on Khotan'] in *Yutian shi congkao* [Collected investigations on Khotan history]. The Khotanese king wrote a letter to the prince of Dunhuang in 970, describing years of war with the Qarakhanids. The English translation is in H. Bailey, *Khotanese Texts*, vol. 2, 125–9 (1964). Citation from Biran 2001a: 86 n. 19.

Tarim, together with Transoxiana and Ferghana. This unit of territory had of course been sporadically unified under the Western Türks earlier, hence the general name of 'Turkestan' used by the Islamic sources to encompass Transoxiana and Xinjiang. For the next several centuries the history of Xinjiang would be closely entwined with that of Transoxiana, even while the fractious tendencies of nomadic powers made it rare that one ruler controlled both Samarkand and Kashgar.

THE QARA KHITAY

The now familiar drama of one set of overlords displacing another played itself out again with the arrival in Xinjiang of another ruling dynasty, the Qara Khitay ('Black Khitay'). The Khitay or Khitan (Qidan) were Mongolian speakers who ruled in north China as the Liao dynasty from 907 to 1125. (Turkic and Mongolian are major divisions of the Altaic language family; early speakers of each were centred on what is today Outer Mongolia. To say that the Khitan were speakers of 'Mongolian' is an anachronistic convention as at this point, before the rise of Chinggis Khan, the Mongols were but one of several tribes speaking Mongolian.) Incidentally, the name of the Khitan ruling clan, via Islamic sources and Russian, gave us 'Cathay', the medieval and early-modern-European name for China.

The Khitan Liao state was destroyed (and many of their number absorbed) by the Jurchens, a people from Manchuria who established their own Jin dynasty in its place. But one of the Khitan royal clan, Yelü Dashi, fled in the late 1120s to Kedun, a garrison on the northernmost frontiers of the Liao in Mongolia, where he gathered followers from among the tribesmen and took control of the Liao imperial horse herds.[27] Then, after a failed attack on the Kirghiz, Dashi marched west to Beshbaliq, where he assembled the chiefs of a large group of tribes and gathered more adherents, including the Uyghurs. He pressed on west, establishing a tent-city capital in the town of Imil, just east of Lake Balkash, and then took Balasaghun, Kashgar, Khotan and eventually Samarkand and Transoxiana from the eastern and western Qarakhanid rulers. (On some of its Central Asian campaigns the Qara Khitay used elephants to besiege walled cities.[28]) By 1142 Yelü Dashi and subsequent '*gurkhans*' (khan of

27 Biran 2001b: 68.
28 Biran 2001b: 67–8.

khans) ruled over the former Uyghur and Qarakhanid empires, a territory that extended from the Amu darya (Oxus) river, Balkh (Northern Afghanistan) and Khotan in the west, to the Tanguts (Xixia) in the southeast, and to the lands of the Naimans, a powerful Mongolian tribe, in the north-east—in other words, today's Xinjiang, Kyrgyzstan, Uzbekistan, Tajikistan and southern Kazakstan.[29] Though not fully subordinated to the Qara Khitay, the Islamic state of Khwarazm on the Aral Sea paid tribute to the *gurkhans*.

The Qara Kitay poses a challenge to any simple imposition of ethno-historical identities upon Central Asian polities. Because of the Qara Khitays' background as rulers of north China for two centuries, they brought with them knowledge of Chinese governing practices and institutions; for example, they used Chinese official titles and minted copper coins bearing their names and reign periods in Chinese characters. Perhaps because of this Chinese imperial background, unlike the Türk and Qarakhanid khanates, the Qara Khitay did not subdivide their empire into eastern and western divisions or dole out appanages to princes—for which one modern Chinese scholar praises the dynasty for avoiding 'feudal' institutions.[30] Nevertheless, Yelü Dashi did not institute a centralised Chinese-style empire in Turkestan. To the contrary, Qara Khitay rule over its vassal countries remained indirect to the extreme. Local rulers enjoyed almost complete autonomy and maintained their own armies as long as they paid their taxes and tributes to the *gurkhans*. Throughout the empire agrarian, pastoral and commercial enterprises continued with no major changes. The Uyghur *idiquts* remained in power in their twin capitals of Qocho and Beshbaliq, and the Qarakhanid khans still reigned in Kashgar and Khotan. Although the Qara Khitay rulers posted financial officials to the courts of conquered regions, they stationed no troops there, dispatching armies only as needed to quell rebellion. Moreover, although Chinese was used for some administrative and prestige purposes (as it was in Uyghur territory), Persian, Turkic and the native Khitan language and script were also employed; it is doubtful to what extent even the Khitan among the ruling élite actually spoke Chinese, though Yelü Dashi himself was well educated in the language.

How, then, should we identify the Qara Khitay? As with the Qarakhanids and many Central Eurasian steppe empires, the label by which

<hr>

29 Biran 2001b: 46.
30 Wei Liangtao in Yu Taishan 1996: 309.

we classify the period and region can be misleading, for it is no more than a handy name for the ruling clan, and by no means fully encompasses the ethnic, linguistic or tribal identities even of the Qara Khitay conquest élite, let alone the people ruled in subject polities in the Tarim Basin or Transoxiana. Yelü Dashi fled China with only 80–200 followers; he gathered 10,000 supporters at Kedun and a similar number from diverse tribes in Zungharia. He subsequently took in some 16,000 Khitan former mercenaries at Balasaghun, and also enlisted local Turkic tribesmen. Ultimately the force he took to Central Asia thus included Khitan-, Turkic-, Mongolian-, Tangut-, Iranian-, Chinese- and maybe Jurchen-speaking soldiers;[31] his administrative retinue included Chinese as well as Uyghurs (a Uyghur judge tutored Dashi's sons). Dashi ruled, moreover, over Iranian-, Turkic-, and any remaining Tokharian-speaking peoples throughout the settled regions of western and eastern Turkestan.[32] Like the Mongol empire that would follow them, the Qara Khitay were a multiethnic polity rather than a particular national or ethnic group.[33]

KÜCHLÜK TAKES OVER THE QARA KHITAY STATE

Juvaini described the Qara Khitay empire as a 'mighty wall' protecting the lands of Islam from Chinggis Khan. The Qara Khitay decline forms an important chapter in the story of the rise of the Mongols. By the end of the twelfth century a succession of weak *gurkhans* permitted Qara Khitay officials to exploit populations under their supervision, engendering unrest throughout Zungharia, the Tarim Basin and Transoxiana. The Qarakhanid khan of Kashgar rose against the *gurkhan* in the first years of the thirteenth century, and was imprisoned in Imil after his rebellion failed. To the west, 'Ala ad-Din Muhammad, the new shah of Khwarazm (on the south-western shores of the Aral sea), challenged Qara Khitay suzerainty in Transoxiana by campaigning against the former Qarakhanids still ruling as Qara Khitay vassals in Bukhara and Samarkand. In Qocho the Uyghurs turned on their overbearing

31   Biran 2001b: 49–50.
32   In his eleventh-century dictionary of the Turkic dialects, Mahmud Kashghari noted that 'the Uighur have a pure Turkic language, and also another language which they speak among themselves.' This other spoken language may refer to Tokharian (Kashghari 1072–7: 1: 83 [I. 29/29]).
33   Wittfogel and Feng 1949: appendix V; Yu Taishan 1996; Ji Zongan 1996.

Qara Khitay supervisor in 1209, beheaded him and threw his head out a tower window.[34] The *idiqut*, Barchuq, then quickly allied with Chinggis Khan (the first head of state to do so). Barchuq proved a loyal vassal, fielding troops and even riding out himself on campaign with the Mongols against the Khwarazm-shah and the Tanguts. Chinggis gave Barchuq one his daughters to marry and the honorific title of 'fifth son.' Barchuq remained *idiqut* of Uyghuristan.[35]

Up to this point Chinggis had been busy subduing and unifying the many tribes in the Hobbesian world of twelfth-century Mongolia. In 1208 his growing confederation defeated an alliance of the Naiman and Merkit tribes, forcing the Naiman chief, Küchlük, to flee west into the protection of the Qara Khitay *gurkhan*. The fugitive Küchlük drew upon his reserves of guile and charisma to convince the beleaguered Qara Khitay *gurkhan* to allow him to re-assemble a force of Naiman and Merkit tribesmen. While the *gurkhan* was engaged with the Khwarazm-shah's forces in Transoxiana, Küchlük gained a strategic footing in Semirech'e, and by around 1211 effectively usurped control of the Qara Khitay state.

The Qara Khitay *gurkhans* had been hospitable to the various religions of their steppe and oasis empire. Kashgar was a Nestorian Bishopric, and Christianity also flourished around the northern capital on the Chu river, as did Judaism in Samarkand. Policies towards Islam, too, were liberal, though the Muslims in the former Qarakhanid lands viewed the Buddhist Qara Khitay as infidels. However, when Küchlük took command of the Qara Khitay empire he reversed this sensible policy. Himself a Buddhist convert from Christianity, he launched a pogrom against Muslims in his new territory. For three years running (1211–13) he sent troops to raid Kashgar at harvest time, starving the city until it submitted to him.[36] The persecution was particularly acute in Khotan, a city already forcibly converted once before, when it fell to the Qarakhanids

---

34 Wittfogel and Feng 1949: 667–8, citing the *Gaochang Xieshi jiapu* (Chronicle of the Xie Family of Gaochang). In Juvaini's version, the tower is pulled down on top of the official (1997: 44–5). In Islamic sources the official's name is given as 'Shaukem', 'Shawkam' etc. (e.g. Barthold [1900] 1968: 362). This is a corruption of the Chinese title *shaojian*, or junior supervisor.

35 Allsen 1983: 247–8.

36 Küchlük evidently had neither siege engines nor elephants at his disposal. Biran 2001b: 66.

two centuries earlier. On conquering this southern Tarim city, Küchlük, in the words of Juvaini,

... compelled the inhabitants to abjure the religion of Mohammed, giving them the choice between two alternatives, either to adopt the Christian or idolatrous creed or to don the garb of the Khitayans. And since it was impossible to go over to another religion, by reason of hard necessity they clad themselves in the dress of the Khitayans .... The muezzin's call to prayer and the worship of monotheist and believer were broken off; and the schools were closed and destroyed. One day, in Khotan, he drove the great *imams* out on to the plain and began to discuss religion with them.

One of the imams, 'Ala ad-Din Muhammad of Khotan (not to be confused with the Khwarazm-shah of the same name), 'girded the belt of truth about the loins of veracity' and engaged the blaspheming Naiman chief in this religious debate. The mullah concluded his presentation with a curse ('Dust be in thy mouth, thou enemy of the faith, thou accursed Küchlüg!'), and Küchlük had him crucified on the door of his own college. But justice was at hand, for 'God Almighty, in order to remove the evilness of Küchlüg, in a short space dispatched the Mongol army against him.'[37]

Indeed, Chinggis Khan harboured a personal animus against Küchlük, and sent his trusted general Jebe ('weapon') against him in 1216–18. Jebe took Almaligh (near modern Ghulja) and accepted the peaceful submission of tribes in Zungharia and Semirech'e; Küchlük fled south and died in an attempt to escape over the Pamirs.

THE MONGOL IMPERIAL PERIOD

After Küchlük's intolerance, the Xinjiang Muslims greeted Jebe and the Mongols as liberators who restored rights of worship and refrained from looting. (That being said, one noteworthy aspect of the Mongol conquest was that Islam became less prevalent on the steppes of Zungharia, as the Mongols, who were shamanist but also favoured Christianity and Buddhism, took control of Muslim Turkic lands.) With the Qara Khitay *gurkhans* and Küchlük out of the way, the Yili, Talas and Chu River valleys, 'Kashgaria' in the south-western Tarim and Uyghuristan in the north-east all joined the empire of 'the world-conquering Khan'. The

37　Juvaini 1997: 63, 71–3.

way was open for the Mongols' westward campaign to Transoxiana, Afghanistan and Persia.[38]

Before his death in 1227 Chinggis Khan divided his vast empire into an *ulus* (a unit of land and people here equivalent to a khanate) for each of his sons. Jöchi, the eldest, received lands in western central Eurasia 'as far as the hooves of Mongol horses have tramped' (including places not yet conquered, where Jöchi's own son Batu would carve out an empire). The *ulus* of the second son, Chaghatai (Chaghatay, Jagatai etc.), comprised essentially the territories of the old Qara Khitay empire, centred near Almaligh (Ghulja), and in theory including the band of oases extending from Turfan to Samarkand. The lands of the third son and Chinggis' designated successor, Ögedei, took in central Siberia and eastern Zungharia, with main pastures on the Imil and Irtysh rivers near modern Tacheng (Chughuchaq, Tarbaghatai) in northern Xinjiang. By custom, as 'prince of the hearth', the youngest son Tolui received as his own *ulus* the Mongol homelands centred on the Orkhon valley, as well as the bulk of Chinggis' army.

This arrangement, though neat in appearance, planted the seeds of centuries of instability, particularly in regard to the territory of the former Qara Khitay empire. It would have been natural for the Chaghatayids, based around Issyk Kul and the Yili Valley, to control the oases of Transoxiana and southern Xinjiang. However, the revenue from these Muslim and Uyghur cities and rights to invest rulers and residents was, in practice at least, the prerogative of the Great Khans further east. Uyghuristan (as the sources now call the Qocho Uyghur kingdom) remained subject to the Mongol Great Khans in Beijing until the start of the fourteenth century, as did Khotan until around 1375.[39]

Another built-in source of tension arose from Ögedei's inheritance of the superior position of Great Khan, while Tolui occupied the symbolically important Orkhon valley lands—where Ögedei would in fact build the Mongol imperial capital of Karakoram. The Ögedeids and Toluids would thus compete over the Great Khanship; conflict would also arise

38 Barthold [1900] 1968: 401–3; Grousset 1997: 233–6.
39 The sources disagree on whether or not Uyghuristan was included in the Chaghatai *ulus*. Juvaini, who wrote most completely and closest in time to the post-Chinggisid dispensation of khanates, implies that the Uyghur *idiqut* initially reigned in his own right, directly subordinate to the Great Khan. Later, Uyghuristan was subsumed within the Chaghatai khanate. See Allsen 1983: 248–50.

later between those Mongols who remained in Mongolia and those ruling from China. All of this assured that Xinjiang would be drawn into the politics of the Mongol imperial centre to the east, and that the region would again play a geostrategic role similar to that under the Han/Xiongnu and the Tang/Türk rivalries. The rich cities of Transoxiana to the west, in theory part of the Chaghatayid legacy, would at times be ruled together with the Tarim and Zungharia, and at other times fall to locally based Mongol descendents and Türkic strongmen. Khans based in Xinjiang would repeatedly raid Afghanistan and northern India. Generally, the fissiparousness, opportunistic alliances and fratricidal struggles of the Mongols and Türks assured a long and—to the student of the region's history—bewildering epoch of military flux throughout Turkestan and neighbouring areas.

Here is a summary of the major political and military events in Xinjiang during the Mongol imperial period. After the death of Chinggis khan (1227), the house of Chaghatai remained closely allied, even subordinate to, the new Great Khan Ögedei (r. 1229–41) and his descendents until 1251. The settled areas of the Tarim Basin, as well as Uyghuristan, were now under administrative arrangement similar to that of the rest of the Mongol empire, with Mongol 'residents' (Mo. *darugha*, Ch. *guanren*) stationed in cities to assure that Mongol demands were met: these included hosting official visits, dispatching royal hostages to the Mongol court, registering the population, paying taxes and irregular exactions, raising a militia, and maintaining postal relay stations. A Khwarazmian Muslim, Mahmud Yalavach, served as darugha overseeing Transoxiana, the Tarim Basin and, by Ögedei's reign, Uyghuristan as well. His son, Mas'ud Beg, succeeded him. The Persian sources praise these governors for wise administration that established consistent taxation systems and rebuilt cities and economies destroyed by Mongol conquest.[40]

Ögedei was succeeded by his widow as regent, by his son for two years, and then by his son's widow. Then, after a bitter struggle, a new house seized the Great Khanship: Möngke (r. 1251–9) was the son of Tolui, and from his reign the Toluids would hold the Great Khanship and the emperorship of China until replaced by the Ming Dynasty in 1368. After coming to power in 1251, Möngke viciously pursued his Ögedeid and Chaghatayid rivals, killing or exiling adult Chaghatayids

40   Allsen 1993: 122–34.

and raising their children within his own court. He selected Chaghatai's widowed daughter-in-law, Orghana, as regent for her infant son Mubarak Shah (the first Muslim Chinggisid). Möngke then struck a deal with Batu, khan of the Golden Horde in what would become the Russian steppe. Together, they would split the steppe along a line running through Semirech'e.

Xinjiang thus came fully under the control of the Great Khan, but only for a few years. After Möngke's death, the Toluids themselves fractured, electing rival khans Arigh Böke (r. 1260–4) in Mongolia, and Khubilai (Qubilai; r. 1260–94) in China. This constellation of power and geography should by now be familiar: Xinjiang became a critical source of grain and tribute for the Mongolia-based Arigh Böke after Khubilai cut off grain shipments from China. Khubilai tried, but failed, to conquer the Tarim Basin and Zungharia, though Uyghurstan remained loyal to him. Arigh Böke sent Chaghatai's grandson, Alghu, to manage the Chaghatai *ulus*, and after rallying Chaghatayid princes in Kashgar, Alghu sent armies to retake Transoxiana from the Golden Horde and extend power into Afghanistan and eastern Persia. But Alghu was no tame puppet. He turned on his former sponsor, Arigh Böke, who lost the support of the nomads in Zungharia and was forced to return east and submit to Khubilai. Alghu married the durable Orghana (his late uncle's wife), but died (1264) before he could enjoy her or his newly reconstituted and consolidated Chaghatayid khanate in Transoxiana, the Tarim and Zungharia. Orghana's son Mubarak Shah thus became the inhertor of the Chaghatai *ulus*.

Khubilai, from his capital in Beijing (Dadu), now moved again to control Turkestan, dispatching Mubarak's cousin, Boraq, with an edict naming him co-ruler of the Chaghatai *ulus*. Boraq quickly took power in Transoxiana, outstripped Mubarak, and then, true to form, rebelled against Khubilai, defeating the latter's armies on the Oxus and in the Tarim, and in the bargain plundering Khotan, once Khubilai's city. Of Xinjiang territories only Uyghuristan now remained subject to the Great Khan in China.

Meanwhile, a new contender from the house of Ögedei had been gathering strength in the north. Qaydu (Khaidu) drew on support from the Golden Horde to the west to challenge Alghu, and after the latter's death took advantage of Boraq's wars with Khubilai's forces to seize control of the Talas river plain. After an uncharacteristically peaceable conference (*quriltai*) in 1269, Qaydu, Boraq and representatives of the Golden Horde divided Transoxiana between them, all the nomad monarchs agreeing to stay out of the way and allow Mas'ud Beg to administer the towns. Upon Boraq's death around 1271, Qaydu became *de facto* ruler of the entire Chaghatai khanate for the next thirty years, though since he was himself an Ögedeid he continued to prop up Chaghatayid princes as formal khans. His rule marks a watershed of sorts, for neither the khans of the Golden Horde to the west nor the khan-emperors of Mongol-occupied China (the Yuan dynasty) had influence in Xinjiang or Transoxiana after Qaydu gained power. Thomas Allsen has pointed out that the same fiscal-military dilemma that undermined Han and Tang power in the 'western regions' made it impossible for the Yuan to hold the area: whereas nomad powers in Zungharia and Mongolia could raid and tax eastern Xinjiang with ease and profit, and in fact relied on grain and commercial connections available there, a power based in north China faced great continuing expenditures to access and defend the region via the Gansu corridor, costs for which the region's produce could not compensate.[41]

UYGHURS IN THE MONGOL PERIOD

Throughout the nine decades between Chinggis and Qaydu, Uyghurs and Uyghuristan occupied a unique position in the Mongol empire. Because of their early submission and continued loyalty to Chinggis, the Uyghur *idiquts* enjoyed a good deal of autonomy; Chinggis did not bestow Uyghuristan as part of an *ulus* upon any of his sons, and not until Ögedei's reign were Mongol residents stationed there. Li Zhichang, chronicler of the journey of Daoist master Chang Chun west from China to where Chinggis' was then encamped near the Amu River, noted the same features of Qocho as had earlier descriptions: the heat, the rich fields watered by *karez*, fruits and ample supplies of grape wine. In Qocho and Beshbaliq the travelling Daoists met Confucians as well as many Buddhist and Manichean[42] priests, indicating the continued local prominence of these religions.

41　Allsen 1983: 261.
42　Waley 1931: 79–81. Although Li Chih-Ch'ang calls them 'Daoists', Waley, who translated this account, argues that they must have been Manicheans; Mani had by this time been incorporated into the Chinese Daoist pantheon (1931: 80 n. 5).

Uyghuristan was not immune to the effects of Mongol succession struggles, however. In the years following Ögedei's death, the *idiqut* Salindi supported Ögedei's grandson, Shiremün, who ultimately lost out to Möngke. When Möngke successfully seized the Great Khanship in 1251, he tried and executed Salindi and several Uyghur nobles. Among the charges levelled at Salindi was his alleged conspiracy with Oghul Khaimish (regent and mother of Shiremün) to massacre the Muslims of Uyghuristan during Friday prayers. While the background and true motivations underlying this incident are unclear, it does suggest that Islam had made inroads into eastern Xinjiang by the mid-thirteenth century.

As they had for the Qara Khitay, Tangut, Naiman and other neighbouring powers, Qocho Uyghurs served the Mongols as a sort of 'steppe intelligentsia',[43] providing crucial administrative skills to the nomads as they built an empire. The Uyghur Tatar Tongga, formerly a secretary in Naiman service, introduced to Chinggis' new state the use of official seals in tax recording as well as the Uyghur script (which was adopted for the Mongolian language and remains in use in Inner Mongolia today). Uyghurs tutored Mongol imperial princes and served as *darughas* and in other official capacities throughout the empire, many reaching high rank.[44] One such figure was Körgüz, a Uyghur, possibly a Christian (his name is equivalent to 'George') from a village near Beshbaliq. Juvaini provides us with a sketch of his career and a sense of what was possible for an ambitious and literate Uyghur in the Mongol era.

Körgüz' father died while he was still young, and although custom dictated that he marry his widowed step-mother, she refused and later prepared to marry someone else. His patrimony at stake, Körgüz went to the *idiqut* who ordered the step-mother to compensate Körgüz with property. Körgüz then learned the Uyghur script and began teaching. Still not well off, he sold himself into bond; with the money he bought a horse and rode off to the camp of Batu, khan of the Golden Horde. Though he entered Batu's service as a herdsman, he soon gained recognition for his literacy and intelligence and began to rise in rank, from tutor to a secretary of the imperial viceroy of Khwarazm, and ultimately to Viceroy himself, governing the eastern Persian province of Khurasan. Instrumental to his gaining this position was the patronage of Chinqay, an important emir who may himself have been a Uyghur, but was at any

43 The term is from Buell 1993: 95.
44 Allsen 1983: 266–7.

rate Turkic.[45] Körgüz is said to have restored the economy and governed justly; he rebuilt the treasury, reduced corruption in the tax collection system, and established the *yam* postal service to free people from arbitrary commandeering of their horses as official mounts. Under his tenure local élites regained sufficient confidence to invest in the underground irrigation canals on their estates and to rebuild the bazaar. Nevertheless, Körgüz fell victim to Mongol politics, first becoming embroiled in an intrigue involving a rival of Chinqay, and later, in the 1240s, when he insulted a Chaghatayid emir and showed disrespect to Ögedei's widow. For this his mouth was stuffed with stones and he was executed.[46]

Despite such vulnerability to political vicissitudes, Uyghurs and Uyghuristan weathered the epoch of Mongol rule better than Transoxiana, avoiding the destructive conquests and subsequent struggles among rivals that all but levelled many Central Asian cities. The kingdom's luck ran out, however, during Qaydu's reign. In the late thirteenth century the territory from Beshbaliq to Hami became the front line in the conflict between Qaydu and the Yuan Dynasty under Khubilai. Raiding by Qaydu and the Chaghatayid princes allied with him inflicted heavy damage to the hydraulic infrastructure so critical to growing crops in the dry heat of the Turfan depression; insecurity forced the Uyghur ruling house to withdraw first from Beshbaliq to Qocho, and then east to the Gansu corridor, where they and a large number of Uyghur refugees became dependents of the Yuan state. The former capital cities of Uyghuristan, meanwhile, were transformed first into Yuan military outposts, colonised by Mongol and Chinese troops, and then in the fourteenth century occupied by Chaghatayids, who enthroned their own pro-Chaghatayid line of *idiquts*.[47]

Qaydu died after a failed attack on Karakoram in 1301, and a series of Chaghatayid khans ruled Xinjiang and Transoxiana in their own right thereafter, also venturing into Afghanistan and north-west India and warring with the Mongol Ilkhanate in Persia. However, by the 1340s another

---

45 Juvaini calls Chinqay a Uyghur, but Chinese sources say he was Kereit; Buell argues that he may have been from a Nestorian Christian clan called the Kereit of the Önggüt people, a culturally Turkicised group from the Sino-Mongolian frontier zone (Buell 1993: 96–7).
46 Barthold [1900] 1968: 474–5; Juvaini 1997: 2: Chapters 28–9; Buell 1993: 102–4.
47 Allsen 1983: 254–61.

geo-historical watershed was crossed when the Chaghatai khanate split in two. One source of this split was religious: the Chaghatayid khan Tarmashirin, who plundered northern India in the late 1320s from his base in Transoxiana, was a convert to Islam. In 1333–4 the Buddhist, Christian and shamanist nomads of Issyk Kul and the Yili region rebelled against him and established a new khan. Tarmashirin's line of Chaghatayids carried on in Transoxiana, where it provided Turkic rulers with figurehead Chinggisid khans. The other branch ruled over the Tarim and Turfan Basins from what now came to be called 'Moghulistan', a geographic notion that included Zungharia as well as the steppe lands between the Syr Darya and Lake Balkash. Like their brothers and cousins in Transoxiana, the Moghulistan Chaghatayids, too, became tools of others: the wealthy and powerful Mongol Dughlat clan served as emirs while playing kingmaker with the Chaghatayid royals in what is now Xinjiang.[48]

MOGHULISTAN: THE MUSLIM CHAGHATAYIDS

In the late 1340s the Dughlats proclaimed as khan a supposed Chaghatayid prince, Tughluq Temür (r. 1347–63), who is famous both as a convert to Islam and as a conqueror. When still a young man, Tughluq met the shaykh Jamal ad-Din, a 'member of the sect of Khwajas', who explained to him the meaning of faith and the 'duties of a Musulman'. Impressed, Tughluq promised that should he ever become khan, he would accept Islam. Some years later Tughluq was indeed the khan, and though the shaykh had died, his son Arshad ad-Din presented himself by calling the prayers outside Tughluq's tent early in the morning. Thus abruptly roused from his bed, Tughluq was at first enraged. When he learned who the holy man was, however, Tughluq not only made good on his personal promise, but agreed to make all his princes convert as well, or put them to the sword. All the princes obeyed except Jaras, who would only accept the faith if the shaykh could defeat a wrestler in Jaras' entourage, a giant famous for having once thrown a two-year-old camel. As is common in such stories of religious contests in Inner Asia,[49] the

48 Except where otherwise indicated, the preceding account of Chaghatai-period Turkestan is based primarily on Barthold [1900] 1968: Chapter 5 (this chapter was added to Minorski's translation) and Grousset 1997: 326–45.
49 On the importance of such contests in the Islamicisation of the Central Eurasian steppe, see DeWeese 1994.

The mazar (mausoleum) of Tughluq Temür, in Huocheng (outside Ghulja)
(photo: J. Millward, 1990)

holy man miraculously prevailed, and the wrestler recited the Islamic
creed as soon as he regained consciousness. Thereupon 'the people raised
loud shouts of applause, and on that day 160,000 persons cut off the
hair of their heads and became Musulmans. The Khan was circumcised,
and the lights of Islam dispelled the shades of Unbelief.'[50] Though the
story is mythologised, the Mongols (or, as they are known in Persian
sources, Mughals) of the Chaghatai khanate were largely Islamicised by
the mid-fourteenth century, the end of the Mongol imperial period
across Eurasia. Outside China and Mongolia, the Mongols were by now
all Muslims.

As a conqueror, Tughluq Temür campaigned in Transoxiana and Afghanistan, temporarily restoring the unity of the Chaghatai khanate on
either side of the Pamirs. After Tughluq, however, the Chaghatayids again
descended into a chaos of puppet khans and concurrent reigns in different parts of what was once the Chaghatai *ulus*. In the west Tamerlane
(Timur-i Lang; r. 1370–1405) built a short-lived empire from India to the

50   Mirza Muhammad Haidar 1972: I: 14–15. Arshad ad-Din is highly revered by
Muslims in Xinjiang. His mausoleum is now a pilgrimage site in Kucha.

Middle East to the Russian steppe as emir under a nominal Chinggisid khan, leaving his own descendents to vie with remaining Chaghatayids for Transoxiana. It was a descendent of both Timur and Chaghatai, Babur (1483–1530), who founded the dynasty in India which has come to be known as 'Mughal'. (In fact, Babur and his successors preferred to think of themselves as Timurids, the term 'Moghul' indicating rather the Chaghatayid rulers of Moghulistan whom they considered false Muslims and uncouth bumpkins.)

Meanwhile, back in Moghulistan, a Dughlat emir, Qamar ad-Din, usurped the khanship following Tughluq Temür's death in 1363 and did away with most of Tughluq's offspring. Other Dughlats in turn challenged Qamar's rule in Moghulistan and Altishahr, as did Tamerlane, whose armies penetrated as far as Karashahr in 1389, driving Qamar into the Altai mountains. Khizr Khwaja, Tughluq Temür's one surviving son, was then placed on the throne by another Dughlat who had sheltered him until he reached adulthood. In the 1390s Khizr personally embarked upon a holy war (*ghazat*) against 'Khitay', conquering Turfan and Qocho (by then called Qarakhoja) in the core of Uyghuristan, and reportedly achieving the conversion of the Uyghuristan populace. In fact, the disappearance of local Buddhism from Turfan took some time. In the early fifteenth century the rulers of Turfan sent embassies to Beijing led by Buddhist priests. Hafiz Abru, a Timurid envoy passing through Turfan and Qarakhoja en route to Ming China in July of 1420 commented on the richness and quantity of 'idol temples' and the prominent image of Sakyamuni. Only by the 1450s were mosques common enough in the area to feature in travellers' accounts.[51] Nevertheless, Khizr's conquest of Uyghuristan does mark the end of Uyghur rule and inauguration of Chaghatayid, or Moghul, control of the Turfan Basin.

Khizr also concluded a truce with Tamerlane, marrying a sister to him, thus giving Tamerlane a Chinggisid connection which allowed him to call himself by the prestigious title 'son-in-law' (of the khans). However, this family tie did not prevent further Timurid invasions of the Tarim Basin: Tamerlane's grandson, Mirza Alexander, attacked Kashgar, Yarkand and Aqsu in 1399–1400; the residents of Aqsu saved their city from sacking only by delivering the city's rich 'Chinese' merchants up to Mirza.[52]

51   Mirza Muhammad Haidar 1972: I: 52; Hafiz Abru 1422: 12–13 (85–6); Rossabi 1972: 210–12.
52   Mirza Muhammad Haidar 1972: 38–9, 51–2; Grousset 1997: 422, 425–6; Bar-

The political and military narrative continues in this vein from the late fourteenth through the seventeenth century, its complexity compounded by the fact that chronologies in the Persian and Chinese sources are hard to reconcile. The fluctuating fortunes of individual rulers and families aside, however, four important developments characterise this Moghulistan period of Xinjiang's history: the decline and disappearance of the Chaghatayid Moghuls; the rise as new regional powers of the Kazaks, the Kirghiz and the Oirats (Zunghars); the revival of trade linking China with Transoxiana and India; and, to be taken up in the next chapter, the further advance of Islam as both religion and political force in the Xinjiang area.

CHAGHATAYID DECLINE AND THE FORMATION OF NEW PEOPLES

The Chaghatayids lost their status as rulers rapidly in Transoxiana, and more gradually in the eastern parts of their former domain. The western Chaghatayids had served as convenient legitimating puppets under the Timurids; however, the Uzbeks (the Shibanid dynasty, 1500–99) who drove the Timurids out of Transoxiana, could boast their own Chinggisid lineage (through Shiban, a son of Chinggis' eldest son, Jöchi), and thus had no need for Chaghatai's descendants. In Xinjiang Chaghatayid khans still reigned and even ruled in some places, but from the late fourteenth through seventeenth centuries the region became subdivided into distinct smaller realms or city-states: in Moghulistan to the north, in Altishahr ('six cities', as the sources begin to refer to Kashgar and the Tarim Basin) and in the Turfan area.[53] Occasionally a single ruler succeeded in uniting the whole region, but more often these realms and cities were ruled separately either by competing Chaghatayid descendants, by the Dughlats, or, as will be discussed below, by the Khojas, ruling

---

thold 1956–62: 141–4. It is unclear to whom this reference to 'Chinese' merchants in the Persian *Zafarname* refers, Chinese from Ming lands or merely easterners from old Uyghuristan, a region that Islamic sources sometimes still referred to as 'Khitay'. If they were Han Chinese operating outside Ming borders they were also well outside Ming law, which theoretically permitted foreign trade only in the guise of 'tribute' presented by envoys. For example, Khizr Khwaja had exchanged envoys and gifts with the Ming court in Nanjing around 1391 (Yu Taishan 1996: 376).

53   The term 'Altishahr', derived from *altä shähär* or 'six cities' (Kashgar, Yarkand, Khotan, Aqsu, Uch [Ush] Turfan and Korla), is equivalent to 'Kashgaria'.

either through a puppet Chaghatayid or in their own right. As the power of the old Moghul khans declined, they lost control of the nomads. New tribal confederations emerged in the steppes and mountains.

One of these was that of the Kazaks, who lived nomadically in Zungharia, Semirech'e and on the steppes north of Transoxiana, roughly the territory of Kazakstan and northern Xinjiang today. The Kazaks as a tribal and political entity emerged from a succession crisis among the remnants of the Golden Horde (also known as the White Horde), the Mongol imperial khanate that Chinggis had bequeathed to his eldest son, Jöchi. In the fifteenth century two Jöchid descendents contested the khanal succession. In the end Abulkhayr (Abu'l Khayr) Khan killed his rival Baraq Khan and emerged victorious as khan. Abulkhayr's grandson, Muhammad, went on to conquer Transoxiana and to found what we know as the Uzbek (Özbeg) state. Meanwhile, Baraq Khan's sons, Janibek and Giray, fled with 200,000 followers to Semirech'e and Zungharia. By the 1520s their confederation numbered a million tribesmen, was known by the name of Kazak (Qazaq, Kazakh), and had expanded its influence south-west to the Syr Darya. The Kazak tribes by the eighteenth century had formed into three subdivisions, known from west to east as the Lesser, Middle and Greater Hordes—or 'hundreds', as the divisions are known in Kazak (*Kishi Jüz, Orta Jüz* and *Ulu Jüz*).[54]

The Kirghiz were not a new people, but many Kirghiz migrated to new lands in western Moghulistan during this period. The Turkic-speaking Kirghiz from the southern Siberian watershed of the Yenesei River had destroyed the Orkhon khaghanate of the Uyghurs in the mid-ninth century. A century later they were themselves forced out of the Orkhon valley by the Khitan, at which point some Kirghiz returned north, and others may have begun migrating to the south-west. Kirghiz participated in Qara Khitay and later Mongol imperial campaigns further west; many joined Qaydu's armies in the later thirteenth century. By the fifteenth century, the Tianshan, Issyk Kul area and Pamir had become a Kirghiz homeland, which they defended against the expansion of the Oirats (see below). Kirghiz tribesmen were the focus of concerted missionary efforts by Sufi shaykhs in the sixteenth and seventeenth centuries, and by the eighteenth century had become fervent Muslims lending military muscle to various factions in the frequent wars of religion and conquest

---

54 A brief discussion of early Kazak history may be found in Olcott 1987 and Soucek 2000: 195–7.

around Kashgar and the Ferghana Valley. They remained largely unassailable in their mountain redoubts, and it was only in the twentieth century that they came under direct control of outside political powers.

A group of non-Chinggisid Mongols, speaking a distinct western Mongolian dialect, also came to power in Zungharia from the fifteenth century. The Oirats (Oyrad, Ölüd, Eleuth; known in Persian and Russian sources as Kalmyk, Qalmuq, Kalmuk etc.) vied for control of Mongolia and put pressure on the Ming in the early 1400s; later they were forced west. By the seventeenth century a sub-confederation of Oirat tribes, the Zunghars, would wrest control of Moghulistan from the last Chaghatayids and form the last great steppe empire in world history (see Chapter 3). As for the Chaghatayids themselves, our best source covers only up to the mid-sixteenth century. Though details are scarce, we know that Chaghatayid princes later paid visits to the court of the Qing dynasty, so they survived at least in the capacity of figureheads. Still, after the mid-sixteenth century no Chaghatayids ruled on a regional scale, and even where they commanded individual cities they remained under the sway of the religious charismatics known as Khojas (Khwajas; see Chapter 3).

CHINESE-CENTRAL ASIAN RELATIONS AND THE EAST-WEST CARAVAN TRADE

The death of Tamerlane (1405) and of his aspirations for far eastern conquest corresponded to the accession of the Ming Yongle emperor (r. 1403–24), a Chinese ruler open to diplomatic and trade contacts with Central Asia. While exchanging letters and envoys with the new Timurid Sultan in Herat on a basis of *de facto* equality,[55] Yongle sent a gift of silk in 1406 to Turfan's eastern Chaghatayid ruler, who reciprocated the following year. In 1408 the Ming court received a Turfani embassy led by Buddhist priests. From this point on, missions to the Chinese court to present 'tribute' in return for gifts and trading opportunities became the focus of Turfan's relations with China for over two centuries. Indeed, the cities of Altishahr, Samarkand and Herat dispatched envoys to and traded with the Ming via Turfan.

These exchanges of goods, through which the Ming received horses, jade and other items from Central Asia in return for gifts, fall within

55 Fletcher 1968.

the 'tribute system' model familiar to students of Chinese history.[56] It is generally agreed that the Ming court covered the envoy's expenses, opened border markets for certain powerful neighbours, and knowingly overpaid for their goods in return for the prestige of having ostensibly obsequious visitors come to the court to present 'tribute'—the Chinese term for these diplomatic presents, *gong*, is usually translated as 'tribute', but it would be better to simply call them 'gifts' since 'tribute' implies a subservient and extractive relationship that did not exist.[57] Though all at the time saw through the charade, official Chinese annals present the official line that emissaries bearing gifts were pledging submission to the Ming emperor. Some writers in the PRC today, in order to enhance China's historical prestige and claim on Xinjiang, still maintain the fiction that envoys presenting gifts were Chinese vassals, as in the following passage on fifteenth-century relations between Turfan and the Ming:

The fact that the latter Chaghatayid princes of Beshbaliq and Turfan repeatedly sought to present *gong* to the Ming court shows us, first, that they saw themselves as Ming vassals (*fanshu*), members of the Chinese nation (*zhonghua*

56 Rossabi 1972 discusses Turfan's relations with the Ming in relation to this Ming approach to trade and foreign relations and the problems it engendered. See also Fletcher 1968 on the rhetoric and reality of Chinese pretensions of imperial superiority.

57 '*Tributum* is one of the Latin words for Roman taxes (another is *vectigalia*) which, after 167 BCE, began to be used exclusively for the direct taxes sent to Rome by the inhabitants of the provinces, both those holding Roman citizenship and those not. … Tribute was either land-tax or poll-tax, levied either in cash or kind. The taxes in kind, of course, included grain from Egypt. … Grain as tribute was also an important levy in Sicily and Africa' (Allison Futrell, personal communication). 'Tribute' thus historically implies a heavy exaction levied by an empire upon a conquered territory. *Gong* in the Chinese context, on the other hand, consisted of symbolic gifts representing their locality of origin, and could be of quite low monetary value—fruit jams from Turfan, for example. Nor were states the only ones to present *gong*: Chinese officials and other subjects of Ming and Qing China presented *gong* to the emperor as well. 'Gifts to the emperor' might be a less misleading translation. By continuing to use 'tribute' as a translation for *gong*, Western scholars unwittingly bolster the imperial Chinese rhetoric of dominion (or at least influence) over the countries it pressed into this particular form of ritualised diplomacy and trade. The problem applies not only to Xinjiang, but to South-East Asia, Korea, Okinawa and others whose emissaries also presented *gong*. More discussion of this problem may be found in Wills 1988 and 1995, and Hevia 1995.

minzu); and second, that at the same time economically they were mutually inseparable [from China] ....[58]

The development of Ming-Central Asian trade relations was punctuated after the 1460s by conflict between the Ming and the Chaghatayids in control of Turfan. In the 1460s and 1470s, Moghulistan (now with a capital at Aqsu) and the Turfan region were reunited by Yunus Khan (r. 1462–81) with assistance from the Timurids. Yunus was Persian-educated and deeply cultured; a visiting cleric from Transoxiana had expected the Moghul chieftain to be 'a beardless man, with the ways and manners of any other Turk of the desert', but upon meeting him had been surprised to find 'a person of elegant deportment, with a full beard and a Tajik face, and such refined speech and manner, as is seldom to be found even in a Tajik'.[59] Yunus was thus more sophisticated and powerful than the Ming perhaps appreciated, for it limited his trade missions and snubbed his requests for such status items as four-clawed dragon robes. The Ming, moreover, attempted to maintain Hami as a military outpost (*weisuo*), under a line of rulers invested by the Ming court, to counter-balance Turfan's regional power. As a result, until the mid-sixteenth century Turfan and the Ming faced off over Hami, which was repeatedly conquered and plundered. Nevertheless, trade missions continued more or less uninterrupted. The Ming needed the horses.[60]

Trade became easier still after 1514, when Yunus' grandson, the Chaghatayid Sa'id Khan (r. 1514–33) put a temporary end to the squabbling among Chaghatayid and Dughlat contenders for power in the west and established himself in 'Kashgaria' (Kashgar, Yarkand and Khotan). He reached a settlement with his brother, Mansur (r. 1503–43) who reigned in Moghulistan and Turfan—that is, in the Yili region, Aqsu, Kucha, Karashahr and Turfan. Sa'id's reign inaugurates what Uyghur and Han Chinese scholars call the Sa'idiyya state or the Yarkand khanate, a distinct dynasty ruling in the south-western Tarim while other Chaghatayids continued to reign elsewhere. The generally amicable arrangement between Sa'id in the west, and Mansur in the north and east, ushered in a rare episode of relative stability, as the main source for this period, the *Tarikh-i Rashidi*, notes:

58   Su Beihai and Huang Jianhua 1993: 154.
59   Mirza Muhammad Haidar 1972: I: 97–8; Barthold 1956–62: 147–8. By 'Tajik' the cleric means Persian-speaking sedentary Central Asian.
60   Rossabi 1972; see also Rossabi's discussion of Yunus in Rossabi 1975.

From this peace and reconciliation between the two brothers, resulted such security and prosperity for the people that any one might travel alone between Kamul [Hami] or Khitai [China] and the country of Farghana without provision for the journey and without fear of molestation.[61]

The Ming initially squabbled with Mansur as it had with his grandfather, but ultimately gave in and allowed larger and more frequent trade missions. For example, Ming annals list 150 'princes' from Samarkand, Turfan, Mecca and elsewhere visiting the Chinese capital in 1536.[62] By the sixteenth century, then, something like regular commerce and diplomatic communication again linked Central Asia and Ming China, and northern and southern Xinjiang (Moghulistan and Altishahr) enjoyed a measure of political unity.

Although the symbolic aspects of the mis-named 'tribute system' have been much discussed, it is perhaps more useful to view this arrangement as an attempt to maintain a state monopoly on foreign trade to use as a diplomatic and strategic tool. One side effect of this Ming policy *vis-à-vis* Central Asia was effectively to afford rulers in Xinjiang a similar monopoly on eastbound trade, which for them proved highly profitable. This much is clear from the records of Bento de Goes, a Jesuit lay-brother who travelled to the Tarim Basin from India in 1603 on a mission to ascertain whether 'Cathay'—known to Europeans from Marco Polo and other medieval travellers—was the same place as 'China'—where Jesuits were recently established at court. After travelling from Kabul, Goes laid over in Yarkand for a year waiting for an eastbound caravan to join. During this interval Muhammad Sultan, Chaghatayid ruler of the Kashgar-Yarkand area, put the right to serve as caravan leader up for sale. The highest bidder (who paid 200 bags of musk for the contract) took on other members, who likewise paid to join the caravan under his authority. In the end Goes and his stocks of jade (recently acquired in Khotan) joined a caravan consisting of the statutory seventy-two members. The merchants then proceeded to the borders of the Ming carrying passports from the Yarkand khan charging them as his 'ambassadors'.[63] After Turfan's rapprochement with the Ming, then,

---

61   Mirza Muhammad Haidar 1972: II: 134. See also Barthold 1956–62: 153. On the Chinese use of 'Yarkand khanate' (*Yeerqiang hanguo*), see Wei Liangtao 1994: 2–6.
62   Rossabi 1972: 223–4. See also Watanabe 1975.
63   Wessels 1924: 25. Goes' diary was apparently destroyed by his debtors after his

long-distance trade between Central Asia and the Ming again became routine, if not exactly trouble-free (Goes died on the Chinese border in Suzhou [Gansu], possibly poisoned by fellow travellers to whom he had unwisely lent sums of money). Despite the formal strictures on the trade imposed by the Ming, moreover, there seems to have been an active trade at the border: Matteo Ricci noted that a community of Central Asian Muslims had established itself in Suzhou (Gansu) by the mid-seventeenth century to broker trade with Kashgar and other western cities.[64]

THE SILK ROAD IN EARLY MODERN TIMES

That historical records indicate a revival of long-distance trade relations from the early fifteenth century (and continuing, despite interruptions, through Qing times) is interesting in light of what has become a common assumption in world history circles: that the rise of European maritime trade in the Indian Ocean and South China Sea rang the death knell of Silk Road trade across central Eurasia, marking the beginning of the region's long decline. This bell apparently tolled for some time, since orbituarists have fixed the patient's death at various points over two centuries: For the authors of the *Cambridge History of Islam*, 'Central Asia was thus isolated from the early sixteenth century ... and ... led an existence at the margin of world history .... The discovery of the sea-route to East Asia rendered the Silk Road increasingly superfluous ....'[65] To Niels Steensgaard, 'the destructive effects of the discovery of the sea route to Asia upon the traditional intercontinental trade routes were not felt until after the elapse of an entire century ... and at the end of the sixteenth century the transcontinental caravan trade reached dimensions which must presumably be regarded as its historical culmination.' Isenbike Togan sees the 'closure of the silk routes' as happening in the latter

---

death; what we know of his journey comes from the Jesuit Matteo Ricci's account, based on a letter he received from Goes and on Ricci's own interview with Goes' travelling companion.

64 Togan 1998: 256 citing L. Gallagher (trans.), 1953, *China in the Sixteenth Century: The Journals of Matthew Ricci, 1583–1610*, New York: Random House, 513–15.

65 P.M. Holt, Ann K.S. Lambton and Bernard Lewis (eds) *The Cambridge History of Islam*, Cambridge University Press, 1970, 471, 483. Quoted in Frank 1998: 118. The argument may originate with Barthold; see Levi 1999: 523.

seventeenth century, when rising Zunghar, Qing and Russian power choked off the independent merchant intermediaries.[66]

Much depends on what one means by 'Silk Road': whether one considers only goods that went from one end of the continent to the other, or choses to include the Chinese, Central Asian, Russian, Indian or Middle Eastern regional segments of the Eurasian trade webs in one's conception of 'Silk Road'; or, indeed, whether one includes 'trans-ecological', 'north-south' necessity trade between sedentary societies and pastoral nomads as well as 'trans-civilisational', 'east-west' luxury exchange between the continent's political and population centres.[67] Silk from China was already considered inferior in Europe to that from the Middle East by the thirteenth century, yet the Mongol period is nonetheless considered a Silk Road highpoint.[68] Trade was, to be sure, disrupted on many occasions by wars and political fragmentation, which made travel unsafe and raised protection costs. Nevertheless, viewed from a long perspective taking in the fifteenth through nineteenth centuries, there is no evidence that competition along sea routes affected the volume of overland trade at the centre of Eurasia, and little indication that this trade entered a secular decline from the sixteenth or seventeenth centuries. Rather, the Ming records of 'tribute trade' furnish a good deal of evidence that large caravans plied both desert and steppe routes across Xinjiang between Transoxiana and north China until the late sixteenth century; thereafter, missions were less frequent, but nonetheless occurred.[69] Moreover, as we will see in the next chapter, following the turmoil of the Ming-Qing transition in China in the mid-seventeenth century, Qing, Zunghar and Russian unification and expansion quelled petty warring khanates and boosted economic activity across the region.

---

66 Rossabi 1990: 352, 360; Frank 1998: 119–20. Despite the title of her article, Togan (1998) in fact provides many examples of on-going trade between China and Central Asia throughout the seventeenth century, suggesting a restructuring rather than a decline of the trade. Indeed, we know that the Zunghar khanate employed Muslim merchants from the Tarim Basin and Transoxiana to conduct their sizeable trade with Qing China and Tibet, and that trade expanded further after Qing conquest of the Tarim Basin and Zungharia (see Chapter 3).

67 The term 'trans-ecological' is from Christian 2000.

68 Lopez 1952.

69 Rossabi 1990: 362–3.

3. Between Islam and China

(16th–19th centuries)

As the survey in Chapters 1 and 2 shows, from the earliest times Xinjiang history has been the history of interaction with other places, be it through migration, trade or imperial conquest. By the sixteenth century, where we begin this chapter, out of the chaos that had followed the decline of the Mongol empire new, larger and more consolidated states were emerging in the agrarian rimlands of the continent—China, India, Persia, Russia. In Central Eurasia as well there were various attempts to reunify, even reimperialise, in Tibet, in Transoxiana, among Mongol groups, and in Manchuria. These efforts involved the mustering of both politico-military and religio-ideological forms of power.[1] Increasingly the ethnic and religious landscape in Central Eurasia resembles that of modern times, with Turkic speakers, Iranian speakers, Mongol speakers, Muslims, Tibetan Buddhists, Mongols, Kazaks, Kirghiz, Uyghurs, Chinese and so on all living more or less where we find them today. Xinjiang was, quite literally, in the middle of all this, and events of these centuries left two legacies that have endured to the present: Xinjiang's sedentary and nomadic population became almost entirely Islamic; and competition among reimperialisers in Mongolia, Manchuria and China resulted in Xinjiang's incorporation and integration to a China-based state in a manner closer than ever before.

Xinjiang was Islamicised by the seventeenth century. This process had begun earlier, its onset signalled by the tenth-century conversion of Satuq Bughra Khan and '200,000 tents of the Turks' discussed in the previous chapter. But while Turkic Central Asia had largely converted to Islam (and Islam had adapted to the nomads' needs), the Mongols were new arrivals in the thirteenth century. They were generally a brand of

---

1 Fletcher 1995b; Millward 2004b.

animist, believing in a universal sky-god (Tenggeri) and various other spirits whom shamans could contact, though some followed Tibetan Buddhism, and many influential Mongols were Nestorian Christians. The Chaghatayid Tughluq Temür's own embrace of Islam in the fourteenth century shows that Islam was making inroads among the Mongols in Xinjiang, but does not yet mark full Islamicisation of either the nomads or Xinjiang's oasis-dwellers. The Ming envoy Chen Cheng, passing through Turfan in 1414, noted many monks and Buddhist temples in that city and environs,[2] and just a few years before that, Turfan had sent Buddhist priests as envoys to the Ming. Even further west, 'those living in felt tents' in the mountains and steppes of Moghulistan were not yet considered true Muslims: until the mid-fifteenth century, the Muslims could still legally enslave 'Moghuls' as infidels. But by the early decades of the sixteenth century inhabitants of the old Uyghur kingdom in the Turfan Basin had followed those of the oases of the Tarim Basin in becoming Muslims. Indeed, within a few decades control over the Tarim cities would fall to shaykhs tracing their lineage to Bukhara, the old Mughal khans reigning as mere figureheads.

Islamicisation linked the Xinjiang region culturally to the west, to the broad zone of Central and South Asia whose high culture was in Persian or Chaghatay Turkic. At the same time, however, Xinjiang remained strategically implicated in the power dynamics between north China- and Mongolia-based powers. There would be one more round in the pattern we have noted above: the north China-based power expanding westward into Xinjiang as part of its campaign against the steppe empire. Despite the repetition of certain patterns, however, history does not really repeat itself. In this final sequel the Qing fought the Zunghars with new technology, a larger agrarian tax base, greater logistical reach, more efficient mercantile cooperation and a different ideology than its predecessors, combining and transcending both Chinese and steppe historical achievements and institutions. The result would integrate Xinjiang within a centrally administered China-based empire far more tightly than it had ever been under Han, Tang or Yuan.

Meanwhile, other empires were converging on the scene. Together with the Qing occupation of Xinjiang, the eastward advance of the Russian empire and northward push of the British Raj effectively hemmed

---

2   Chen Cheng, *Xiyu fanguo zhi*, excerpted in Yang Jianxin 1987: 292–3.

in Xinjiang and the rest of Central Eurasia, marking the end of the
nomadic steppe empire and bringing the region into unprecedented
contact with a wider world.

SUFI PROSELYTISATION IN THE TARIM BASIN

Muhammad Oghlan Khan, a Chaghatayid raised to the khanship by the
Dughlat clan, took the business of Islamicisation seriously. He issued
an edict in Kashgar around 1416 to the effect that any Mongol nomad
or member of the ruling clan who did not wear a turban would have
a horseshoe nail driven into his head. 'May God recompense him with
Good', comments the historian.[3]

Others took a subtler approach. Sufis, or Islamic mystics, spread Islam among the Turkic and Mongol nomads on the Kazak steppe in
Zungharia, in the Tianshan and Pamir, as well as throughout the oases
of Central Asia. Their claims of descent from the prophet Muhammad,
chains of initiation, networks of lodges, close ties to merchants and rulers, tombs which served as pilgrimage sites and their often considerable
wealth made the larger Sufi orders (tariqa) especially the Yasawiyya and
Naqshbandiyya[4] powerful institutions with growing religious and political influence in the Mongol imperial period and after. Stories about
famous Sufi shaykhs stress their healing powers and the miracle-working
upon which their success as missionaries hinged—the defeat of the giant
Mughal wrestler by Arshad ad-Din (the shaykh who converted Tughluq
Temür) is one example of such a miracle. The life of the Khoja Ishaq
Wali (d. 1599) provides many others. He spent several years spreading
the faith in Kashgar, Yarkand, Khotan, Aqsu and among the shamanist
and Buddhist Kirghiz tribes in the nearby mountains. In one story, Ishaq
sends a disciple to the camp of a gravely ill Kirghiz chief, Seryop Qirqiz,
whose followers were making offerings to idols in an effort to cure him

---

3 Mirza Muhammd Haidar 1972: I: 58.
4 The Yasawiyya were active proselytisers among the Turks of Transoxiana and
Semirech'e from the twelfth century, and were influential among the Uzbeks and
Moghuls of Moghulistan. From the fifteenth century the Naqshbandiyya Sufis became more active, especially their branches the Ahraris and Juybaris, who gained
great influence and wealth under the Shibanid Uzbeks. As discussed below, branches
of the Naqshbandiyya also proselytised among the Kirghiz and in the oases of the
Tarim Basin from the fifteenth century.

by shamanic ritual. The disciple had the Kirghiz bring their idols—one of silver and a thousand of stone and wood—to Ishaq, who pointed out their uselessness. Ishaq and his disciples then prayed, and the Kirghiz ruler 'suddenly sneezed and, standing up, gave voice to the Muslims' famous profession of faith: "I bear witness that there is no deity but God, and I bear witness that Muhammad is His servant and His prophet."' The Kirghiz thereupon accepted Islam to a man, and donated the silver from the idol (which they had smashed) to the Sufis.[5]

In demonstrating healing powers, deciding battles by magical tricks or surviving trials by fire, Sufis acted like the shamans associated with Turko-Mongol rulers across Eurasia.[6] In fact, in some ways the form of popular Islam that took root in the Xinjiang region following centuries of Sufi missionary work was overlaid upon, without displacing, pre-existing beliefs and cults. This is evident at many smaller shrines in Xinjiang, especially those not dedicated to well-known historical figures but to nameless 'khojas' or masters.[7] One such shrine is at Qumartagh (Chinese name Niujiaoshan) on a hill overlooking the floodplain of the Qaratash and Yurongkash rivers south of Khotan. This striking site was once sacred to Buddhists; now it commemorates a hunter who, after a snake-spirit came to his aid, promised to build a place of worship on this spot. The tombs on the site, supposedly of the hunter, his parents and the snake, resemble similar cairns in Mongolia and Tibet, festooned with sticks, flags, sheep's horns and yak-tails—all reminiscent of shamanic practice. Clearly an older tradition at Qumartagh has been recast as Islamic, as it has at similar shrines throughout the region.[8]

Folklore reveals a similar process. According to a legend recorded in the sixteenth century *Tarikh-i Rashidi*, Khoja Jamal ad-Din (who would later meet Tughluq Temür, and whose son would convert him) once lived and preached in a town between Turfan and Khotan known as Lob Katak. The populace, however, had treated him with disrespect. One day he announced from the pulpit that God would soon deliver a calamity upon the town. Jamal ad-Din and the muezzin (the man who delivers

5   Fletcher 1976:V: 171–2.
6   Fletcher 1986: 43–5.
7   Hamada 1978: 79–81.
8   A cave shrine in the village of Tuyoq (Tuyok), near Hami, is another example. Cable and French (1942: 195–7) describe the 'cave of the seven sleepers' and its shrine adorned with sticks, yak-tails, horns and hair on an *obo*, or cairn of stones.

Shrine at Qumartagh, south of Khotan
(photo: J. Millward, 1992)

the call to prayer) then fled, but after they had journeyed some distance,
the muezzin changed his mind and returned to the town to attend to
some last business. While he was delivering the call to prayer one final
time, sand began to rain from the sky. Only because he was in the minaret was the muezzin able to escape inundation himself; the town was
completely buried. When he rejoined the Khoja, they immediately fled
together. 'It is better to keep at a distance from the wrath of God,' Jamal
ad-Din said.

The seventh-century Chinese Buddhist traveller, Xuan Zang, had
related a very similar story in his account of the states of the 'Western
Regions': A sandalwood image of the Buddha had flown miraculously
to the city of Helaoluojia in the southern Tarim Basin. It was neglected
by the city residents, however, and when a strange arhat (Ch. *luohan*)
arrived to worship the image, the people buried him in the sand and
starved him. Nevertheless, one of the townsmen who had himself prayed

to the Buddha image took pity on the arhat and secretly brought him food. The arhat then warned this kind man to make preparations, for his city would soon be buried in sand. So saying, the arhat suddenly disappeared. The man's relatives and neighbours dismissed his warnings of the coming disaster and one week later the sandstorm came. As the town was inundated, only the kind man was able to escape through a tunnel he had prepared. The Buddha image later magically reappeared in Pimo, the nearby town to which he had fled.

Both Buddhist and Islamic versions of the story seem to concern cities in southern Xinjiang—Lob or Lop of course echoing the name Lop Nor—and echo the fate of the buried city of Loulan (Kroraina) on the shores of the defunct lake.[9] The later Islamic legend was built upon an existing substratum that may have already been old by the time of Xuan Zang.

THE NAQSHBANDIYYA AND THE 'KHOJAS'

Despite this continuity in popular religious belief, the Sufis operating in Kashgaria, Uyghuristan and Moghulistan from the fifteenth century also represented a new and potent force, one that accelerated the Islamicisation of the southern townsfolk and among all the nomads except the Buddhist Oirats. Branches of the Naqshbandi order were even able to seize control of political and military affairs in the Tarim Basin and Turfan.

The Naqshbandis trace the lineage of their leaders back to the prophet Muhammad. The religious aura this lent them, together with their miracles and reputation as religious authorities, made them popular as advisers to temporal rulers in Central Asia. The order's name derives from Baha' ad-Din Naqshband (1318–89), who revitalised the order of the 'masters' (khoja or khwaja) in a village north-east of Bukhara, contributing three innovative teachings which henceforth characterised the Naqshbandiyya. First, Baha' ad-Din believed and himself exemplified that certain Sufis, known as uwaysis, could be guided not only by living teachers, but by masters who were dead or separated by distance from

9 Mirza Muhammd Haidar 1972: I: 11; Xuan Zang, Datang xiyuji, j. 12, under Qusadana guo; see also Hamada 1978: 81–3. The descendents of Jalal al-Din and Arshad al-Din are known as Katakis after Jalal's place of origin, the Lob Katak of the story. They became rich and powerful in Kucha.

their disciples. (This is reminiscent of the 'discovery' by reformist Tibetan lamas around the same time of 'treasure texts' buried in the consciousness of departed lamas but conveyable to the minds of their incarnations and successors.) Baha' ad-Din also taught that the Sufi need not seclude himself from the community in order to maintain his mystical relationship to God (this had been a much debated issue in the eleventh century, when Yusuf Khass Hajib took up the contradiction between worldly and otherworldly in his *Wisdom of Royal Glory*). By justifying his followers' active involvement in worldly affairs, Baha' ad-Din set the stage for the Naqshbandiyya in the fifteenth century to champion strict observance of the *shari'ah*. They were also staunch Sunnite activists, reacting against the triumph of Shi'ism in Safavid Persia.[10] Baha' ad-Din's third innovation was to advocate use of the silent *dhikr* (*zikr*), or remembrance of God. This form of prayer usually consisted of unison chanting by groups of dervishes of 'there is no God but Allah'. The Naqshbandis, however, believed the remembrance could be mentally intoned to oneself.

The Naqshbandi order gained strength rapidly in Ferghana, Bukhara, Samarkand, Herat and elsewhere, as Naqshbandis married into the families of local rulers and accumulated land and rights to tithes for the support of shrines, schools and religious work. One of Baha' ad-Din's most important successors was Khoja Ahrar (1404–90), a Naqshbandi grand master who assisted Timurid rulers Abu Said (1451–69) and Sultan Ahmad (1469–94), maintained contacts with the rulers of Moghulistan through a network of his own disciples, and greatly expanded the wealth and landholdings of the Naqshbandi order through charitable endowments (*waqf*) and family businesses in Samarkand, Herat and elsewhere. The influence of the Ahraris continued under the Shaybanids (Uzbeks) who displaced the Timurids from Transoxiana in 1500.[11]

One of Ahrar's disciples, Khoja Taj ad-Din, became a fixture in the Moghulistan court of Ahmad Khan and his successor Mansur Khan—the

10   That the Naqshbandiyya was later an exponent of 'the eighteenth century reform tide [which] fused shari'ism and Sufism together, permeating virtually the entire network of the Sufi mystical paths' vast geographical outreach' is one of Fletcher's more provoking points (1995a: 22–4). This posthumously-published article on the Naqshbandiyya in Xinjiang and China proper was the culmination of Fletcher's work in the last years of his life, and provides direct evidence of the influence of early modern Islamic movements in China. My section on the rise of Naqshbandi power in Altishahr is based on Fletcher's work, except where otherwise noted.
11   Fletcher 1995a: 6; Soucek 2000: 140 has a biographical sketch of Khoja Ahrar.

Turfan ruler who repeatedly fought with the Ming over Hami and who, with his brother, helped revitalise the Tarim trade routes. The *Tarikh-i Rashidi* claims that these khans were Taj ad-Din's disciples, and its highly favourable account gives a sense of how these saintly masters worked and the power they could obtain in southern Xinjiang:

He [Taj ad-Din] was in attendance on [the two Chaghatayid khans] for fifty years .... And he accepted, during all this period, neither offering nor gift, whether it were from the Khans or the Sultans or the generals of the army, or from peasants or merchants. The Khwaja occupied himself, also, with commerce and agriculture. And from these occupations there accrued to him, by the blessing of the Most High God, great wealth. And what urbanity did he not show, every year, towards the Khans and the Amirs! The poor and indigent—nay, more, the peasant, the villager, the artisan and the merchant all profited [by his wealth]. For this reason no one denied him anything, and all the affairs of the kingdom were laid before him in detail.[12]

Khoja Taj ad-Din was evidently a man possessed of great land-holdings and other wealth, and a respected adviser to the military and political rulers of Moghulistan and Turfan privy to affairs of state. (The claim that he accepted no gifts may be read as evidence that most khojas did so, and in any case is contradicted by the statement that nothing was denied him). The extent of Taj ad-Din's involvement in the business of khans is clear from the manner of his death *c.* 1533: in battle against the Ming.

Taj ad-Din was also a direct descendent of Jamal and Arshad ad-Din, the father and son shaykhs who a century earlier had converted Tughluq Temür and the Moghuls to Islam. Arshad's line of Sufi masters, probably originally Yasawi, had in the early fifteenth-century 'transformed itself into a line of Naqshbandi saints' and continued to promote Islam not only in the oases but among the nomads of Xinjiang.[13] As mentioned above, as late as the early 1400s Buddhist temples still dotted the landscape around Turfan, and Buddhist monks were dispatched as envoys from Turfan to the Ming court. However, by the time of Mansur and Taj ad-Din in the early decades of the sixteenth century old Uyghuristan was virtually all Islamic.

In Kashgaria members of another branch of the Naqshbandiyya not only advised the khans and proselytised but ultimately took power in

12 Mirza Muhammad Haidar 1972: I: 127.
13 Fletcher 1995a: 5.

their own right. The progenitor of this branch, Ahmad Kasani (1461–1542) or Makhdum-i A'zam ('Supreme Teacher'), was another disciple of the Naqshbandi master Khoja Ahrar. Makhdum-i A'zam's own influence spread in his lifetime from Transoxiana to the Tarim Basin, but the penetration of the Makhdumzadas (as his successors are called) into Xinjiang truly began with one of his sons, Ishaq Wali (d. 1599)—the same shaykh who worked miracles among the Kirghiz. Khoja Ishaq enjoyed high repute as a Sufi master in Transoxiana, where he enjoyed the patronage of several Uzbek khans. In the late sixteenth century he and his disciples journeyed to the Tarim Basin, and after several years had established the Ishaqiyya (as their order came to be known) in the Kashgar region. Ishaq made the Chaghatayid khan of Kashgaria, Muhammad Sultan (r. 1592–1609) his disciple. (Muhammad was the ruler who arranged Bento de Goes' caravan to the borders of China.) Before his death Ishaq even named Muhammad Sultan the Naqshbandi grand master—Ishaq's spiritual successor—thus assuring the Ishaqiyya's continued status in the region.

A short time later Khoja Muhammad Yusuf (d. 1653), descended from Makhdum-i A'zam through the patriarch's eldest son, also came east. He preached in the cities of the Tarim and Turfan Basins and in western China. Ishaqis, jealous of his success, poisoned Khoja Yusuf, leaving his work to be carried on by disciples under his son Hidayet Allah (d. 1694), also known as Khoja Afaq ('Master of the Horizons'). Their branch of the Makhdumzada Naqshbandis in Xinjiang thus came to be known as the Afaqiyya.

Khoja Afaq was a powerful presence in Kashgar until the 1670s, and he may even have served as governor of that city under the khan 'Abdullah, whose capital was in Yarkand. When 'Abdullah went on hajj, however, his son, Isma'il Khan, in league with the Ishaqiyya, drove Khoja Afaq out of Kashgar. Afaq fled to Kashmir and then to Lhasa, where he sought the intervention of the Dalai Lama. There are differing versions of Afaq's encounter with the Shaykh of the Brahmans—as the Afaq's hagiography calls the Dalai Lama. In one story, the two holy men engage in a contest of miracles, in which Afaq's magic proves the more powerful.[14]

Today both the reputation and political position of Tibet's leading cleric have changed greatly, but in the seventeenth century the Fifth

14   Papas 2004: 152–3; See also Zarcone 1996.

Khoja Afaq Mazar, an important Naqshbandi tomb and tourist site outside
Kashgar (photo: J. Millward, 2004)

Dalai Lama (1617–82) was a forceful ruler, leading the reformist Gelugpa (dGe-lugs-pa, Yellow Hat) school of Tibetan Buddhism to supremacy over other schools and over the kings in Tibet proper, and expanding his political influence into Khams (eastern Tibet), Qinghai (Amdo
or Kokonor) and even among the Oirat, Khalkha, Chahar and other
Mongol peoples in Zungharia and Mongolia. Today's sense of Tibetan
Buddhism as a quietist, pacifistic religion is not borne out by events in
seventeenth- and eighteenth-century Inner Asia. In fact, Joseph Fletcher
compared the rising Gelugpa to the Naqshbandiyya in both its reform-
mindedness and its engagement with worldly affairs.[15]

Khoja Afaq represented himself to the Dalai Lama as the legitimate
secular ruler of Kashgaria, and the Dalai Lama agreed to help by calling
on Galdan, ruler of the Zunghars, the confederation of Oirat Mongols
who had since the early seventeenth century been forming a steppe
empire north of the Tianshan, in the region since known as Zungharia.
'Isma'il Khan has seized [Afaq's] country', the Dalai Lama wrote Galdan,

15   Fletcher 1995b: 25–7.

who gladly lent a hand by conquering the Tarim Basin oases in 1678 and placing Afaq and his sons in power, in return for an annual payment.[16] The Afaqi-Ishaqi rivalry continued, however, while the Zunghars were preoccupied elsewhere. After Khoja Afaqs' death, for example, his wife earned the nickname 'Jallad Khanum' ('Butcher Queen') for the way she pressed the bloody feud with the Ishaqis. Kirghiz tribes in the mountains ringing the western Tarim Basin joined both sides of the struggle, and for this reason the Ishaqiyya is also called Qarataghliq—Black Mountain—and the Afaqiyya known as Aqtaghliq—White Mountain—after Kirghiz factions in different areas.[17]

In the late seventeenth and early eighteenth century, then, the Tarim Basin had reverted to an old pattern: local rulers in the oases (now a lineage of Sufis) paying tribute to nomad overlords north of the Tianshan. As in previous periods, moreover, the political dynamic across the Tianshan was but part of a larger geostrategic picture, a rivalry between the northern nomadic power (the Zunghars), the ruling power in China (the Manchu Qing dynasty) and even Tibet under the Gelugpa Dalai Lamas. More than that, however, another continental empire had emerged over the western horizon: Muscovite Russia, together with the Qing, would definitively change the steppe-sown dynamic, and with it Xinjiang's place in Central Eurasia.

ZUNGHAR-MANCHU RIVALRY AND THE QING CREATION OF 'XINJIANG'

'Zunghar' is a political term, referring to a confederation of Oirat tribes, including Choros, Dörböts and Khoits, that coalesced under Zunghar tribal leadership in the early seventeenth century in northern Xinjiang. There is considerable confusion regarding the terminology, and one may find the terms Oirat and Zunghar (and their variants Wei-la, E-lu-te, Wei-lu-te, Wei-la-te, Ölöd, Eleuth, Junghar, Jegün Ghar, Dzunghar, Zhun-ge-er) used interchangeably. Islamic and Russian sources call all

---

16 The source regarding Khoja Afaq's dealings with the Dalai Lama and Galdan is the *Tazkira-i Khwajagan* of Muhammad Sadiq; see Shaw 1897, and Zarcone 1995; Zarcone 1996 is a fuller version, in French, of Zarcone 1995.

17 Schwarz 1976: 275–80. Chinese sources, with imprecision, also use the terms *heimao* and *baimao* (black and white hat) for factions of the Naqshbandiyya in Xinjiang. See Fletcher 1995a: 10 n. 3.

Oirats 'Kalmyks' (Qalmuqs), and sometimes use this term even for eastern Mongols and Manchus.

While all Zunghars were Oirats, not all Oirats were Zunghars. In fact large numbers of two Oirat tribes fled the intense struggle for control of lands and people in Zungharia in the 1620s and 1630s in search of more open pastures elsewhere. The Khoshuuts moved from grazing lands in the region of today's Urumchi south to Qinghai and Tibet, where they lent their military muscle to the Gelugpa cause. The Torghuts migrated west from the Tarbaghatai region of northern Xinjiang all the way to the banks of the Volga. There, known as Kalmyks, they dominated local Muslim Nogay Turks, but eventually fell under Tsarist rule and were forced to pay taxes and fight in Moscow's wars against the Ottoman empire. To escape this oppression, in 1771 some 150,000 Torghuts migrated back east to seek asylum with the Qing. They were received with much pomp, and resettled in northern Xinjiang. This episode, with its ripple effects reminiscent of the Xiongnu displacement of the Yuezhi, was history's last great 'billiard ball' movement of nomadic peoples across Central Eurasia.

Through the seventeenth and first half of the eighteenth century the Zunghars gained strength and built a powerful state, constructing stone-walled towns, adopting Tibetan Buddhism, expanding trade with Russia and the Qing, and ultimately deploying gunpowder weapons—by mounting small cannon on camel back, the Zunghars even fielded mobile 'tanks'. Though still less militarily effective in open battle than mounted horsemen, cannon and guns were useful in conquering cities and made an impressive amount of noise. As Peter Perdue points out, the fielding of cannon on camelback shows that the Zunghars were more than mere raiders, but were rather engaged in a full-scale imperial project.[18]

Indeed, under their ruler Batur Khongtaiji the Zunghars expanded at the expense of the Kazaks, and in 1635 concluded a treaty with the Russians over territory, jurisdiction and rights to tribute from tribal peoples, like the Yenesei Kirghiz, caught between their growing imperial realms. The Russians had been expanding westward across Siberia since the sixteenth century; the Russian merchants and rough frontiersmen who came in search of sable and other furs were followed by Tsarist troops and officials. Before long a string of frontier forts and trading towns dot-

18   Perdue 2005: 305.

ted the banks of Siberia's major rivers. The Zunghars obtained gun-casting and cartographic technology from Russians and Swedes formerly in Russian service. The Zunghar state also drew on labour and manufactured goods from southern Xinjiang, and mined iron, copper, silver, gold, steel and minerals for gun-powder. With copper from Xinjiang mines, the Zunghars minted coins bearing the mint name 'Yarkand' in Arabic and their khan's name in Oirat script. The Zunghars manufactured paper and printed books in the Todo script specifically designed for the sounds of the Oirat Mongolian by a Tibetan prelate (who thus repeated a service rendered to the Chinggisids by another lama centuries before).

The Tibetan connection was critical to the growth and legitimacy of the Zunghar state. Though some Chinggisid Mongols had adopted Buddhism during the imperial period (Khubilai, in particular, had close relations with Tibetan lamas), Tibetan Buddhism did not predominate among the tribesmen of Mongolia until after the mid-sixteenth century, when the political and missionary activity of the Gelugpa won over rulers among both eastern and western Mongol groups. In 1640 Batur Khongtaiji participated in a *quriltai*, or congress, of Mongol and Oirat tribes, attended by representatives of the Khalkhas, Khoshuuts from Qinghai and Torghuts from the Volga, as well as Tibetan lamas. From this meeting emerged a pan-Mongol law code in which Tibetan Buddhism was designated the religion of the Mongols, and marriages were concluded linking Batur with the Torghut and Khoshuut ruling clans. Political marriage was not an option for the Tibetan lamas, but one of Batur's sons, Galdan, went to Lhasa as a novice monk, establishing a similar sort of linkage. (His name is a Mongolised version of the Tibetan 'Dga' ldan', the Tushita Paradise of Maitreya Buddha, also the name of a famous monastery built in Lhasa by the reforming founder of the Gelugpa school.)

The 1640 *khuriltai* thus signalled the potential of the Zunghar state to unite the Mongols under the banner of Tibetan Buddhism and forge a new Mongol empire in Inner Asia. When Galdan returned to Zungharia in 1670 and resolved the succession struggle that had ensued upon Batur Khongtaiji's death a few years earlier, he began to make good upon that promise. He seized the Tarim and Turfan Basins in 1678–80 with the Dalai Lama's blessing. The Dalai Lama also bestowed upon Galdan the title 'Boshugtu Khan', khan by divine grace, essentially licensing Galdan to use the khanal title despite his lack of Chinggisid ancestry. Now possessed of a tax-base in the oases to his south, Galdan pursued an interest in the affairs of the Khalkhas, those Mongols still ruled by Chinggisid khans to the east. This brought Galdan into direct competition with the other rising Inner Asian power, the Qing (Ch'ing) empire founded by the Manchus.[19]

From their beginnings in the frontier lands between north China, Korea and Siberia, the Manchus had been closely involved with Mongol groups. The confederated military force (the 'Eight Banners') which they deployed against the Ming and ultimately led into Beijing contained many Mongols. The Qing had assumed control of tribes and lands in Inner Mongolia in the 1630s, and by the time the Manchus took Beijing (1644), they exercised considerable influence over the Khalkhas to the north as well. Thus Galdan's advance into Outer Mongolia in 1688 was a direct provocation to the Qing. The Qing Kangxi emperor (r. 1662–1722) responded to the threat methodically, through both diplomatic and military means. He stabilised relations with the Russians, who had come into conflict with the Qing in the north-east, and whose fort at Albazin on the Amur River (Heilongjiang) the Qing had razed twice (1685 and 1686). In the treaty of Nerchinsk (1689), the Qing and Russia regularised trade relations, demarcated their eastern border, and set rules governing the unsettled peoples in frontier territories. Kangxi also took steps to secure the lasting loyalty of the Khalkhas, of whom some 140,000 had fled the Zunghars into Qing territory. The Qing dispatched grain, livestock and other supplies to these refugees. While the Khalkha khans and their highest lama deliberated over whether to cast their lot with the Qing or the Russians, the Qing's own court lama lobbied hard for the Manchus, stressing that unlike the Russians, the Qing patronised the Gelugpa church. In the end the Khalkhas came over to the Qing, an event celebrated in 1691 with a great feast at Dolonnor 250 kilometres north of Beijing. This new reserve of Khalkha manpower would serve as a mainstay of the Qing military, especially in its Inner Asian campaigns. Moreover, to have the Khalkha Chinggisids as subjects of the Manchu emperors lent the Qing political legitimacy in Inner Asian affairs, aiding in their efforts to assume the Chinggisid mantle and the role of patron and protector of the Gelugpa church. Finally, the Kangxi emperor

19 Perdue 2005 provides a monumental history of the Zunghar state, in the context of rising Qing and Russian power in Inner Asia. I have drawn specifically on pp. 102–6 and 304–7 here. See also Perdue 1996 and 2004.

launched a military campaign against Galdan, and a Qing army crushed the Zunghar force in 1696 at Jao Modo (on the Tula River just east of modern Ulaan Baatar). Abandoned by his army, Galdan died the next year, perhaps poisoned by one of his few remaining followers or a victim of sudden illness. The Qing court and historians knowingly falsified the record in the service of the Qing imperial myth, claiming that Galdan had committed suicide.[20]

Meanwhile, fighting continued among the Ishaqiyya, Afaqiyya, remaining Chaghatayids and Kirghiz groups in the south-western Tarim Basin, prompting the new Zunghar khan, Tsewang Rabdan, to invade again in 1713 and restore the revenue stream from the oases. The Zunghars took the leaders of both khoja factions as royal hostages back north to Ghulja; a few years later they would restore the Ishaqiyya to power in Altishahr as Zunghar vassals.[21]

The Zunghars did not govern the Tarim Basin so much as extract from it, in the manner of the Qara Khitay before them. However, we have more information for this period about precisely what this meant. The *Tazkira-i Khwajagan* reports that the Zunghars assessed an annual levy on Kashgar of 48,000 ounces of silver; other cities likewise owed a cash tax. In the mid-eighteenth century a Qing official reported that Kashgar had annually paid the Zunghars 40,898 silver ounces and 67,000 *patman* of grain (a *patman* was approximately four piculs and five pecks). These levies were supplemented by payments of grain, cotton, saffron, *corvées* of labour and taxes on distilling, milling and trade. The exactions could be arbitrary: Zunghar bands arrived each harvest season to collect the tax, and had to be wined, dined and supplied with women.[22]

One way in which the pattern of Zunghar control over Xinjiang differed from that of earlier nomadic powers was in their efforts to develop the agricultural potential of Zungharia. Captive Kazaks, Kirghiz and prisoners from western Turkestan and China, along with some Zung-

20 Perdue 2005: 202–3.
21 Schwarz 1976: 281–2.
22 Schwarz 1976: 277 n. 40, 282 n. 59, citing Muhammad Sadiq Kashghari, *Tazkira-i Khwajagan* in Shaw 1897 for the figure of 48,000. Schwarz points out severe miscalculations and exaggerations in the figures given by Courant 1912: 51 n. 4 and Valikhanov. The Qing had reason to exaggerate the size of Zunghar exactions, yet its figures are an order of magnitude less than the 400,000 cited by Courant. Millward 1998: 54, and Wang Xilong in Yu Taishan 1996: 420, give citations from Qing sources on Zunghar taxation.

hars, constructed irrigation and worked the land in the rich Zungharian river valleys and the Urumchi area; most numerous were Muslims transported from the western Tarim to the Yili valley to be farmers, or 'taranchis'.[23] This demonstrates the importance the Zunghar state placed on regularising its sources of grain and other produce. Incidentally, but significantly for the future, this policy marks the beginning of the process by which Zungharia came to be inhabited by non-nomadic Muslim Turkic-speakers from the south—a group that by the twentieth century would be called Uyghurs.[24]

Commerce provided another source both of revenue and of items the Zunghars could not grow or manufacture for themselves, including silks, tea and cotton cloth. High-value satins and tea could be trans-shipped to the west and sold at profit; cloth and coarse brick tea was consumed by common nomads in Zungharia. Having taken control of southern Xinjiang, the Zunghars also seized the monopoly on licensing caravans that had once been the prerogative of the Chaghatayid khans and other rulers of the Tarim oases. The merchants in Zunghar caravans, referred to as 'Bukharans' in the sources, were themselves likely to come from the Tarim Basin, Turfan or western Central Asia. (For example, Chinese sources list the name of the 'ambassador' leading the Zunghar delegation to Beijing in 1744 as 'Tur-er-du'—certainly a transcription of 'Turdi', a Turkic—not Mongolian—name.) By contracting such merchants, the Zunghars exchanged goods with Tashkent in the west and the Qing in the east. In peacetime, trade with China followed the same pattern and engendered the same aggravations as during the Ming period, with the Zunghar caravans exceeding the quotas both on 'tribute missions' to Beijing and at the frontier trade fairs in Suzhou, Gansu. The Zunghars also traded with Tibet, in the guise of pilgrimages to donate tea to monasteries in Lhasa; the Qing was forced to sanction and even subsidise these trading ventures, much to the annoyance of officials. Thus the Zunghars

23 Wang Xilong in Yu Taishan 1996: 426, citing a 1739 Grand Council memorial in the Beijing Qing archive. Fletcher 1995a: (XI) 35.
24 The term 'Uyghur' was not used in this sense in the eighteenth century. Rather, Chinese sources simply called these people Muslims (Huizi), and they called themselves either by their city names (Kashgarliq, Quchaliq, Khotanliq) or more generally as musulman (Muslims). I use the term Uyghur here for the Turkic Muslims of the Tarim and Turfan Basins as well as for the transplanted Taranchis; I do so for this period out of convenience, albeit somewhat anachronistically, as it was a century before the term Uyghur was used in its current sense.

provide a good and well documented example of the importance of the caravan trade to the nomadic states of Inner Asia.[25]

For fifty years after Galdan's death Zunghar relations with the Qing alternated between open warfare and tense truces. Following the pattern now familiar to us, the two powers sparred for control of eastern Xinjiang (the Hami, Turfan and Urumchi areas), passing control of these cities and their peoples back and forth. The struggle spread into Tibet in 1717, when the Zunghars intervened in the politics of Dalai Lama succession. Their defeat there by the Qing in 1720 marks the beginnings of the Qing protectorate in Tibet. The Zunghars also invaded western Turkestan in 1723, sacking Tashkent and other cities; these Zunghar attacks greatly weakened the Middle and Great Hordes of the Kazaks, facilitating Russian penetration of Central Asia. The Zunghars also fought periodically against the Russians, whose chain of fortified outposts pressed upon Zunghar lands and who were demanding submission and tribute from tribes already subject to the Zunghars.

The attitudes of Chinese sources towards the Zunghars have changed little since the Qing emperors in the seventeenth and eighteenth centuries berated their untrustworthy, bellicose and rebellious natures. A more neutral perspective is possible. The Zunghars, like the Qing, Tsarist Russia and, indeed, several European states, were engaged in a self-strengthening, state-building effort. As Peter Perdue points out, however, in the eighteenth century the great continental empires of Russia and the Qing could draw upon larger agrarian bases and more highly centralised administrative systems than could the Zunghars in the Tarim Basin and Zungharia; these empires could also effectively limit the Zunghars' access to strategic materials and tributes from Siberian peoples.[26]

By the mid-eighteenth century succession troubles, the bane of all steppe empires, fatally weakened the Zunghar state. Following the death of the khan Galdan Tsering (r. 1727–45), internecine struggle split the confederation. In 1752 chieftains Amursana and Dawachi assassinated the currently reigning candidate; when Dawachi declared himself khan, Amursana went to war against him, but was defeated and fled east to the Qing with 20,000 followers. The Qing Qianlong emperor (r. 1736–95) saw this as a great opportunity, and personally received Amursana along

25   Millward 1998: 29; Lin Yongkuang and Wang Xi 1991: 82–130 provide a general account, with much archival data.
26   Perdue 2005: esp. 518–20.

with Tsereng, another defecting Oirat chief, with great ceremony in the Manchu summer capital at Chengde on the Mongolian border. (Inner Asian luminaries preferred not to visit Beijing, where the chance of contracting smallpox was high.)

With these new allies in the vanguard, Qing armies marched on Zungharia, taking it easily in 1755. This was not a victory of firearms over primitive weapons: documentary portraits of the battles, as painted by Jesuits in the Qing court, reveal that both sides used cannon and small arms as well as bows and arrows. The Qing could, however, more effectively mobilise its agrarian, economic and military resources. After years of fighting among themselves, moreover, the ragged Zunghar confederation offered little resistance.

After capturing Dawachi and taking Ghulja without a fight, the Qing felt secure in withdrawing most of its forces. The Qianlong emperor initially planned to break up the Zunghar confederation and divide the region's pastures and people between four main Oirat tribes, each under their own khan. By this formula, similar to how the Qing had pacified Mongolia, Amursana would have become khan of the Khoits. But Amursana hoped to command the whole of the former Zunghar peoples and pastures himself. He announced this intention in a memorial to the Qing court and slaughtered the remaining Qing forces in Ghulja. (Though treated as a traitorous rebel in Chinese historiography, Amursana is a hero in the Mongolian Republic, where a street is named for him in Ulaan Baatar.)

The enraged Qianlong emperor had Amursana's impudent missive printed and circulated to all the officials in China, and launched a massive Qing retaliation to resolve the Zunghar problem. Qianlong repeatedly urged his reluctant generals to exterminate all the Zunghars except women, children and the elderly, who were to be enslaved to Manchu and other Mongol banners. Starvation tactics, smallpox and the suppression of tribal identities of surviving Zunghar slaves led to the disappearance of the Zunghar people and depopulation of the region. The name Zunghar was expunged; there were surviving Oirats, but no Zunghars. Perdue calls the episode a deliberate ethnic genocide unprecedented in Qing practice, a '"final solution" to China's north-west frontier problems'.[27]

27 Perdue 2005: 282–7, quote from 285.

When Qing forces first took Ghulja in 1755 they found two Afaqi khoja brothers, Burhan ad-Din and Khoja Jahan, whom the Zunghars had detained there as hostages. The Manchus gave Burhan the military support to retake the Tarim Basin, hoping to establish him as a client in the south. However, when Amursana rebelled, Khoja Jahan fled south to join his brother and they renounced their allegiance to the Qing, executed an envoy, and attempted to reinstitute independent Afaqi rule in the Tarim Basin. Without ever having intended to, therefore, the Qing found itself campaigning oasis by oasis south of the Tianshan, an enterprise that required enormous logistical efforts to move men, grain, livestock, silver and other supplies from Zungharia across the Tianshan passes and from north-west China over the Gobi desert to Xinjiang. When Qing banner armies took Yarkand and Kashgar the Khojas escaped west through the passes to Badakhshan. In the course of their campaigns against the Zunghars, the Kazaks who supported the Zunghars, and the Khojas, Qing armies in the late 1750s penetrated the mountain pastures of the Kirghiz and the Ferghana valley beyond; one detachment reached the city of Talas—the first China-based army there since the famous battle a thousand years earlier. Another reached the city of Khoqand, and another camped outside Tashkent. Though this show of force beyond the Pamirs was temporary, it served its purpose: cowed local rulers hastened to help the Qing apprehend fugitives. In particular, Sultan Shah bent to the will of the wrathful Manchu superpower and sent first Khoja Jahan's head, and later Burhan ad-Din's remains, back east with his compliments.[28]

Thus the Qing extended its imperial rule to Muslim Central Asia, adding the Zunghar empire to its already vast holdings in north-east Asia, China and Mongolia. The Qianlong emperor had carried on the campaigns in the face of domestic opposition from Chinese officials concerned about the cost of conquering and holding territory they judged to be 'wasteland'. The emperor and the court justified the conquest in financial and strategic terms, arguing that a forward position allowed banner troops to be stationed on the steppe, where they herded livestock and, in theory (though never in practice), supported themselves without adding to the burden on the population of China proper. Certainly the threat from the steppes north of China, which had comprised the most serious strategic issue for Han, Tang, Ming, Yuan and other states based

28 Newby 2005: 22–6 gives the best English account of the advance of Qing forces beyond the Pamirs.

in north China, was no longer a concern after the Qing annexation of outer Mongolia and conquest of Xinjiang. Holding Xinjiang, the emperor argued, saved money and enhanced security. Many Chinese officials and literati remained unconvinced of this at first, but got used to the idea over subsequent decades. From this line of reasoning would develop the argument that Mongolia was essential to the security of the Beijing capital, and that Xinjiang was an essential bulwark to the defence of Mongolia, and ultimately the argument that Xinjiang was an essential, inalienable part of China—something no Chinese would have argued before the nineteenth century.

QING XINJIANG

Although the Qing followed some Han and Tang precedents in Xinjiang, the structure of Qing imperial control over Xinjiang recalls the type exemplified by the Qara Khitay or other nomad powers in that it ruled the oases of the Tarim from a base in Zungharia, north of the Tianshan. This differed from the Han and even the Tang dynasties, which had located their Xinjiang headquarters in the east of the region. The Qing military forces in the 'New Frontier' (the literal meaning of Xinjiang, a term first introduced in the late eighteenth century) were mostly banner troops, accustomed to a steppe lifestyle, and the vast majority of them were maintained on grasslands north of the Tianshan, where their horses could feed on good pasture and they could raise livestock for food and portage. Local government in the southern oases remained in the hands of Muslim élites, and the imperial state did not in its first century of rule (1760–1864) interfere much in the Islamic legal system or religious matters. Like the Zunghars and its other predecessors, moreover, the Qing taxed the agrarian peoples of the Tarim and Turfan Basins in cash and kind to support the military occupation in the north, and any uprisings were quelled with great violence. It also actively promoted agriculture in both south and north. Overall, however, the Qing overlords intervened relatively little in the local society of what it called the Muslim Region (*Huibu*) of southern Xinjiang.[29]

---

29 The term 'Muslim region' was balanced by the term *Zhunbu* (Zungharia) for northern Xinjiang. The character *zhun* is short for Zhun-ge-er, or Zunghar, and the place name *Zhunbu* is thus the only vestige of the Zunghar state, the existence of which the Qing tolerated. Qing usage also divided Xinjiang into three 'routes':

However, comparisons with previous nomad rulers are deceiving, for in other ways Qing rule in Xinjiang was a departure from the pattern of previous overlords controlling the Tarim from Zungharia. In fact the Qing broke the geostrategic standoff that had in the past characterised relations between China-based, Mongolia-based and Tibet-based powers and Xinjiang. The dynasty did this by itself absorbing, or at least controlling, Mongolia, Zungharia, Qinghai and Tibet. Moreover, unlike the Mongol empire under Chinggis Khan, which had conquered the same territories, the Qing did not divvy Inner Asia up into appanages, but rather ruled it all as a centralised empire through a combination of bureaucratic methods derived from China and the Qing ruling élite's own linguistic, cultural, historical and military experience of Inner Asia. Xinjiang under the Qing was thus not passed back and forth between warring powers like a goat carcass in the nomad game of *boz-kashi*, but rather enjoyed a century of stability (with some interruptions) under a single authority.

To consolidate its hold on Zungharia and the Tarim, the Qing developed communications and agricultural infrastructure, systematised the monetary system, and colonised parts of Xinjiang with Han and Muslim Chinese (Tungans or Hui). The dynasty also embarked upon a project to gather and publish knowledge about Xinjiang, likewise in the service of imperial rule. In many ways, then, Qing rule in Xinjiang resembles the empires of European powers and Russia more than it does those of earlier Inner Asian regimes such as the Xiongnu, Turks, Mongols or Zunghars.

Defence and administration

Until the 1880s Qing administration in Xinjiang took a form different from that in China proper. Rather than divide the region into prefectures and counties, each under a magistrate as in the provinces of 'inner' China, the empire employed the hierarchy of the Qing banner system to create an overarching administration that saw to the needs of military personnel and supervised local government by indigenous élites. For this reason, some western scholars have referred to Xinjiang as a 'protector-

---

northern, southern and eastern (the eastern route including Urumchi, Turfan and Hami). This scheme divides Xinjiang much as I have been in this book with the terms Zungharia, Tarim Basin and Turfan Basin.

ate' or 'vassal' of the Qing, implying that it was not fully part of the empire. Likewise, Xinjiang, along with Qinghai, Mongolia and Manchuria have sometimes been depicted on historical maps in a manner setting them off from China proper. Though there is an important distinction to be made between these Qing Inner Asian areas (once called 'Chinese Tartary') and the provinces of China, all (with the partial exception of Tibet[30]) should be considered fully parts of the Qing empire. In most of Qinghai, Mongolia, Xinjiang and Manchuria the primary form of administration was the banner military hierarchy.

The Qing initially stationed some 40,000 troops in Xinjiang, and boosted that number to around 50,000 by the mid-nineteenth century. About half of the initial deployment were Manchu and Mongol bannermen, many transferred west after the conquest. (The Sibe [Xibo] people of the Chapchal [Chabucha'er, Qapqar] Xibo Autonomous County, today the last living native speakers of a Manchu dialect, are descendents of tribal cousins of the Manchus transferred from Manchuria to Zungharia by the Qing.) The other half were Chinese troops. These military forces were distributed unequally across Xinjiang, with four times as many troops based in Zungharia (mostly in nine garrisons along the Yili Valley and in Urumchi) as in southern Xinjiang. Moreover, while the forces in the north were posted permanently, with their family members, and were supposed to be a self-perpetuating force, the troops stationed in Kashgar, Yarkand, Khotan and other southern cities were rotated after three-year tours of duty. This light military presence in Kashgaria, which would prove a great vulnerability, reflects the region's north-controls-the-south tradition, the greater availability of fodder in Zungharia and the desire not to overburden Muslim city-dwellers and so destabilise Qing rule.

Military government. A military governor based in Huiyuan (today's Yining) held ultimate authority over all Xinjiang and answered to the emperor and the Grand Council in Beijing, the empire's highest executive body. Below him, councillors based in Yili, Tarbaghatai and Kashgar/Yarkand supervised important sub-regions of the province, and superin-

---

30 Qing power in Tibet was never as extensive as in China and elsewhere in Qing Inner Asia, and for much of the nineteenth century lapsed to a mere formality. Numbers of Qing officials and troops in Tibet, except for two noteworthy military interventions, were minimal.

tendents were responsible for individual cities. Till the 1880s, aside from a very few Manchuised Han (*Hanjun*) and Uyghurs, only Manchus or Mongols served in these high offices. These officials were known collectively by the Manchu word *amban* or its Chinese equivalent *dachen*, and thus European travellers in nineteenth- and early-twentieth-century Xinjiang refer to Qing authorities as 'da-jin' and the like.

Jasak system. Local government in Qing Xinjiang varied with the ethnic makeup and political background of the people governed. As in Mongolia and Qinghai, nomadic groups in Xinjiang were formed into companies and governed by rulers known as *jasaks*, who though hereditary, served at the pleasure of the Qing government and could be replaced. When some 50,000 to 70,000 Torghut and Khoshuut Mongols returned from the Volga region and sought Qing asylum, they were resettled as several companies in scattered parts of Xinjiang, including just north of Bosteng Lake (for this reason PRC leaders carved out the massive Bayin Gol Mongol Autonomous Prefecture including the former Torghut reservation, but also a huge swath of the Taklamakan Desert where few Mongols ever ventured). There were miscellaneous companies of Chahars, Oirats and Kazaks under the jasak system in Zungharia. More important, the cities of Turfan and Hami were likewise governed under this system, their 'princes' (*wangs*) having aided the Qing during the conquest. Amin Khoja, the ruler of Turfan, led his own troops alongside the Qing banners during the campaigns in southern Xinjiang, and together with the Hami *wang* was put in charge of Kashgar and Yarkand in the aftermath of the Qing takeover. Jasaks enjoyed much autonomy. Hami and Turfan rulers, known as 'princes' (*wang*) in Chinese, were exempt from paying taxes to the state, were granted titles like members of the Qing royal house, had their own retainers, and commanded the people in their home territories as serfs (*yänchi*).

Beg system. Elsewhere in southern Xinjiang, and in parts of the Yili Valley where Uyghurs had been relocated as *taranchi* farmers, local governance fell to Muslim officials known as *begs*. *Beg* is a Uyghur word which meant 'noble', and had applied to the landed aristocrats descended from the Moghuls, a class whom the Qing wished to co-opt.[31] The Qing

---

31 Kim 2004: 10–11.

adopted existing administrative titles in the Tarim Basin, added the word *beg* to them, ranked each position in the Chinese manner, and thus created a relatively systematic bureaucracy consisting of local élites with supervision and appointments in the hands of Qing *ambans*, in consultation with Beijing. The highest ranked beg officials, the *hakim begs*, were old Qing allies, descendents of Turfan and Hami ruling families allied with the Qing during the conquest, and served in key positions overseeing Uyghur affairs for whole cites—though not their own cities. Lower-ranking begs, for whom there were over thirty different offices dealing with taxation, clerical work, irrigation, post stations, policing, legal and penal matters, commercial affairs and even some religious and educational duties, were in theory assigned outside their own villages or neighbourhoods. Begs received small salaries from the Qing government, and were granted lands and serfs to work them in proportion to their rank. Region-wide there were nearly 300 begs.

In addition to the begs the Qing maintained relations with the *'ulama*, or Islamic learned community, who handled certain judiciary tasks involving *shari'ah* law, which pertained in local matters.

Chinese-style administration. Finally, in Urumchi, Barkol, new colonies north of Urumchi, and gradually elsewhere in Zungharia as the population of Chinese farmers and merchants increased, the Qing created counties, prefectures and circuits, and established magistracies. These were similar to those in the provinces of China proper except that the vast majority of cases magistrates were Manchus and Mongols, and their grain taxes were retained locally to support the military, rather than remitted to the imperial centre. Chinese-style administration could exist side-by-side with other forms in Xinjiang, as in the Turfan area, or even overlap: and although they fell geographically within the territory of the Yili military government, the civil officials within Xinjiang's Chinese-style administrative areas were theoretically answerable to the Governor-General of Shaanxi and Gansu province.

Qing administration in Xinjiang, then, was complex, multilayered and more sophisticated than any imperial government in the region that had preceded it. It permitted a degree of local autonomy while maintaining a monopoly on military force, and cultivated and employed a cadre of local officials under the supervision of imperial officers. It managed ethnic diversity through multiple administrative and legal systems, and did not attempt to proselytise or culturally assimilate. And although far from the imperial capital, the Xinjiang administration kept in close contact with Beijing through lengthy written memorials in Manchu and Chinese, which were dispatched by fast-horse over well-maintained post roads. The Qing imperial archives still hold tens of thousands of these documents from Xinjiang—like imperial bureaucracies elsewhere, the Xinjiang administration ran on paper.[32]

Indeed, one may draw many parallels between Qing administration in Xinjiang and that of the British in India or Russia in Central Asia, both of which relied on diverse administrative forms and local personnel. And there is no particular evidence that the Qing imperial regime in Xinjiang was any more or less effective, malevolent or benevolent than European versions in their earlier stages (by later in the nineteenth century, when European imperialism implemented the rhetoric and policies of 'civilising mission' backed by industrial power they become qualitatively different from the Qing). Of course, corruption was endemic across the Qing empire, in China proper as well as in Inner Asia. Local officials were well positioned for aggrandisement, and often even needed to embezzle to make ends meet. However, when such peculation and 'squeeze' on the people remained within limits, supervisors took no notice, local populations did not rebel and the officials did not get caught. It may be said that with one notable exception (discussed below), Xinjiang's military government, beg and other administrative systems, while by no means entirely honest or enlightened, nevertheless functioned for decades in a manner efficient enough to allow economic development to prevent local uprisings. By the mid-nineteenth century, however, the region would become a tinderbox.

Infrastructural and economic development

Having come upon its empire in Xinjiang almost by accident, as a side-effect of wiping out its Zunghar rivals, the Qing faced an on-going problem of financing rule so far from the Chinese agrarian heartlands of its empire. The Qing Qianlong emperor, whose 60-year reign dominated the eighteenth century, tried to finesse the issue by arguing, in

32 On general aspects of Qing administration in Xinjiang, see Millward 1998 and Wang Xilong in Yu Taishan 1996. On the beg system, see Saguchi 1963, Miao Pusheng 1995, and Millward and Newby 2006.

effect, that the tax-payers of China enjoyed a 'peace dividend' as a result of Manchu conquest and control of Inner Asia. Though this is in one respect true, Xinjiang could not generate sufficient revenue to fully support the military forces required to hold it, and millions of ounces of silver had to be shipped annually from China to Xinjiang to pay military salaries. (Xinjiang today still requires large central government subsidies, as will be seen in Chapter 7.) In attempts to lessen the required stipends and consolidate Qing rule in the Tarim Basin and Zungharia, Qing officials engaged in a variety of infrastructural projects, commercial ventures and schemes to stimulate handicraft and agricultural production. They opened state farms (discussed below) to provide needed grain, and managed stock-rearing to provide meat. They used tax policy to encourage increased production of cotton cloth in southern Xinjiang that could be shipped north to supply the banners and trade with Kazak nomads for more needed livestock. They opened iron and copper mines and nationalised copper to normalise currencies, and then manipulated the exchange rates between silver and copper currency to state benefit. They dabbled in running pawnshops, commissaries, textile shops, lumber yards, apothecaries and rental properties to provide other revenue, and joined in partnerships with private merchants to purvey tea and other products at a profit. They gathered jade from the mountains and rivers south of Khotan to ship back to Beijing.

These endeavours were facilitated by the Qing development of Xinjiang's roads, roadside inns, water depots and post-horse stations on the major routes leading from China and Mongolia and around the Tarim Basin and Zungharia. It was military necessity that kept key passes passable, but these improvements benefited merchants as well. Chinese merchant firms engaged in long-distance trade via the steppe route from Mongolia and along the Gansu corridor, either purveying supplies for the military or opening branch stores in Xinjiang's larger cities. Also many smaller-scale merchants peddled goods or smuggled jade from Xinjiang, where it was a controlled commodity, back to China proper, where it was a freely traded luxury item. (Border guards often caught smugglers with jade in false-bottomed carts or sewn into their trousers.) Additionally, Central Asian and Indian merchants congregated in Kashgar, Yarkand and Khotan and exported tea, Chinese medicinals and silver, bringing in gems, livestock, hides, furs, opium and various other products.

The focus of Qing development policies in Xinjiang was agricultural development on the old state military farm (*tuntian*) model. The Han dynasty, it will be recalled, was first to open military farms in Xinjiang. Later China-based powers did the same when stationing forces in the far west. The Qing implemented the *tuntian* model to an unprecedented extent, thus not only building on tradition but also furnishing the immediate forerunners of the twentieth-century Xinjiang state farms, the Xinjiang Production Construction Corps (PCC or *Bingtuan*), as well as of the Xinjiang gulag.

The Qing military founded its first state farms in eastern Xinjiang early in the 1700s, while still at war with the Zunghars. After 1759 the Qing established state farms in various categories; besides setting Chinese soldiers to work the land, authorities employed exiled convicts, Han and Hui (Muslim) Chinese civilian colonists and local Uyghurs. After the defeat of the Zunghars, northern Xinjiang was, in the words of one writer, 'an empty plain for a thousand *li*, with no trace of man'.[33] Most of the state farms were thus in Zungharia, especially in the vicinity of Urumchi, where there was fertile, well-watered land and few people. But the Qing also organised Uyghurs into state farms in some Tarim Basin cities and in the Yili Valley. Even in far northern Tarbaghatai (Tacheng) settlers attempted to open state farms on the steppe.

Given the controversy about Han migration to Xinjiang today, some have seen the Qing agricultural colonies as an effort to displace Uyghurs from their homeland. In fact, however, from 1760 to 1830, when most of the farms were opened and the Chinese population in Xinjiang grew to around 155,000, Qing authorities prohibited Chinese from settling permanently or bringing their families to the Tarim Basin.[34] Only a few hundred Chinese, mostly merchants, resided in the Tarim oases during these decades. Rather, the Chinese settlers were concentrated in Urumchi (then a new city) and Zungharia, where few Uyghurs yet lived. That being said, the main goal of the Qing *tuntian* was nonetheless strategic, and it was hugely successful. The Qing military, based primarily in Zungharia, needed grain. The state farms provided this grain and a

33 From Wei Yuan's 'Tangping Zhunbu ji' [record of pacifying Zungharia], cited in Fang Yingkai 1989: II: 605.
34 For this estimate of Chinese (including Chinese Muslim) population in Xinjiang and other Qing population estimates, see Millward 1998: 51 and 271–2 n. 21. See also the discussion of migration in Chapter 7 ('The Peacock Flies West').

surplus: grain supplies were often greater, and prices cheaper, in Qing Xinjiang than in China proper.

After 1831 the Qing permitted and encouraged Chinese migration into the Tarim and stationed permanent troops, with dependents, on the land there as well. To people the Tarim with Chinese had by then become the great hope of some Chinese statecraft thinkers and of the Qing Daoguang emperor, but in those troubled decades there were few Chinese farmers available in the remoter Tarim cities. A major survey of available land conducted in the 1840s by Lin Zexu (banished to Xinjiang from Guangzhou for mishandling the opium crisis with the British) concluded that in most areas of southern Xinjiang, new lands reclaimed by the state should be given to local Uyghurs to farm, thus raising the tax base, as there were simply no Chinese around to farm them. In Karashahr and Barchuq (outside Kashgar) some Chinese colonists secured a foothold in these decades, but they were mostly killed or driven out by the uprisings of the 1860s. As we will see in the next chapter, moreover, Uyghurs also ended up farming lands promoted for reclamation by the Qing after it reconquered Xinjiang in 1879. Qing officials on the spot in Xinjiang were primarily concerned about revenue and stability. Although after 1831 Qing authorities saw Chinese colonists as an ideal means to achieve this, settling and taxing Uyghur farmers on new or abandoned lands could serve the same purposes.[35]

Imperial Ideology

In recent years, some historians have approached the subject of European imperialism by studying ideology and rhetoric, the ways in which imperial powers thought and spoke of themselves, of the peoples they colonised, of their mutual relationship, and the ways in which empire was represented and commemorated. Following the Enlightenment and in tandem with scientific developments that reflected a new outlook towards the natural world in general, Europeans applied new concepts and technologies to the lands and peoples they encountered in Eurasia, Africa and America, thinking about them in ways very different than, say, Marco Polo had a few centuries previously. Besides the political and

35 Zhao Yuzheng 1991: 111–21. There is a large literature in Chinese on agricultural development in Xinjiang. See Millward 1998: 50, 270–1 n. 15 for an introduction, and Borei 1992 and 2002.

economic goals of empire (extending dominion, extracting wealth), early-modern and modern Europeans sought also to map, categorise, catalogue and curate the flora, fauna, landforms, cultures and languages of places newly under their control. This was the period when such disciplines as modern cartography, ethnography, historical linguistics and comparative biology got their start, relying upon the wealth of data available from the colonies. This endeavour has been described as the 'imperial gaze' or the assembly of an 'imperial archive'. Edward Said coined the term 'Orientalism' to describe European scholarly work on the Islamic world and Asia that was distorted by the inequality of power relations between coloniser and colonised. The term may be applied to analogous phenomena elsewhere.[36]

The Qing engaged in a similar imperial project, aside from its tangible efforts to control and finance the occupation of Xinjiang. The court produced massive volumes to codify knowledge about the region. These include dictionaries of Xinjiang place names and the genealogies of its ruling élites; lengthy works of history, geography and local description; large scale maps of the empire produced with the latest cartographic technology under supervision of European Jesuits in the Qing court; a series of engravings depicting key battles of the conquest, so detailed that military historians use them to study contemporary weaponry; and ethnographic accounts of the various peoples in Xinjiang. That these works were meant to commemorate conquest, as well as collect knowledge, is clear from the triumphant poems by the Qing emperor that serve as prefaces to court-sponsored works. There were also essays carved on tall stone steles, portraits of meritorious generals, lyric poems and ceremonial parades and executions of Central Asian 'rebels'. Though the nuances differ, and though the Qing seldom espoused a 'civilising mission' or 'manifest destiny' in Xinjiang (that would come later, under the Chinese Republic and People's Republic), there are ample similarities between Qing and various European imperial projects to justify comparison.[37]

And what about Sinocentric ideology? Until recently many historians of China accepted without question the notion that the tribute system

36 Works on this subject—which touches on both studies of imperialism and the relatively recent rubric of 'post-colonial studies'—are voluminous for European, though not for Qing, colonialism. See for example Said 1978, Pratt 1992, Edney 1997, Richards 1993.

37 Hostetler 2001; Millward 1994 and 1999; Waley-Cohen 1996.

(discussed in Chapter 2) and the process of sinicisation governed China's relations with neighbouring countries and non-Chinese peoples. The concept of sinicisation is a problematic one, however. It has been used in at least two senses. First, it was once assumed that both neighbouring peoples and conquerors of China acculturated spontaneously to the superior Chinese civilisation once they encountered it. This idea, derived from classical Chinese texts, has been dismissed or highly qualified on both empirical and theoretical grounds.[38]

The second sense of 'sinicisation' is that of direct state attempts to eradicate non-Chinese cultural elements and convert a people or region to Chinese ways. Qing officials occasionally implemented such assimilative policies among Miao groups in south-western China.[39] Uyghur exile groups and their sympathisers often accuse the PRC government of such a project in Xinjiang today—a question we will take up below—and some assume the Qing was interested in doing the same thing. In fact, however, as mentioned above, before the mid-nineteenth century the Qing operated parallel administrations and legal systems for Turkic Muslim, Mongol and Chinese inhabitants of the region, and maintained a loose segregation of the populations, restricting Chinese farmers to northern and eastern Xinjiang. This was a deliberate policy to limit Chinese influence, and the friction it would cause, in the Tarim Basin. Moreover, such an approach was in keeping with the efforts of the Qing rulers in Tibetan and Mongol areas to rule not as an emperor in the Chinese mode, but as an Inner Asian great khan, with legitimacy derived from Chinggisid descent and patronage of the Gelugpa Tibetan Buddhist church. The 1830s policy to encourage Chinese settlement in the Tarim marked the beginnings of a shift away from this stance; by the end of the century some Chinese literati would be advocating the full-scale assimilation of Xinjiang to Chinese norms as a means of securing the territory, an approach to which the Qing court would increasingly acquiesce

Even before that, however, Qing imperium suffered from an ideological shortcoming in the Tarim Basin. Descent from a great khanal line, like that of the Turks or especially the Mongol Chinggis Khan, had long been a major component underpinning the legitimacy of rulers in Xinjiang. This the Qing emperors could claim, and they were known in lo-

---

38 Crossley 1990; Rawski 1996.
39 Rowe 2001: Chapter 12.

cal Muslim sources as *Khaqan-i Chin* (Khaghan of China) or *Ulugh Khan* (Great Khan).[40] Since the Qarakhanids, however, Chinggisid descent had been complemented, and was ultimately eclipsed by the religious charisma of those claiming descent from the prophet Muhammad or lineages of Sufi saints, especially the Makhdumzadas. As Joseph Fletcher and Kim Hodong have pointed out, despite some patronage of Islamic sites and the employment of local Islamic beg officials, as non-Muslims, the Manchus could not co-opt Islamic sources of legitimacy.

The Ush Uprising

Ideology aside, the Qing position in Xinjiang in the mid-eighteenth century suffered from two serious weaknesses. The first was the scanty military deployment in southern Xinjiang. The second was the failure of the Xinjiang tax-base to support fully the Qing military government, and the consequent need for annual silver stipends that the dynasty, by the early nineteenth century in increasingly straitened fiscal circumstances, could ill afford. The first of these flaws left the south-western Tarim vulnerable to invasions from Central Asia, which could be repulsed only by expensive mobilisation of troops from elsewhere in Xinjiang and even China proper. The second flaw made such repeated mobilisations an unattractive option from Beijing's point of view, but it also made increasing troop strength in Kasgharia fiscally difficult to implement and maintain.

However, the first outbreak of unrest in Xinjiang after the Qing conquest was not directly related to these factors, but rather to egregious misrule and exploitation by local officials in the first years after the conquest. 'Abd Allah, younger brother of the Hami ruler, was appointed Hakim Beg of Ush Turfan in the western Tarim Basin (not to be confused with Turfan). He and his retainers used his position to extort money from the population. Meanwhile, the Manchu *amban*, Sucheng, and his son were abducting local Muslim women into their compound and holding them there for months. As one Manchu observer put it, 'Ush Muslims had long wanted to sleep on [Sucheng and son's] hides and eat their flesh.'[41] When in 1765 Sucheng decided to join an official caravan

40 Kim 2004: 69.
41 Qi-shi-yi, *Xiyuji*, j. 6, 'Wushi panluan jilue', cited in A-la-teng-ou-qi-er 1996: 31.

conveying official gifts to Beijing, and dragooned 240 men to carry his luggage, the porters and townspeople rebelled. When the Qing court learned the reasons for the uprising it was initially not unsympathetic, and expected that the situation could be quickly returned to normal. After the fortified town held off a besieging Qing force for several months, however, the emperor became enraged and ordered a massacre. When starvation finally drove the townspeople to turn their leaders over to the Qing and open the gates, some 2,350 surviving adult men were executed, and around 8,000 women and children sent to Yili and enslaved, thus depopulating the town. The Qing then undertook a reform of the beg system, cutting *corvée* taxes, restricting higher begs' privileges and opportunities for collusion with Qing military officials, and intensifying supervision.[42] The court issued stern warnings and rebukes to Manchu and Mongol as well as Uyghur officials in Xinjiang.

The Khoja and Khoqandi invasions

The main threat to Qing rule in Xinjiang before 1864 did not in fact arise directly from the Uyghur population itself, but from Central Asia. One reason for the heightened Qing anxiety that led to the Ush massacre were rumours that the leaders of the Ush rebellion had communicated with other oases and with Central Asian Muslim monarchs, from whom they expected aid. During the siege Qing forces went so far as to round up the leaders of nearby Kirghiz tribes to prevent the nomads from joining the revolt. In the early 1760s the states and tribal powers in Central Asia had reacted to the Qing arrival on their doorstep with alarm and some talk of holy war 'to deliver the Muslim world from the attack of the unbelievers'. Did the advance of the Manchu forces seem like a repeat of the Mongol onslaught on Transoxiana five and a half centuries earlier? Whatever the case, the powerful Ahmad Shah of Afghanistan massed his troops and corresponded with other Central Asian rulers to raise a united resistance. These efforts came to naught when the Qing

---

42 Millward 1998: 124–5. There are many accounts of the Ush rebellion in published Qing sources and modern secondary accounts; they differ over the exact events which sparked the rebellion. One careful secondary account may be found in A-la-teng-ou-qi-er (Altan Ochir) 1996: 30–3. Altan does not whitewash events, but he is sympathetic to Qing officials in the field, placing blame for the massacre on the Qianlong emperor, whose edicts to this effect he quotes.

appeared content to stop at the Pamirs, but Ahmad Shah, in alliance with Bukhara, invaded Badakhshan and killed its ruler, citing as justification the fact that the Badakhshani Sultan Shah had betrayed Burhan ad-Din and Khoja Jahan to the Qing.[43]

One Central Asian power which benefited from the new situation was Khoqand, centred in the Ferghana valley over the passes west of Kashgar. The Qing conquest had eliminated the Zunghars as military threat and as intermediaries in the China trade, and brought Chinese goods right up to Khoqand's back door. Khoqandi rulers began calling themselves khan and expanding their territory. They petitioned the Qing for trading privileges, not always adopting the proper honorific forms of address, a fact which Xinjiang translators concealed when they transmitted the documents to the capital. (Khoqandi rulers referred to themselves as 'khan' and, with appalling *lèse-majesté*, to the Manchu emperor as *dost*, 'friend'.) The trade in Chinese products became especially profitable from 1785 to 1792, when the Qing closed the market at Khiakhta on the Mongolian-Russian border, and Khoqand could trans-ship Chinese tea and rhubarb to supply frustrated Russian buyers. Rhubarb, or, more precisely, the dried yellow root of a strain of rhubarb that grows best in the highlands of Gansu and Qinghai, was highly valued in early modern Europe as an efficacious astringent, purgative and all-round wonder drug, almost as important a commodity as tea.[44]

As early as 1760 Khoqandi rulers sought to secure relief for their merchants from Qing customs taxes and repeated these demands through subsequent decades. Later they would seek the right to levy the tax themselves on Khoqandi and other non-Chinese merchants in Kashgaria. Khoqand had some leverage in dealings with the Qing, moreover, because the descendents of the Afaqi Khoja clan lived in Khoqand under their control, and enjoyed a following both locally and within Kashgaria. Together, Khoqand and these Afaqi revanchists who sought to restore their ancestral control over the Tarim Basin would be the primary source of instability in Xinjiang till the 1860s.

---

43 Kim 2004: 20–1, direct quote (p. 20) from Valikhanov's account relating contents of a letter from Fadil Bi, ruler of Khojent, to Ahmad Shah of Afghanistan. My account of Khoqand's involvement with the Khojas and Qing Kashgaria relies on Kim's excellent account (2004), which is based on Persian, Turkic, Russian as well as Chinese sources and Japanese and English secondary literature.
44 Foust 1992.

City walls of Kashgar (1926) (photo: W. Bossnard; Swedish Riksarchivet
Samuel Fränne Östturkestan Samling, karton 120 ark 9)

Sarimsaq, Burhan ad-Din Khoja's son, began communicating with
supporters in Xinjiang and raising funds in the 1780s. It was not until the
time of Sarimsaq's own son, Jahangir, that open Khoja attacks on Kashgaria began.[45] In 1820 Jahangir escaped and led a band of Kirghiz living
in the mountains north on a raid into the Kashgar region. He was driven
back by Qing forces, only to escape from house arrest again two years
later following an earthquake and lead another failed raid in 1825. From
a base in the mountains outside Kashgar Jahangir maintained secret contact with Afaqis in Kashgaria, who sent him money for the war effort.
In the summer of 1826, when Jahangir and a larger army of Kirghiz
and Khoqandis invaded again, they had local support. After stopping
in Artush to visit the shrine of Satuq Bughra Khan (the Qarakhanid

---

45 According to Kim Hodong (2004: 22), the Qing paid Khoqand a stipend to
keep Jahangir under house arrest; Laura Newby, however, argues that what scholars
have interpreted as a Qing pay-off was actually the trade caravans returning from
Beijing; in addition to on-going trade in Kashgar, the dynasty periodically allowed
Khoqand to send more lucrative 'tribute' missions to the capital (2005: 58–61).

convert to Islam—see Chapter 2), Jahangir took Kashgar's old city, and, with the help of local Muslims, captured Yengisar, Yarkand, Khotan and Aqsu as well. The Qing garrison citadels in each city held out for a time, but after lengthy sieges the forts fell in every city but Aqsu, with much slaughter of Qing troops, Chinese merchants and Uyghur begs. The following spring Qing reinforcements finally arrived from the north and east, defeated Jahangir's army, and eventually managed with the help of spies to capture him in the mountains.

Jahangir was transported back to Beijing for execution by slicing. A special commissioner to Xinjiang, Nayanceng, then undertook a review of fiscal, military and administrative regimes in the territory. The review resulted in major changes, including an increase in troop levels in Kashgaria and a punitive boycott on Khoqandi trade. Using moneys confiscated from Khoqandi merchants and local Jahangir supporters, the Qing rebuilt its westernmost cities and constructed stronger fortifications behind high tamped earth walls at some remove from the old Muslim quarters of the towns. Chinese merchants then located their shops and houses in between the old and new cities, on land the government now rented to them. The lingering effects of this pattern of settlement are still visible today in Kashgar, where as one proceeds east from the old town around the Id Kah Mosque the neighbourhoods become newer and more heavily inhabited by Han residents. Notably, the Qing took no measures for the defence of the native Uyghur sections of these cities.

The boycott of Khoqand proved an abject foreign policy failure. Three years later the Khojas were back, this time in the person of Muhammad Yusuf Khoja, Jahangir's brother. Unlike Jahangir's, this 1830 invasion was primarily the work of Khoqand, who made Yusuf nominal head of an army of Khoqandi merchants and other refugees from Kashgar, with Khoqandi generals as real commanders. This time, though the invaders sacked the old Muslim quarter of Kashgar, Yarkand's Uyghurs offered stiff resistance, and in neither city did the Qing citadel fall. Yarkand had long been a bastion of the anti-Afaqi Ishaqi branch of the Makhdumzada Khojas (see above), and Ishaqis in Kashgar actually took refuge in the Qing fortress (there over-zealous Chinese merchant militia, who refused to distinguish between 'good Muslims' and 'bad Muslims' massacred many Ishaqis despite orders from Manchu officials to desist). It was in great part the ferocity with which the Chinese merchant community in Kashgar and Yarkand resisted the Khoqandi and Afaqi Khoja invaders that led the Qing court to revise its policy and allow permanent Chinese settlement and farming in the Tarim Basin (see 'Infrastructural and economic development' above).[46]

Following these debacles the Qing was again forced to reassess its policies towards Khoqand. As the Qing official who oversaw the defence of Yarkand analysed the situation, 'The officials in Kashgaria are, so to speak, shepherds, the [Uyghur] Muslims are sheep, Khoqand is a wolf and the Qirghiz, surrounding us, are like dogs. In 1826 and 1830 Khoqand invaded the frontier again, and the dogs, following the wolf, also devoured our sheep. Therefore, even the barking of the dogs is hard to trust.'[47]

The problem thus derived primarily not from unrest among Uyghurs, but from Khoqand, and involved foreign trade and frontier defence. Starting in 1827 the Qing court and officialdom debated the question of retrenchment from the western half of the Tarim Basin (as far as Aqsu), the Daoguang Emperor himself even cautiously embracing the idea at one point. It was determined, however, that there was no secure place east of Kashgar to establish a new boundary.[48]

Thus the empire was forced to accede to Khoqandi demands, which would be far cheaper than further emergency mobilisations (the 1830–1 campaign had cost the state 8 million ounces of silver, and the military requisitions of grain, draught animals and carts caused great hardship throughout the region). Having abandoned trade sanctions as a policy tool, between 1832 and 1835 the Qing agreed to pardon Kashgari supporters of Khoqand, indemnified Khoqandi merchants for confiscated land and goods, and granted Khoqandi and other foreign merchants the right to trade tax-free in Xinjiang.

Though forced upon the Qing, this arrangement was really not detrimental. In effect the Manchu authorities in Kashgar allowed control of the bazaar to pass from the hands of begs in the Qing system to similar figures, known as *aqsaqals*, or white-beards, in the employ of Khoqand.

---

46 I have narrated the events surrounding the 1830 invasion in detail, based on Qing archival documents, in Millward 1998: 211–26.
47 Bi-chang made the comment which was quoted by Wei Yuan in his *Sheng wu ji* (1842: 1: 196–7), and translated and quoted in Kim 2004: 27. I have substituted Western years for those based on imperial reigns in Kim's translation.
48 Millward 1998: 226, based on a report by En-te-heng-e held in the First Historical Archives, Beijing.

Both powers now shared an interest in border stability and the smooth functioning of commerce, and this showed in the region's relative quiet over the next two decades. Qing duties on foreign imports to Xinjiang had been low to non-existent since 1760 in any case; the dynasty did not tax Xinjiang's exports. In fact the Qing taxed the considerable Silk Road trade through Xinjiang only indirectly by charging rents and levying property taxes on those Chinese merchants who set up shop in Tarim Basin cities. Uyghurs and foreign merchants had always been exempt from local commercial taxes.[49] Thus the Qing was giving up little by allowing Khoqand to trade freely in south-west Xinjiang.[50]

Joseph Fletcher suggested that the terms of the 1832 agreement with Khoqand were later echoed in the Qing concessions made to Western traders following the 1839–41 Opium War with Britain. Moreover, many of the same Qing officials in Xinjiang during the Jahangir crisis were also involved in negotiating and implementing the terms of the later Treaty of Nanjing (Nanking) with the British. He argues, further, that major elements of this 'unequal treaty', including extraterritoriality, most-favoured-nation, and the ceding of tariff collection to a foreign power were in fact not new in the 1840s, but had been tried and found workable in Kashgaria for a decade. (Laura Newby, with the benefit of Qing archival materials, argues that the Qing never ceded to Khoqand the right to collect taxes from foreign merchants in Xinjiang, though Khoqand in various sources seems to have claimed this right.[51]) One should not downplay the arrogance and might-makes-right attitudes of Western imperialists, who despite much mouthing of high principles did after all use gunboats to open China's markets to Western drug dealers, and eagerly banked the laundered profits at home. Nonetheless, Fletcher's and Newby's studies of this incident suggest that the Qing exercised a good deal of influence in shaping the agreements with both Khoqand and Britain, managing to insert into the treaties elements drawn from a traditional Chinese repertoire of techniques used to manage foreign trade and traders. The British were but red-faced *aqsaqals* with boats.[52]

49 Millward 1998: 100, table 8, and Chapter 3 *passim*.
50 Newby 2005 provides the most recent and detailed account in English of Qing-Khoqandi relations, based on thorough research in Qing archival, British, Russian and Central Asian sources.
51 Newby 2005: 192–9.
52 Fletcher 1978c: 375–85. On Qing-Khoqandi relations, see also Fletcher 1978a:

Despite the Qing's convenient arrangement with Khoqand, Khoja revanchists continued to cause trouble. Small bands of Kashgari exiles and Kirghiz under the Khoja Wali Khan and others staged attacks on Kashgar in 1847, 1852, 1855 and 1857. In the last Khoja invasion, Wali Khan led a band of Khoqandi and Kirghiz adventurers to Kashgar, surprised the Qing guard (who'd been smoking opium) and rode into the old city through Kashgar's Qum Darwaza, Sand Gate. The usual massacres of Chinese merchants ensued, and their wares and women were divided up among Wali Khan's men. But in the seventy-seven days before the Qing army arrived, Wali Khan was unable to take the citadels of Kashgar or nearby cities, though he did make the most of his brief reign: gathering a harem, staying intoxicated on *bhang*, and erecting a pile of skulls (including that of one European) on the banks of the Qizil River. When the Qing reinforcements arrived, Wali Khan escaped and the imperial forces slaked their own bloodlust with hundreds of executions of local Muslims. Ahmad Shaikh, caretaker of Satuq Bughra Khan's shrine in Artush, 'was crimped from heel to head and disembowelled; and his heart plucked out, whilst yet beating with life, was thrown to the dogs. He was then decapitated, and his head exposed in a cage on the main road leading to the city, together with a long row of those of other victims of Chinese revenge.'[53]

The pillage of the invaders and the reprisals by Qing soldiers and Chinese militia led local Uyghurs to become disaffected with the Khojas. As Kim Hodong's research shows, Islamic sources also abhorred Wali Khan's brutality, viewing his minaret of skulls with distaste. The Khoqandi khan threatened to execute Wali Khan for massacring fellow Muslims, and reprieved him only after the *'ulama* intervened on the grounds that Wali Khan was a *sayyid*, a descendent of the prophet. With support from neither Khoqand nor the populace of Kashgaria, their jihad tarnished by indiscriminate bloodshed and plunder, the Khoja cause slipped into irrelevance and oblivion. Future movements against Qing and Chinese rule in Xinjiang would share no direct link to those of 1826–57.[54]

58–90 and Pan Zhiping 1991.
53 Bellew 1875: 81–3. That Wali Khan added the skull of the 'scientific traveller' Adolphe Schlagentweit to his riverside cairn greatly insensed European followers of events in Chinese Turkestan.
54 Kim 2004: 29–32.

THE REBELLIONS OF 1864 AND THE EMIRATE
OF YA'QUB BEG

Contrary to a common misconception, the Qing presence in the Tarim Basin did not face unrelenting resistance from the local Uyghur population during most of its run. For sixty years, from the Ush rebellion (and reforms which followed it) to the Jahangir invasion, there were no major incidents. The Khoqand/Khoja troubles of the 1820s through 1850s initially enjoyed the support of Afaqis in Kashgar, but little elsewhere. The Tarim as a whole did not rise against the Qing, even when the Khoja occupations of western Tarim cities presented an opportunity. Apart from the dispute with Khoqand and the activities of the Khoja revanchists in Kashgar, for its first hundred years Qing governance elsewhere in Xinjiang could be called stable. Given the relative calm, expanding agriculture, thriving local and long-distance commerce, and growing populations of both Uyghurs and Chinese, it might even be called good.

All this changed in the 1850s. As noted above, though self-sufficient in foodstuffs, Qing rule in Xinjiang depended on silver stipends from the provinces of China proper, as well as taxes on Chinese merchants, to pay the salaries of soldiers and officials. Many of the Chinese merchants doing business in the western Tarim had been killed in the 1820s–1840s, and few came to replace them in subsequent years. Foreign merchants complained of the lack of Chinese goods in the bazaars, and military officials agonised over grain shortages. More serious still, by 1853 the Qing central treasury had been depleted, and provincial tax-bases in China were ravaged by rebellions, especially the Taiping onslaught in the rich southern and central Yangzi provinces, China's ricebowl and base of its silk industry. From this year silver stipends to Xinjiang fell into arrears, soon stopping entirely. In response, authorities in Xinjiang first began to expend their savings, invest funds at interest with pawnbrokers and commandeer Uyghur labour to mine for precious metals. They also imposed crushing new taxes on Chinese and Uyghurs and allowed the begs to do the same. Offices were sold to the highest bidders, who then pressured the populace under their jurisdiction to extract a return on their investment. The begs were given free rein in return for kickbacks to the Manchu authorities. Meanwhile, the Qing banner troops in both northern and southern Xinjiang fell into decrepitude, depleted and demoralised by disease, starvation and opium addiction, even as the populace in the Tarim grew increasingly restless.

The 1864 rebellions

The spark for the 1864 uprisings in Xinjiang came not from the Uyghurs (Turkic Muslims) but from the Tungans or Hui (Chinese Muslims). Tungan rebellion against the Qing had been raging since 1862 in Gansu and Shanxi provinces. Tens of thousands of Tungans originally from these provinces were now in Xinjiang farming, running small businesses, or serving in the Qing military. Tensions between the Tungans and Han Chinese and Mongol and Manchu authorities had grown in Xinjiang as well, until in June of 1864 a rumour spread that the Qing Tongzhi emperor had ordered authorities to massacre Tungans in Xinjiang cities as a pre-emptive measure. Tungans rebelled first in Kucha, followed rapidly by Urumchi, Yarkand, Kashgar and Yengisar. Manas, Changji, Qutubi, Jimsar and Gucheng, north and east of Urumchi, all rose over the next few months. Other cities fell as expeditions from Kucha helped topple Qing hold-outs in the Turfan-Hami region, in Karashahr, Ush Turfan, Bai and Aqsu. In the complex of cities in the Yili valley, Tungans and Taranchis attacked Qing authorities in November 1864. In Khotan, where there were few Tungans, Uyghurs rebelled in the same period. In fact, though Tungans generally rose first, they were quickly followed everywhere by Turkic Muslims, and leadership of local rebellions soon shifted from Tungans to local Turkic élites, except in eastern cities where Tungans were in the majority.

The 1864 rebellions are now often treated as a Uyghur independence movement. While certainly fuelled by hatred of the Qing regime and its begs, and cast by Muslim writers such as Molla Musa Sairami in the rhetoric of holy war, such depictions greatly oversimplify a complex and confusing series of events, involving a variety of mutually antagonistic actors. Moreover, Ya'qub Beg was no Uyghur freedom fighter, but a Khoqandi who imposed his regime upon the populace of the Tarim Basin.

In most cities the Tungans rebelled first, and were later joined and displaced by Turkic Muslims. Thereafter, a variety of candidates for local and regional power took leadership positions. These included Tungan military figures; Uyghur, Tungan and one Afghani scion of noble families; Sufi *shaykhs*; former begs; and other would-be padishahs and khans, most with religious credentials. Notably absent were the Afaqi Khojas. Results of the rebellions were specific to particular cities. In Tarbaghatai Muslim rebels were victorious, but then fled south, leaving the city to a group of Mongols. In Yili the Tungan rebellion gave way to a Taranchi government that endured until Russian intervention in 1871 (Taranchi was the name used for those Turkic Muslims brought from the Tarim by the Zunghars and the Qing to farm the Yili valley). Kucha, under the leadership of Rashidin Khoja, a descendent of Arshad al-Din, attempted to dominate the other oases, dispatching armies east as far as Hami, west as far as Kashgar and south to Yarkand and Khotan.[55] Far from being a unified movement, Xinjiang in 1864–5 is more reminiscent of Afghanistan in the immediate post-Soviet period, with its warlords, inter-ethnic and inter-regional rivalries.

Nor should these rebellions be viewed as motivated primarily by religious concerns. Islam did provide the unifying ideology that joined Tungans with Turkic Muslims and rulers of different oases, albeit only briefly, and contemporary Muslim writers described the hostilities as a holy war to rid the land of infidel occupiers. However, Xinjiang Muslims had lived in relative peace and stability under Qing rule for a century before these events, and faith in Islam did not lead to unrest in that period. It was economic distress and rampant misrule from the 1850s that created the conditions underlying the uprisings.[56]

Ya'qub Beg's emirate

Powers to the west of the Pamirs closely observed the collapse of the Qing regime in the Tarim Basin and endeavoured to take advantage of it. In 1865 Alim Quli, ruler of Khoqand, itself lately free of Bukharan occupation, sent a Makhdumzada Khoja, Buzurg, under the direction of a military official, Ya'qub Beg, with an army to join the Kirghiz who had besieged and then plundered the Muslim town of Kashgar.

Details of Ya'qub Beg's background are obscured by myths: that as a young man he worked the teahouses as a dancing boy, and that later, after appointment to serve as beg of an important trade *entrepôt*, he led local forces in a heroic resistance to the Russian invasion of Aq Masjid. Whatever the truth of these stories, he proved a successful commander and shrewd ruler in Kashgaria, soon displacing Buzurg. In 1865 Ya'qub Beg drove the unpopular Kirghiz out of Kashgar, and soon thereafter took Yengishahr (Yengihissar). (When this city fell, Ya'qub presented his pa-

55 Kim 2004: Chapter 2 is the most detailed account, based primarily on Russian and Muslim sources.
56 Kim 2004: 66–71.

Ya'qub Beg (drawing from Veselovskii 1898)

tron, Alim Quli, with a tribute in the traditional Turko-Mongolian manner, in multiples of nine: nine Chinese cannon, nine Chinese charming
virgins, nine young Chinese boys, eighty-one silver ounces, eighty-one
horses and eighty-one porcelains.[57] He finally took the Qing fortress
in Kashgar after striking a secret deal with the Tungans within the city.
His forces massacred thousands of Chinese merchants and militia, and
the Manchu officials blew themselves up with the powder stores. Over
the next year Ya'qub conquered the cities to his south-east, including
Khotan, where thousands of Uyghur defenders died, and then in the
north-east, where his advance was hastened by internal strife among the
male relatives of Rashidin Khoja, the Kucha ruler.

   Kucha fell in the spring of 1867. A few years later conflict broke out
between Ya'qub Beg and the Tungan regime in the Urumchi and Turfan
area. The events leading to Ya'qub Beg's conquest of Urumchi well illus-
trate the opportunism that governed military alliances among the various

57   Kim 2004: 85.

actors in Xinjiang in this period. In his first attack on the Tungan–held city, in 1870, Ya'qub Beg was joined by Xu Xuegong, a non-Muslim Han Chinese militia leader who had taken to the hills with 1,500 troops following the Tungan uprising. The Tungan leader in Urumchi, Tuo Ming (Daud Khalifa) surrendered after a siege; however, he later again took up arms against Ya'qub, and this time Xu and the Han guerrillas joined forces with the Tungans. After he once again took Urumchi, in the early summer of 1871, Ya'qub Beg controlled all of southern Xinjiang, from Kashgar to Turfan.[58] He also enjoyed some influence among the Mongols nomadising in Zungharia, but the Yili valley remained under the separate Muslim rulership of 'Ala Khan, a 'Taranchi'.

Ya'qub Beg established his Kashgar *orda* (camp or, here, court) in the 'new city' built by the Qing after the Jahangir invasion, a multi-gated fortress locally known as the *gulbagh*, or rose garden. Foreign visitors to the *Ataliq ghazi* (fatherly holy warrior), as Ya'qub was also known, were led by silk robed attendants through courtyards under the eyes of his ethnically diverse personal guard to a pavilion with potted poplars and lattice-work walls, where the emir received them with a mixture of Central Asian and European ceremony: once seated for the traditional meal of tea, fruits, nuts and bread, one group of English envoys were honoured with a fifteen-gun salute. Not far away in the citadel could be found one of Ya'qub's three harem quarters (others were in Kashgar proper and Yengisar), where he was said to keep two hundred wives and concubines, a group reputedly just as diverse as his guard, consisting of 'representatives of almost every people from the cities of China on the east to the markets of Constantinople on the west, and from the steppes of Mongholia on the north to the valleys of the Himalays on the south'.[59] From this imposing court, Ya'qub appointed governors (*hakims*) and other officials to administer, police and collect taxes in provinces and townships throughout southern Xinjiang.

Having positioned himself as a defender of the faith and holy warrior against the infidel *khitay* (Chinese), Ya'qub Beg pursued a strict Islamist policy. His officials enforced adherence to Islamic law, cracking down on male and female prostitution, consumption of alcohol, and sale of such

58   Again, Kim is the best source on this period (2004: Chapter 3). Except where otherwise indicated, the rest of my discussion of Ya'qub Beg is based on his book.
59   Quote from Bellew 1875: 303–4; description from 295–301, and Shaw 1871: 260–2.

haram meats as cat, dog, rat, pig and ass said to be common in the bazaars under Qing rule. *Qadi Ra'is* (religious judges) patrolled the streets
with squads of police to maintain the *shar'iah*, dealing out floggings to
improperly veiled women or men without a turban. Ya'qub Beg also
restored, endowed and visited key shrines in the Kashgar area: the tombs
of Afaq Khoja, Satuq Bughra Khan and Bibi Miriyam (a locally revered
saint, matron of the Qarakhanid Arslan Khans, whose progenitor she
conceived immaculately when the Angel Gabriel visited her through the
smoke hole of her tent).[60]

Local Uyghurs did not entirely welcome these changes. Not only
were they not accustomed to the strict adherence to Islamic law Ya'qub
Beg's regime enforced in its bid for legitimacy, but many suffered from
a heavier tax burden and an economy that was slow to recover. The turmoil of 1864–7 had cut off the last trickle of trade from China, putting
an end to the important *entrepôt* business of re-exporting Chinese tea,
silver and other items. Even the jade mines were abandoned. Moreover,
the population had declined during the wars, especially in Yili and the
eastern part of Ya'qub Beg's domain. Economic crisis was exacerbated
by high taxes: provincial and city officials received no salaries, and lived
off the population. The regime maintained an army of some 40,000
soldiers. Unlike the Qing forces, which had been mainly stationed in
Zungharia and paid with silver from China, Yaq'ub Beg's force had to be
locally supported in Altishahr, increasing the burden on the population.
Indeed, Ya'qub Beg's was for the most part an occupation regime. As he
took control of the oases cities, he eliminated the local religious leaders
who had taken power in the immediate aftermath of the 1864 rebellions.
The majority of his governors, and the core of his army were Khoqandis, supplemented by Kashmiris, Badakhshis, Afghans, Kirghiz, Mongols, Tungans and even some recent Chinese converts, known as 'new
Muslims' (*yengi Musulman*). British envoys in the 1870s, who were for
strategic and economic reasons keen on Ya'qub Beg's state, nonetheless
noted that the populace appeared cowed into submission by mounted
Khoqandi guards, who were dressed in the Uzbek fashion.[61] Although
people still remembered the Qing with hatred, and welcomed the idea
of rule by Islamic authorities, some at least grudgingly acknowledged
that times were better under the Manchus.

60 Bellew 1875: 324–35, 373.
61 Bellew 1875: Chaper 7.

What you see on market day now ... is nothing to the life and activity there was in the time of the *Khitay* [Chinese]. Today the peasantry come in with their fowls and eggs, with their cotton and yarn, or with their sheep and cattle and horses for sale; and they go back with printed cottons, or fur caps, or city made boots, or whatever domestic necessaries they may require, and always with a good dinner inside them, and then we shut up our shops and stow away our goods till next week's market day brings back our customers. Some of us go out with a small venture in the interim to the rural markets around, but our great day is market day in town. It was very different in the Khitay time. People then bought and sold every day, and market day was a much jollier time. There was no Kazi Rais with his six *muhtasib* armed with the *dira* to flog people off to prayers, and drive the women out of the streets, and nobody was bastina-doed for drinking spirits and eating forbidden meats. There were musicians and acrobats, and fortune-tellers and story-tellers, who moved about amongst the crowds and diverted the people. There were flags and banners and all sorts of pictures floating at the shop fronts, and there was the *jallab*, who painted her face and decked herself in silks and laces to please her customers. ... Yes, there were many rogues and gamblers too, and people did get drunk, and have their pockets picked. So they do now, though not so publicly, because we are now under Islam, and the *Shariat* is strictly enforced.[62]

Even the guardian of Satuq Bughra Khan's shrine admitted that Muslims could be as brutal as the Qing, the major difference between regimes being the booming trade of earlier days. Of the *Khitay* he said, 'I hate them. But they were not bad rulers. We had everything then. There is nothing now.'[63]

Although he managed to extend and consolidate his power over the Tarim Basin, Urumchi and Turfan, Ya'qub Beg faced many threats. Ya'qub was wary of potential rivals within his own government and army, as such was the way of Central Asian regimes. Russia, which in the 1850s and 1860s had conquered Transoxiana (Turkestan), including Khoqand, loomed over the border, and indeed in 1871 would annex the Yili valley, wiping out the Taranchi rulers in just a few days. The main threat, however, was an expected return of Qing forces. This concern

---

62 Forsyth 1875: 36.
63 Bellew 1875: 354–5. Such sentiments were commonly noted by British visi-tors to Xinjiang in the 1870s. One may question their objectivity, but they had no apparent interest in denigrating Ya'qub Beg's regime, which the British imperial authorities hoped would succeed in establishing a buffer state in eastern Turkestan, blocking further Russian penetration.

drove Ya'qub Beg's shrewd and, for a Central Asian regional leader, unprecedented foreign policy. Though his relations with Russia remained tense, he ultimately signed a commercial treaty allowing Russian traders and commercial representatives in his cities (1872). He actively sought out good relations with the British, welcoming their envoys, hosting a 350-member delegation in 1873–4, signing a commercial treaty granting access to British subjects, and posting an ambassador to London. (Unlike Tibet, which would try desperately to achieve this a few decades later, Ya'qub Beg's emirate enjoyed full diplomatic recognition from the British.) In return, Britain provided the emirate with some international support and covert military aid. Ya'qub became famous in the Islamic world as an infidel-fighter, and ultimately accepted a status as emir of the Ottoman sultan, an arrangement that contributed to the aura of both rulers, but which had no effect on Ya'qub's own autonomy. The Ottoman Porte also proved a more generous source of military aid than the British, providing cannon, thousands of modern and old rifles and military officers to help Ya'qub train his army in the new drill which the Ottomans themselves had acquired from Europe.

Ya'qub Beg, then, is a fascinating transitional figure. On the one hand he was a Central Asian strongman of the familiar type, claiming descent from Tamerlane, patronising the religious establishment, and leading his troops on a group hunt like a tribal chief.[64] Yet on the other hand he was also cognizant of the new strategic situation which left Central Asia struggling for room between expanding British and Russian and the declining Qing and Ottoman empires. Cannily recognising that Chinggisid and Islamic legitimacy and a personally loyal following would be insufficient to sustain his regime under these circumstances, he entered into long-distance diplomacy with the imperial powers and sought to equip his military with modern weapons and techniques. Whether intentionally or not, he garnered international publicity in Europe as well as Central Asia. Under Ya'qub Beg, Xinjiang for the first time became visible to the whole world, merging with the larger drama of imperial expansion and globalisation.

---

64 Bellew 1875: 346.

4. Between Empire and Nation

(late 19th–early 20th century)

The Qing recovery of Xinjiang was the last imperial campaign of a dying empire. That the dynasty pulled it off at all surprised Westerners at the time; since then Western historians have treated the decision to reconquer Xinjiang as an example of backward continental thinking, an anachronistic echo of the Qing's Inner Asian strategic heritage at a time when more important matters demanded attention along China's coasts. Yet the Qing reconquest of Xinjiang was the prologue to something new: an attempt to expand China into Central Asia. Hitherto in this book I have carefully distinguished between the terms 'Qing empire' and 'China'; from the late nineteenth century, however, this distinction fades. From this point, the Manchu and Mongol ruling élites of the Qing no longer brokered between the interests of Xinjiang's Turkic peoples and its Han settlers and merchants. After the reconquest in 1878 and the creation of Xinjiang province in 1884 Qing authorities in Xinjiang were themselves Han, and Qing policies in Xinjiang increasingly reflected a sinicising agenda, albeit an incompletely realised one.

Meanwhile, Xinjiang remained linked economically and culturally to places to its west. The Russian empire had consolidated its control in Transoxiana and on the Kazak steppe. The mass-produced, modern products of industrialised societies would enter Xinjiang from Russia and Russian Turkestan; some Indian goods competed with Russian manufactured goods in southern Xinjiang, but Chinese goods were not in the running. Ideas moved along those same trade channels, just as they had when religions followed the Soghdian caravans eastward or Sufis proselytised among traders and nomads. Like peoples under colonial rule throughout the world, the Islamic and Turkic peoples of Central Eurasia were thinking in new ways about their situation, questioning aspects of their tradition, proposing new approaches to knowledge and promoting

124

political reform. Xinjiang fell within the circuits of this new discourse in Central Eurasia, which increasingly defined the object of concern as the *khälk* ('the people') or *millät* ('the nation'). Nationalism came to Xinjiang from two directions.

RECONQUEST

In many ways, the hardest struggles in the reconquest of Xinjiang were fought before the first Qing soldiers marched into the region. These were the battles for political, logistical and financial support necessary before the campaign could be launched. Once again, troubles in the distant territory had raised doubts for many Qing officials regarding Xinjiang's place within and value to the empire. It took a mixture of new and old arguments and intense lobbying to overcome opponents and convince an ambivalent Qing court that Xinjiang should be recovered. The chief proponent of Xinjiang reconquest, commander of the campaign and mastermind of post-war reconstruction was Zuo Zongtang (Tso Tsung-t'ang; 1812–85).

Zuo was a scholar from Xiangyin, Hunan, who made his name not by success in the civil service examinations but by forming and leading a local army of Hunanese soldiers in victorious battles against rebels in south China. As such, he was one of several Han Chinese figures (including Zeng Guofan and Li Hongzhang) commanding regional Chinese armies who became prominent during the mid-nineteenth century when the Manchu banner soldiers proved ineffective against rebellions in China. Their rise, and the influence the desperate Qing court was forced to cede to them, marks a stage in the ongoing devolution of centralised Manchu power over the empire to a more regionalised arrangement under powerful Han generals and officials.

After his successes in campaigns against the Taiping and Nian rebels, in November 1868 Zuo Zongtang took up the post of Governor-General of the north-western Chinese provinces of Shaanxi and Gansu, bringing his Hunanese force with him. There he began the pacification of Tungan (Chinese Muslim, Hui) rebels in these provinces and in Qinghai.[1] This he accomplished by 1873 (at a cost of 40 million taels), but Zuo was forced to delay his planned march west into Xinjiang due to court concerns

1 On the Hui rebellions, see Lipman 1997; Chu Wen-djang 1966; and Fields 1978.

over its merits. The Japanese invasion of Taiwan in 1874 had alerted the court to the inadequacies of Qing defence on the coast, and a group of officials in China, led by Li Hongzhang, began advocating that the Xinjiang campaign be postponed and the money allocated instead to naval development. (Li was then Governor-General of Zhili, the capital province, and active in the dynasty's foreign relations with the West.) There then ensued what Immanuel Hsü has called 'the Great Policy Debate in China: Maritime Defence *vs* Frontier Defence'—but which we may see as simply the latest episode in the long-running debate over Xinjiang that began with the conquest of Zungharia and Altishahr under the Qianlong emperor in the 1750s. What differed this time, however, was the presence of a coastal threat from Western nations and Japan to balance the traditional security challenge on the north and north-western frontiers (now embodied by Russians rather than Mongol groups).

The 'maritime defence' party argued along sinocentric lines that retaking Xinjiang was not worth the massive expense, as it would always be a trouble-spot. Xinjiang was a barren waste, the government of which had required annual subventions from China since Qianlong times. Zuo and supporters of reconquest countered that nations threatening China along the coast were primarily interested not in penetration or territorial conquest but in establishing peripheral bases for trade; on the other hand, British and especially Russian aspirations in Xinjiang were more dangerous. Arguing, in essence, that 'as goes Xinjiang, so goes Mongolia; as goes Mongolia, so goes Beijing', the frontier defence advocates claimed that recovering Xinjiang was more critical to the defence of the capital than building more ships or coastal gun emplacements, for which standing funds existed in any case. Finally, the fact that Beijing lies relatively close to the ocean, but as far from Yili as New York from Denver, or London from Moscow, was less compelling to the frontier defence advocates than the hard-to-answer moralistic point that failure to recover Xinjiang would amount to unfilial conduct on the part of the present, Tongzhi, emperor, towards his illustrious ancestors.[2]

In their responses to the throne, both sides employed a corporeal metaphor, disputing which threat, frontier or coastal, amounted to a sickness of the heart, and which a disease of the limbs. (That lobbyists cast the dynasty's options in terms of death or dismemberment reflects the des-

2 Hsü 1965a and 1968; Zeng 1936: 365–9.

peration of the times.) Though the idea of the Russian-controlled Yili valley as a dagger pointed at the heart of Beijing may seem far-fetched, this view was in line with the Qing's earlier strategic emphasis on Inner Asia, and Zuo ultimately won the debate of 1874 and prevailed against further arguments from Li to abandon the Yili region in 1879.

In English-language accounts this debate has often been used to highlight the supposed backwardness of Qing strategic and diplomatic thinking. Li was a famous proponent of Chinese self-strengthening, and his advocacy of coastal defence and ship-building has seemed relatively modern to Western scholars of Chinese history. For example, in his influential textbook *Tradition and Transformation* John King Fairbank wrote that Zuo's victory in the debate against Li and other 'self-strengtheners' and subsequent reconquest of Xinjiang led conservatives into complacent opposition to Westernisation—though Zuo himself promoted and employed Westernising methods: modern military drill, factories, arsenals to produce modern weapons and Western loans. Even S.M. Paine's recent study of Qing-Russian relations calls Li's arguments 'logical' in contrast to Zuo's 'traditional' ones.[3] In Chinese-language historiography and any ideological stripe, on the other hand, Zuo has been and remains a hero for his reconquest of Xinjiang against apparently great odds. One might add, moreover, that a stress on continental security has characterised PRC policy as well, at least from the rupture of Sino-Soviet relations in 1960 till the 1990s. It is only in recent years that the People's Liberation Army has begun to focus seriously on development of its maritime capability.

In April of 1875, Zuo Zongtang was appointed imperial commissioner for Xinjiang military affairs, becoming the first Han Chinese to take charge of a region that had hitherto been the preserve of Manchu and Mongol officials. He then began careful preparations for the Xinjiang campaigns, selecting an army of some 60,000 soldiers and service personnel, well-trained and armed with imported Western guns and Chinese-made versions of new Western weapons. During 1874–6, while preparing for the campaigns, these solders farmed, adding to the army's grain stockpiles. Other grain was brought in by the massive logistical

---

3 Fairbank *et al.* 1978: 600; Paine 1996: 141–2.

apparatus Zuo mobilised, with 5,000 wagons, 29,000 camels and 5,500 donkeys and mules to transport and store a reserve of some 16 million kilograms of grain in staging areas along the Gansu corridor, Hami and Barkol. Zuo even obtained grain from a Russian supplier in Siberia.

Zuo's greatest problem was financing. Despite opposition from various quarters, the court provided funds from customs on maritime trade, and from the provinces of China proper. In addition, the court authorised Zuo to borrow 8.5 million taels from a foreign bank, the Hong Kong and Shanghai Banking Corporation. Overall, Zuo spent 26.5 million taels on the military phase from 1875 to 1877, and another 18 million on reconstruction work in 1878–81. Though he remained within his initial budget, from 1876 he spent, annually, an amount equivalent to one sixth of the annual expenditure of the Qing treasury.[4]

After Zuo's meticulous preparations, the Qing forces marched west with very few difficulties while Zuo himself directed operations from Gansu. Qing columns, including one comprising Zuo's Hunan Army under command of Liu Jintang (a Hunanese colleague of Zuo's) moved into northern Xinjiang in the summer of 1876. The Qing forces first took towns in the agricultural belt north of Urumchi, defended primarily by Tungans, including the followers of Bai Yanhu and Yu Shaohu whom Zuo had driven from Qinghai three years earlier. The Tungans defending Urumchi fled, and Qing troops captured it in a day (August 18). In all of northern Xinjiang only the city of Manas offered serious resistance; its Tungan defenders, fighting for their lives, received no reinforcements from Ya'qub Beg. Manas finally fell in early November 1876 after a siege of two and a half months by the entire Qing force. The reconquest of Zungharia (except for the Yili valley, which remained under Russian control) took only three months.[5]

Ya'qub Beg had opted to leave defence of the east and north to Tungans. In fact Ya'qub Beg did not wish to engage the Qing forces himself, but rather hoped to reach a diplomatic agreement with the Qing. In 1873–4 Ya'qub Beg discussed the matter with British envoy T.D. Forsyth. Those Qing officials who favoured 'maritime defence', including Li Hongzhang and Prince Gong in the Zongli Yamen (the Qing's new modernised foreign office), seem to have cautiously encouraged such a settlement; Li Hongzhang asked Forsyth in 1876 if Ya'qub Beg would

4 Hsü 1968: 53–60; Kataoka 1991: 182–3.
5 Kim 2004: 166–7; Yu Taishan 1996: 480.

be willing to 'submit' to the Qing formally. The British mediated talks between the Emir's plenipotentiary in London and the Chinese ambassador, Guo Songtao. They agreed in principle in July 1877 that Ya'qub Beg would acknowledge Chinese suzerainty if he could retain control over Kashgaria, though the two sides had not ironed out all the details. Such a deal would have been in line with an option explored by the Qing in 1758, and then again in the 1830s, by which the dynasty hoped to leave the Tarim Basin under the control of a local power willing to send tribute and acknowledge Qing suzerainty. Li Hongzhang, Prince Gong and Guo Songtao were at least initially open to such a possibility with Ya'qub Beg, and the proposal was discussed at one point by the Qing Grand Council and promoted in Beijing by the British ambassador Thomas Wade. Zuo Zongtang, not surprisingly, remained cool to the idea.[6]

In any case, by the spring of 1877 the new military situation in southern Xinjiang led the Qing court to change its mind. In April 1877 Qing forces took Turfan, Pijan, Dabancheng and Toqsun with little resistance. In fact the Muslim commander in Turfan, Hakim Khan, fled before the Qing arrival, although he had 20,000 troops and a large store of supplies. In Dabancheng the besieged defenders waited in vain for Ya'qub Beg to send reinforcements. Toqsun, where Ya'qub Beg had built a new fortress the year before and at one point made his headquarters, was abandoned before General Liu Jintang's force approached the city.

Kim Hodong suggests that this lack of resistance on the part of Ya'qub Beg's forces was due not to overwhelming Qing strength—Muslim troop numbers were roughly comparable to those of the Qing columns—but to an order issued by Ya'qub Beg (reported in Muslim, though not Chinese, sources) to avoid engaging the Qing in combat. Ya'qub Beg was apparently still hoping that the negotiations in London would result in an agreement, and thus sought to avoid antagonising the Qing. His armies, however, were demoralised and confused by this command. Moreover, when Ya'qub Beg himself died suddenly in Korla in late May, probably of a stroke, what remained of organised resistance to the Qing collapsed. Qing sources report that Ya'qub Beg committed suicide, but this is the usual self-glorifying imperial spin (they said the same about Galdan). Kim points out that Ya'qub Beg had as yet sent none of his troops to

6   Kim 2004: 170–1; Zeng 1936: 375.

fight Liu Jintang's battalions, so was thus far from defeated at the time of his death.[7]

Following Ya'qub Beg's death, several rivals vied to succeed him as ruler in Kashgaria. These included his sons Beg Quli and Haqq Quli; in Korla, soldiers enthroned their commander Hakim Khan, who was one of the last surviving Afaqi khojas (son of Kättä Khan); Niyaz Beg, one of the antebellum Altishahri begs who had come to resent rule by Ya'qub Beg and the Khoqandis, took control in Khotan. Beg Quli overcame his Turkic rivals by October, 1877, though independent Tungan forces still remained active. Meanwhile, the Qing juggernaut rolled on. In early October Liu Jintang sent a force from Toqsun to Karashahr, and the Tungan leader Bai Yanhu cut the dikes on the Kaidu River, flooding the Karashahr-Korla area. Despite this impediment, the Qing occupied Karashahr on October 7; Bugur fell soon after, followed rapidly by the other cities along the westward road. Driving Bai Yanhu and his few thousand followers before them, the Qing reached as far as Ush Turfan by the end of the October. Bai Yanhu and his followers fled over the border, where they formed the core of the Russian Tungan population that remains as a small minority in Kyrgyzstan and Kazakstan today. Beg Quli, by then besieging his own capital of Kashgar in a vain attempt to recapture it and free his relatives from the Tungan Ma Daluya, escaped to Ferghana in mid-December when the Qing vanguard reached the area. With the Qing occupation of Khotan in January 1878, the reconquest of Xinjiang was complete.

The Qing retook the entire territory from Korla to Kashgar in seventy days; this, as Kim Hodong has pointed out, is only twice the thirty-five days a trade caravan needed to cover that route in peacetime.[8] The Qing thus advanced almost unimpeded, owing to Ya'qub's order not to fight Qing troops, his reluctance to commit his Turkic forces, the chaos that followed his death, and Uyghurs' disaffection with the harsh Khoqandian regime. Many native Altishahri residents defected to the Qing army as it marched into the region.

---

7 Kim 2004: 167–9. Muslim sources themselves disagree over whether Ya'qub Beg was killed or died of natural causes after beating an underling. The nature of the Emir's decline (he lost memory and speech several hours before dying), suggests cerebral hemorrhage.
8 Kim 2004: 178.

RECONSTRUCTION

The Qing had reconquered a ruined land. From Gucheng to Kashgar, forts and city-walls were flattened, villages burnt out, and irrigation canals filled in. The broad, formerly fertile area around Karashahr lay flooded by the Kaidu River, and the city itself stood under several feet of water. Throughout Xinjiang refugees roamed while fields lay fallow.

Besides the physical damage, moreover, the conflicts and Ya'qub Beg's regime had swept away the institutional foundations of Qing governance in Xinjiang. Many of the begs (the hereditary local officials employed by the empire) had been killed or displaced and stripped of their estates. Likewise, in Turfan and Kucha, while the Muslim princes enfeoffed by the Qing had survived, they had largely lost their source of sustenance: the lands and the agricultural serfs which were the source of their economic and political power. The Manchu and Mongol bannermen, the former backbone of Qing military in Xinjiang, were dead or scattered. One Qing official reporting to his new post in Gucheng compared the banner garrison there, with only a dozen remaining soldiers, to 'a handful of straw'. When the Qing marched into Urumchi they found the Manchu citadel razed without even any rubble left to mark where it had stood; only one Manchu soldier remained of the former garrison. To the north, the Yili valley, where the majority of the Manchu and Mongol bannermen had once been quartered, was of course now occupied by Russia, but when the Qing finally recovered the Yili region (see below) officials found the old Qing residences, barracks, guard posts, granaries and so on to be just as dilapidated as in the south.[9] Ghulja could no longer serve as Xinjiang's capital.

Not all Chinese had fled or perished in the conflicts. Bellew, who accompanied the British party on its embassy to Yarkand and Kashgar in 1873–4, reports that numbers of Chinese converts—'new Muslims' (*yengi Musulman*)—frequented the bazaars of Yarkand and Yängihissar, and there was even a private army of Tungans and 'new Muslims' in the Emir's service.[10] And there were still many Tungans, especially further east. But even after Chinese refugees, new immigrants and some of Zuo's troops resettled in Xinjiang, farming populations in the agricultural settlements north of Urumchi in 1878 amounted to only between a tenth

9 Yu Taishan 1996: 484; Kataoka 1991: 150–1.
10 Bellew 1875: 266, 270–1, 311–15, 381.

and a quarter of what they had been before the rebellions.[11] This limited the state's ability to provision soldiers and support a governing apparatus in the territory.

General Liu Jintang, who would soon become the first Governor of Xinjiang Province (in office 1884–91), wistfully contemplated the ruins of a century of Qing rule there: 'Since the chaos, the old system has been entirely swept away, and to contemplate restoring it involves myriad difficulties.'[12] He and others believed only a sweeping reform of Xinjiang's administrative system, though it would require an initial investment, could consolidate Qing control in the region for the long term.

Before the reconquest was complete Zuo Zongtang had already officially suggested making Xinjiang a province: 'To cut costs and save effort, in order to draft policies ensuring enduring peace and stability in Xinjiang and reduce the court's anxiety ... [we must] establish a province and change to *junxian*-style administration.'[13] Zuo thus proposed putting all of Xinjiang on the same administrative footing as the provinces of China proper, replacing the old system of local rule by Uyghur begs and princes and Mongol *jasaks* under a supervisory Qing military government, with the system of counties, prefectures and so on each under Confucian-trained civil magistrates (the system known in Chinese as *junxian*). The idea of provincehood for Xinjiang had been around since the 1820s, when Gong Zizhen (Kung Tzu-chen, another Hunanese) raised it in a famous essay as a way to control costs in Xinjiang. Zuo himself had even alluded to Xinjiang provincehood in a poem he wrote forty years earlier. Even in the 1870s, however, the Qing court had not yet been ready to commit to such a radical reform before the reconquest was complete and while the issue of the Yili valley awaited solution. Nonetheless, the court did authorise Zuo to take the first steps towards a Chinese-style administration in Xinjiang as part of his 'post-pacification' (*shanhou*) reconstruction programme in both north and south Xinjiang.[14]

11 Wang Xilong 1990: 190.
12 Liu Jintang 1898 (1986): 3: 44b; Miao Pusheng 1995: 74.
13 Zuo Zongtang, *Zuo wen xiang gong quanji*, j. 50, 'zunchi tongchou quanju zhe', cited in Feng Jiasheng *et al.* 1981: 2: 395. Cf. Kataoka 1991: 155.
14 Yu Taishan 1996: 484; Kataoka 1991: 128. Kataoka's research on the policy debates and procedures leading to Xinjiang provincehood is thorough, and the following is largely based on his *Shinchô Shinkyô tôji kenkyû* (1991).

Thus under the rubric of reconstruction the Qing army began establishing for the first time the rudiments of a Chinese civil administration in south Xinjiang, from Hami to Kashgar. There were specialised Reconstruction Agencies to collect taxes, promote production of grain, mulberry and silkworms, and institute a collective responsibility and security system (*baojia*) at the village level. More general tasks included reconstruction of city defences, government offices and barracks, bridges, roads and canals; sorting out land ownership; minting a new currency; and opening schools. The work was carried out by Zuo's Hunanese soldiers and their officers—by default the main governing body in post-war Xinjiang—and funded from China proper. Although, as we will see below, reconstruction plans were not immediately realised due to budget constraints, these efforts represent a definitive departure from earlier Qing policy, which had left local-level affairs in Muslim areas almost entirely to the begs.[15]

RECOVERY OF THE YILI VALLEY

The rapid collapse of Ya'qub Beg's emirate and the swift reconquest of Xinjiang took even foreign observers by surprise. When Governor-General Kaufman of Russian Turkestan sent troops into the Yili valley in 1871 in the name of protecting lives and property of its citizens from the chaos of the rebellions, he surely did not expect to be discussing its return to the Qing eight years later. Indeed, the Russians seemed to have intended a long stay in Ghulja, for they restored major irrigation canals, built a hospital, established bilingual schools and other cultural institutions, including a Russian Orthodox Church.[16] However, since Russia had initially promised to return all occupied Qing lands outright, its negotiating position was poor as it sought concessions from the Qing. Moscow was, moreover, feeling the strains of rapid imperial expansion, having just waged a war with the Ottoman empire which left it little energy or funds for another conflict in Central Asia. Besides, the victorious Qing army was just over the border, and far outnumbered the Russian troops in Yili.

Despite all these factors in the Qing favour, the Manchu representative, Chong-hou, agreed in the Treaty of Livadia (1879) to terms so scan-

15 Kataoka 1991: 151–5.
16 Roberts 2003: Chapter 2, n. 41, citing Russian historians.

dalously detrimental that he was sentenced to death immediately upon his return to Beijing, and spared execution only after appeals on his behalf from the international diplomatic community. The treaty, which the Qing court refused to ratify, promised only the partial return of the Yili lands occupied in 1871; in addition, it would have allowed Russia to open seven new consulates in Xinjiang and Mongolia, permitted duty-free trade in both these regions; afforded Russian traders access to trade routes extending to Beijing and the Yangzi river through China proper; opened the Sungari (Songhua) River in Manchuria to Russian navigation, and paid Russia an indemnity of 5 million roubles (2.8 million taels).

The usual explanation for this diplomatic debacle, following Qing sources, is that Chong-hou was inexperienced and over-eager to return home to China. However, in her recent study of the diplomatic history of the Sino-Russian frontier, S.C.M. Paine has shown that Chong-hou was in fact a seasoned diplomat and no homebody, having dealt with Western nations on several occasions over thirty years in France, England and the United States. Moreover, so absurd were the concessions to Russia in the Livadia treaty (Russia even attempted to keep them secret, fearing objections from other powers), especially those regarding overland trade privileges in the Chinese interior, that no sane Qing official could have expected them to be accepted by the court had he agreed to them independently. Thus, Paine reasons, Chong-hou must have had the approval of the terms of the treaty from others in the Zongli Yamen before his return to Beijing. It was only later, after the Empress Dowager sought general comment on the treaty from officials at large that the scandal broke. With appalled officials calling for war with Russia, Chong-hou was made the scapegoat, first hurriedly by the court and then over time by historians.[17]

In February of 1880 the Qing court announced its refusal to ratify the Treaty of Livadia. Although both sides began preparations for war, neither wanted it; hostilities were averted after the Qing dispatched Zeng Jize (Tseng Chi-tse), former minister to Britain and France, as minister

17 Paine 1996: 132–45, esp. 136–7. Paine's conclusion is strengthened by her discovery that key documents including some of Chong-hou's correspondence with the court during the negotiations have been removed from the documentary record in Beijing (p. 146, n. 31). Contrast the general thrust of Hsü 1965b: Chapter 2, or the characterisation of Chong-hou in Ji Dachun 1997: 134–5.

to Russia to renegotiate the return of Yili. During the latter half of 1880 and early into the next year Zeng and his Russian counterpart Biutsov worked to reach a new agreement despite the largely incompatible demands behind which both courts staked their imperial dignity. Ultimately the Russian need for cash, and Qing willingness to pay a larger pecuniary indemnity in return for reduced territorial and commercial concessions, led to the Treaty of St Petersburg (February 1881). By this treaty the Qing paid 9 million roubles for the return of Yili east of the Khorgos River; Russia retained the westernmost part of the Yili valley to resettle some 50,000 Tungan and Taranchi (Ghulja Uyghur) refugees who feared Qing reprisals, and who had appealed to the Tsar to accept them as subjects.[18] Commercial concessions were limited to only two new Russian consulates to be established immediately (as opposed to the seven stipulated by the Treaty of Livadia), though others were to follow. Russian traders gained customs-free trade rights in Xinjiang and Mongolia, but not in the interior of China. Border issues in other parts of Xinjiang, from Khobdo (in Mongolia) to Kashgar, were to be decided separately in five ancillary treaties following field surveys (Zeng thus avoided Chong-hou's mistake of making territorial decisions based on Russian maps).

Both Qing contemporaries and later Western scholars have considered the Treaty of St Petersburg a diplomatic victory for the Qing, and when judged against the disastrous Treaty of Livadia, it certainly is.[19] Zeng Jize was an informed and hard-nosed negotiator who convinced the Russians to retreat from territory already occupied—something unprecedented in the history of Tsarist expansion in Central Asia. However, the Russians nonetheless gained considerable territorial and commercial benefits for returning a portion of the lands they had forcefully occupied—and which they had originally promised to return free and clear in their entirety upon the repression of the rebellion in Xinjiang. The exact extent of the lands ceded to Russia depends on one's assess-

18   This figure, based on an 1884 Russian military report, includes 45,000 Taranchis and 5,000 Tungans, amounting to some 80 per cent of the population (Roberts 2003: Chapter 2). In addition, some 20,000 Kazaks also migrated. By the 1890s Uyghur (Taranchi) population on both sides of the border was about equal. On the community of Yili Uyghurs and their experience in the Soviet Union, see Roberts 2003.

19   See Hsü 1965b: 187–93, and Paine 1996: 163. Cf. Yu Taishan 1996: 482–3.

ment of where the westernmost boundary of Qing Xinjiang lay prior to the treaty. Views differ: Hsü's map shows a relatively narrow strip of land, but a late-twentieth-century Chinese historical atlas claims that Qing territory originally included lake Balkash and beyond, at its furthest point extending some 900 kilometres west of Yili to Baykadam (now in central southern Kazakstan). Based on complaints about the border revisions conducted as riders to the St Petersburg treaty, Chinese today view it as an 'unequal treaty' by which China lost 70,000 square kilometres to Russia. Moreover, Chinese historians write that many Yili residents, called 'refugees' by Russian and Soviet historians, were forcibly deported by Russia. This is said to have led to a shortage of manpower that slowed subsequent agricultural development in the Yili region.[20]

CREATING XINJIANG PROVINCE

Despite the indemnity and other concessions in the Treaty of St Petersburg, Qing court and officials alike were pleased to recover control in 1881 of the most densely populated and strategically important part of the Yili valley. In particular, the retrocession of Yili cleared the way for Xinjiang's full provincehood.

As discussed above, Zuo Zongtang began reforming Xinjiang's administration in tandem with the reconquest, with the ultimate goal of instituting the *junxian* system of China proper in this frontier territory. Zuo was recalled from the north-west before the conclusion of the St Petersburg treaty, but along with his successor, Liu Jintang, he continued to press for provincehood—a reform which would require an initial outlay of more funds, but which in theory promised future savings to the Qing court and provinces of China. When the court solicited input on the question from officials at large, some prominent Qing figures, especially the 'maritime defence' party, continued to object to provincehood or any further outlays for Xinjiang. Li Hongzhang did not memorialise publicly on this issue, but in letters to acquaintances, including ambassador Guo Songtao in England, he opposed provincial status for what he called 'useless Xinjiang' (*wuyong zhi Xinjiang*).[21] The objections

20 Yu Taishan 1996: 482–3. The atlas is Tan Qixiang, ed., 1982–7: vol. 8, map 52–3.
21 *Li wen zhong gong quanji* (Collected letters of Li Hongzhang), j. 17, cited in Kataoka 1991: 133, 146 n. 16.

were familiar: Qing forces were too weak in the area, Chinese were too few, and there was insufficient fertile land to support a full-scale *junxian* system or a military presence of requisite size.[22] In the end, however, the court agreed to Liu Jintang's slightly modified scheme for Xinjiang provincehood.

At the same time as the Qing court and officialdom discussed Xinjiang provincehood, they debated whether Taiwan, under threat from Japan, should likewise receive this status. Kataoka Kazutada has shown that in these debates Li Hongzhang and others stressed the differences between Taiwan and Xinjiang, while Zuo, by then posted in southern China, argued for the similarities. That the court ultimately acceded to both proposals, making Xinjiang a province in 1884 and Taiwan in 1887,[23] demonstrates that provincialisation of the frontier, with the concomitant promotion of Han migration and implementation of Chinese institutions in areas with sizeable non-Han populations, was part of the beleaguered dynasty's attempt to shore up its position on all frontiers. (To similar purpose, the provinces of Fengtian, Jilin and Heilongjiang were established in 1907 out of lands beyond the Great Wall in the north-east.) That Taiwan's provincial status was linked to Xinjiang provincehood is interesting in light of the informal alliance today between advocates of formal independence for Taiwan with those pressing for rights of Uyghurs and Tibetans. The reverberations of Qing imperial expansion echo and re-echo.

Some historians have misinterpreted the shift in Xinjiang's status in 1884, seeing it as representing 'Chinese' 'annexation' of Xinjiang, a region that had hitherto been a 'mere dependency' or 'protectorate'.[24] Journalists writing about the background to Xinjiang's separatist problems often repeat this mistake. To say that China 'annexed' Xinjiang in 1884 is wrong, first, because it was the Qing empire, and not China, that changed Xinjiang's status. Secondly, this interpretation wrongly implies

22 Kataoka 1991: 135–6.
23 The office of Taiwan governor was created in late 1885, beginning the transition to full *junxian* style administration. The Qing court announced formal Taiwan provincehood two years later.
24 See, for example, Liu and Smith 1980: 242, or Owen Lattimore's mistaken assessment that 'Manchu policy in Hsi Yü [the Western Regions, i.e. Xinjiang] was militarily much weaker than that of the Han Dynasty, and politically inferior to that of the T'ang' (1950: 46).

that from 1759 to 1864 Xinjiang was less a part of the Qing empire than was China. In fact, as shown in Chapter 3, Xinjiang, like Mongolia, northern Manchuria and other frontier territories, was an imperial holding on a par with China proper, despite being administered for the most part under different systems. The implementation of provincehood in Xinjiang represented not annexation of a former protectorate by 'China,' but rather a fundamental shift in the governing principles of the Qing empire as a whole. The late Qing state took an administrative model employed in the agrarian core of its sprawling empire and applied it to the ecologically and culturally different regions of the periphery. The debates over the pragmatics of provincehood thus hinted at deeper issues involving the nature of the empire and the status of the Manchus, Mongols and other Inner Asians in a realm dominated demographically by Han Chinese. Though proponents of provincehood stressed the fiscal savings and reduction in troop numbers to be realised by the reform, and it was for these reasons that the court approved it, underlying these claims was the assumption that a Xinjiang that was demographically and culturally more like China proper would be both easier and cheaper to govern. This implication was already present in Gong Zizhen's essay in the 1820s; it was amplified in some of the 1870s arguments. For example, Zhu Fengjia, who published an essay in favour of Xinjiang provincehood in a large collection of works devoted to frontier matters, argued that while the military government of mid-Qing Xinjiang could only guard the people, the Chinese-style provincial system could truly govern and teach them. Once counties had been established there would have to be schools to teach the classics, so that under the *junxian* system, 'Confucian learning can be taught, laws established, and the Rites will flourish.'[25] Xinjiang government, then, would have to be didactic and assimilative to be effective. By this theory, sinicisation of the local non-Chinese population went hand-in-hand with provincialisation.

Planners pinned hopes on another type of sinicisation as well, that achieved by sponsoring resettlement in Xinjiang of Chinese from further east. To expand the tax-base, populate ravaged lands and 'consolidate control of the frontier' (*shibian*), Liu Jintang enlisted exiles and homesteaders from China in a civilian agricultural reclamation programme which provided settlers with land and loans of seed, tools and draught

25   Cited in Kataoka 1991: 141, 147 n. 34.

animals. By their third year settlers were expected to have repaid the loans and begin paying taxes. For the most part the state-sponsored homesteading was focused on northern Xinjiang, but early in the twentieth century it was expanded to southern regions as well.[26]

Administrative reforms

Xinjiang provincialisation was thus a grand design on which the Qing court and Han officials pinned high hopes. The scheme was based on a reworking of the region's administrative and military arrangements. Starting in 1884 circuits, prefectures, sub-prefectures and counties were established in both northern and southern Xinjiang. Liu Jintang was appointed First Governor, headquartered in Urumchi, the new provincial capital, but he in theory answered to the Governor-General of Xinjiang, Gansu and Shaanxi, who was based in Gansu, through which Xinjiang's budget subventions were channelled. These changes stripped much importance from the former top post in Xinjiang, the Yili Generalship, which had always been held by Manchus or Mongols answering directly to the Qing emperor and Grand Council. The bulk of Xinjiang's troops now fell under the command of the Governor in Urumchi, not the Yili General. The overall size of the army had been reduced as well, to just over 30,000 (compared to some 40,000 in mid-Qing times), but now more troops were permanently stationed in the Tarim Basin than before the wars of the 1860s and 1870s. To achieve these reduced levels of permanent forces, large numbers of the 50,000 man army of reconquest were demobilised and enrolled in the land reclamation programme.

The creation of so many new administrative districts required officials to fill the posts, and this is one of the most striking changes in the new Xinjiang province. Whereas the upper ranks of the military government of mid-Qing Xinjiang had been staffed by Manchus, Mongols and the occasional Uyghur, the formal bureaucracy now became almost entirely Han Chinese. Moreover, because Zuo Zongtang's Hunan Army had composed the core of the reconquest force, Liu Jintang drew upon this pool of fellow Hunanese in making appointments, with the result that from 1884 to 1911 an average of 55 per cent of men in office in Xinjiang were Hunanese, primarily from Zuo's and Liu's own home counties in

---

26 Yu Taishan 1996: 484–5, 487; Kataoka 1991: 173–5, 275–7.

Hunan. Moreover, none of these men held the metropolitan, or highest, degree in the state civil service examination system, which county magistrates were in theory expected to have obtained. Very few could boast even the lowest *shengyuan* degree status. In short, thirty years before the dynasty abandoned the examination system in the empire as a whole, the system was all but replaced in Xinjiang by native-place patronage, as the Hunanese clique took control of the new province.[27]

The creation of this Chinese bureaucratic network represented an unprecedented attempt by the Qing state to govern directly at the local level in non-Han as well as Han areas of Xinjiang. As such, it assigned to new Chinese magistrates responsibilities which had under the previous system belonged to the upper echelons of Uyghur begs. Nevertheless, these reforms did not entail the wholesale elimination of native Turkic officials. Despite the wishful thinking of some of the provincehood visionaries, implementing *junxian* administration could not immediately address the fact that most of Xinjiang's Turkic population did not speak Chinese, and the Hunanese and other Chinese officials certainly spoke no Uyghur. Since the eighteenth century the Qing had relied on begs and *ahungs* (Muslim clerics) for interpreting, implementation of decrees, collection of taxes, police work, adjudication of minor disputes and a range of other clerical and administrative matters. Moreover, the higher-ranked *hakim* and *ishiqagha* begs were eminent personages who governed cities and communicated directly with the emperor; they frequently bore the titles and trappings of the Qing nobility—honours shared by élite Manchus and Mongols but generally not Han.

After 1884 the *hakim* and *ishiqagha* begs, higher-ranked than the new county and prefectural officials, were stripped by Liu Jintang of their duties (though they initially retained their noble titles and stipends). Otherwise, however, some 3,300 Turkic functionaries (many of them the same men, or descendants of men who had served as begs before 1864) remained in service as clerks in government offices, as 'runners' conducting official business in the field, and as village headmen—this in contrast to only eighty-two formal civil government posts. In Chinese the native functionaries were no longer officially called *boke* (beg) but rather 'clerks' or *xiangyue*—a term used in China proper for village elders. In Uyghur, however, they were generally still known by such

27 Kataoka conducts a minute statistical analysis of the Hunan connection among Xinjiang provincial officialdom (1991: 246–59, 263–96, 270–1).

traditional terms as beg, *onbashi* (head of ten households) *yüzbashi* (head of a hundred) and so on.[28]

Zuo Zongtang had anticipated retaining the begs, who were after all very useful in local matters, but drew this distinction: 'they are official servants, not officials' (again, this was a departure from earlier Qing practice, when the higher-ranked begs were clearly Qing *officials*).[29] And Chinese officials apparently treated downgraded begs accordingly. One British visitor to the southern Tarim in the early twentieth century writes of the contempt displayed by the Chinese 'ambans' for the 'native officials', whom they called by the derogatory term *chantou* (turbaned-head) and with whom they shared little if any social interaction. 'The manner assumed by an Amban in speaking to his native entourage would,' he writes, 'if used by an Englishman to a native in India, be described at least as "unconciliatory"—by the native press probably in far stronger terms .... Judged by our own method of treating Asiatics, this must tend to weaken the central authority by preventing mutual understanding.'[30]

Foreign travellers' accounts also make clear, however, that although these new begs were vetted and supervised in their positions by local Han officials, they still retained a good deal of autonomy. They collected their salaries from the households under their jurisdiction, which left ample opportunities for extortion, and linguistic and cultural barriers prevented Chinese magistrates from monitoring the begs too closely. Despite Confucian idealism, then, even under the reformed administrative system a gulf divided central government officials from people and affairs in southern Xinjiang.

Of course the Chinese central government had throughout late-imperial history always assigned officials to postings far from their homes, where they often encountered a strange language (many dialects of Chinese are mutually unintelligible) and novel conditions—this was true throughout China, not only in Xinjiang. The standard solution relied on class solidarity and the workings of traditional education: the sons of local élites received training in the Confucian classics in academies or from private instructors in preparation for the civil service exams; this gave them a cultural idiom in common with officials posted to the

---

28 Kataoka 1991: 171–3, 205–12.
29 '*Shi yi, er fei guan*'. From Zuo Zongtang 1888–97 (1968): *shu xu*, j. 21, cited in Kataoka 1991: 170, 180 n. 47.
30 Bruce 1907: 12–13.

district. They also learned to communicate in Mandarin. Administration by means of the *junxian* (provincial) system was thus closely linked to Confucian education and the civil service exams, as Zhu Fengjia noted. However, the difference in Muslim Xinjiang after the reconquest was that the local élites—the families from which the begs were drawn—educated their children in the Islamic, not Confucian, tradition. To change this, Qing authorities embarked on a programme to establish Confucian academies throughout Xinjiang.

Introducing Chinese education

In keeping with the sinicising thrust behind his planned reforms for post-conquest Xinjiang, Zuo Zongtang advocated a programme of educating Muslims in the Chinese fashion: 'If we wish to change their peculiar customs and assimilate them to our Chinese ways (*huafeng*), we must found free schools (*yishu*) and make the Muslim children read [Chinese] books, recognise characters and understand spoken language.'[31] Another goal was to replenish the supply of local interpreters and clerks to promote communication between officials and the people. Therefore, as soon as the Qing armies had reconquered each Xinjiang city, the Reconstruction Agencies set up free Confucian schools. By 1883 there were seventy-seven of these schools in Xinjiang, fifty of them in predominantly Turkic Muslim areas (including Aqsu, Kashgar, Yarkand, Khotan and so on), each with a teacher and attended by some fifteen to twenty boys, eight years old and above. Although students in theory did not pay tuition, they did purchase books, paper and ink from the Reconstruction Agency. Teachers received a salary and materials stipend from revenues on public land, based on enrolments.

The curriculum in these schools was similar to that of Confucian schools in China proper where students learned to read through rote memorisation of the classics, character by character. However, some modifications were necessary in light of the fact that many of the matriculating pupils in Xinjiang did not even speak Chinese and therefore experienced more than the usual difficulty with this standard pedagogical method.[32] In addition to such standard works as the *Trimetrical Classic*

31 Hamada 1990: 28–9; Zuo Zongtang 1888–97 (1968): *zougao*, 56: 22b–25a, 'Banli Xinjiang shanhou shiyi', quote on 22b.
32 Xinjiang Regional Archives, document 15-11-53 (GX5.6). This and subse-

(*Sanzi jing*), the *Classic of Filial Piety*, the *Book of Odes*, the *Analects* and other classics, officials prepared various bilingual texts, such as a parallel Chinese-Uyghur version of the Sacred Edict (sixteen homilies by the Kangxi emperor) and a glossary called *Chinese and Muslim (Language) Juxtaposed* (*Han Hui he bi*).[33] In 1879 one of the reconstruction agencies was ordered to print 500 copies of an *Annotated Arabic Character Sampler* for distribution to Turfan (forty copies), the four eastern and four western cities of Xinjiang (230 copies each).[34]

Teachers gave students Chinese names. Unlike the Chinese versions of Uyghur names used today for official PRC documents which transliterate the names syllable by syllable into long strings of characters, these school names took the usual form of three Chinese characters. As is familiar to any foreign student of Chinese today, such names, chosen to vaguely emulate the pronunciation of the original foreign name, often have an outlandish quality or convey a didactic message through the meaning of the characters or a pun on their sound. One ten-year-old student of beg descent who entered a Chinese school near Turfan in 1883 was dubbed Ai Xueshu ('loves to read books'); his classmates included Bi Deming ('must make a name for himself'—as in the civil service exams) and Tui Dalun ('promotes the great Analects').[35]

Following the Boxer Rebellion in north China (1900) the Empress Dowager, Cixi (Tz'u-hsi) approved a series of reforms in a desperate effort to save the Qing dynasty. The most significant of these were the elimination of the civil service examination system and the establishment of 'modern' schools to include study of science, mathematics, foreign languages, Western nations, physical education and other subjects deemed necessary for the strengthening of the country, particularly in regard to the Western attack on Qing territorial and commercial sovereignty. The modern schools came to Xinjiang following the appointment in 1907 of Du Tong as provincial superintendent of schools. Du had studied pedagogy in Japan, then a model for many Qing reform

---

quent documents cited in this section were dispatches from officials in the Turfan area. Records are listed in the Xinjiang Regional Archives catalog #Q15-11.

33 Kataoka 1991: 202–4. Kataoka provides an illustration of the *Han Hui he bi* on p. 204.

34 Xinjiang Regional Archives 15-11-51 (GX5.2), second document in packet. The Chinese title of this work was *Zhushi Huizi yangben*.

35 Xinjiang Regional Archives, 15-11-309 (GX12.9.25).

efforts, and attempted to establish a broad-based lower, middle and vocational school system in Xinjiang to provide instruction in these modern
subjects as well as Chinese language and physical drill. By around 1911
this programme had resulted in an expansion in the number of schools
(to over 600) and an approximate ten-fold increase in the numbers of
students matriculated (to about 15,000). Unlike the Confucian schools,
which were designed primarily to train the sons of Uyghur notables to
be government functionaries, the modern schools had broader social
and political goals. They thus included 'common' as well as 'upper level'
(élite) schools, and were located in villages as well as urban communities.
Attendance was in theory compulsory, at least for boys.

The Xinjiang government took its educational efforts seriously, during both the first, 'Confucian', and second, 'modern', phases. In the late
nineteenth century seasonal grade reports for all students were forwarded by teachers up the government hierarchy to the provincial governor
himself. These reports listed each student by Chinese name, commented
on their ability and improvement, and even noted the text and exact
sentence up to which they had successfully memorised. It was proposed
that teachers receive bonuses on the basis of the number of their students who could speak Chinese clearly (with light accent), and although
Governor Liu dismissed this idea, he threatened to investigate any school
where students did not improve.[36]

Despite attention at both gubernatorial and national levels, neither
phase of the plan to educate Xinjiang Muslims was a success. The last
governor of Qing Xinjiang admitted just before the fall of the dynasty in
1911 that after twenty years in operation the Confucian academies had
at best served only to train 'mullahs'—here indicating, in a somewhat
derisive way, men with bare functional literacy, capable of serving as
secretaries, but little else. The mass cultural assimilation once envisioned
remained an unlikely prospect. Moreover, there was great resistance to
all Chinese schools on the part of the very people they were designed
to educate. Students who matriculated put little effort into studying,
according to their instructors. Of course, the teachers themselves were
less than stellar: most were impoverished and embittered Han who had
themselves failed the civil service exams and wound up teaching in Xinjiang as a last resort. The implementation of the modern curriculum

36 Xinjiang Regional Archives, 15-11-255 (GX10.12).

after 1907 was impeded by the fact that most available instructors had been trained only in the traditional curriculum, if at all.[37]

In fact élite Uyghur families sought to avoid sending their sons to Chinese schools, where they were required to participate in Confucian rites considered idolatrous by Muslims. Whenever possible, rich families hid their sons or hired poor boys to attend in their place. Isa Yusuf Alptekin, the Uyghur separatist leader, told of his father's experience with the late Qing Chinese school system. When Isa's grandfather first heard that Uyghurs would be sent to Chinese schools, he arranged to have Isa's father hidden in the Taklamakan desert and sent a poor neighbour to school as a stand-in. When the local magistrate uncovered the ruse, Isa's father was forced to matriculate. At the school he was given a Chinese name and was required to don official Qing dress with his hair in a queue. Thereafter the boy reportedly was not allowed into his own house until he changed out of these clothes, and his own mother (Isa's grandmother) could not bear the sight of the long pigtail; she found herself unable to demonstrate affection for her own son.[38]

Xinjiang education commissioner Du Tong himself held quite a liberal attitude toward educating the Uyghur population of Xinjiang, writing that literacy and technical education to improve agriculture and textile production were priorities, whereas changing Uyghur customs and converting them from Islam was not an urgent task. Some of the new state schools even taught the Qur'an as well as the subjects of the new curriculum. Du furthermore forbade corporal punishment of pupils by teachers. Nonetheless, even after 1907 Turkic Muslim resistance to state education policies continued, especially at the primary level. Part of the problem lay in the costs and manner of implementation of the new education programme. Although the provincial government was supposed to cover some costs of establishing the new schools, this support was in practice directed to northern districts populated primarily by Han. Elsewhere special taxes were levied to raise funds for the new schools, and Kataoka has shown that many of the new village schools were in fact located in local mosques and madrasas—the only buildings available for the purpose—an imposition which may also have engen-

---

37 Yuan Dahua, comp. 1910 (1992): 38: 4; Kataoka 1991: 204–5, 323–4; Hamada 1990: 30–1.
38 This story is cited in Hamada 1990: 31, and Kataoka 1991: 323 from different original sources, both by Isa Yusuf Alptekin. The versions differ in some details.

dered resentment. Moreover, although Du had initially intended Uyghur to be the medium of education, the 'common' lower schools switched around 1908 to instruction in Chinese only, on the grounds that the Uyghur language 'does not communicate' (*yuyan butong*)—that is, with the Han Chinese teachers—and that it contributed to the gulf between Chinese and Uyghur. This led to complaints that boys and girls, some of whom boarded at their schools, could no longer speak to their own parents without interpreters. Overall there was considerable agitation in southern Xinjiang regarding the taxes, corruption by Chinese officials involved in tax-collection and school construction, and the apparent sinifying intent of the new education. Some families fled to Russian Turkestan to avoid sending children to the Chinese schools.[39]

Islamic education in Qing Xinjiang

The Chinese schools were not, of course, introduced into a pedagogical vacuum, and understanding the role and meaning of the autochthonous education system sheds light on why the Qing-era Confucian schools and especially the new Chinese modern schools were abhorrent to many Uyghurs. In Muslim Xinjiang in the late nineteenth century Islamic education was available to boys between the ages of roughly six to sixteen (and in some places by the late nineteenth century to girls under twelve as well) via the traditional institution of the maktap (*mäktäp*). Maktap were informal neighbourhood schools established in a mosque, at the house of a teacher, or that of a wealthy member of the community; teachers could be any literate man, usually either a mullah or *qurra* (Qu'ran reciter), and were paid by occasional donations in kind or cash from students' parents. The curriculum was primarily religious and oral, including instruction on the religious festivals, certain Qu'ranic verses and some poetry in Turki and Persian. Arabic script was taught after a fashion, but not the language, so much of the Qu'ranic study took the form of rote memorisation without comprehension. (As such, maktap education was similar to that in the Confucian schools.) According to foreign observers in Xinjiang and Adeeb Khalid's study of contemporary maktap in Bukhara, this training provided pupils with minimal reading and no writing skills; by the end of their studies they often could read only those texts

39 Kataoka 1991: 309–27; Hamada 1990: 31–2; Skrine and Nightingale 1987: 162.

they had memorised and nothing else. What students did garner from their time in the maktap, however, was the acquisition of 'basic elements of culture and modes of behaviour through interaction with an older, learned man'. Maktap were common in the Tarim Basin region—as in Central Asia generally—with some seventy to eighty in Kashgar before 1930. Substituting a state-run institution for the interaction of student and teacher in maktap intervened in a basic way with the practices of intergenerational transmission of culture in southern Xinjiang.[40]

The larger oases of southern Xinjiang also supported madrasas (*mädräsä*): colleges attached to shrines and run as charitable foundations supported by income from endowed lands (*waqf*). In the last decades of the nineteenth century there were dozens of madrasas in Yarkand, several in Kashgar and two important ones in Aqsu. Many of the mullahs who taught at these Xinjiang colleges had themselves studied in Bukhara, which remained until the twentieth century a major centre of scholarship drawing students from throughout Central Asia, including the Tarim Basin oases, and elsewhere in the Islamic world.

Madrasas in Kashgar, Aqsu and Yarkand attracted young men (aged fifteen and up) from throughout the Xinjiang region, who were housed in cells at the college. Well-to-do students paid tuition; poor students worked for the school and could sometimes receive financial assistance from the college's charitable foundation. The curriculum stressed the study of texts relating to Islamic law, Arabic grammar, logic and dogma, as well as some poetry. Like the maktap, madrasas employed oral-aural methods of teaching and learning. After some time in the madrasa, students could recite the Qu'ran and understand it, at least in part; they could read and write in Arabic and Persian (and presumably Turkic as well). By the early twentieth century some madrasa curricula also included Islamic history, astronomy, geography, literature and medicine—an indication of the influence of the jadidist or 'new method' movement (see below), and perhaps of the Chinese new curriculum, even in these traditional institutions.

---

40   Quote from Khalid 1998: 26; on Russo-native schools, see 157–160. When the Russian government attempted to institute Russo-native schools in Turkestan from the 1880s, local peoples resisted in precisely the same ways as in Chinese Turkestan. See Bellér-Hann 2000: 44–8 for general background on maktap in Xinjiang. On Islamic education in the Kashgar region on the eve of the Chinese Communist takeover, see Wang Jianping n.d.

Opinions on the quality of Xinjiang's madrasa education vary with place, time and the outlook of the observer (most available information comes from Westerners), but while some of the colleges may have served as little more than hostels for the urban poor, permanent students and other hangers on, some at least were vital centres of scholarship where influential mullahs trained students from a wide catchment area in Islamic jurisprudence and thus linked Xinjiang's Turkic Muslims to intellectual trends in the broader world represented by Bukhara. Training at a madrasa allowed men to become mullahs and opened the way for employment in the (Qing) beg bureaucracy as a judge (*qazi* or *qazi räis*) or as a teachers in madrasas.[41]

After reconquering the region in 1878, then, the Qing shifted its approach to Xinjiang to one that was more assimilative and sinicising. Personnel with top political and military authority were for the first time predominantly Han, not Manchu, Mongol or Uyghur. The beg officials were down-graded, though they remained essential. And the state attempted to implement in Xinjiang education systems based on the same content and pedagogical style as those in China proper, first through Confucian education for Uyghur élites, and then through 'modern' Chinese-language education for, in theory if not practice, all Uyghur children. Both educational initiatives joined and in some ways challenged local educational systems already in place. In fact, a parallel effort to modernise Islamic education had already appeared in Xinjiang from the 1880s and 1890s, inspired by the jadidist movement in the Crimea and Central Asia and by developments in Turkey. We will examine Xinjiang's jadidist education and its influence below (see 'Islamic modern education'); first, however, we will look at the results of Xinjiang provincialisation and the political upheavals that followed the fall of the Qing dynasty.

ACHIEVEMENTS OF PROVINCIALISATION

Provincehood for Xinjiang, and the administrative and other reforms that accompanied it, emerged from the debate over Xinjiang's status and place in the empire, a debate which began in the mid-eighteenth

41   These paragraphs are based on Bellér-Hann 2000: 48–55.

century. Roughly following the model proposed by Gong Zizhen in the early nineteenth century, Zuo Zongtang and his successors lobbied hard for provincialisation, in the face of court reluctance and opposition from other officials, on the grounds that making the region a province would best address the dilemma of security *versus* cost along the north-western frontier. Provincehood, it was hoped, would encourage Han migration to Xinjiang, promote assimilation of native peoples, allow for more effective taxation, and thus reduce the costs to the centre of controlling Xinjiang, while simultaneously increasing stability and defending against foreign encroachment in the area. However, the new province would require a sizeable initial investment, on top of annual operating budgets, before the enhanced security and savings could be realised.

For several reasons, that investment did not materialise. As described above, the education effort did not achieve wide-spread assimilation in part because of native resistance, but also in part because the shortage of funds transferred the financial burden of building a Chinese school system in southern Xinjiang onto the population. Moreover, few of the other grandiose predictions of the advocates of Xinjiang reconquest and provincehood were fully realised in the decades that followed 1884. At the core of these problems lay Xinjiang's continued fiscal weakness.

Fiscal matters

After the creation of Xinjiang Province (1884) Xinjiang's annual subvention from the treasury and provinces of China proper was formally stabilised until 1901 at 3.4 million taels (passed on each year out of 4.8 million sent to Gansu-Shaanxi-Xinjiang Governor-General's office). This was a considerable reduction from the annual average of 11 million taels which Zuo and his armies had drawn since 1876 for military and reconstruction expenses, and only covered Xinjiang governmental and military salaries and operating costs. The 3.4 million taels provided nothing for the continued reconstruction or enhancement of infrastructure that in the long term might have increased revenues locally available to the Xinjiang government. Moreover, once Russia relinquished Yili (1881), the court considered Xinjiang's crisis resolved, and turned its primary attentions to the next looming disaster, tensions with France over Annam (northern Vietnam). War with France would erupt in the south in 1884–5, intensifying the need for coastal defences. Thereafter no extra funds to be invested in Xinjiang were available; for example, the court refused a request by the Yili General for 1.9 million taels for reconstruction in the newly recovered Yili territory, and all non-essential work was suspended. Moreover, the court exerted political pressure on Xinjiang governors to cut costs below their allotted subsidy, and the budgeted 3.4 million taels did not always arrive in timely fashion, if at all.

The Boxer debacle in 1990 burdened the Qing and China for thirty-nine years with an annual 30–40 million tael indemnity to the foreign powers, which the court paid from both commercial and customs tax revenues and by docking provincial budgets. Xinjiang province, despite its perennial deficit status, was charged an annual 700,000 taels as its share of the indemnity payment. As a result of this and other budget cuts, Xinjiang's annual subsidy fell in 1901 from 3.4 million to 2.58 million taels. But in fact the situation was even worse than this. Kataoka Kazutada has established that the actual amounts forwarded to the new province after 1900 fell short even of this reduced quota, occasionally by over a million taels. In 1900, for example, the province received only 1.78 million taels; in 1909 only 1.21 million.[42]

The plan for a provincial administration and slimmed-down military deployment implemented in Qing Xinjiang after 1884, with its promises of more security at lower cost, was predicated on the potential to increase local revenues in tandem with Chinese immigration and land reclamation. However, the Sino-French War diverted funds that might have been available for Xinjiang's reconstruction, and the Boxer indemnity then halved the province's basic operating budget. This is one way in which the military and diplomatic pressure of the Western powers and Japan on the Qing directly affected the dynasty's security on the Inner Asian frontier. To compensate for lost revenues, after 1902 Xinjiang authorities increased tax rates and imposed a variety of surtaxes. By 1910 the total revenue from the land tax (*tianfu*) had quintupled compared with 1887; this was despite the fact that overall land area under cultivation during this period actually declined from 11,480,190 *mu* (about 1,740,000 acres) to 10,554,705 *mu*. Various commercial taxes, including internal customs (*likin* or *lijin*) also provided increased revenues. Local revenue sources had thus been expanded, but the burden on taxpaying farmers increased substantially.[43]

42   Kataoka 1991: 166–7, 182–8.
43   Based on a detailed analysis in Kataoka 1991: 189–94.

Land reclamation and resettlement

Though expansion of arable land and encouragement of Chinese in-migration were priorities of Xinjiang's reconstruction and provincialisation programmes, the results of these programmes between the 1880s and 1911 were mixed and somewhat unexpected. While there was an initial rush of Han population into Xinjiang, these migrants included many peasants temporarily fleeing the devastation in their hometowns in Gansu without plans to settle permanently. They were reluctant to homestead more distant sites with harsher environments, preferring Xinjiang's eastern and northern areas that were already relatively thickly settled. Furthermore, for various reasons, neither the demobilised soldiers from Hunan and Gansu nor the exiled convicts made good farmers. Many of the lands reclaimed in the 1880s were later abandoned, and for this reason the total area registered as under cultivation actually declined by the turn of the century. Xinjiang would not become intensively populated by Han until after 1949.

But there was an important demographic shift of a different sort underway in Xinjiang. Attracted by the fertile lands in the north and east left empty by the wars, poor Uyghurs had begun migrating from the south to the Yili area, Tacheng (Tabarghatai), Kur Kara Usu, Jinghe and Urumchi and even the chain of settlements (previously almost entirely Chinese) from the capital to Qitai. Uyghurs were also migrating, some with government assistance, to the nearly vacant lands on the lower reaches of the Tarim River, the Lop Nor area and around today's Ruoqiang. The walled city of Buchang Cheng was built in 1893 as the administrative centre of the area's growing population. In the first years of the twentieth century Governor Tao Mo acknowledged both this fact and the mixed record of post-reconquest Chinese resettlement programmes in a memorial requesting a halt to intensive efforts to resettle Chinese. The 'turbaned people (Uyghurs) have lived on the frontier for generations. ... Their bodies are acclimated to the land, and their hearts content with the work .... If we resettle a household [of Uyghurs], we will get a household's worth of results', or if the household is large, he added, two household's worth. The government would also be spared the sizeable expense of relocating people across hundreds of kilometres of desert from Gansu.[44]

---

44 Hua Li 1994: 215–18, citing Tao Mo, *Tao le su gong zouyi*, 2: 9–10 and 3: 10–11.

The spread of Uyghurs from the western cities of the Tarim Basin throughout the entire province is a Qing period development with significant long-term consequences. The Qing conquest and administration of Zungharia and Altishahr led ultimately to the belief by nationalistic Chinese that a territory known as 'Xinjiang' (New Frontier) was part of the Chinese motherland. However, the Qing imperial experience had an analogous effect on the sedentary Turkic-speaking population of the Tarim Basin oases, the group now known as Uyghurs. The Qing destroyed the Zunghars and scaled back the nomadic population in the north; it unified Zungharia and the Tarim Basin administratively under a single name and political aegis; it relocated Uyghurs from the Tarim Basin to farm the Yili valley; it promoted the conversion of forest and rangeland in northern and eastern sections of Xinjiang into farmland; it improved communications throughout the region. These factors, and the death and flight of many Chinese between 1864 and 1878, made possible the fanning out of Uyghur farmers and merchants from the south-west to northern, eastern and south-eastern parts of Xinjiang, where they had not dwelt in appreciable numbers before.[45] By the end of the nineteenth and beginning of the twentieth century, though the Uyghur population was still concentrated in the south-west and the Chinese in the northeast of the province, Xinjiang *in its entirety*, beyond just the Tarim Basin, Turfan and Hami, was becoming a Uyghur homeland.

Overall the population of Xinjiang was recovering from the turmoil of the 1860s and 1870s and resuming the pattern of increase which began in the mid-eighteenth century. A census taken in 1887 in the three circuits of Zhenxi-Dihua, Aqsu and Kashgar—i.e. all Xinjiang except the sparsely inhabited Yili-Tarbaghatai circuit—counted 1,238,583 people (including some 66,000 Han, 33,114 Tungans and 1,132,000 Uyghurs). At that time Han and Chinese Muslim numbers remained well below their antebellum levels—at the start of the nineteenth century, some 155,000 Chinese settlers (including Muslim Chinese) had lived in Xinjiang. The Uyghur population, on the other hand, increased rapidly through the nineteenth century, almost doubling since 1831, the trou-

---

45 Of course, from the point of view of nationalistic Uyghurs today, their ancestors include the nomadic Uyghurs who ruled and settled eastern Xinjiang from the ninth through thirteenth centuries, and the Qarakhanids who controlled northern and western Xinjiang from the tenth through twelfth centuries.

Buchang cheng, a walled city built in 1893 to administer and protect new
Han migrants to south-east Xinjiang (photo: J. Millward, 1992)

bles notwithstanding.[46] By 1907–8 the combined population of all four
circuits was in the range of 1,650,000 to 2,000,000 (the two available
sources disagree). Although these later figures are not broken down by
ethnicity, the bulk of the population (1.4–1.8 million) lived mostly in
the Aqsu and Kashgar circuits, which were predominantly Uyghur.[47] (On
Xinjiang population, see also 'The Peacock Flies West' in Chapter 7.)

Security

Military readiness was another aspect in which provincehood did not
entirely live up to the expectations of its early proponents. Military

46 Hua Li 1994: 218, citing figures from Liu Jintang, *Liu xiang le gong zouyi*, 12:
38b and Guangxu edition of the *Da Qing huidian*, j. 17, *hubu*. There are no hard
figures for the population of Xinjiang as a whole or of large subregions in the early
nineteenth century. Hua Li estimates that there were 620,000 people (mostly Uyghurs) in southern Xinjiang in 1831 (1994: 147–8), projecting by means of growth
rates calculated by Miao Pusheng.
47 Hua Li 1994: 219, citing Song Bolu, *Xinjiang jianzhi zhi* (1907), j. 1, and Yuan
Dahua, *Xinjiang tuzhi* (1910): j. 43–4.

forces in Xinjiang and Gansu did deal effectively with Muslim (Salar) uprisings in Gansu in the 1890s. But just as during the 1850s and 1860s, when the expenses related to the Taiping and other rebellions in China cut into the silver shipments on which the Qing banners in Xinjiang depended, Xinjiang's budget strictures after the imposition of the Boxer indemnity again contributed to a hollowing out of the Qing military in the far west. British visitors in the first decade of the twentieth century, who took special notice of troop levels owing to their perennial fear that Russia would annex Xinjiang, commented on the low numbers and poor condition of Qing soldiers throughout the cities of Xinjiang and Gansu. Their comments indicate a great discrepancy between paper quotas of soldiers supposedly stationed in each city and actual numbers present and able to pass muster. Budget crisis, corruption, opium addiction, the aging of the military population, and unwillingness of Qing local authorities to raise local Uyghur troops all contributed to this military unreadiness.[48] The military reforms that followed province-hood and accompanied the 'New Policies' programme in the first decade of the nineteenth century were primarily aimed at cutting costs through troop reductions, and had little substantial effect; moreover neither was the command structure unified nor the forces thoroughly modernised (despite some units adopting the moniker 'New Armies' after 1905).[49]

Commerce and trade

From the time of the Qing conquest commerce had become an increasingly important part of Xinjiang's economy, in part because the Qing personnel and growing local population needed provisions, and in part because peace in the region allowed merchants of many backgrounds to restore the Xinjiang region's traditional position as commercial conduit between China and India, Central Asia and, more recently, Russia. However, the commercial pattern changed in certain ways following the 1864–78 hiatus in Qing rule, with new Chinese merchant groups replacing those most active earlier, and with Russian traders gaining a predominant position in the region.

48 Bruce, 1907: 14–16; Skrine and Nightingale 1987: 143.
49 Skrine and Nightingale 1987: 156; Kataoka 1991: 333–7, cf. Zeng 1936: 406–11.

The principal merchant group in eighteenth- and early-nineteenth-century Xinjiang had been the Shanxi traders, whose family-owned businesses dominated the long-distance trade between China and Xinjiang. Shanxi firms ran chains of retail operations and pawnshops, and provided the remittance banking services that facilitated both private and official transfers of money. After 1879 these firms lost part of their lucrative tea monopoly, as the Hunanese-controlled Xinjiang government handed the loose tea business to Hunanese merchants (Shanxi merchants continued to ship and sell brick tea to Xinjiang's Mongol and Kazak consumers). A more serious challenge came from merchants from the capital province (Zhili), known as the Beijing-Tianjin clique or 'Eight Great Houses' (Ba Da Jia). These merchants had originally contracted to supply Zuo Zongtang's reconquest campaigns and used this opportunity to establish shops in each Xinjiang city. They linked the capital and the coast (Tianjin) with Xinjiang via the Gobi desert route and Qitai, moving such luxury items as dried vegetables and seafood, textiles and other manufactured goods. The Zhili houses outstripped the Shanxi merchants in the twentieth century after the silver subsidy from China proper to Xinjiang fell off and the Shanxi banks which had handled those silver transfers lost business. By the 1930s the Beijing-Tianjin clique controlled some 60 per cent of Xinjiang's domestic trade with the rest of China.

Another change involves Tungan (Hui) merchants. Many Chinese Muslims had been small-scale traders earlier in the Qing period. According to Zeng Wenwu (a Chinese historian of Xinjiang who wrote in the 1930s), after the reconquest and provincehood of Xinjiang, Tungan merchants developed more highly-capitalised businesses, extending their trading operations to Sichuan, Beijing and even overseas by the first decades of the twentieth century.[50] Some Uyghur merchants, such as the Musa Bay (Musabayov) brothers discussed below, likewise expanded operations to the Russian empire and Europe.

Russian trade

However, the most dramatic commercial developments in this period involved not Chinese but Russian merchants. Russian subjects (Central

50   Zeng 1936: 750–1; Kataoka 1991: 278–80.

Asians, and some disguised European Russians) had been trading in Xinjiang since the early 1800s, often through Kazaks who participated in annual trade fairs at designated zones in Yili and Tarbaghatai. In 1851 this trade was codified by the Sino-Russian Treaty of Ghulja (also known as the Yili-Tarbaghatai Commercial Treaty). This agreement allowed for duty-free entry of Russian goods into Xinjiang (and for this reason is considered by the Chinese an 'unequal treaty'), but it also allowed the Qing to monitor the trade more closely by restricting it to designated zones in Yili and Tarbaghatai where the Russian merchants were allowed to warehouse and exchange goods and reside for part of the year under the supervision of a Russian consul. For the most part the Qing exported brick tea and some cloth in return for Russian livestock, hides, furs and manufactured goods.[51]

Following a conflict with Russians over a gold mine in disputed territory south-west of the city, Chinese miners looted and burnt the Russian warehouses in Tarbaghatai in 1855. Qing officials quickly sought to defuse tensions; after negotiations with the military officer, explorer, scholar and modern Kazak hero Ch. Ch. Valikhanov the Qing eventually agreed to rebuild the Tarbaghatai trade zone and compensate Russia for lost goods. Modern Chinese scholars have portrayed this event as patriotic resistance to Russian imperialism, but trade continued to grow thereafter, with little apparent popular dissent.[52]

The rebellion and inter-oasis fighting of the mid-1860s brought almost all of Xinjiang's foreign trade, including that with Russia, to a halt. Russian trade gradually recovered after that, and from 1870 to 1871 more than doubled to a value of over 600,000 roubles. Russia concluded a commercial treaty with Ya'qub Beg in 1872, and trade volume expanded to a million roubles of trade thereafter.[53]

The treaty of St Petersburg (1881) opened Xinjiang further to Russian traders, with new consulates in Tarbaghatai, Yili and Kashgar the next year, and one in Urumchi four years later. Most important, the treaty extended Russian merchants' duty-free status. This proved a great

51 Li Sheng 1990; Fletcher 1978b: 330–1.
52 *Chouban yiwu shimo*, 1851–61: (1979): 11: 414–18, Zha-la-fen-tai memorial, 1 October 1855 and Ying-xiu memorial, 25 October 1855; Fletcher 1978b: 331; cf. Xinjiang shehui kexueyuan minzu yanjiusuo 1980–7: 2: 26–34, or Ji Dachun 1997: 118–21, for the official PRC view.
53 Kim 2004: 127–8.

advantage in a period when *likin* taxes were a major source of provincial income throughout China. Not only did Russian subjects (or those, including some Uyghurs, who successfully passed themselves off as Russians) pay no tax, but Chinese merchants who did pay were at such a palpable disadvantage that Xinjiang authorities could not levy the tax consistently without driving them completely from the market. Moreover, compared to Chinese merchants, who had to transport goods by caravan hundreds of kilometres, paying *likin* many times en route, Russians in Xinjiang enjoyed the advantages of geographic proximity further enhanced by the completion of the Trans-Siberian Railroad (1904). (The Turkestan-Siberian Railroad, completed in 1929–30, would provide still greater access, as it passed close to the Xinjiang border). Russian liquor, metal goods, fabrics, lamps, ceramics, watches, cigarettes and so forth were all much cheaper than their Chinese counterparts on Xinjiang markets, a fact reflected in the Russian-derived Uyghur names for many modern Western products imported from around this time through the twentieth century: *lampa* (oil lamp), *sharpa* (scarf), *pilati* (women's Western-style dress), *nefit* (petrol), *pechinä* (biscuit). The rouble circulated freely in the bazaars of Kashgar.

Russian merchants mainly imported raw materials from Xinjiang, including 60 per cent of the cotton crop from Turfan, the largest cotton producer in Xinjiang. Russian demand for cotton was great: in 1902 Kashgar exported some 1,350,000 roubles worth of cotton cloth out of 3 million roubles total exports to Russia. Altogether in 1902–4 the Russian consulates of Yili, Urumchi and Kashgar recorded annual exports worth almost 5.9 million roubles, and Russian imports to Xinjiang of 3.4 million roubles. The prominent position of Russian trade in the Xinjiang economy would continue until it evaporated during the Russian Revolution, and then pick up again.[54]

Chinese historians generally view the implementation of provincial status in Xinjiang in a highly positive light. In a recent synthetic history by several prominent Chinese historians of Xinjiang, Wang Xilong writes that after provincialisation 'Xinjiang's political and economic connections to the rest of China (*neidi*) grew closer, and objectively speaking,

[54] Kataoka 1991: 234–8.

for Xinjiang's socio-economic development and for the development of a unified multi-nationality state, the significance of this cannot be underestimated.' Advocates of Uyghur autonomy or independence, on the other hand, who usually cite 1884 as the date of Chinese 'annexation' of Xinjiang, are rueful, even speculating that if the Qing had not chosen to reconquer Xinjiang and the territory had fallen under Russian control, then Eastern Turkestan would be independent today along with the former Soviet Central Asian Republics.[55]

Symbolically significant as reconquest and provincialisation was, from the Qing imperial point of view it fell far short of its goals of tight integration and fiscal independence. On the eve of the 1911 'revolution' that brought down the Qing dynasty, the new Xinjiang province was governed under a Chinese-style administrative structure more intrusive than the mid-Qing military government, but which still relied on indigenous élites to manage local affairs. Resettlement of Xinjiang by Chinese had proceeded more slowly than expected, and mass conversion of local population to Chinese ways had proceeded not at all. Fiscally, Xinjiang government still depended in theory upon subsidies from other Chinese provinces and the court, though in fact the shortfalls in those subsidies led to *ad hoc* taxes and increased corruption. The military could not maintain its designated troop strength. The Faustian bargain concluded with Russia for the return of the Yili Valley in the treaty of St Petersburg left the province wide open to penetration by Russian merchants, thus severely limiting commercial integration with China proper.

LIFE IN THE TARIM OASES AT THE TURN OF THE TWENTIETH CENTURY

Though Turkic society was by no means stagnant or passive during the decades following Ya'qub Beg's reign and the Qing reconquest, our knowledge of what life was like, and how it was changing for Uyghurs or Kazaks in Xinjiang in this period is limited by the type and quality of sources. Uyghur sources are not yet easily available or greatly exploited by scholars. And Chinese sources from the late Qing period are not greatly helpful in this regard, as Chinese writers of the time rarely de-

55 Yu Taishan 1996: 485. For 1884 rather than 1759 as 'annexation', see the article 'Who Are the Uyghurs' on the Uyghur Human Rights Coalition Homepage <http://www.uyghurs.org/who.htm>, 2000 (accessed 17 August 2000).

Ferry on the Yarkand River, 1920 (Swedish Riksarchivet Samuel Fränne Östturkestan Samling, karton 142a ark 19)

picted local life at all, and when they did, tended to do so in picaresque verses or brief stylised and often cribbed passages in the local surveys known as gazetteers.[56] European writers were given to their own stereotypes. As was common in Westerners' visions of 'natives' or 'Asiatics' in the nineteenth and early twentieth century, British visitors to southern Xinjiang, and even George Macartney, the long-time British representative in Kashgar, tended to consider the Tarim oasis dwellers lethargic and apathetic. Colonel Francis Younghusband referred to them as 'the essence of imperturbable mediocrity'.[57]

While the smug racism of imperialists should hardly be taken at face value, there is nevertheless a clear sense that after the frequent bloodletting and palpable anxiety of the era of rebellions and Ya'qub Beg, the oasis cities of the Tarim Basin moved to calmer rhythms for the next two to three decades. Life revolved around the marketplace, mosques and *ma-*

---

56 For an examination of Chinese ethnographic and literary treatments of Xinjiang and Uyghurs in the mid-Qing, see Newby 1999; for a discussion of how Xinjiang travel writing and cartography was influenced by Chinese history and imperial agendas, see Millward 1999.

57 Quoted in Skrine and Nightingale 1987: 18.

Girls spinning cotton, playing dutar (centre) and dap (right), Chini Bagh
by the British Consulate in Kashgar, 1930 (Swedish Riksarchivet Samuel
Fränne Östturkestan Samling, karton 147 ark 17)

zars (Sufi shrines) as well as the low mud-brick homes with their shaded
courtyards. These houses were densely packed in the cities and more
comfortably spaced along willow-shaded lanes in the villages. Most Uyghurs had little contact with Chinese officialdom in their fortified 'new'
or 'Chinese (Khitai) cities' walled off or at a remove from the city proper,
except possibly for a sighting of the Qing Amban abroad in his sedan
chair, escorted by soldiers. Chinese and Tungan merchants—and gamblers with their dice and cards—were of course a presence in the bazaars.
And on rare occasions a legal dispute would have to be brought before
the Chinese magistrate, as when two well-paid rainmakers in Kashgar,
around the year 1900, produced excessive precipitation and were caned
and thrown in the Chinese stocks for their negligence.[58] The tax burden
was not light, but indications are it was less than under Ya'qub Beg,
at least initially after reconquest. Corruption was ubiquitous, from the
onbashi and other begs who collected the head-tax, sales and other taxes,
to the Chinese officials (such as the Hunanese ex-military officers from

58 Jarring 1979: 14.

Fabrics, imported from Russia, for sale outside Kashgar Chinese city (Hancheng) (Swedish Riksarchivet Samuel Fränne Östturkestan Samling, karton 145 ark 25)

Zuo's army). Officials often paid to obtain their postings and strove to make a return on the investment before their transfer or retirement.[59] The burden in taxes and bribes on common people grew in the early twentieth century, as the Xinjiang government's financial underpinnings became more precarious.

In southern Xinjiang, on farms irrigated with river water, many people grew cotton, which they spun and wove into cloth for export, generally via camel caravan. Others grew wheat and rice; vegetables and especially fruits were plentiful. A simple meal of apricots, almonds, peaches, grapes with flat-bread (*nan*) and tea was common, and was served as the standard manner of greeting a guest. Few could afford to eat mutton daily, but yak and horsemeat were cheaper alternatives, as was fish from larger rivers. Rice *polu* (pilaf or biryani) steamed with sheep's fat, carrots

59   In Cherchen *c.* 1904 the *amban* took 20 per cent on sales of goods in the bazaar (Bruce 1907: 14).

Old Kashgar, *c.* 1926 (Swedish Riksarchivet Samuel Fränne Östturkestan Samling, karton 120 ark 22)

and onions was a festive meal: the presentation of the *polu* crowned the all-night feasts held in rotation by men belonging to village or city-neighbourhood clubs known as *mäshräp*. After a night of eating, tea-drinking, music and dancing, men ate *polu* with the tips of their fingers from copper platters and rubbed the grease from their hands onto their boots before departing, just in time for the dawn prayer.

Everyone, men and women alike, came out during festivals, such as the ancient Persian new year Nawruz (still celebrated, despite the remonstrances of mullahs), or on market days to 'make *tamasha*': they would stroll about, greet friends, and see what was happening in the market-place or covered bazaar. In addition to foodstuffs, tea, hardware, carpets, furniture, notions, dyes, medicines and imported Indian or Russian clothes and manufactured goods, each in its own section of the bazaar, there were beggars, male and female soothsayers by the town gates and a variety of entertainments to enjoy. One of these, the manual predecessor of a well-known arcade ride, a tall pole with a wagon wheel mounted at its apex was driven into the ground. People grasped ropes hanging from the wheel and ran around, to be swung into the air as the wheel spun atop the pole. There was story-telling and singing, and musicians played while dancers whirled on a large carpet spread on the ground.

Sometimes there were animal acts in the bazaar—one man had trained a goat to balance on a platform atop a high pole. Another led a dancing bear on a chain. Someone else stood a donkey on top of a cart, antlers lashed to its head to resemble a deer. Chinese opera was performed in a tent outside the city walls; even Uyghurs could recognise Guan Gong by his red beard and fierce demeanor. On weddings and other special occasions young men would *oghlaq tartish*—play the 'kid game': a kind of all-against-all rugby on horseback, common throughout Central Asia (where it is also known as *boz kashi*), in which mounted competitors strove to seize the carcass of a baby goat and haul it over a finish line.

The spiritual world of the oases was active. Harmful spirits (*jin*), ghosts and the evil eye were omnipresent, especially threatening to children; remedies included verses from the Qur'an sewn into a cap or other amulet, musical exorcisms or simply addressing children in unflattering terms ('thief') so as not to attract evil. Many people took their requests for divine help to the *mazars*, like the Hazrat-i Afaq (Afaq Khoja) Mazar outside Kashgar. At these saints' shrines (see Chapter 3) people prayed tearfully for health, children or other miracles. The shrines were also pleasant retreats and gathering places, with a pond and shade trees under which to drink tea. Young men and women found ways to meet here, and this neutral territory was often used by matchmakers to conduct their business.

Formal prayer and services in mosques were restricted to men, but some women took part in devotional gatherings in prayer halls (*khaniqa*) with a female master to whom they swore themselves disciples. The meetings consisted of swaying, vigorous breathing, chanting, reading of passages from religious books and recitation of Arabic verses from the Qu'ran, followed by energetic dancing. We have a detailed description of such a prayer rite, as practised by men in Kashgar:

[In the] *khaneka*, a mud hut without windows or ceiling … men of all ages gather. The *ishan* [master] has a venerable position. His disciples (*murid*) present him with their offering of food or money. After they have assembled they sing religious hymns accompanied by stringed instruments, like the *dutar*, *sutar* [both long-neck lutes] and *kalon* [a hammer dulcimer]. Thereafter follows the wild music of the *dap* [frame drum] and the clarinet (*surnai*). When the music has stopped there follows a dance of an indescribably wild nature. They jump and run like veritable madmen. Many of them fall unconscious to the ground because of the exertion. In a circle around the dancers the other people sit rhythmically rocking their bodies and inhaling and exhaling with a noisy, snorting sound. This sound represents the words *ya-hu* [Arabic *ya huwa*, 'oh Him!']. When the dance has stopped food is offered whereafter they all lie down and sleep.[60]

THE FALL OF THE QING

Nowhere in China were the events of 1911–12 revolutionary in the sense of constituting a broad and deep social upheaval, or even a thorough political housecleaning. This was even less the case in Xinjiang, where the immediate impact was restricted to the military and upper echelons of government, and involved neither a popular movement nor great changes in the structure of administration. Nevertheless, with the fall of the imperial court and loss of a strong central power in Beijing, Xinjiang's subsidy from the imperial government, already attenuated and unreliable as a source of revenue, came to an end (it would be revived under the PRC). For the next thirty-eight years new rulers in the region had to rely on local resources, which they had freer rein to exploit, or on aid from Russia or the Soviet Union.

The 1911 'Revolution' in Xinjiang

The main instigators in Xinjiang in 1911–12 were similar to those in contemporaneous events elsewhere in China: revolutionary elements in the new army, working closely with secret society members. Zuo Zongtang's Hunan army included many members of the Gelao hui (Brothers and Elders Society), a secret brotherhood with eighteenth-

---

60 Quotation from Jarring 1979: 17–18; Jarring is quoting from missionary reports from 1907 and 1925. Instruments are pictured in Zhou Jingbao 1987. Glosses in parentheses are Jarring's; explanations in square brackets are mine. Zhou 1987: 413–15. In 1988 the ethnomusicologist Jean During recorded a similar Sufi or *Ishan* chanting ceremony in Yarkand (Smithsonian Folkways 2002: disc 2, track 19, 'Zikr'.) The section above on turn of the century life in Kashgar is based on Jarring 1975 and 1979, Skrine and Nightingale 1987: 17–20, the Pelliot photo collection at the Musèe Guimet, Paris, and photographs in the Samuel Fränne Östturkestan Samling at the Riksarkivet in Stockholm, especially those in karton 147 on folk festivals. Some of these date from the 1930s; others are from photos taken in 1905–7 by the missionary Gustaf Raquette, from the negatives of which later Swedish missionaries in Kashgar made new prints.

century origins and anti-Qing aspirations. There is even a story that Zuo himself was forced to join the society as a 'Dragon Head' chief before leading his army to campaign in the Chinese north-west.[61] Once in Xinjiang, the Gelao hui spread beyond the army through members who had been demobilised when some 30,000 troops were cut after the reconquest. Although many of these soldiers were given government support to settle and farm new lands, many were unsuccessful at agriculture and left the land. They then often turned to the Gelao hui and became involved in organised crime, especially the cultivation and selling of opium, which had become a major business in the Qitai region in north-eastern Xinjiang. Other, non-military settlers likewise gravitated to the opium business and the Brothers and Elders. The Gelao hui also recruited among Tungans and, according to future Governor Yang Zengxin, among Turkic Muslims as well. For the most part, however, it was among Han soldiers and new settlers in Xinjiang that employment and the mutual aid network provided by the Brothers and Elders Society were most welcome.

Revolutionaries worked primarily within the ranks of the New Army units, which had been created in Yili and Urumchi as part of the New Policies reforms of the late Qing. Yili General Chang-geng was a strong proponent of the reforms, and formed a new-style infantry brigade around a core battalion of New Army troops transferred from Hubei. In Urumchi (at that time referred to as Dihua, 'guided to civilisation'), Governor Lian-kui began drilling his troops in accordance with Western and Japanese models; the force was renamed the 'Xinjiang Army'. Both regions opened military academies and hired instructors from China proper. To command his New Army in Yili, Chang-geng retained Yang Zuanxu, a graduate of a Japanese military academy, who was secretly a member of the anti-Qing Revolutionary Alliance (Tongmeng hui). A dozen other revolutionaries with experience propagandising in the New Army in central China found their way to Yili with Yang after being driven out of Hubei in a Qing crackdown. Among them were Feng Temin (a.k.a. Feng Yi), a journalist and graduate of the Self-Strengthening Academy and member of the Society for Daily Improvement (Rezhi hui) in Wuhan. In Yili Feng and other conspirators involved themselves in various institutions connected to the New Army, and in particular

61 Quoted in Kataoka 1991: 298.

produced the *Yili Vernacular Newspaper* (Yili baihua bao) in Chinese, Manchu, Mongol and Uyghur editions. This paper was effective in politicising soldiers, merchants, Gelao hui members and Muslims in the region. In propaganda directed at Turkic Muslims, the revolutionaries drew an association between Zuo Zongtang's massacre of Muslims during the reconquest of Xinjiang and the famous Yangzhou and Jiading massacres during the Qing conquest of China in the seventeenth century. The implication was that although he was Han, Zuo had been doing the bloody work of the Manchus, and Muslims should thus make common cause with the Han to bring down their common oppressors.[62] Such definition of the Republican revolution as specifically anti-Manchu, a common theme throughout China, would require modification later, as the 1911 Revolution's chief ideologue, Sun Yat-sen, would discover: One could not easily denounce the Qing empire and Zuo's reconquest of Xinjiang without opening the question of whether the territory was rightfully 'Chinese'.

In Urumchi the leading revolutionary organiser was Liu Xianjun, likewise a Hunanese returned from study in Japan. Liu arrived in Xinjiang with a relative's introduction to 'offer his services' to Governor Yuan Dahua. Yuan first tried to assign Liu to a position where he could keep an eye on him, and then to pay his fare to send him back east, but Liu lingered in Urumchi, forging connections with Gelao hui elements and agitating within the army.

The mutiny in Wuchang in October 1911 and subsequent proclamation of the Republic of China raised tensions in Xinjiang. In Urumchi Liu Xianjun's plans for a coup were leaked to Yuan Dahua, who arrested and executed two of Liu's co-conspirators. Liu was forced to act prematurely in late December with only some 100–200 troops, and was unable to convince the rest of the army to join them. Qing forces repressed the uprising within days. However, after executing the leaders Yuan allowed many of Liu's supporters to return to farms outside Urumchi, and simply transferred others to southern Xinjiang. This had the effect of spreading the Brothers and Elders members and revolutionary influence to southern Xinjiang.

In Yili disaffection in the army had increased after the energetic Chang-geng was transferred to Shaanxi-Gansu in 1909 and replaced as

62   Zeng 1936: 532.

Yili General by Guang-fu, an illiterate who failed to carry through on his predecessor's military reforms and remained unaware of the corruption, inequalities and the degree of revolutionary sentiment among the rank and file in the army. Guang-fu was replaced in turn in 1911 by Zhi-rui, a strong Manchu loyalist and cousin of two of the Guangxu emperor's concubines. Zhi-rui was reportedly party to a secret plan to create a fall-back Manchu state out of Mongolia, Xinjiang and Gansu should the Chinese revolutionaries expand their influence beyond the Yangzi Valley. With Chang-geng, Yuan Dahua and others, Zhi-rui would then welcome the Xuantong emperor to carry on the dynasty from a new capital in Outer Mongolia.[63]

After taking office Zhi-rui discovered the extent of revolutionary activities in Yang Zuanxu's New Army and promptly disbanded it (he maintained personal command of remaining banner forces). Zhi-rui also demanded that the soldiers return their official-issue leather outergarments before travelling to their distant homes—in dead of winter. This order, not surprisingly, promptly drove the entire New Army force to the revolutionary side. With Yang Zuanxu urging action, in January 1912 Feng Temin and associates led the uprising. Virtually all significant groups in Ghulja (Yining) joined the revolt, including military units, officials in charge of the key South Arsenal, the Gelao hui, Tungans and even local Uyghurs. The last hold-outs, a division of Manchu garrison troops, eventually surrendered after Yang Zuanxu persuaded Guang-fu to broker and guarantee a truce in the name of 'five peoples republicanism' (*wuzu gonghe*). After executing Zhi-rui in front of the old drum tower in Ghulja, a provisional government proclaimed itself on 8 January 1912, with Guang-fu as nominal head (*dudu*) and influential ministries controlled by Yang Zuanxu and the revolutionary leaders.[64]

Yang Zengxin comes to power

For neither the first nor the last time, Xinjiang now had two rival governments, that of the republican revolutionaries in Yili, and Yuan Dahua's rump Qing administration in Urumchi. Fighting soon broke out

63 Zeng 1936: 533; Kataoka 1991: 342.
64 The above account of the background and events of the uprisings in Urumchi and Yili is drawn from Zeng 1936: 527–42; Kataoka 1991: 301–4, 333–8; and Xinjiang shehui kexueyuan minzu yanjiusuo 1980–7: 2: 307–16.

between them, with major battles occurring in severe winter conditions during the first months of 1912. Yuan's forces, including Uyghur cavalry, defeated the Yili army at Jinghe in January and February; but after Yang Zuanxu, leading his own troops, won a major victory in March, a stand-off ensued.

Already in February the Dowager empress in Beijing had arranged for the Xuantong emperor (Pu-yi) to abdicate, and Yuan Shikai had taken effective control of the new Chinese Republic. In Urumchi Yuan Dahua recognised the Republic and soon thereafter stepped down from his post. As talks began with the Yili forces to distribute power in the province, a complex struggle ensued. The Gelao hui, in communication with the Yili leaders, launched a campaign of terror, assassinating eleven former Qing officials in Zhenxi, Karashahr (Yanchi), Aqsu (Wensu), Kucha, Luntai and Kashgar in April and May. One of their victims, Yang Houyou, was Yuan Dahua's chosen successor as governor. Military figures who were also Gelao hui members began to take control of the south.

Meanwhile, former Urumchi Circuit Intendant and Commissioner for Judicial Affairs, Yang Zengxin (1867–1928), had quietly seized the capital. Yang Zengxin was originally from Yunnan, and had served as circuit intendant and district magistrate in Gansu and Ningxia before his posting to Xinjiang. There was a high concentration of Chinese Muslims in each of these places, and Yang enjoyed good relations with them. While Yuan Dahua's Urumchi troops were tied down fighting the Yili revolutionaries, Yang deputised an exiled convict, Ma Fuxing, to raise a force consisting of some 2,000 personally loyal Tungans and with this personal guard pressured Yuan Dahua into retiring and fleeing the province. Yang Zengxin then himself accepted Yuan Shikai's appointment as Civil and Military Governor. Yang came to terms with the Yili group, and in June convinced their leaders to accept positions in a unified provincial government. Yang Zuanxu, for example, became military commander in Kashgar, and Feng Temin became commissioner for Xinjiang foreign affairs.

Over the next three years Yang consolidated his control over the entire province, appointing fellow Yunnanese and relatives to many posts, creating a provincial spy network to report personally to him, and effectively eliminating both the Yili revolutionaries and the Gelao hui. He managed the latter task by first incorporating his rivals into the government, scattering them to posts throughout the province, then quietly having them arrested and executed one by one. It was a technique he would employ again.[65]

Hami and Turfan uprisings

In the last years of Qing rule, while the far west remained relatively quiet, the Hami and Turfan region in the east became Xinjiang's new hotspot. One cause of unrest involved the khan or prince of Hami (Qumul) who had assisted Zuo Zongtang in the reconquest, just as his ancestors had aided the Qianlong emperor's campaigns. As a reward, after province-hood in 1884 the Qing allowed him to keep the serfs and lands that had been his under the Qing hereditary politico-military system. The Hami khan oversaw agrarian, pastoral, religious and legal affairs for some 6,500 people in thirteen companies (designated by the Mongolian term *sumu*, arrows). He required *corvée* service of them in his fields and mines. The khan had recently greatly increased the *corvée* requirement from three to seven days per month, and his labour bosses forced peasants to perform a similar amount of private work for them, with the result that farmers had insufficient time to work their own fields. Another source of tension was the flow into the Hami and Turfan area of Chinese settlers who paid agricultural tax to the Qing authorities but were exempt from the *corvée*. In 1907 some one thousand Uyghur peasants converged on the prince's compound demanding to be put on a par with Chinese farmers, as rent payers rather than serfs of the prince. This unprecedented demand arose, no doubt, from Chinese migration, increased foreign demand for Turfan cotton, and other recent changes in Xinjiang that had problematised the old Qing system of differing administrations for different ethnic constituencies. (Chinese scholars writing from a Marxist perspective understandably highlight this event as marking Uyghur discontent at the 'feudal' society of the Qing. While Chinese historiography has been derided for its loose use of the term 'feudal' to cover the entire Chinese imperial period, in this case the word more or less fits the personalistic relationship of the khan with his *sumus*.)

The Qing helped the Hami khan repress the uprising and carted the ring-leaders off to Urumchi for execution. Despite some pressure from the state to reduce the *corvée*, the Hami prince successfully maintained

65 Kataoka 1991: 348–56; Forbes 1986: 11–13.

the *status quo* until early 1912. At this point, while the battles with the Yili revolutionary army occupied Governor Yuan Dahua's troops and attention elsewhere, Hami Uyghurs rebelled again. This time, under a leader named Timur, they successfully defeated the forces Urumchi sent to repress them, and retreated to a base in the mountains north-east of the city. The following year Yang Zengxin opened negotiations with the rebels, sending a commander of his own Tungan troops, Li Shoufu, as emissary to Timur's redoubt. Li swore on the Qu'ran that the Hami Uyghurs would be relieved of the *corvée* if they came out of the mountains, and on the strength of this oath concluded a deal whereby Timur and 500 of his men were incorporated into the provincial army as a cavalry unit based in Urumchi.

The Turfan oasis too had been restive. In early 1910 Uyghur farmers rioted following a bad harvest and price inflation. Armed with knives and agricultural tools they attacked and burned Han settlements, stealing grain, money and horses, before being put down by Qing forces and those of the Turfan khan. Two years later there was a similar uprising, which Yang dealt with as he had the rebellion in Hami: by co-opting the rebel leader, Mu-yi-deng, and incorporating his followers into the provincial army. Through such an apparently conciliatory approach, Yang successfully defused the situation in Hami and Turfan. In fact, however, Yang never forced the Hami khan to lessen the burden of *corvée*, and he kept Timur and Mu-yi-deng under close watch. Their men complained of mistreatment. When the Uyghurs conspired to rebel again in September of 1913—or perhaps Yang trumped up the charges—Yang had an excuse to round up and execute the two leaders and some two hundred of the Uyghur soldiers, thereby eliminating yet another source of resistance to his rule in Xinjiang.[66]

ISLAMIC MODERN EDUCATION

The events in Hami and Turfan centred on local issues concerning the economic well-being of Turkic peasants. Although the reference to Chinese tax status at Hami and the attacks on Chinese in Turfan hint at an element of ethnic awareness, these riots and rebellions in the early twentieth century were not attempts to throw off Qing or Chinese rule—had

66 Kataoka 1991: 357–8.

they been so, the acceptance by the rebels of positions in Yang's armed forces would have been ludicrous as well as unwise. Nor were these uprisings more than opportunistically connected to the events of the 1911 'Revolution' in Xinjiang. Unlike in Tibet and Mongolia, where the fall of the Qing *empire* led indigenous élites to declare their own national independence from a new *nation*, the Republic of China, there were no such élites in positions of sufficient prominence in Xinjiang to make any such proclamation, and no unified Uyghur response to the fall of the Qing.

Nevertheless, there were stirrings of nationalistic thought among more worldly Turkic Muslims in Xinjiang. This spirit is reflected most strongly in the creation of new-style Turkic schools in the province, a movement led by affluent, well-travelled merchants in several Xinjiang cities. There were various influences underlying this movement. Xinjiang merchants trading abroad had contact with progressive Muslim intellectuals and educational trends in Kazan (Crimea) and other Russian cities. There they learned of the jadidist movement for modern schools which in the last decade of the nineteenth and first decade of the twentieth century was challenging the dominant maktap- and madrasa-based Islamic education in Central Asia. In Ottoman Turkey, where Uyghur merchants also travelled, a similar push was underway for enlightenment through education in subjects outside the traditional Islamic school curriculum, including mathematics, history and geography. Moreover, merchants from Russian Central Asia, especially Crimean Tatars, were numerous in northern and western Xinjiang, thanks to the Treaty of St Petersburg. The connection between the madrasas of Bukhara and the *'ulama* of western Xinjiang is another channel by which new subjects and ideas for Islamic curricular reform, including the *usul-i jadid* (see below), came to Qing territory. And finally, the Chinese schools of the New Policies period, established throughout the province from 1907, brought their own version of modern education, ultimately derived from Japanese models, to towns and villages of Xinjiang; despite their limitations and the unpopularity of their Chinese-language focus, the challenge presented by these new schools doubtless had the effect of raising concern among Uyghurs regarding their own communities' level of scientific or 'modern' knowledge.

The earliest efforts to modernise the Islamic schools in Xinjiang were those of Hüsäyin Musa Bay Hajji (Hüsän Musabayov), a wealthy merchant based in Artush, near Kashgar, and his brother, Bahawudunbay (Baha' al-Din; Bawudun Musabayov). Hüsäyin had travelled widely, including trips to Paris, Berlin, Moscow and Istanbul, in the course of building up his trading company in Artush; he also owned a factory in Ghulja. Made aware during these travels of Kashgar's backwardness, in 1885 he opened a primary school in Artush organised differently from the traditional maktap. The first cohort of teachers was local, and included one graduate of a maktap in Kashgar that a few years earlier had attempted to teach modern science along with religious subjects. Hüsäyin later sent the local teachers to Kazan, where they studied at the normal college before returning and expanding the Artush primary school. The Artush school curriculum followed those of contemporary Kazan and Istanbul, influenced by the jadidist programme: language and literature, arithmetic, history, geography, nature, art, physical education, Russian, Arabic and eventually Chinese. Hüsäyin also sent talented students abroad for further study.[67]

In 1913 Hüsäyin sent a delegation from Kashgar to Istanbul to request a modern-educated teacher from Mehmed Talat Pas, who was then in charge of an organisation promoting pan-Turkism and pan-Islam outside Turkey. Mehmed sent Ahmed Kemal, who had been exiled from his home on Rhodes when the Italians took the island the year before and had since been teaching in Istanbul. By March 1914 Ahmed Kemal was in Kashgar.

Ahmed Kemal, working with Bahawudunbay, first attempted to establish a modern school in Kashgar city. Their efforts there were frustrated, however, by 'Umar Akhund Bay, another rich merchant, who feared the reaction of the Chinese authorities. Thus the new school, a normal college, was established in nearby Artush with funding from Hüsäyin and a charitable foundation to provide continuing support. As the goal of the new school was to train modern teachers quickly, Ahmed Kemal drafted a special cohort of students from local madrasas who already displayed a strong command of Arabic and Persian; they joined other boys from influential Artush families. Later the school offered a programme for girls.

---

67   Niyaz 1985: 80–1. Niyaz gives 1883 as the date for Husayn's founding of his school; more recent Uyghur secondary sources give 1885 as the founding year (Seyit *et al.* 1997, Tekin 2000). Niyaz also has Ahmed Kemal arriving in Kashgar in 1907 (1914 in other sources) and remaining in the Kashgar area in 1925 (he had been repatriated to Turkey by 1920). Thus Niyaz' dates are generally imprecise.

The pedagogy at the Hüsäyniyä Mäktäpi, or Artush Normal School, reflects both the jadidist curriculum and Pan-Turanian ideology then popular in Turkey. Ahmed Kemal used textbooks produced in Istanbul. Besides their courses in religious subjects, history and geography, the students performed a play written by Ahmed Kemal and sang Turkish marches. The school uniform was a version of Ottoman court costume, and students were told the Ottoman sultan was their supreme ruler.

These innovations disturbed local conservatives, including 'Umar Akhund, who petitioned Governor Yang Zengxin in Urumchi to shut down the primary and normal schools. Yang ordered local Kashgar authorities to do so, and had Ahmed Kemal and others involved with the school arrested in the summer of 1915. However, this decision aroused considerable local agitation. Moreover, Ma Shaowu, the new Prefect of Kashgar and nephew of Ma Yuanzhang, a Naqshbandi leader in Gansu, personally appealed to the governor on behalf of the new schools. Thanks to this appeal (and to a financial contribution from Bahawudunbay), Yang relented and allowed Bahawudunbay to reopen the schools, provided that Chinese language and physical drill were added to the curriculum—thus bringing their format closer to that of the Chinese new schools.

Bahawudunbay reopened his school, this time in the centre of Kashgar. Though the numbers of students reportedly declined immediately after that, the school and its Artush sister retained their influence as students fanned out to other communities to found and teach in new schools. Physical education apparently caught on in later years: Uyghur new school students won back-to-back victories in football matches against teams fielded by the Swedish missionaries and the British consulate. It was said that the British consul was so put off to see the European defeated by the native that he fled the scene without making good on his promise to give a horse and saddle to the winning team. Thus, with an opportunity to capitalise on his rival's discomfiture, the Russian consul stepped in to grandly present the Kashgarians with his congratulations and a new football.[68]

Several of the Turks who accompanied or followed Ahmed Kemal from Turkey to Kashgar wound up in various Xinjiang cities as schoolteachers, a fact which worried British and Russian consuls during the First World War. After China joined the Allies and broke relations with

68 Niyaz 1985: 85–6.

Germany in 1917, Ottoman Turks in Xinjiang lost their diplomatic representation, formerly provided by Germany. Yang Zengxin then brought Ahmed Kemal to Urumchi and kept him busy as a translator until finally sending him to Shanghai for repatriation with other POWs at the end of the war.[69]

In Urumchi, as in Kashgar, a similar mix of native and foreign merchants and intellectuals was working to promote enlightenment for Turkic peoples under Chinese rule, mobilising the same linkages between foreign trade, Islamic philanthropy and nationalism. In the early twentieth century there were thousands of Russian subjects in northern Xinjiang, including Tatars strongly influenced by jadidist modernisation ideology. As early as 1908 the Tatar merchants in Ghulja opened a school teaching Turkish to girls. There were likewise a large number of prosperous traders in Urumchi. Even under the wary eye of Yang Zengxin, Ahmed Kemal maintained a correspondence with this community, who provided him with Tatar journals and other materials. One of his correspondents was Burhan Shähidi (Shahidullah), the Tartar who would later become Xinjiang Provincial Chairman during the transition period between Chinese Nationalist (Guomindang) and Chinese Communist Party rule. In the late 1940s Burhan would espouse *Chinese* nationalism, but in the 1920s he and other Tartars in northern Xinjiang were concerned about the *Turkic* nation—Ahmed Kemal wrote in his memoirs that he and Burhan were collaborating 'to defend their nation against the forces of decline'.[70] We know from these memoirs also—though not from Burhan's own, published later in the PRC—that Burhan was a reader and fan of Ismail Bey Gasprinskii (1851–1914), the Tatar founder of the jadid movement, and that he published a journal in Urumchi entitled *Turan* (a romantic designation for the Central Asian land of the Turks).

Burhan and other local Russian Turkic merchants and intellectuals also directed their energies towards education. In spite of criticism from conservative Uyghur mullahs and merchants (often egged on by the governor), in 1920 the Turkic progressives in Urumchi invested money to open a modern school in a mosque and donated funds for tuition and teachers' salaries. The school, initially for boys but later offering separate instruction for girls as well, was nicely appointed with a small library stocked with textbooks, newspapers, journals and books on literature

69   Hamada 1990: 35–40; Niyaz 1985: 85–6.
70   Hamada 1990: 34–5; quote from Ahmed Kemal's memoirs, cited on p. 40.

and art. The school also ran a teacher-training course whose students included not only Uyghurs, but Kazaks who upon completion of the course returned to the mountains and opened schools in their yurts.[71]

Islamic and Turkic modernism was also manifested in, and disseminated by, new-style Turkic schools in Ghulja, Yarkand, Khotan, Aqsu, Kucha, Shanshan, Hutubi, Qitai and Hami. One of the most influential of these schools was that founded by Maqsud Muhiti in Astana, just outside Turfan. Muhiti, the son of a wealthy family, had been educated in maktap and madrasa before embarking on trading trips to Urumchi, Tarbaghatai, Semipalatinsk, Kazan, Moscow and elsewhere in Russian territory, where he encountered Turkic nationalist ideals. After 1911 Muhiti and associates sent representatives to Nanjing to lobby Sun Yat-sen for native schools in Xinjiang. The Nanjing Government's promises of support were never realised under Yuan Shikai. In 1913, therefore, Muhiti recruited a teacher from Kazan and started his own school in a deluxe (for the time and place) two-story structure opposite his home. The school was furnished with blackboards and student desks—equipment unknown in the rote maktap pedagogy but essential to the new goal of producing fully literate students.

This 'rebel school' incurred local opposition, so its male and female students were initially drawn not from Astana but from the larger cities of Turfan, Urumchi and Qitai. After the October 1917 Revolution Muhiti again travelled to Russia and recruited more teachers to teach in a network of schools he opened in Turfan city proper, Gucheng, Urumchi and Tarbaghatai. Several of these teachers and their students were later involved in newspaper publishing or held government posts; in the 1930s eighteen students from the tiny village of Astana went on to study in the Soviet Union.[72]

XINJIANG JADIDISM AND TURKIC NATIONALISM

From what little we know about the curriculum of the Turkic new schools in Xinjiang, it appears they were similar to the jadidist schools in Russian Central Asia. Besides maths, geography and natural science, they taught Islam and the local Turkic language as discrete subjects. As Adeeb Khalid has pointed out, Islam alone had been focus in the maktaps and

71 Mai-ji-te Ai-bu-zha-er 1985: 78–9.
72 Muhiti 1985: 91–6.

madrasas of Central Asia, to be taught through repetition of texts in Arabic and Persian, a mimetic practice which was a goal in itself. The new schools, on the other hand, fenced off Islam as a distinct discipline. Conservative 'ulama objected to this approach, which implicitly put Islam on a par with other forms of knowledge.[73]

There were many changes on the horizon in the 1910s and 1920s, all notable challenges to old ways. One traditionalist Islamic scholar in Yarkand, Ghulam Muhammad Khan, compiled a list of these dangerous evils, which to his mind all fell into the same camp by virtue of their novelty. His list included Bolsheviks in Bukhara and China (the 1920s Guomindang, whom he called *jadidi khitaylar*—Chinese jadids); the Turks who forced the abdication of the Sultan, exposed his harem to public view, and forbade wearing of the turban; and the Wahabbists who were now occupying Mecca and Medina, destroying mausolea, and prohibiting worship at shrines. Perhaps worst of all, Ibn Saud and his son were said to know French.[74]

Teaching about the Uyghur language and using texts written in vernacular Turki was another innovation, one closely tied to an evolving Turkic nationalism. At Maqsud Muhiti's school in Astana, for example, the students sang songs glorifying the national language:

> Mother tongue! Oh beautiful language
> the wisdom of our ancestors is its source.
> I understand much about the affairs of the times
> all by means of you—miraculous language.

Ironically, the lyrics of this paean to the 'national' language were in Tatar, not Uyghur.[75] This highlights the fact that that the jadidist discourse emerging among Turkic merchant and intellectual élites in Xinjiang in the 1910s and 1920s remained vague about the actual nature and locus of the 'nation' it promoted. It was not focused on a 'Uyghur' nation— popularisation of and identification with this term would come later. Rather, this nation was that of Turkic Central Asian Muslims, to which the merchants and intelligentsia, be they Russian or Chinese subjects, saw themselves belonging. Furthermore, a nation-state free of colonial rule was not an explicit goal of these educators and publicists in Xinjiang.

73   Khalid 1998: 173–6.
74   Hamada 1990: 38.
75   Muhiti 1985: 94.

If jadidism in Russia is any guide, the widely-travelled merchants who promoted new education in Xinjiang hoped primarily to modernise the Turkic nation and allow youth to function effectively in the current political and commercial environment—thus as the schools developed, they came to include Chinese, Russian, Turkish and accounting among their new subjects.

Nevertheless, it is not a long step from more general Turkic nationalism to aspirations for an 'East Turkestan' within the boundaries of Chinese Xinjiang: many of the leaders of the rebellions and independence movements of the 1930s were connected with the reformist educational movement of the 1910s and 1920s.[76]

76 For example, Hüsäyin and Bahawudun's brother, Obülhäsän, served as Commerce and Agriculture Minister in the government of the first Eastern Turkestan Republic. I have not been able to determine if this is the same Abu'l Hasan who travelled to Istanbul to find a teacher for the Artush school in 1913 (Tekin 2000: photo p. vi). Besides Burhan, mentioned above, Mas'ud Sabri, who would serve in 1947–9 as Guomindang chairman of Xinjiang province, had once taught at a private school highly influenced by pan-Turkic ideas (Shinmen 1990: 3).

5. Between China and the Soviet Union

(1910s–1940s)

In 1933 Dr Khalid (*né* Bertram William) Sheldrake (Muslim convert, Life President of the Western Islamic Association, Honorary President of the Islamic Cultural Union, Honorary President of the Pan-Islamic Society of London, founder of the Western Islamic Movement, editor of *The Minaret*, Honorary Ecuadorian Consul to the UK, and sometime leader of prayers at the mosque in Peckham) left his wife Ghazia (*née* Sybil) in their South London home to embark upon an international speaking tour. He reports that a delegation from Chinese Turkestan approached him at his Beijing hotel that summer and entreated him to be their monarch. He agreed, and Sheldrake appeared in subsequent newspaper accounts and speaking engagements across Asia as 'His Majesty King Khalid of Islamestan'.[1]

King Khalid never actually bothered to go to Xinjiang, and there is no reason to expect anyone there ever knew of his existence. But from the late nineteenth century through the mid-twentieth increasing numbers of European archaeologists, geographers, diplomats, missionaries, spies and other adventurers did. The Greco-Armenian Sufi, hypnotist, occult charlatan and Tsarist agent G.I. Gurdjieff chose Keriya and Yengisar as spots to recuperate from the death of a colleague and his own gunshot wounds, respectively.[2] Sven Hedin, Aurel Stein, Albert Van de Coq, Paul Pelliot, Count Kozui Otani and others reaped from the barren Xinjiang soils a rich harvest of archaeological artefacts to supplement the written accounts of the region's early history. These provided the first material evidence of the remarkable early communication of goods and ideas between India, China and the Mediterranean—a history of intercultural

---

1 Everest-Phillips 1990 gives Sheldrake's story.
2 James Moore, 'Chronology of Gurdjieff's Life', *Gurdjieff Studies* at <http://www.gurdjieff.org.uk/gs9.htm> (accessed 20 July 2005).

exchange captured in the term 'Silk Road'. Despite the turmoil of those years, Swedish missionaries in Kashgar and missionaries including Mildred Cable, Francesca French and G.W. Hunter with the Chinese Inland Mission opened schools, ran a printing press, took care of orphans, and found many welcome recipients of their medical, if not spiritual care. Agents of foreign governments, most notably the great gaming British and Russians, their Indian, Kazak and Uzbek proxies, but also the first field casualty of the American CIA, drew maps, learned languages, dined with local dignitaries, promoted their national products, and gathered intelligence from consulates in several Xinjiang cities. European travellers endured insufficient food, brackish water and the ever-troublesome camels to attempt extraordinary journeys (or, rather, journeys that were unexceptional in the context of Xinjiang travel but which sounded extraordinary when written up for European readers).

And they wrote many books.[3] These enjoyed brisk sales, no doubt because of their seemingly remote and exotic settings. However, the very fact that so many European, Russian, American and Japanese accounts of Xinjiang ('Chinese Turkestan') were issued between the 1870s and the 1940s suggests something quite different: that Xinjiang was increasingly linked to global events and trends. Expansion of modern communications (rail and telegraph) brought Xinjiang closer to political, commercial and cultural centres to the east and especially the west; the new ideologies of nationalism, modernisation and socialism inspired members of both Turkic and Chinese élites in the region. At the same time, Anglo-Russian rivalry, revolutions in Russia and China and two

---

3 A search of the books under Library of Congress subject heading 'Xinjiang Uygur Zizhiqu China Description And Travel' will yield a large number of titles from any good library, though earlier accounts are often catalogued under such names as Sinkiang, Turkestan and Kashgaria. Firsthand narratives of the late nineteenth through mid-twentieth centuries include Bellew 1875; Cable 1948; Cable and French 1942; Eleanor Lattimore 1934; Fleming 1936; Grenard 1897–8; Hedin 1925, 1931, 1936, 1938, 1940; Kuropatkin 1882; Lattimore 1930; Maillart 1935; Schuyler 1877; Shaw 1871; Skrine 1926; Stein 1904, 1912, 1933; Teichman 1937; and Valikhanov 1961. Kamal 1940 is a lively though highly embellished (if not invented) account of a trip to southern Xinjiang in the 1930s. Prokosch 1937 is spy fiction set in the same place and time. Hopkirk 1980 is an entertaining history of the European archaeologist explorers in Xinjiang in the early twentieth century; Dabbs 1963 is a more academic treatment of the same subject. Some more recent travel accounts are Davies 2001; Jarring 1986; Myrdal 1979; Seth 1983 and Stevens 1988.

world wars created a shifting political and economic context from which emerged new models for the region's political status. These included Chinese warlord satrapies paying lip-service to weak Chinese central governments, hopeful Turkic republics and satellites of the Soviet Union. Neither Chinese warlords nor Turkic nationalists could escape outside influences, however, especially that of the Soviet Union, and the region's political fate ultimately turned upon the vicissitudes of Sino-Soviet relations more than on the aspirations and efforts of local residents.

YANG ZENGXIN'S ADMINISTRATION

Yang Zengxin (1867–1928), the Yunnanese mandarin who took control of Xinjiang after 1912 (see Chapter 4), has a mixed reputation. Some have credited him with firm rule and successful foreign policy, by which he maintained stability during an unsettled period. Wu Aizhen, a Chinese official who served Yang's successor, called Xinjiang under Yang Zengxin 'an Earthly Paradise' where robbery had been eradicated along with more serious crimes. Even Sir Clairmont Percival Skrine, British Consul-General in Kashgar from 1922 to 1944, praises Yang for keeping tax rates low and for maintaining law and order, allowing Europeans to travel more safely about the province. Lattimore judges Yang 'an honest and a competent official by old mandarin standards' even while noting the pervasive corruption in Xinjiang and Yang's own schemes to bank profits in Tianjin and Manila.[4] Others, however, including PRC scholars and Andrew Forbes (author of the most detailed English-language account of Xinjiang from the 1920s through the 1940s) have condemned Yang as a 'feudal warlord' and a dictator who cloaked his greed and lust for power with a veneer of self-serving Confucian moralism. Yang Zengxin himself, despite a penchant for secrecy in most matters, certainly did not hesitate to demonstrate his particularly brutal form of governance in public, and to record and justify his actions in voluminous published journals. In fact there were fewer checks on his autocratic rule than on any 'mandarin' official under the Qing.

4   Wu 1940; Skrine 1926: 59–61; Lattimore 1950: 52–64, quote on 59. On Yang Zengxin, see also Richard Yang (1961), which is informative if hagiographic.

British consulate in Kashgar, c. 1935 (photo: Sigrid Larsson; Swedish Rik-sarchivet Samuel Fränne Östturkestan Samling karton 144 ark 43)

A bloody banquet

One famous incident sums up the cold-blooded real politic by which Yang Zengxin dominated Xinjiang for seventeen years. He later described his strategy with the adage, 'when a cat catches a mouse, the cat emits no cry; when a hawk attacks a bird, it does not reveal itself.'[5] In 1915, when Yuan Shikai, President of the young Chinese Republic, proclaimed a restoration of the monarchy with himself on the imperial throne, politicians, officials and generals throughout China opposed him. Yunnanese General Cai E launched a rebellion against Yuan, which many progressive Yunnanese military figures in Xinjiang planned to join. Yang Zengxin, however, did not believe the republican form of government suited China, and announced his support for Yuan Shikai. The group of Yunnanese officers in Xinjiang then began conspiring against Yang. When a Sichuanese officer, Xie Wenfu, brought the plot to Yang's attention, Yang feigned disbelief, calling in his Yunnanese subordinates to reassert their loyalty personally, which of course they did. Yang then had Xie Wenfu executed, 'to set his officers' minds at ease', and had them move their families into the governor's compound for safety.

5 Yang Zengxin, *Buguozhai wendu*, j. 6, cited in Chen Huisheng 1999: 157 n. 3.

Soon after, in February 1916, Yang invited the same group of officers to a Chinese New Year's banquet at the ministry of education. After a few cups of wine Yang gave a signal and his guards beheaded three of the plot organisers, Xia Ding, Li Yin and Ma Yi, where they sat at table. Yang then calmly finished his dinner. (Yang may have seen himself as a latter-day Ban Chao, the Han dynasty general who had staged a similar dinner party ambush while pacifying the Western Regions). Later the governor deported some seventy Yunnanese cadets implicated in the plot back to China proper.[6]

As discussed in Chapter 4, Yang came to power in Xinjiang by out-manoeuvring and then executing his rivals, including the Gelao hui, republican revolutionaries in Yili and Turkic rebels in Hami and Turfan. Yang's main goal in Xinjiang remained the retention and enhancement of his personal power. He thus at first relied heavily upon relatives, his coterie of fellow Yunnanese and a personal army of Chinese Muslims. He appointed a trusted aide, Ma Shaowu, a Hui from Yunnan, as Military Commander at Kucha. He put Ma Fuxing, a commander who had helped him seize power and another Yunnanese Muslim, in charge at Kashgar. However, Yang was also perfectly capable of turning on his allies when necessary, as the banquet executions of Yunnanese officers shows. For example, Ma Fuxing installed himself up as padishah in Kashgar, gathered a harem of Uyghur women, manipulated the local economy to his personal benefit, and hung the amputated limbs of criminals and opponents on the city gates. When by 1924 Ma Fuxing's vicious despotism threatened to destabilise the south, Yang dispatched troops to arrest and execute him in a carefully planned coup.[7]

Yang Zengxin also recognised that in a region with such complex local and ethnic interests, maintaining centralised control required patronising and balancing various élites, and allowing them, within limits, to enrich themselves off the territory under their control. Yang gave the Turkic Muslim local headmen (the institutional descendents of the Qing begs), nomad chiefs and the khans of Hami and Turfan latitude to enrich

---

6 Chen Huisheng 1999: 156–9; the most colourful account of this incident is that of Wu Aizhen (Aitchen Wu), who heard the story from a witness at the dinner party (1940: 43–4). Wu writes that only Xia Ding and Li Yin were killed at the party. Lattimore writes mistakenly that Xie Bin was present at the banquet; Xie was not yet in Urumchi at the time of the executions (1950: 53 n. 12; cf. Xie Bin 1925: 135).
7 Forbes 1986: 21–8.

themselves from their populace. Though his writings reveal chauvinistic views about the non-Han peoples of Xinjiang, he did not implement any new sinifying policies or attempt wholesale replacement of local and non-Han leaders with Chinese. Rather, he played groups off against each other, as, for example, when he supported Kazaks against Mongols and the conservative Islamic *'ulama* against the jadids.

Yang's isolationism

Yang was particularly keen to prevent outside economic and intellectual influences from penetrating his territory. Thus he refused to use provincial budget funds for inter-provincial road projects, and actively impeded private efforts to build paved roads linking Xinjiang to north China. He censored mail, kept tight control on the telegraph (Xinjiang's first lines had been built in the 1890s),[8] and attempted to keep newspapers and other publications from China and Soviet territory out of Xinjiang. After coming to power he closed many of the new provincial Chinese schools, allowing others to languish or to continue only Confucian-style education; he allowed conservative Muslims to shut down jadidist schools. Although his administration's dire need for trained personnel eventually forced him to open a teacher's college, a provincial middle school, and a Russian language political and legal academy, there were never more than one hundred students enrolled in these schools at any one time. Indeed, both Uyghur and PRC historians consider Yang's 'ignorant people policy' to be one of the most damaging aspects of his regime.[9]

In keeping with his isolationist goals, Yang encouraged development of Xinjiang's infrastructure and economy only in ways that could enhance provincial revenues. Thus he improved irrigation systems between 1915 and 1918, resulting in an almost 40 per cent increase in grain yield per acre, a total increase in grain production of 1.4 million hectolitres (cubic metres).[10] He also constructed a system of motor roads within Xinjiang and purchased a fleet of automobiles and trucks for transport. However, Yang did little to alleviate Xinjiang's shortage of medical fa-

8 Chen Huisheng 1999: 171 n. 2 for the development of the telegraph system in Xinjiang.
9 Bughra 1940: 375 cited in Tursun 2002; Chen Huisheng 1999: 172–81.
10 Chen Huisheng 1999: 162–3, citing statistics from *Zhongguo nianjian* (China Yearbook).

cilities or doctors and epidemics raged unchecked in southern Xinjiang from 1912. Only in 1917, after British and Russian consular officials in Kashgar complained through their embassies to the Foreign Ministry in Beijing, was Yang pressured into a belated and underfunded effort to train medical personnel. Yang publicly called for development of industry and commerce, but those enterprises that depended on substantial investment, imported technology or external markets, including iron and steel, oil and electric power, gold, copper and other mineral extraction, and cotton textile production, stagnated during the 1910s and 1920s. In 1927, near the end of Yang's rule, Xinjiang investment in construction and communications amounted to only 0.13 per cent of Xinjiang's reported annual budget, while the military took over 72 per cent.[11]

Yang's fiscal policies were driven by the need to cope with the chronic revenue shortfall that followed the fall of the Qing and the end of annual subsidies from China proper. Yang achieved some success increasing his government's share of tax revenues by eliminating abuses in collection. But as deficits continued, he also printed money: four separate paper currencies (in tael denominations) with different exchange rates circulated in Urumchi, Turfan, Yili and Kashgar areas. Annual deficits deepened nonetheless, and the provincial debt accumulated during Yang's tenure amounted to almost 50 million Chinese dollars in 1927. Although printing unbacked paper money did little to help with the persistent budget shortfalls and produced high inflation, the multiple currency systems did allow Yang to manipulate exchange rates and control Xinjiang's external trade. Yang's administration forced merchants—and even the Sino-Swedish geographical and archaeological expedition under Sven Hedin—to exchange specie for Xinjiang currency in order to do business in the province. Much of this bullion fell into the hands of Yang and other high provincial officials, who in turn shipped it to China proper and elsewhere. Yang himself reportedly opened a bank account under American protection in the Philippines.[12]

All of this merely demonstrates that Yang Zengxin was a warlord not unlike others of the same era in China. One important difference, however, lies in Xinjiang's distance from the centres of political and military power in China and relative proximity to Russia and the Soviet Union. While voicing nominal allegiance to the national government, Yang en-

11   Chen Huisheng 1999: 164, 183.
12   Bai and Koibuchi 1992: 122–4; Lattimore 1950: 58–9; Forbes 1986.

joyed virtual autonomy from power-holders in the fragmented Chinese state. He was less protected from influence across his other borders.

Impacts from Russia/the Soviet Union

Soon after coming to power in 1912, Yang faced a threat from newly independent Mongolia, where followers of the new Mongolian ruler, the Jebtsundamba Khutukhtu, massacred Chinese in Khobdo (Khovd), near the Xinjiang border. Yang reinforced military defences in the Altai region, and in the process consolidated his own control in this nomadic area. A little later, during a Tsarist settlement campaign in 1912–14 and a revolt in 1916, tens of thousands of Kazaks fled Russian territory for Xinjiang. Still later, in the 1920s, Soviet collectivisation stimulated a further mass migration from the Kazak Soviet Socialist Republic into Yang's Xinjiang. During each of these refugee crises, Yang negotiated repatriation agreements with the Russian or Soviet authorities. He also played the nomadic peoples against each other, arming Kazaks in northern and eastern Xinjiang to counterbalance Mongol groups and potential threats from Outer Mongolia.[13]

The October Revolution and civil war that followed it drove a total of 30,000 to 40,000 Russian refugees and armed White Russian soldiers into Zungharia, including defeated forces under Generals Annenkov and Bakich. Around twenty thousand of their troops camped in the Ghulja and Tarbaghatai (Tacheng, Chughuchaq) areas, plotting revanchist assaults on the Soviets, communicating with White Russian forces in Mongolia and causing trouble locally. Yang did not want his province to become a base for opponents of his powerful neighbour, whose historical designs on Xinjiang were well known. He thus attempted to close the border and prevent the White armies and refugees from entering. When that did not work (Yang had few troops at his disposal) he used his favourite trick of scattering his enemies and dealing with them individually over time. He invited Annenkov and his force to Urumchi where they camped in the old Russian trade enclosure; later Yang had Annenkov detained and eventually repatriated via China proper to Soviet territory, where he was executed. Yang invited the Soviet Red Army into Xinjiang to deal with Bakich's forces; an attack into the Tarbaghatai region drove the Whites

---

13 Benson and Svanberg 1998: 61–3.

to Altai; a second invasion defeated them badly. The remnants fled to Khobdo, in Mongolia, and the Red Army withdrew north. Yang thus dealt successfully with a series of refugee crises.

The proximity of Russia and the Soviet Union also posed challenges in economic matters. Russian commercial interests in Xinjiang had been growing since the mid-nineteenth century, and since the Treaty of St Petersburg (1881) Xinjiang's exchange of raw materials for Russian manufactured goods played a large role in the Xinjiang economy. However, as the political situation in Russia deteriorated after 1914, trade declined. The collapse of the Russian rouble undermined the Xinjiang tael, contributing to escalating inflation and fiscal troubles. By 1919 Russian trade had evaporated, with grave effects on the Xinjiang economy as cotton and pastoral products found no ready market and imported Russian cotton cloth, ceramic and metal products, sugar and fuel fell into short supply. Soviet trade picked up again in the 1920s, and Yang concluded temporary trade treaties with the Soviets even before the Chinese Republic had recognised the government of the Soviet Union. By these agreements, Russian merchants would no longer enjoy exemption from customs duty or extraterritorial privileges. Once the Republic of China and the Soviet Union had restored relations, Yang finalised a treaty (1924) allowing Soviet consulates in Ghulja, Tarbaghatai, Urumchi, Kashgar and Sharasume in the Altai. The institution of the restricted 'trade pavilion' was abandoned, and these cities were completely open to traders. For the first time, moreover, China opened reciprocal consulates in Alma-ata, Tashkent, Semipalatinsk, Andijan and Zaisan. Xinjiang's trade with the Soviet Union boomed and by 1928 had reached a total value of over 24 million roubles—almost ten times the value of Xinjiang's trade with China. Northern Xinjiang was only a few days land travel from the nearest Soviet railhead, so Soviet products were much cheaper than Chinese goods, which reached Xinjiang only after a three-month caravan journey. After the completion in 1929 of the Turkestan-Siberian Railroad, which ran parallel to the Xinjiang border from Semipalatinsk to Frunze (today's Bishkek, Kyrgyzstan) rail transport became relatively accessible to southern Xinjiang as well. Despite some trade with India and Afghanistan, and a continued small-scale trade with central China, Xinjiang was gravitating closer to the Soviet economic sphere.[14]

14 Forbes 1986: 28–9; Lattimore 1950: 59; Li Sheng 1993: 324, cited in Benson and Svanberg 1998: 64; Chen Huisheng 1999: 189–200.

Yang's fall

Through iron-fisted rule, a wide-ranging intelligence network and his willingness to use guile and violence, Yang managed to defuse a series of challenges to his rule over seventeen years, though the province was far from calm during that time.[15] His relationship with the Chinese central government was cordial, and he filed detailed memorials regarding the situation in Xinjiang and his policies. Nevertheless, he remained free from any substantial political influence from Beijing. On the other hand, his attempts to isolate the Turkic population from intellectual currents flowing from Turkey, Russia and Central Asia were less successful. To a large degree this was because of the relative openness of trade and communications with Soviet territory and the porosity of the border to merchants, refugees, migrant labourers, students and others. Finally, Yang's autocratic rule multiplied what Marxist historians like to call 'contradictions' among his ministers, officers and subjects, Chinese and non-Chinese alike. These would bring him, and the whole province, to grief.

Yang's downfall stemmed from political factionalism within his own provincial government. After crushing the Yunnan clique in 1916, he relied increasingly on a group of officials from the north-west provinces of Gansu and Shaanxi; a rival faction originating in Hunan and Hubei coalesced around an official named Fan Yaonan, a moderniser and supporter of republican government. Fan had studied law at Waseda University in Tokyo before coming to Xinjiang with a personal recommendation from President Li Yuanhong and an understanding that Beijing would like to see him replace the intractable Yang as provincial head. Yang allowed the well-connected and well-educated Fan to advance through a series of lower posts eventually to become the *daoyin* of Urumchi, all the while contriving to deny Fan any real power. Frustrated by this treatment, and uneasy under Yang, whose murderous treatment of other rivals was legendary, Fan submitted his resignation several times, only to have it refused by the governor. Yang preferred to 'raise a tiger' close by, rather than allow Fan to return to Beijing and tell tales of Yang's regime.

In 1928 Chiang Kai-shek's Northern Expedition defeated or co-opted the warlords and established national government in Nanjing under

---

15 Chen Huisheng 1999: 203–8 lists a number of small uprisings during Yang's tenure in both agrarian and pastoral areas, mostly directed at local officials over tax, *corvée* and other impositions.

the Nationalist Party (Guomindang). Yang immediately proclaimed his allegiance to the new government, changed his own title to match Guomindang (GMD) nomenclature and effected paper reforms of Xinjiang government structure. This was mere charade, of course, but Nanjing promised to take a more direct interest in Xinjiang affairs than had the various warlord governments in Beijing. Against the background of this shift in the national political terrain, Fan Yaonan decided to move against Yang.

That year, following the graduation ceremony at the Russian-language political and legal college Yang, Fan, assorted officials, the Soviet consul and the consul's wife attended a banquet. At one point during the meal Fan asked meaningfully if the wine was ready. A colleague replied that it was, and banged a wine-pot on the table. At the next toast, soldiers emerged and shot Yang Zengxin seven times. (The assassination took place on the seventh day of July and is thus known as the 7-7 Incident.) 'The revolution is not a dinner party', Mao Zedong once famously said, but Xinjiang history is thick with banquet *coups d'etat*.

Fan Yaonan failed to seize control of Xinjiang for himself. He and his supporters quickly moved into the Provincial yamen (headquarters) to take control of the seals of office, but were surrounded there by government troops loyal to Jin Shuren, Yang's second in command and Xinjiang Commissioner for Civil Affairs. Jin executed Fan and his supporters and appointed himself Provincial Chairman and Commander in Chief, positions in which Nanjing officially invested him five months later.[16]

THE DELUGE: CONFLICTS OF THE 1930s

Dissatisfaction with Chinese warlord government accumulated during Yang's long tenure and Jin Shuren's egregious misrule, Turkic nationalism nurtured in two generations of jadidist-educated students, and the eager intervention of Gansu Huis, White Russians and the Soviet Union plunged 1930s Xinjiang into a chasm of rebellion and inter-ethnic blood-letting. Though there is no single point of origin for modern Uyghur nationalism and separatism, this period is a major milestone.[17]

16   Wu 1940: 46–52; Chen Huisheng 1999: 210–17.
17   The rebellions of the 1930s have received a good deal of historical coverage in English. The most comprehensive and generally reliable account is Forbes 1986. Shinmen 1994 on the Eastern Turkestan Republic of 1933–4 corrects Forbes' in-

Governor Jin Shuren

Jin Shuren (1883–1941), originally from Gansu, came to Xinjiang in 1908 and rose through official ranks as Yang Zengxin's protégé. After coming to power, he followed precedent and placed his relatives and fellow-provincials in key military posts. As or more obsessed with security than his mentor, he nonetheless lacked Yang's self-discipline and—if the word can be applied to such a man—restraint. Whereas Yang printed 10 million taels worth of unbacked paper bills, Jin increased that value to 145 million to meet his sky-rocketing deficits. Jin raised taxes and added new ones, such as a much-resented levy on the butchering of livestock. He monopolised the gold, jade, lambskin and other industries for his own benefit, and exported personal profits to Beijing. Peter Fleming (one of the European travellers who chose these sanguinary years to pass through Chinese Turkestan), summed Jin up as 'an official whose rapacity was insufficiently supported by administrative talent'.[18]

Most disruptive for Xinjiang, however, was Jin's abandonment of Yang's careful balancing act with regard to the regions' non-Han élites, in favour of a return to the sinicising approach first envisioned in the mid-nineteenth century by Gong Zizhen, and which Qing governors had attempted to implement in the years after the reconquest and creation of Xinjiang province. Whereas Yang had followed early Qing precedent and co-opted indigenous élites, Jin Shuren alienated many of them with his policies. Besides such culturally inflammatory acts as banning Xinjiang Muslims from going on hajj, Jin sought to replace local non-Chinese leaders with Han officials. In one case he appointed Han officials to take charge of Mongol and Kirghiz nomads in mountain regions, sparking armed resistance. In another he attempted to replace the Torghut Mongols' ruler (a holy emanation like the Dalai Lama in Tibet or Jebtsundamba Khutukhtu in Mongolia) with Han officials. He

---

terpretation that this was an extremist Islamic state controlled from Khotan. Other accounts by historians or by visitors to Xinjiang who were caught up in the war include Nyman 1977, Clubb 1971, Whiting and Sheng 1958, Lattimore 1950, Cable and French 1942, Wu 1940, Teichman 1937, Fleming 1936, Hedin 1936. There are many Chinese accounts. Of special interest is that by Burhan Shahidi (Bao-er-han 1984), as he was later an important political figure in Xinjiang. My narrative here of the military and political events is based on Forbes 1986, Shinmen 1994 and memoir articles in Tang Yongcai 1994, except where otherwise noted.

18 Fleming 1936: 253.

also eliminated the status of the 'khanate' of Hami. This third move set off a conflagration.

As discussed in preceding chapters, the Turkic khans (called *wangs*, or princes, in Chinese) of Hami and Turfan (the Turfan khanate was known as Luqchun) had enjoyed special privileges since Qing times owing to their assistance in the Qing wars against the Zunghars. They held their territories as personal sultanates, with Muslim Turkic subjects owing them labour service as well as annual livestock tribute. Allowing such a khanate a quasi-independent status within the empire was an Inner Asian arrangement that the Manchus not only tolerated but promoted, as they had the similar domains of the Mongol aristocracy, and various non-Chinese chieftains (*tusi*) throughout the empire. After remaining loyal to the Qing during the great rebellions of the nineteenth century, the Hami khanate survived the administrative changes accompanying Xinjiang's conversion to provincial status in 1884. However, in the post-Qing period, Chinese rulers were trying to extend state power and replace the patchwork of local arrangements made by the Qing in non-Han frontier areas with regular administration, a process known as *gaitu guiliu*, to gain control of new territory and potential tax revenues. When traveller Xie Bin spent a few days in Hami in 1917, he reported that there was much 'unopened land' in the area, and suggested a settlement and reclamation programme in Hami such as the Qing and Zuo Zongtang's troops had employed. (A Turfan official had proposed opening such lands to Han settlement in the early nineteenth century, but the Manchu He-ning had overruled him on the grounds that so doing would upset relations between Uyghurs and Han.)[19]

Under Yang, and when Jin first took office, the khan of Hami (the Hami *wang*) was Maqsud Shah, purportedly a Chaghatayid descendent. In Qing times he had travelled regularly to Beijing for audiences at the Qing court, to which he also dispatched tributes of melons. He was fluent in Chinese, designed his palace garden in imitation of Beijing gardens, and dealt well with Chinese authorities, who provided a Chinese garrison to back up his Uyghur guard. He had his own staff to collect taxes and conduct other business in the city, which had a mixed population of Uyghur and Chinese and was a busy commercial crossroads. Immigration by Han and Hui, who owed only rents and tax, not Maqsud's

---

19   Xie Bin 1925: 78, 80. See Millward 1998: 288 n. 46.

heavy labour service, had contributed to resentment and rebellions by Uyghur subjects of the khan in 1907 and 1912 (see Chapter 4).[20]

Maqsud died in 1930, and Jin Shuren, eager to assert Urumchi's control over the large Hami district that commanded the east-west route into Xinjiang, abolished the khanate and in its place established three new administrative districts: Hami, Yihe and Yiwu. (The latter names were historical Han dynasty names for outposts in this general area; the replacement of indigenous Turko-Mongolian place names with historical Chinese names was a common practice in Republican period Xinjiang, one partly reversed by the PRC.)

Though there may have been some Uyghurs who initially welcomed the end of khanal rule and *corvée* duties, hopes were dashed when Urumchi immediately assessed double agricultural taxes for the first year after abolishing the khanate. To make matters worse, Chinese refugees were at the time fleeing into eastern Xinjiang to escape famine and war in Gansu. The government expropriated farmlands left fallow by Uyghur farmers, and gave them to Han settlers as 'wasteland' to reclaim, in addition providing the settlers with tools and seed and waiving their taxes for the first two years. In compensation Uyghurs received unimproved, unirrigated lands abutting the desert. Corruption, extortion and commandeering of grain and livestock by Chinese military forces deployed around the region by the new county governments further frustrated and angered Uyghurs.[21]

The Hami Rebellion, 1931

A Chinese named Zhang, the tax collector and police chief in the village of Xiaopu outside Hami, has the distinction of touching off the rebellion in February 1931 that would enflame southern Xinjiang. He coerced a Uyghur father into giving him his daughter in marriage, and while he and his men were carousing at the wedding, a gang of angry Uyghurs attacked and killed them. The mob grew, and next stormed the hated police garrisons throughout the county, capturing weapons at each one. They slaughtered some one hundred families of Gansu Chinese and buried the settlers' heads under their own fields—thus clearly expressing their feelings about the recent settlement of Chinese in Hami. The Hami

20 Cable and French 1942: 132–45.
21 Forbes 1986: 42–6; Chen Huisheng 1999: 243–7.

Muslim town fell as well, but soon a relief force from Urumchi forced the rebels to retreat to the mountains.

At this point the character of the rebellion shifted from that of a peasant *jacquerie* to a somewhat more organised movement, and adopted as one goal the restoration of the Hami khanship. This fact has given Chinese Marxist historians pause, for while they are obligated to view peasant uprisings as progressive, the desire to restore a 'feudal' ruler in preference to Chinese provincial governance is, from their point of view, most certainly reactionary.[22] Of course, historical materialism aside, ethnic concerns and fury at the Chinese warlord government adequately explain Hami Uyghurs' nostalgia for Maqsud Shah. The rebellion now came under the leadership of two former khanal ministers, Khoja Niyaz (? –1937) and Yulbars Khan (1888– ?).

Over the following months Jin Shuren gravely mishandled the situation, particularly in contrast to the finesse with which Yang Zengxin had dealt with the Hami and Turfan rebellions two decades earlier. After retaking Hami, Jin's military, especially brigade commander Xiong Fayou, gave no quarter, massacring Muslim townspeople and villagers in reprisal for Chinese casualties. When it became evident that surrender meant death, the Uyghur rebels in the surrounding countryside saw no choice but to continue fighting. Other dissatisfied groups, including Kazaks, Kirghiz and Huis, joined the rebellion. In an attempt to even the military balance *vis-à-vis* the provincial forces, Yulbars travelled east to seek help—ostensibly, according to his own memoir, from the Nationalist government in Nanjing. In the event, however, he called upon the services of a young Muslim Chinese warlord named Ma Zhongying.[23]

Ma Zhongying

Ma Zhongying (1911–?) was a product of the near apocalyptic devastation of Gansu and Qinghai in the 1920s. The region had been ravaged by earthquake, drought, famine, opium, floods of refugees and battles between Han warlord Feng Yuxiang and several Hui militarists, all surnamed Ma, most related to Zhongying. Zhongying (originally named

---

22   See, for example, Chen Huisheng 1999: 248–9.
23   According to Forbes, Ma Zhongying may have been covertly involved with the Hami uprising from an earlier point, and Yulbars' account of an accidental meeting with the warlord is unlikely (1986: 53–4).

Ma Buying), was a cousin of Ma Bufang, one of the infamous Mas who dominated north-western China. Ma Zhongying has inspired much colourful reporting (Cable and French call him the 'Baby General'; Hedin dubbed him 'Big Horse'). He seems to have emerged early as a charismatic leader, commanding an army ostensibly in the service of his uncle Guzhong in Qinghai, Gansu, Ningxia and Suiyuan while only a teenager in the 1920s. According to some accounts, Ma studied briefly at a Guomindang military academy in Nanjing in 1929 or 1930 before returning to Gansu and reassembling his personal Hui force. Whether or not he actually attended the academy, the Nationalist government appointed Ma 'Commander of the 36th Division', though the government in fact exercised no real authority in north-west China. His exalted title notwithstanding, by the spring of 1931 Ma Zhongying had exhausted his cousins' patience and they jointly drove him to far north-western Gansu. There Yulbars Khan found him eager to move in a new direction and lend a hand against Jin Shuren.[24]

In the summer of 1931 Ma's ill-armed cavalry force of some five hundred men accumulated weapons, recruits and notoriety from a series of successful engagements with Jin's forces on the westward road to Hami. Combining forces with Uyghurs under Khoja Niyaz, they laid siege to the Hami Chinese town and dispatched a sortie to take nearby Barkol.

Jin Shuren sent a force of one thousand men to relieve the siege of Hami, but Ma's force ambushed and destroyed it. His options shrinking fast, Jin called upon the Torghut Mongols in the Korla area for help, but they resented Jin's earlier efforts to replace their own Torghut regent with Han officials, and remained aloof. (Jin would later execute this Torghut regent—at a banquet.) Finally, provincial forces from Yili in the north, including 250 experienced White Russian troops, rode south in October under the command of Zhang Peiyuan and met Ma Zhongying between Hami and Urumchi. Ma was wounded in the engagement and retreated to Gansu with most of his army. (Missionaries Cable and French tended his wounds there.) Zhang Peiyuan relieved the Han Chinese in Hami, who by the end had mounted a defence with little more than opium, boiled leather, bales of wool and incendiary arrows from a

---

24 Boorman 1967: II: 463–4 has a basic biography, but all authors writing about this period cover Ma Zhongying's career, with differing details. See Forbes 1986, Cable and French 1942, Hedin 1936, Nyman 1977, Chen Huisheng 1999 and Yuan Dirui in Tang Yongcai 1994.

buried Qing arsenal. As was now the norm in Xinjiang warfare, Zhang's men took horrible reprisals among Muslims in Hami and the surrounding countryside. Surviving rebels took refuge in a mountain fortress above the old summer palace of the Hami khan, and for several months waged guerrilla war against provincial forces.

Rebellion in Turfan

During his recuperation, Ma Zhongying dispatched a lieutenant, Ma Shiming, to Xinjiang to fight beside Khoja Niyaz and Yulbars Khan. Many accounts of the period attribute further rebellions in eastern Xinjiang cities in late 1932 to this coalition. However, also deeply involved in the 1932 Turfan rebellion was a secret society consisting of Mahmut Muhiti (brother of the jadidist school founder Maqsud) and several others, including the son of the khan of Turfan and a camel-driver from Artush who gathered intelligence throughout the Urumchi-Qitai-Turfan area. In the course of the Turfan uprising rebels captured and killed the reviled commander Xiong Fayou. Soon after, despite Mahmut's suspicion of the Hui leaders, he and Ma Shiming jointly led a force in an attack on Pizhan (Shanshan).[25]

During the winter of 1932–3 rebellion spread quickly throughout the province. These events are sometimes depicted as simple bilateral conflicts, as Muslims against their infidel rulers, or as an ethno-nationalist revolt of Uyghurs against Chinese authorities. For example, a brief history of the Uyghurs that appears on many Uyghur advocacy websites states that 'The Uighurs, who also wanted to free themselves from foreign domination, staged several uprisings against the Nationalist Chinese rule during this [1911–49] period. Twice, in 1933 and 1944, the Uighurs were successful in setting up an independent Islamic Eastern Turkestan Republic.'[26] Although communal and ethnic concerns were important factors in the strife of the mid-1930s in Xinjiang, and certainly con-

---

25   Bay Aziz (Bai-ai-ze-zi), *Tulupan nongmin baodong*, in Tang Yongcai 1994: 55–60; Shinmen 1994: 5–6. Cf. Forbes (1986: 72) who follows Aitchen Wu with a story that makes the revolt in Turfan a more exclusively Hui affair.

26   Erkin Alptekin, 'The Uighurs', downloaded from <http://www.taklamakan. org/erkin/aliptekin.htm> on 17 May 2002; this article or similar versions is frequently quoted and cross-linked on other sites. The article has also been printed as Alptekin 1987.

tributed to its bloody character, the reality is complex and multi-sided. In fact, besides Hui and Uyghur fighting in concert, there were also struggles among Turkic and Chinese Muslims. Besides the Uyghurs and Huis, forces arrayed against the provincial government included Kazaks, Kirghiz and other Chinese commanders and armies. Moreover, outside influence and intervention played a role: the Nationalist government dispatched 'Pacification Commissioners' and Guomindang party agents, and muddied the waters by extending recognition and official titles to Huis who were themselves fighting the recognised Xinjiang provincial government. Ultimately it was the Soviet Union's support and military intervention on behalf of certain Chinese and Uyghur groups that proved decisive against both Hui and Uyghur rebel movements. (Claims of significant and substantial Japanese or British influence or support of rebel groups in Xinjiang in the 1930s are exaggerated.[27]) It was a time when ethnic, religious and political alliances were fungible; even the 'White' Russian troops in the employ of the Xinjiang government were by 1934 largely commanded and armed by the Soviets.

The events of 1932–4 are most easily treated by dividing them into two 'theatres': the northern and eastern region, where the fighting focused on Urumchi, and the Tarim Basin, where various early rebellions later converged in a struggle for control of Kashgar and the proclamation of an independent Turkic state.

Northern and eastern Xinjiang

After the fall of Turfan at the end of 1932 a coalition of Hui and Uyghur forces under Ma Shiming and Khoja Niyaz gathered in the Turfan, Toqsun and Pijan area, preparing an attack on Urumchi via the pass at Dabancheng. Other Huis approached Urumchi from the north. The Hui and Uyghur rebels fought frequent engagements with provincial troops, including the White Russians, under Sheng Shicai (1895–1970), the new Commander of Bandit Suppression on the Eastern Circuit.

Sheng, originally from Liaoning province, had studied both at Waseda University and at military academies in Japan and Guangdong before serving on the staffs of warlord Zhang Zuolin (in Manchuria) and then under Chiang Kai-shek on the Northern Expedition in 1928. A year

27 Nyman 1977: 75, 78.

later he was recommended to a delegate from Jin Shuren's government who was hoping to recruit officers in Nanjing to help reorganise Xinjiang's forces. Sheng took up the job in Urumchi in early 1930.

From January through March 1933 rebels attacked the Urumchi area and refugees poured into the city; food became scarce and disease rampant. Late in March the Soviet Union repatriated a force of some two thousand experienced Chinese troops who had fled into Soviet territory after the Japanese invasion of north-east China in 1931. As a North-easterner himself, dismayed by the Japanese occupation, Sheng established a rapport with this 'Manchurian Salvation Army' (*Dongbei yiyong jun*). With these battle-hardened men reinforcing the Xinjiang provincial force, Sheng Shicai successfully relieved the capital.

True to form, Jin Shuren managed to alienate these new allies, who conspired with similarly aggrieved White Russians, Han Chinese in Jin's own government and Guomindang representatives to stage a coup against him on April 12. Sheng kept his hands clean during this '4-12 Incident', and even executed the leading Chinese conspirators, but ultimately emerged as formal military commander-in-chief, and *de facto* ruler, of Xinjiang's provincial government. Russian exiles in Urumchi met each other after the coup with a play on a traditional Easter-time greeting: 'Khristos voskres, Sinkiang voskres' (Christ is risen, Xinjiang is risen).[28] Certainly Soviet representatives were pleased to have a vehemently anti-Japanese leader in charge at Urumchi.

Next, Ma Zhongying re-entered the fray in person, and Zhang Peiyuan, Chinese commander from Yili, turned against Sheng. By the spring and summer of 1933 Sheng in Urumchi faced Hui adversaries to the south and east, and Zhang Peiyuan to the north. However, for reasons that remain unclear, but which may have involved Soviet incentives, in June Khoja Niyaz, Mahmud Muhiti and their Uyghur army also switched sides. They declared support for Sheng and began fighting occasional battles against the Huis from a new base in Kucha. Despite this defection, by the winter of 1933 Huis throughout Zungharia were at war, and Ma Shiming had occupied the northern frontier town of Tarbaghatai while Ma Zhongying led the attack on Urumchi with his core force.

28 Forbes 1986: 105–6; Hedin 1936: 10. Chen Huisheng 1999: 253 claims Guomindang representatives joined the plot against Jin. Jin Shuren managed to escape Xinjiang and returned to China via Siberia. There he was incarcerated by the Chinese Nationalist government.

Southern Xinjiang

From late 1932 uprisings and rebel movements spread around the Tarim along two main trajectories. One branch of Huis proceeded westward along the northern edge of the basin from Karashahr. They joined forces with the Uyghurs commanded by Timur,[29] then in control of Kucha. Then Huis and Uyghurs, under Ma Zhancang and Timur, marched on to Bai and Aqsu, and eventually, after battles with troops dispatched by the Kashgar *daotai* (circuit governor) Ma Shaowu, entered Kashgar.

Along the southern rim of the Tarim Basin a rebellion which started among gold miners in Khotan led to the declaration of an Islamic government by Muhammad Emin Bughra (1901–65) and his two brothers, who had been organising for a rebellion in Khotan for some time. The Bughras styled themselves 'emirs' of the new state. Muhammad Emin was a member of the Islamic scholarly community and had worked as head of a madrasa in Karashahr, but, according to Yasushi Shinmen, he was also sympathetic with the modernising thrust of the jadidist education movement and belonged to secret societies working to overthrow Chinese rule.[30] The Khotan regime established after the rebellion extended its power into neighbouring towns of Chira, Niya and Keriya, and pushed towards Yarkand, where its army ousted and, with Kirghiz help, massacred Chinese and Hui soldiers in April 1933.

From the spring through the fall of 1933 the Muslim city of Kashgar changed hands with bewildering frequency. First, it was occupied in early May by the Kirghiz army of Osman 'Ali whom Ma Shaowu had originally commissioned to help defend the city. Soon thereafter Timur and his Uyghur army arrived, followed closely by the Hui force of Ma Zhancang. In this uneasy period ethnic affiliations trumped political and religious ones. Though the Huis claimed to be allied with Ma Zhongying, who had been warring against the Xinjiang provincial authorities for two years, they nonetheless rode to join the *daotai* (and fellow Hui) Ma Shaowu, then defending himself in his yamen. Later all Huis and Chinese would retire to the walled Chinese city (known as Hancheng, or Shule) a few kilometres from the Muslim old town. There they were

29 Forbes (1986: 73) calls this Timur a local Kucha leader, but Shinmen (1994: 6) links him to Maqsud Muhiti's secret society in Turfan. See also Bay Aziz (Bai-ai-ze-zi) in Tong Yongcai 1994, who mentions a Timur as one of the leaders of the Turfan rebellion.
30 Shinmen 1994: 6; cf. Forbes 1986: 83–7, who gives a different impression.

besieged and occasionally stormed by the Turkic groups. Then relations soured between the Uyghur, Timur, and the Kirghiz, Osman. Having by now already looted Kashgar, Osman led his men back to the hills in late July. Timur rode in pursuit but failed to capture him. Upon his return in August Timur encountered a regiment of Ma Zhancang's men, who killed him and displayed his head on a spike at Kashgar's Id Kah mosque. Osman returned to Kashgar, again attacked the Chinese cantonment with much violence and few results, and then once more sacked the old city.

Meanwhile, the Khotan regime had sent its own representatives to this busy neighbourhood. In early July 1933 Muhammad Emin's brother, 'Abd Allah Boghra, arrived in Kashgar accompanied by Sabit Damulla, a publisher and author from Artush who had met Muhammad Emin Bughra some years earlier while they were both returning from Mecca. Timur had arrested the pair, but after Timur's death in August they were released and opened up a 'Kashgar Affairs Office of the Khotan Government' (Khotan Idarasi). Here Sabit Damulla gathered Uyghurs and west Turkestanis with progressive views. In September this group metamorphosed into the East Turkestan Independence Association; in October Osman retired to his mountain camp once again; and in November 1933 Sabit Damulla proclaimed the foundation of the East Turkestan Republic (about which, see below). The constitution of this new state declared Khoja Niyaz 'president-for-life' in absentia, and Sabit Damulla and his cabinet emerged for a time in control of Kashgar, with Ma Zhancang and the Hui forces still holding out in the Kashgar Chinese city.

Soviet intervention

Jin Shuren had continued Yang Zengxin's pattern of relations with the Soviet Union, rebuffing Nanjing's attempt to take the 'Chinese' consulates in Central Asia away from Xinjiang provincial control, and concluding a new trade treaty with the Soviet Union in 1931 (only revealed to Nanjing a year later), through which he received some Soviet planes and other military and economic aid in return for lower tariffs on Soviet goods. Trade continued to expand between Xinjiang and Soviet territory, with Xinjiang exchanging raw materials (wool, cotton, livestock, hides) for Soviet manufactured goods. Xinjiang ran continuous trade imbalances with the Soviet Union.

Besides this economic interest, after the Japanese invasion of Manchuria and Inner Mongolia, Soviet strategic and political interests in Xinjiang also developed rapidly. Japanese pan-Turkic and pan-Islamic propaganda stimulated Soviet fears that Japan planned to roll on to Xinjiang in order to create an Inner Asian buffer between China and the Soviet Union. Rumours of Japanese military aid to Ma Zhongying and the discovery of a Japanese among Ma Zhongying's entourage (he also had Turkish *aides-de-camp*) lent substance to this concern. Should they take control of Xinjiang, the Japanese would not only have been expected to cut off trade with the Soviet Union, but to use forward bases to launch air strikes on oil facilities at Baku. Moreover, the Soviets did not like the establishment of an independent Islamic republic in southern Xinjiang, just across the border from its own Central Asian territories, where the religiously-inspired Basmachi guerrilla movement remained a recent memory.[31] Thus a first step in pursuing its strategic interest in the region was to facilitate the transit and repatriation of the Chinese Manchurian Salvation Army to Xinjiang. Once the anti-Japanese General Sheng had taken provincial power with the help of these troops, the next step was to save him and Urumchi from the Huis. In October of 1933 Sheng appealed to Garegin Apresoff, Consul-General in Urumchi, for military assistance. (A few months earlier Sheng had paved the way for this request by inviting the Urumchi Soviet consul-general in Urumchi to dinner and showing off volumes of *Capital*, *The Communist Manifesto* and *Problems of Leninism* on the shelves of his library.[32]) In January 1934 two brigades of Soviet troops entered Xinjiang via Ghulja and Tarbaghatai and quickly crushed Zhang Peiyuan and the Hui forces in north Xinjiang. After two months of fierce fighting, during which Soviet aircraft dropped chemical weapons on Ma Zhongying's forces, the Huis were driven from the Urumchi area towards the south-west. Xinjiang provincial forces pursued them, Soviet officers now in command of the White Russians.

As they fled, the Huis entered territory occupied by Uyghur armies. Khoja Niyaz had arrived in Kashgar to a warm welcome as President of the new Eastern Turkestan Republic (ETR) in January 1934, and his lieutenant, Mahmut Muhiti, revived the assault upon Hui and Han Chinese in the Chinese city. Units of Ma Zhongying's Hui army were not far behind Khoja Niyaz, however, and in February they attacked Kashgar

31   Clubb 1971: 280–4.
32   Bao-er-han 1984: 188; Chen Huisheng 1999: 299.

in the name of the Nanjing Government. After driving Khoja Niyaz and the government of the Eastern Turkestan Republic to Yengisar, Huis from the Chinese city recaptured old Kashgar and proceeded to slaughter the Uyghur civilian population: one primary source estimates 4,500 dead.[33] In April Ma Zhongying himself drove into Kashgar, where he delivered a speech at the Id Kah mosque exhorting the local populace to show loyalty to Nanjing.

Then in early July Ma Zhongying reached a very strange decision. He dispatched the bulk of his '36th Division' to Khotan, while he and 280 men rode across the border into Soviet territory in the company of Soviet representatives. They journeyed to Moscow, supposedly to undertake military training. He later sent letters, a voice recording and photograph of himself in the uniform of a Soviet Red Army cavalry officer to his compatriots in the Khotan region, but after 1937 no more was heard from him. What happened? A recent Chinese source lists three explanations in current circulation: He died (1) while training to be a fighter pilot (2) in the Spanish Civil War, or (3) as a soldier defending the Soviet Union from Nazi attack. A Western source suggests that Stalin simply liquidated him, but the case remains open.[34]

Khoja Niyaz and Mahmud Muhiti, meanwhile, having themselves made contact with Soviet agents on the border near Tashkurghan, moved on to Yengisar and Yarkand, where they found Sabit Damulla and a few of the other ETR ministers. Khoja Niyaz then took prisoner the very people who had named him president-for-life. Eluding the Huis on their own trail, Niyaz and Muhiti delivered the erstwhile leader of the Eastern Turkestan Republic into the custody of Soviet forces in Aqsu. Other members of the ETR government fled to Afghanistan and India. Sheng appointed Khoja Niyaz Vice-Chairman of the Xinjiang Provincial Government, and made Mahmut Muhiti Deputy Commander of the South-

33 Shinmen 1994: 38, citing Muhämmät Imin Qurban, 1983, 'Qäshqär tarixidiki Fewral pajiäsi' in *Shinjang Tarix Matiriyalliri*, Urumchi: Shinjang Hälq Näshriyati, 12: 167–81.
34 Exactly why Ma Zhongying chose to put himself in the custody of the Soviets, who only a few months earlier had been gassing his army, remains unclear. Of the possible explanations and accounts of Ma's activities after crossing the border, the one I follow here derives from a source with a good deal of detail, at least, behind it. Yuan Dirui, 'Ma Zhongying junshi huodong biannian' [Chronology of Ma Zhongying's military activity] in Tang Yongcai 1994: 228–50, at 249–50; Fleming 1936: 306 describes the photograph; See also Forbes 1986: 126.

ern Xinjiang Military Region at the head of a division of Chinese and Uyghur provincial troops garrisoning Kashgar. The remnants of the Hui army concluded a truce with Sheng and established a rapacious government of their own in the southern Tarim Oases under Ma Zhongying's half brother, Ma Hushan.[35] Sheng kept Muhiti under close watch, and in various ways chipped away at his authority. In 1937, when Muhiti fled to Afghanistan and Uyghurs and Huis in the south rose up again, Sheng called on Soviet troops to repress both the Uyghurs and the independent Huis, thereby securing control over the whole province.

THE EASTERN TURKESTAN REPUBLIC, 1933–4

The establishment of the Eastern Turkestan Republic, or Eastern Turkestan Islamic Republic, in Kashgar on 12 November 1933 was an event of great historical moment in the development of Uyghur nationalism. It is also an ambiguous one, due to confusion over exactly how 'Islamic' the state was intended to be; due to its odd gesture in appointing as its President Khoja Niyaz, the former vizier of the khan of Hami and present ally of the provincial warlord; and because the government was destroyed by Ma Zhongying's Huis before it had much chance to develop.

Politicised Chinese sources now routinely equate Uyghur separatism with religious extremism and foreign incitement. For example, a document released in early 2002 by the State Information Council of the PRC claims that 'in the beginning of the twentieth century, a handful of fanatical Xinjiang separatists and extremist religious elements fabricated the myth of "East Turkestan" in light of the sophistries and fallacies created by the old [European] colonialists.' This is clearly propaganda, but the main account of the period in English also stresses Islamic aspects of the 1933–4 Eastern Turkestan Republic, arguing that it was inspired and controlled from Khotan by the madrasa teacher Muhammad Emin Bughra, and pointing out that after the Khotan rebellion, the new regime in that city mistreated Christian missionaries.[36]

Shinmen Yasushi presents a different picture in a study based on various Uyghur-language publications, Eastern Turkestan Republic documents, contemporary memoirs and British consular reports from

---

35 Travels through 'Tungganistan', as some have called this regime, are the subject of a large part of Peter Fleming's *News From Tartary* (1936).
36 PRC State Council Information Office 2002; Forbes 1986: 83–9 *passim*.

Soldiers of the Eastern Turkestan Republic, *c.* 1933–4 (Swedish Riksar-chivet Samuel Fränne Östturkestan Samling, karton 148 ark 37)

Kashgar.[37] He argues that the Republic, as reflected in its constitution, was founded not only on Islam, but on the modernising, nationalistic ideals of the jadidist movement of the 1910s and 1920s. Indeed, this ambiguous nature is reflected in confusion over the names used for the new state: although some primary sources refer to this proclaimed state as the 'Eastern Turkestan *Islamic* Republic', in other places, including the constitution itself, it is simply called 'Eastern Turkestan Republic'.[38]

37   Shinmen 1994 is based in part on a thorough reading of the print-runs of *Shärqi Türkistan Hayati* (Eastern Turkestan Life), *Erkin Türkistan* (Free Turkestan) and *Istiqlal* (Independence). The latter journal published the constitution of the Eastern Turkestan Republic. These materials, preserved by the Swedish scholar Gunnar Jarring, are archived in Lund. The Library of Congress has microfilms of part of the collection.

38   This ambiguity in references to the 1933–4 state by Uyghurs continues. The passage from Erkin Alptekin's 'The Uyghurs' quoted above refers to 'an independent Islamic Eastern Turkestan Republic', where it is published on the website <www.taklamakan.org> and in the print version (Alptekin 1987). However, on the East Turkestan page of the website of the Unrepresented Nations and People's Organisation (UNPO), based in The Hague, the same passage appears without the word

There was also ethno-nationalistic ambiguity: the new government struck its first copper coins in the name of the Republic of Uyghuristan (*Uyghuristan Jumhuriyiti*), but later coins and passports were labelled 'Eastern Turkestan Republic'.[39] According to one man present at the time, the government decided upon 'Eastern Turkestan Republic' only after some debate, on the grounds that there were other Turkic peoples besides Uyghurs in Xinjiang and in the newly established government.[40]

This confusion over the ethno-religious identity of the new state may stem from the nascent government's precarious position betwixt the Khotan emirs, the Hui armies and the pro-Soviet provincial government. In any case, Shinmen's analysis of the membership of the East Turkestan Independence Association and the subsequent leadership of the (Islamic) Republic of Eastern Turkestan is revealing. One would expect that if Muhammad Emin Bughra was behind the independence movement much of its leadership would come from Khotan; in fact only a few did. Rather, a high percentage of the ETR leaders were educators or rich merchants from the Kashgar-Artush area and had been associated with the 'Uyghur enlightenment' movement of the 1910s–1920s. These included, first of all, Prime Minister Sabit Damulla himself, whose Artush publishing business had been shut down by Yang Zengxin. Another was Abuhasan, Minister of Agriculture, said to be the younger brother of the merchant industrialist Musa Bay brothers who founded the first jadidist schools in Artush and Kashgar. The Minister of *Waqf* Affairs (mosque and shrine endowments), Shams al-Din Damulla, was formerly a teacher in the Artush schools, and is mentioned in the memoir of Ahmed Kemal (the Turkish consultant brought in by Hüsäyin Musa Bay) as a progressive participant in the modern education programme of the 1910s . The Turfan jadid educational movement launched by the international trader Maqsud Muhiti was also represented in the Kashgar Republic: Yunus Beg, a peasant from Turfan, had been the secretary of Maqsud's secret organisation, and held the post of Minister of Internal Affairs in the Republic. Later, of course, Maqsud's brother, Mahmud, also briefly held an ETR position.[41]

'Islamic' (<www.unpo.org/member/eturk/eturk.html>, accessed 20 May 2002).

39   Shinmen 1994; Abduqadir 1986: 60–2; Chen Huisheng 1999: 283.

40   Personal communication with Nabijan Tursun, who obtained the information from an interview with Gholamidin Pahta.

41   Shinmen 1994: 7–9, 15.

Besides this prosopographic evidence, further indication of the found-ers' vision for the Eastern Turkestan Republic can be adduced from the political theatre surrounding the declaration of independence on 12 November 1933. Some 7,000 troops and 13,000 people, prominent-ly featuring students and teachers from local schools, attended a mass rally on the Tumen river. The streets around the area were festooned with blue banners reading 'Eastern Turkestan Islamic Republic'. Sabit Damulla presided over a rally at which the principal ministers delivered speeches; at noon a cannon was fired forty-one times, and the crowd waved Eastern Turkestan flags and shouted 'Amen, amen!' The students of the Normal College then sang a song with the lyrics, 'Our flag is a blue flag, our horde (*orda*, i.e. our people, our khanate) is a golden horde, Turkestan is the homeland of our Turk people, it has become ours.'

Following the ceremony Sabit Damulla led a parade back into town, where the crowd reassembled in the square before the Id Kah mosque at the centre of old Kashgar. Here the leaders gave more speeches from the roof and minaret of the mosque. A published programme of the day's events, including the formal proclamation of the Eastern Turkestan Re-public, pledged the new government to the goals of restoring peace and security, and included assurances to foreigners in Kashgar that the new government would not interfere in their activities. The proclamation invokes God at the beginning and end (somewhat less frequently than an average US presidential inaugural address), but the document's tone is not religious overall. Shinmen points out that the techniques of mass mobilisation utilised here were unprecedented in the region's history. Although people had been roused to rebellion and holy war in the past, the promulgation of printed speeches and political promises, parading of school children and soldiers, and the introduction of a national flag and anthem all draw from the repertoire of modern nationalism.[42]

The constitution of the 'Eastern Turkestan Republic'[43] (the name used in the constitution title itself) likewise reflects modernising, nationalis-tic ideology, while nonetheless highlighting the Islamic character of the East Turkestan nationhood then in the process of conception. In its first

42   Shinmen 1994: 11–13.
43   A copy of the constitution, printed in the journal *Istiqlal*, is held in the Jar-ring collection at the Lund University Library, ref. no. PFK 1933.1. My thanks to Eric Nicander, Deputy Keeper of Manuscripts, for locating this reference. Shinmen 1994 analyses the constitution.

Cover of the 1933 publication *Istiqlal*, which contains
the proposed political programme of the Eastern Turkestan government in Kashgar (Lund University Library,
Jarring Collection, PFK 1933: 1)

clauses the constitution announces that the new state is founded and will
govern in accordance with *shari'ah*; the next clauses stress the new government's democratic character and state that it is to be a republic. Taken
as a whole the document underlines the reformist and developmental
goals of the founders, emphasising the importance of education, promising to support foreign study, recruit foreign specialists, create libraries
and promote publishing; there is a similar approach to the medical and
other infrastructures. The state defined in this constitution would no
doubt have been highly centralised; despite vague references, the national assembly was not defined in the same detail as were the central
executive organs; in particular, there were no indications as to how and
when this assembly would be convened. Likewise, the document pro-

vides few specifics about local government or local representative bodies within the region claimed by the state (which in theory encompassed Aqsu, Kashgar and Khotan).

Of course, with few resources to carry out any of its ambitious goals, the new government focused mainly on survival. Military requisitions, the printing of new paper currency (with cooperation of the Swedish mission, which ran the only press in town) and the looming threat from the Hui and Soviet armies all contributed to runaway inflation. Food prices doubled between October and December 1933. The new government, moreover, failed to receive international recognition or help from any foreign source. From Turkey came professions of solidarity, but no military or economic aid. The Soviet Union actively opposed this independent Turkic or Islamic Republic on its doorstep. Although Chinese sources routinely assert that Britain supported the ETR, and historians have found evidence of contacts, interest and even enthusiasm for Sabit's government on the part of the British consulate in Kashgar, they have found no evidence of material support. Rather, it appears that concern on the part of both the Indian government and London not to harm relations with the Nationalist Chinese government was a restraining factor.[44] Nanjing, of course, denied the legitimacy of the ETR, and continued to recognise Ma Zhongying, Ma Zhancang and other Chinese Muslims as well as Sheng Shicai as its official representatives in Xinjiang, despite the fact that Nanjing had no real control over these figures, who were in any case busily savaging each other and the people of the province. (In retrospect, of course, the policy of defiantly maintaining their claims to Xinjiang through thick and thin, even absent any real influence or monetary investment, proved successful for the Chinese government).

THE SHENG SHICAI ERA

Sheng became beholden to Soviet economic as well as military aid. He negotiated two loans totalling 7.5 million gold roubles to develop Xin-

---

44 In their close studies of the period, neither Wang Ke nor Shinmen found any evidence of British aid; in addition, Shinmen points out that while Sabit Damulla and the East Turkestan Independence Association was planning the ETR in September and October of 1933, there was no British consul-general in residence in Kashgar, Fitzmorris having left Kashgar on 25 September, and his replacement Thompson-Glover not arriving until 29 October. Shinmen 1994: 29–30.

jiang, especially its communications and extractive industries; he also used the funds to purchase weapons. In so doing he all but mortgaged his government and Xinjiang to Stalin. The Soviet Union gained valuable concessions to Xinjiang's gold, tungsten, manganese, tin, uranium and other minerals in rich supply in Zungharia, and soon began mining and exporting these resources. Soviet engineers opened the Dushanzi oil fields at Wusu, north-west of Urumchi. Large-scale survey teams and hundreds of Soviet military, economic, political and technical advisers came to Xinjiang; Soviet personnel penetrated the Xinjiang military and helped organise Sheng's various security agencies (secret police) along KGB lines; A Soviet NKVD regiment was stationed near Hami as a defence against the feared Japanese invasion.[45] Guomindang partisans and the Japanese complained that Sheng's Xinjiang was 'going red'.[46]

Ethnic policies under Sheng

Taking his cues from the Soviets, Sheng gave the Xinjiang government a public posture that involved non-Han groups more prominently than had his Qing and immediate post-Qing predecessors. Soviet policy towards the many non-Russian peoples of the Soviet Union was to categorise them and promote aspects of their cultural and even political identity, while working in other ways (such as gerrymandering the boundaries of their 'republics') to undermine separatist and nationalistic impulses. Sheng brought Stalinist-type ethnic taxonomy to Xinjiang, the same approach the PRC would later apply to minorities throughout China.

A few words about how the Nationalist Chinese regime conceived China's ethnic diversity will underscore the significance of Sheng's shift. Sun Yat-sen had considered nomad and sedentary, Chinese and Turkic Muslims all as one 'race' in his scheme of the 'five races of China'—Han, Manchu, Mongol, Tibetan and Hui (Muslim—oddly translated as 'Tartar' in English versions of Sun's speeches). Chiang Kai-shek's version, expounded in his book *China's Destiny* (*Zhongguo zhi mingyun*) and serving as official line in the 1940s, employed the same five categories. However, in a bizarre marriage of ancient mythology and modern racialist thinking, Chiang argued that they were all actually offshoots of the original

45 Benson 1990: 21–2; Chen Huisheng 1999: 297; Forbes 1986: 136, 144–52; Lattimore 1950: 75.
46 Chen Huisheng 1999: 299.

Chinese stock, all descendents of the Yellow Emperor, which had di-
verged only by unfortunate accidents of geography and history.[47]

Under Soviet influence Sheng departed from Guomindang ideology
to recognise fourteen ethnic categories in Xinjiang: Uyghur, Taranchi,
Kazak, Kirghiz, Uzbek, Tatar, Tajik, Manchu, Sibe (Xibo), Solon, Han,
Hui (Tungan or Chinese Muslim), Mongol and Russian. This represented the first time 'Uyghur' entered official and common use to apply to
the Turki-speaking, non-nomad population of southern Xinjiang, while
continuing the use of 'Taranchi' for people in north Xinjiang who call
themselves Uyghur today. Russian Orientalist scholars in the late nineteenth century had proposed that the Muslim inhabitants of the Xinjiang oases were Uyghur by virtue of descent from the Turfan Uyghur
kingdom and the Qarakhanids. Starting in the 1910s Uyghurs in Tsarist
and Soviet-controlled Ferghana and Semirech'e embraced this historical
connection, and at a 1921 conference in Tashkent, 'The Organisation
of Workers and Farmers of Altishahr and Zungharia' took a new name,
'the Organisation of the Revolutionary Uyghur'. Some activists with
Russian and Soviet connections in the Turfan area had also adopted the
term in the 1920s and 1930s (notably the poet Abdukhaliq 'Uyghur'),[48]
and as we have seen, the 1933–4 Kashgar republic considered calling
itself 'Uyghuristan'. But up till Sheng Shicai, Chinese governments distinguished Turkic Muslims from Chinese Muslims by referring to the
former as 'wrapped-head' or 'turbaned Muslims' (*chantou, chanhui*) after
the turbans some Uyghur men wore. Sheng gave the term 'Uyghur' its
first official currency.

Ethnic categories such as Uyghur seem natural today, and insofar as
they often reflected real cultural, linguistic and occasionally physical differences between communities of Xinjiang's peoples, they were generally accepted in the late 1930s and 1940s. Sheng's government reinforced
them, moreover, assigning representation in the provincial legislature on
the basis of the fourteen categories and creating an official cultural association for each.[49] However, the shift from a broadly defined sense of
'Türk' to narrowly drawn categories had political implications, threaten-

47   Sun Yat-sen 1933:165, 168; Chiang Kai-shek 1947: 40, see also 29–43.
48   Rudelson 1997: 149. In personal communication, Nabijan Tursun informed
me of the Russian reclamation of the term Uyghur for the modern people. See
also Tursun 2002.
49   Benson and Svanberg 1998: 67.

ing to divide Muslim and Turkic peoples against each other. In fact, from his new home in Chongqing (where he had settled after his flight from Khotan), Muhammad Emin Bughra criticised Sheng's adoption of these categories, maintaining that 'Türk' or 'Türki' was sufficient designation for the Turkic Muslims of Xinjiang.[50] However, with some exceptions Sheng's categorisation stuck, and his identifications as continued by the PRC remain the basis of 'minority nationality' policy in the region.

Sheng's ethnic policies appear liberal in some ways. Each of his major policy statements (the 'Eight Great Proclamations' of 1934, 'Nine Duties' of 1935 and 'Six Great Policies' of 1936), contained, along with pledges of friendship to the Soviet Union, language guaranteeing the equality of Xinjiang's various nationalities (*minzu*), or promising to protect the status and rights of princes (*wanggong*), ahongs and lamas—i.e. the non-Han élites. He employed prominent non-Chinese in his government (though as the cases of Khoja Niyaz and Mahmut Muhiti show, the warlord's sincerity in so doing is doubtful). Sheng also promoted publication and education in languages other than Chinese, although, as in the Soviet Union, the main intent of the literacy programme was to extend the reach of propaganda. In other ways as well Sheng Shicai achieved some positive results. He implemented a currency reform, promoted agricultural recovery, constructed schools and roads, and expanded medical facilities. Soviet investment and renewed commerce led to an economic recovery, especially in the north.

Stalinism in Xinjiang

The darker side of this pro-Soviet turn was the flowering of Stalinism in Xinjiang. Sheng and his Soviet advisers wove an elaborate network of intelligence and secret police agencies to spy on, incarcerate and eliminate potential rivals, especially Turkic leaders suspected of nationalistic leanings.[51] Stalin was purging the Turkic political élites and intelligentsia of the Central Asian republics at the same time that Sheng faced a renewed challenge to his rule in 1937 from Turkic forces (followers of Mahmud Muhiti) and Huis (under Ma Hushan) in southern Xinjiang. Sheng dealt with the military threat with Soviet troops, killing an estimated 50,000 rebels, and then launched his own series of purges

50 Benson 1990: 31.
51 Chen Huisheng 1999: 292–6; Tursun 2002.

against 'traitors', 'pan-Turkists', 'enemies of the people', 'nationalists' and 'imperialist spies'. These detentions and executions swept up an entire cohort of Uyghur and Hui intellectual and political leaders, including Khoja Niyaz (accused of spying for the Japanese), Ma Shaowu and many of the White Russian generals who had helped Sheng come to power. In a later wave of purges, Sheng arrested as 'Trotskyites' a group of Han Chinese originally sent to him by Moscow. In the midst of this terror in Xinjiang, Sheng travelled to Moscow, where Stalin and Molotov regaled and enrolled him in the Communist Party of the Soviet Union. Estimates of those killed in Sheng's purges range from 50,000 to 100,000.[52]

Having so thoroughly cleaned house, Sheng found his government short-staffed. He thus approached the Chinese Communists in Yan'an. In the same spirit of wartime 'united front' through which it was co-operating with the GMD, the CCP seconded dozens of its cadres to Xinjiang. The CCP members worked mostly in high-level administrative, financial, educational and cultural ministerial positions in Urumchi, Kashgar, Khotan and elsewhere, helping to implement Sheng's Six Great Policies and maintain the communications corridor with the Soviet Union—the CCP's one open route from Yan'an. Mao Zedong's younger brother, Mao Zemin, served as Deputy Finance Minister in Sheng's Xinjiang government.

Sheng misplays his hand

There is evidence that Turkic leaders in Kashgar were in indirect contact with the Japanese ambassador in Afghanistan, and Sheng played up the alleged Japanese threat in his political propaganda. Despite (or because of) his education in Japan, Sheng had been strongly anti-Japanese since the Japanese occupation of his home in north-east China. Indeed, these anti-Japanese credentials made Sheng an attractive ally to the Soviet Union in the late 1930s.

However, balanced as it was between world powers, Xinjiang's situation was highly sensitive to shifts in their strategic alignments. The 1939 Nazi-Soviet Pact and supplies of raw materials had allowed Hitler to expand in Europe. However, in April of 1941 the Soviet Union signed

52 Tursun 2002: 31–76, citing Soviet scholar A. Narenbayev on the numbers killed in the uprising. Forbes 1986: 135–44, 161 and Benson 1990: 27; Bai and Koibuchi 1992: 344.

an anti-aggression pact with Japan to protect its eastern flank while concentrating on the upcoming conflict in the west. In June Hitler invaded the Soviet Union with three million men, and in December 1941 the United States joined the war against Japan, throwing its weight behind the Guomindang regime still holding out in south-west China. Sheng Shicai, whose hold on Xinjiang depended upon outside aid, thought the tide had turned against his Soviet backers and reopened channels to the Nationalist Government, which with US aid now had the wherewithal to assert its hitherto theoretical sovereignty in Xinjiang. Beginning in the spring of 1942 Sheng closed Xinjiang to trade with the Soviet Union, dealing a major economic blow to the region. He started purging Chinese communists and pro-Soviet Turkic Muslims, and ultimately had Mao Zemin and many others executed in prison. By mid-summer Sheng concluded negotiations with the Guomindang (GMD) with a ceremony attended by Madame Chiang Kai-shek (Soong Mei-ling). The GMD began moving its own troops into Xinjiang and founded a Xinjiang party branch with Sheng as official Chairman. In the spring of 1943, on Chongqing's invitation, the United States opened a consulate in Urumchi, and by the autumn the Soviets had withdrawn their military units, advisers and technical teams. They capped the Dushanzi oil fields and took their drilling equipment with them.

Sheng's mercurial career took one last twist. When the Soviets finally prevailed over the German armies in February 1943 in the Battle for Stalingrad, Sheng yet again attempted to switch patrons. He arrested Guomindang representatives in Xinjiang, wrote to Stalin claiming that they were Japanese spies and informing Chiang Kai-shek that they were Communists. (With this last about-face Sheng had incarcerated just about every Xinjiang political figure of any persuasion from the late 1930s to the early 1940s.) By now, however, Stalin was fed up with Sheng. He refused Sheng's request for a resumption of support and passed Sheng's letter on to Chiang Kai-shek. This forced Sheng to crawl back to the Nationalist Chinese government, who finally removed him from Xinjiang in September 1944. It is said that only a donation of 500,000 Chinese dollars to the GMD treasury allowed him to escape execution. He served out the war as Minister of Agriculture and Forests in Chongqing, and retreated to Taiwan with the Guomindang in 1949.[53]

53 Benson 1990: 28; Forbes 1986: 157–62; Tursun 2002: 37–8; Lattimore 1950: 74.

GUOMINDANG XINJIANG

The direction Nanjing's Xinjiang policy would take was already evident in 1942, while Sheng Shicai was still in power in Urumchi. In this year the Nationalist Government announced a campaign to develop and populate north-western China; the goal was to provide an economic base for Nationalist control of the north-west for resistance against Japan, and to undermine Communist organisation in the dirt-poor region. Magazines with titles like 'Come to the North-west!' (*Dao xibei lai*) had encouraged migration since the 1930s. The influential scholar Gu Jiegang did extensive fieldwork in Gansu and Qinghai and wrote that the diverse ethnicities of the north-west frontier were the best hope for salvation of the Chinese nation. In its 1942 'North-west Development' programme the Nationalist government proposed subsidising the migration of 10,000 officials and their families to Xinjiang to serve as administrators, teachers and technical experts. A Guomindang report of 1943 claimed that at least one million Chinese refugees could be resettled comfortably in Xinjiang (the region's total population was then under 4 million), and the government began actively promoting colonisation of Xinjiang, comparing it to California and Alaska before their respective gold rushes. Homesteading and land reclamation by Han Chinese was to be accompanied by a programme for 'converting nomads to a semi-pastoral, semi-agricultural economy'. Some 4,000 Han, fleeing famine in Henan, came to Qitai and Urumchi in 1942–3 (few got their promised 15 acres); another 7,000 arrived in Hami by April 1944.[54]

In the first half of the nineteenth century Gong Zizhen, the Chinese statecraft thinker, had imagined that the Qing empire in Xinjiang could be saved by Chinese immigration, Chinese style administration, Chinese-style agriculture and Confucian education. Zuo Zongtang and Liu Jintang attempted to implement similar policies after reconquest and provincehood in the 1880s (Chapter 4). Restoring central Chinese control to the region after a thirty-year hiatus, the Nationalist government's approach still reflected this outlook and ignored the ethnic and nationalistic sentiments of Xinjiang's non-Chinese peoples, who had been nourished by bloody war, moulded by Soviet theories and fired in the crucible of Sheng's harsh rule.

---

54   Whiting and Sheng 1958: 98 (from Whiting's analysis); Lattimore 1950: 79, 106; Benson 1990: 38–9, quote from 39.

Thus the newly appointed GMD Governor of Xinjiang, Wu Zhong-xin, while claiming in his first major speech that his first two priorities were 'promoting mutual trust among the races (*zongzu*)' and 'guarantee-ing religious freedom', reiterated in that same speech Chiang Kai-shek's theory that non-Han peoples in what had been the Qing empire were all racially Chinese, and that the various categories of national identity newly employed in Sheng Shicai's Xinjiang (Kazak, Uyghur, Kirghiz etc.) did not as such exist. Wu was, of course, charged with pacifying the area and consolidating central Chinese control. This he hoped to accomplish by integrating Xinjiang economically with China proper, maintaining an army of some 100,000 Han and Hui troops in Xinjiang, and repressing any local ethnic national movements.[55]

Sheng's about-face and the process of reintegration with China proved disastrous for Xinjiang's economy. The closure of the Soviet bor-der had cut off pastoral and agricultural producers, particularly those in northern Xinjiang, from their primary market. It also led to shortages of manufactured goods. To deal with its towering deficits in Xinjiang, the new GMD government printed Xinjiang dollars with abandon. Infla-tion took off in the summer of 1944, with prices of staple foods more than doubling between July and August, and quadrupling in the autumn. The heaviest blow came with the programme to replace Xinjiang's cur-rency with the Nationalist Chinese dollar, which was still more severely inflationary. The forced rates of exchange were highly unfavourable to holders of Xinjiang dollars, but Chinese merchants purportedly ben-efited greatly.[56]

The new government also raised taxes. The US consul in Urumchi, Robert Ward, reported that land taxes, often assessed at more than the land was worth, were in places collected up to ninety years in advance. The GMD radically increased the fees charged for official exit papers required for foreign travel, a policy which directly affected Uyghur and other Turkic businessmen accustomed to trading with the Soviet Union. Moreover, only service or goods in kind, not Nationalist Chinese dol-lars, were accepted for payment of many of the new taxes. The increased revenues were needed to support the large resident army, and to pay back the Soviet Union for an aircraft factory it had sold to the Xin-jiang government upon departure. In October of 1944 Wu Zhongxin

55 Chen Huisheng 1999: 381; Lattimore 1950: 83–4; Bai and Koibuchi 1992: 395.
56 Benson 1990: 36; Chen Huisheng 1999: 385; Forbes 1986: 163–70.

reported a provincial deficit of almost 38 billion Chinese dollars (7.5 billion Xinjiang dollars).[57]

Rebellion in Zungharia

As the Guomindang government transferred troops into Xinjiang, Kazaks were already in revolt in the north. Kazak tribes had moved into northern Xinjiang after the Qing eliminated the Zunghars in the mid-eighteenth century. They traded with the Qing authorities and private Chinese merchants, but remained autonomous during Qing times, coming to trade fairs and making winter camps in Zungharia, then returning north beyond Qing watch-posts in the spring. Maintaining such a status became increasingly difficult over time as the Kazaks of the Middle and Greater Horde were caught between expanding Qing and Tsarist empires and forced to conclude agreements with both imperial governments. Moscow and Beijing each chose to interpret these treaties as proof that Kazaks had accepted their exclusive sovereignty. As the Qing and Russia demarcated their mutual border in the late nineteenth century, and as Russian and Soviet policies towards Kazaks grew harsh in the early twentieth century, more Kazaks moved south from Tarbaghatai and the Altai to the Tianshan range north of Hami and around Qitai. Still, Kazak migrations across the border remained an issue into the twentieth century.[58]

Sheng Shicai's policies, especially the closure of the Soviet border, had angered many Kazaks, especially those in the Tianshan area. The Guomindang did nothing to alleviate their dissatisfaction. Kazaks frequently raided Han settlement and military posts during the 1930s and 1940s, which of course brought on reprisals from provincial forces. In 1940 nomads attacked a Soviet investigation team in the Ashan district, killing the team leader and torching its vehicles. In 1939–40 Sheng began trying to disarm the Kazaks, sending units from camp to camp to confiscate privately owned firearms, including those most Kazaks used for hunting. (Yang Zengxin had helped arm Altai Kazaks in the 1910s and 1920s as a hedge against Mongols in the region). The disarmament law caused anxiety and resentment, especially when Sheng attempted to

57 Consul Ward cited in David Wang 1999: 89–90. Forbes 1986: 167; Chen Huisheng 1999: 385.
58 Benson and Svanberg 1998: 33–44; Millward 1992.

enforce it through a campaign of kidnapping and intimidation. Those who fled to avoid the order *ipso facto* became 'bandits'. The cessation of Xinjiang's trade with the Soviet Union also created hardships for the Kazaks, who lost the major market for their wool and livestock. Then in 1943–4 Sheng demanded 'contributions' of horses, ostensibly for the benefit of the Nationalist war against Japan. The bulk of the 10,000 head of horses to be assembled were to be levied from nomads in north Xinjiang; others were to 'donate' 700 dollars (more than a horse's market value). Furthermore, the Guomindang-sponsored settlement of Han refugees on Kazak grasslands near Qitai in 1943 had been accompanied by forced evictions of nomads from the lands; Lattimore reports that camps of non-cooperative Kazaks were machine-gunned from trucks by GMD soldiers.[59]

From the autumn of 1943 Kazak groups in the Ashan (Altai Mountain) region and north slopes of the Tianshan were in sporadic revolt, staging guerrilla raids on provincial targets under the leadership of a tribal chief, Osman Batur ('Uthman Batur, 1899–1951), who received Soviet military aid channelled through Outer Mongolia and who hoped to establish his own state in the Altai. By the time Sheng Shicai left Xinjiang in September 1944, the provincial government had lost control of north-eastern Zungharia and unrest was spreading into the Yili valley.

'THE THREE DISTRICTS REVOLUTION' AND A SECOND 'EASTERN TURKESTAN REPUBLIC'

In October 1944 rebellion broke out in the small town of Nilka (Gongha, south of Ghulja/Yining) and advanced towards the district capital. The rebels gathered supporters, including a unit of escapees from Xinjiang who had been trained, armed and repatriated by the Soviet Union to coordinate the rebellion. In early November anti-government forces fighting under a green banner converged on the city of Ghulja, which was strongly garrisoned by both Sheng's and Nationalist troops. In preparing to defend the city, the Guomindang arrested hundreds of individuals whose loyalty it questioned. The attack began on November 7th and by the 14th rebel forces had prevailed; after finding some 200 mutilated corpses in a well in GMD police headquarters, they began

---

59   Benson 1990: 36–7, 62; Chen Huisheng 1999: 384–5, 388; Lattimore 1950: 156.

massacring Han Chinese remaining in the city; later rebels would conduct similar pogroms elsewhere in the Yili district.[60]

On 12 November Ali Khan Töre, an Islamic scholar and charismatic orator usually said to be of Uzbek nationality, declared

The Turkestan Islam Government is organised: praise be to Allah for his manifold blessings! Allah be praised! The aid of Allah has given us the heroism to overthrow the government of the oppressor Chinese.[61]

This declaration came eleven years to the day after the foundation of the Kashgar East Turkestan Republic. This new government, also called the East Turkestan Republic (ETR) and initially led by Ali Khan Töre, fought a fierce war against the Guomindang. Osman Batur joined the anti-Chinese offensive and captured the main cities of Tarbaghatai and Ashan districts. Hostilities broke out simultaneously in Tashkurghan (Puli), on the Soviet Border in the Pamirs above Kashgar, and in the Aqsu and Yanqi regions. Meanwhile, having held off a GMD attempt to retake Ghulja in the bitter winter of 1944–5, the newly organised Yili National Army (whose tunic buttons bore the Cyrillic letters 'BTP', Russian for ETR) pushed the GMD back in a south-east direction during the summer, using air power successfully against Chinese divisions at Wusu and Jinghe. By September 1945 the ETR controlled northern Xinjiang and faced the GMD forces across the Manas River, not far from the capital, Urumchi. ETR troops had also taken the city of Aqsu to the south, and Kirghiz pushed the GMD from the frontier post of Tashkurghan, in the Pamirs above Kashgar.[62] Chiang Kai-shek dispatched Zhang Zhizhong, formerly the Commander of the North-western Military Headquarters in Lanzhou, to Urumchi to deal with the situation; he would later replace Wu Zhongxin as Xinjiang Governor.

Immediately upon his arrival in Urumchi, Zhang contacted Soviet Consul-General Abasoff. Apparently encouraged to do so by the Soviet Union, the ETR government soon thereafter cabled the Nationalist government in Chongqing to request a ceasefire. The two sides began negotiations to form a coalition government, the ETR leadership having promised to abandon its call for an independent Turkic state and replace

60   Forbes 1986: 170–6; Sadri 1984: 301.
61   Translation provided as enclosure in a US consular report, cited in Benson 1990: 45.
62   Forbes 1986: 186–90; Sadri 1984: 306.

the name 'Eastern Turkestan Republic' with the geographic designation 'Eastern Turkestan'.

That the ceasefire came about, with Soviet involvement, soon after China and the Soviet Union signed their Treaty of Friendship and Alliance on 14 August 1945 is no coincidence. Underlying this was the Yalta Agreement of February 1945 between the United States, Britain and the Soviet Union. At Yalta Stalin had agreed to join the United States in the war with Japan in return for territorial concessions in Sakhalin and the Kuriles, as well as the right to operate jointly key railroads in north-east China (Manchuria) where Russia had lost her sphere of interest to Japan after 1905. Chiang Kai-shek was not a direct party to this agreement, but the United States promised, in effect, to urge him to accept it when precise terms were worked out between the Chinese and Soviet parties. The Treaty of Friendship and Alliance was the result of negotiations towards this end; and in one of the notes exchanged by their respective foreign ministers, the Soviet Union stated its intention not to interfere in the Xinjiang crisis, which it referred to as 'internal affairs of China'.[63]

The coalition government

Zhang Zhizhong is unique in Xinjiang's modern history as a governor who was appreciated by virtually all of the region's rival parties, and who enjoys the respect even of historians. By GMD standards he was incorrupt and free of factional entanglements and gangland connections. We may also credit him with what would today be called multicultural sensitivity. Zhang recognised not only that most of Xinjiang's inhabitants were not Han Chinese, but that rhetorical assertions to the contrary would not help. Quite remarkably, he wrote, 'We Chinese comprise only 5 per cent of the population of Sinkiang. Why have we not turned over political power to the Uighurs and other racial groups who constitute the other 95 per cent?'[64] It is a pity that Zhang's acknowledgement of Uyghurs' desire for a degree of self-determination, in contrast to the Han chauvinism more characteristic of the Guomindang approach to its non-Chinese frontiers, leads one scholar to label Zhang 'pro-Soviet'.[65]

---

63 Both Forbes (1986: 193–5) and David Wang (1999: 69–70 *passim*) associate these treaties with the halting of the ETR offensive at the Manas River.
64 In *Xinjiang Ribao* (Urumchi), 14 August 1947, cited in Forbes 1986: 199–200.
65 David Wang 1999: 230, 413 *passim*.

Zhang consulted with three Uyghur leaders who had wound up in Chongqing: Muhammad Emin Bughra, Isa Yusuf Alptekin (1901–95) and Masud Sabri (1886–1951). Bughra, as noted above, was associated with madrasas and secret societies in southern Xinjiang; he had led the Khotan rebellion in 1933 and made himself emir of Khotan after its success. After the destruction of the 1933–4 ETR and invasion of southern Xinjiang by Hui armies, he fled to India and Afghanistan before moving to Chongqing in 1943, where he was appointed a Xinjiang representative within the National Assembly. Isa, a Uyghur whose early education included both Islamic study and time in a Chinese school in Xinjiang (see Chapter 4), was likewise an advocate for autonomy for Turkic peoples in Xinjiang. He became Xinjiang member of the Legislative Yuan (the Nationalist government's parliament) in 1939. Together with Bughra in Chongqing, he ran the Altai Publishing House and edited Turkic nationalist periodicals which were often critical of GMD policy with regard to Xinjiang, stressing such things as the Turkic background of Xinjiang's people and defending the name 'Turkestan' for the region. Masud, a Uyghur from the Yili valley, trained as a medical doctor in Istanbul before returning to Xinjiang in 1915 to found a pharmacy and several schools in Ghulja. He was arrested by Yang Zengxin in 1924, and later supported the first ETR from Aqsu until he too escaped to India. He returned to China in 1934 and like his two compatriots joined the GMD. He likewise wrote in favour of an autonomous 'East Turkestan' within China.

Zhang brought these three knowledgeable Uyghurs to Urumchi as his advisers; they steered him toward more liberal policies in education, publishing and other cultural areas, use of Turkic language in government offices, and greater freedoms of speech, assembly and religion, justifying their stance in favour of Xinjiang autonomy within China by reference to Sun Yat-sen's call for self-determination of non-Chinese peoples. All later served as ministers in the provincial coalition government.[66]

Zhang's opposite number in the negotiations to create a coalition government was Ahmetjan (Äkhmätjan) Qasimi, a Soviet-educated Uyghur originally from the Yili valley who had spent time in Sheng's prisons. Although the most prominent early leaders of the anti-Chinese uprising

66 Benson 1990: 52–3. For fuller biographies of these men and a defence of their credentials as Uyghur nationalists, despite their GMD association, see Benson 1991.

in the Yili valley were religious figures (including Ali Khan Töre, who became Chairman of the new government), by the spring of 1945 control of the movement had shifted to more secular and pro-Soviet figures, Ahmetjan Qasimi pre-eminent among them. Indeed, a year later, a few weeks before the conclusion of the negotiations, Ali Khan Töre would depart for the Soviet Union, possibly for medical treatment but more likely kidnapped, in a disappearance reminiscent of Ma Zhongying's a decade earlier.[67]

The negotiations between the Guomindang and the Yili government took months, and it was not till July 1946 that an agreement was eventually concluded. Zhang Zhizhong would be Chairman and Ahmetjan Qasimi Vice-Chairman of the new Xinjiang provincial government. Both sides consented to direct elections for representatives to county assemblies; these assemblies would in turn elect magistrates and representatives to a provincial assembly. Each of Xinjiang's ten districts (including the three northern districts controlled by the Yili group) would recommend a portion of the ministers in a provincial council, with Nanjing appointing the remainder. Higher-level provincial offices were divided among various ethnicities, including Han, Hui, Uyghur, Kazak, Manchu, Mongol and Tatar, and across political lines with Guomindang and Yili partisans each holding influential positions. Zhang Zhizhong also agreed to work towards an eventual apportionment of civil service jobs in the proportion of 70 per cent non-Han to 30 per cent Han. Uyghur and Kazak were both declared official languages along with Chinese; education at all levels would be in native languages, and non-Chinese cultures were to be promoted in other ways as well. The real stumbling block in the negotiations had been the extent to which the north could keep its own military and police forces. In the end the Yili group retained some 12,000 men in six regiments under Muslim command, though three of these regiments were in theory to be stationed in southern Xinjiang. Zhang was nominal commander-in-chief of the entire Xinjiang military.[68]

---

67 Sadri writes that his family saw Ali Khan Töre dragged into a Soviet jeep. Töre had reportedly been unwilling to follow all the dictates of Soviet 'advisers' (1984: 308–9).

68 The text of the Peace Agreement of January 1946 (with a supplement dated 6 June 1946) is in Benson 1990: Appendix A. See also Benson 1990: 55–61 and Forbes 1986: 190–3.

This new coalition government enacted a number of needed reforms and development projects. Zhang released political prisoners, including CCP members, still mouldering in prison. In 1946 he disbanded a provincial import-export monopoly, dating from Sheng's tenure, that competed unfairly with private traders. Commerce with the Soviet Union resumed, as did Soviet extraction of oil and mineral resources in Zungharia. Zhang's government lent money to poor farmers in some areas, and mobilised GMD troops stationed in some southern areas to construct irrigation works. He cancelled arrears of the excessive taxes of his predecessors, and limited the collection of tax in kind. In the cultural arena he prohibited marriages between Muslims and non-Muslims (a regulation sought by the former ETR members and popular among Muslims in southern Xinjiang). He revived the Nationality Culture Promotion Association (dating from the time of Sheng Shicai), which made grants to Uyghur, Kazak and Kirghiz culture associations and promoted publication in Turkic languages (including a Uyghur-Chinese- Russian dictionary edited by Burhan Shähidi). And of course, Xinjiang under Zhang sent song and dance troops to Beijing, Shanghai and Taipei, thus bringing Soviet-style showcasing of minority song and dance to China. Chinese performers also visited Urumchi.[69]

Zhang may be praised for open-mindedness, but other Chinese leaders in Xinjiang were less conciliatory; furthermore, the Yili group had not entirely abandoned its hope of establishing an independent Turkic state. Neither side of the coalition truly trusted the other, and each continued to manoeuvre for position. The Yili group did this through political organisation and propaganda throughout Xinjiang, and the GMD through its control of the police and key military units. The limitations of the coalition were clear in the run-up to the elections for county assembly in the autumn of 1946, which were disrupted by violence, intimidation and the failure to allow voting or to post results in many counties. Although the election process may have served to politicise people in rural areas, and familiarise them with democratic procedures, the fact was that ultimately not a single Turkic representative from southern Xinjiang (districts under GMD control) made it onto the Provincial Council.[70]

During the year following its formation, neither party in the coalition fully lived up to the spirit or letter of the coalition agreement. The Yili

69 Forbes 1986: 196–9; Bai and Koibuchi 1992: 439–42.
70 Benson 1990: 77–82, 114.

group disseminated propaganda in the southern seven districts and or-ganised Turkic nationalist opposition to the GMD presence in Xinjiang, particularly that of the Chinese military. This it accomplished through a party known as *Sharqi Türkistan Yashlar Täshkilati*, the East Turkestan Youth League. This group and its renamed successors gained supporters rapidly in Urumchi, Aqsu, Kashgar, Khotan, Hami, Yarkand and Korla, to the point where it could challenge the GMD organisation.[71] The old ETR leaders maintained control of their military forces, kept the GMD military out of the three northern districts, and refused to open com-munications between Urumchi and the north via the bridge over the Manas River. The north maintained its separate currency and remained, in fact, an independent regime.

In the southern seven districts educational reforms moved slowly and few native-speakers of Uyghur and other Turkic languages were recruited as schoolteachers. A number of Han were displaced from com-fortable provincial, district and county level government jobs, though not enough to approach the 70:30 proportion. Zhang's 'Turkicisaton' policy thus became a source of resentment both to the Chinese, who were threatened by it, and to Turkic peoples, who felt it remained unful-filled. In February 1947 there were demonstrations and counter-dem-onstrations in Urumchi over this and other issues related to the terms of the coalition treaty. GMD General Song Xilian, who opposed Zhang's conciliatory approach, declared martial law and dispatched soldiers and police on destructive house-to-house searches for Uyghur suspects in the city, further exacerbating tensions.

Meanwhile, both Osman Batur, nominally a member of the coalition government, and another Kazak leader, Ali Beg Rahim, had broken from the ETR, possibly because of the disappearance of Ali Khan Töre and the ETR's pro-Soviet tilt. Osman and Ali Beg led their nomad followers into the Altai and Tianshan, where they received covert military aid from the GMD. A parallel rift divided Uyghur and some Kazak members of the coalition, reflecting the split between Osman and the ETR leaders. News organs in Urumchi and Yili embarked upon a propaganda war, each side accusing the other of bad faith.[72]

Furthermore, the Nationalist Government, now back in Nanjing and dealing with the threat from the Chinese Communists, was not happy

---

71 Bai and Koibuchi 1992: 442–3.
72 Benson 1990: 83–118, 151–2; Forbes 1986: 201–4.

about Zhang's cultural pluralism or his apparently soft policies with regard to the Yili group. Frustrated by his increasingly untenable position, Zhang Zhizhong relinquished his position in May 1947 in favour of the anti–Soviet, but also Turkic nationalist, Masud Sabri. Despite the fact that Masud was a Uyghur and had publicly advocated autonomy for Xinjiang's Turkic peoples, his appointment provoked a storm of opposition. The Provincial Assembly even passed a resolution against his chairmanship (Masud dissolved the assembly in June). Much of this opposition derived from the Yili group and from the Soviet Union, who rightly saw Masud as a threat because he, along with fellow ministers Isa Alptekin and Muhammad Emin Bughra, continued to espouse a political and ethnic model for Xinjiang peoples at odds with approaches promoted by the Soviet Union. For years these men had opposed the subdivision of Xinjiang's Turkic peoples into the categories Uyghur, Kazak, Kirghiz, Tatar, Uzbek and so on, arguing instead that these groups were all Turks, or Turki, divided only by dialectical differences and in following an agrarian/urban or pastoral way of life. As Soviet Central Asia was founded on the policy of creating competing nationalities among the Muslim Turkic peoples of former Turkestan, such an assertion of overarching Turkic identity was dangerous from the Soviet point of view. And Masud, Isa and Bughra supported, publicly at least, full autonomy for East Turkestan within a Chinese state, not formal 'independence' with actual dependence on the Soviet Union.[73]

Despite these nationalistic credentials, however, Masud appeared even to some Uyghurs in southern Xinjiang as at best a figurehead, at worst a corrupt stooge of the most thuggish GMD elements. Indeed, the influence of General Song Xilian, Minister of Information Liu Mengchun, and Xinjiang GMD party head Chen Xihao increased after Masud's appointment.[74] In July the GMD military repressed an uprising in Turfan, Toqsun and Yanqi (the Tushantuo incident), which may have been organised or supported by the Yili regime. The Nationalist government probably also stepped up its support of Osman Batur—and his 15,000 Kazaks—who precipitated a clash in June with Mongolian troops at Beidashan in the Altai mountains on the Xinjiang-Mongolia border, and in the autumn attacked the city of Chenghua (Sharasure) in the north. The Kazaks were soon driven out, allegedly by Soviet troops and armour.

73 Sadri 1984: 310, 318 ns 61–2; Benson 1991.
74 Benson 1990: 129, 154–5.

By the summer of 1947 the coalition treaty, never well adhered to, fell apart in a storm of mutual recriminations. Ahmetjan Qasimi returned to Ghulja in early August. Although he remained nominal Vice-Chairman of Xinjiang province, in effect he was again Chairman of the Eastern Turkestan Republic; some sources say the ETR name once again came into use and its flag was again unfurled. Politically, power in the ETR was channelled through an organisation known as the Union for the Defence of Peace and Democracy in Xinjiang, which despite the name was the party behind Ghulja's one-party system, also under Ahmetjan's control. By all accounts, this government, which lasted until northern Xinjiang was reunited with the south under the CCP in late 1949, achieved some positive results. Insulated against the severe inflation of China proper, the three districts of northern Xinjiang enjoyed relative good times thanks to a subsidy from the Urumchi government, trade with the Soviet Union and renewed Soviet investment in mining enterprises. The Ghulja government stabilised the economy and developed a regular and efficient tax system; provided increased elementary education and higher technical training; loaned money and seed to encourage agricultural development; and invested in medical facilities and publications in the region's five main languages, with the result that rates of typhus decreased and literacy increased. Even US consular reports from 1945 noted that the ETR regime was locally popular, and there is no indication that it declined in popularity thereafter.[75]

The same cannot be said for the GMD regime in Urumchi. The end of co-rule with the Yili leadership did not bring an end to ethnic and nationalistic tensions in southern Xinjiang. While keeping some Yili representatives of the former coalition on the books, the Masud administration held new district elections and reshuffled the government to create a semblance of Uyghur and other non-Han participation. Where a district inspector-general was Turkic, his assistants were Han, and *vice versa*; where a Uyghur held a ministerial post, his vice minister was in most cases Han or Hui. (The Manchus used such a diarchic device in controlling the Chinese bureaucracy during the Qing period, and a similar system pertains in the PRC's Xinjiang Uyghur Autonomous Region today.) Uyghur nationalists, advocating not separatism but greater Turkic

---

75 Chen Yanqi 1998; Tursun 2002: 40; Benson 1990: 144–51, US consular report of Robert Ward cited p. 149 n. 83. For a negative assessment of the Yili regime's social and economic achievements, see David Wang 1999: 321–36.

autonomy in the GMD state, were elected to the provincial assembly, where they agitated for a return to the policies of Zhang Zhizhong's era. Isa Alptekin and Mohammad Emin Bughra each held ministerial positions and managed to promote moderate nationalism through schools and print media. They ultimately distanced themselves from Masud, especially when the latter became associated with GMD repression and mired in a corruption scandal. Meanwhile, the economy plunged. Severe inflation undermined confidence in the Xinjiang dollar, which was pegged at a fixed rate to the nearly worthless Nationalist *yuan*. Merchants and consumers hoarded goods, and grain, meat and fuel grew scarce.[76]

Finally, in January 1949 Nanjing replaced Masud Sabri with Burhan Shāhidi (1894–1989), a Tatar born in Kazan to a family with roots in Aqsu, who had travelled and studied in Germany and the Soviet Union, been imprisoned by Sheng Shicai as a 'Trotskyite' and later served as one of Zhang Zhizhong's deputies. Burhan presided over the transition between GMD and CCP rule in Xinjiang; he was partly successful in stabilising Xinjiang's finances by taking the province off the newest Nationalist currency, the gold *yuan*, and restoring the Xinjiang dollar; and he allowed the expansion of Turkic nationalist organisations. However, besides negotiating with the Soviets to reopen full trade relations (the Soviets wanted, but did not get from Chiang Kai-shek, a return to the unlimited access and tariff concessions they had enjoyed under Sheng Shicai), there was little he could do about the deteriorating economy or political situation before the victory of the CCP in China once again realigned the outside forces that were shaping Xinjiang's fate.

The character of the second Eastern Turkestan Republic and the Soviet role

Though some Uyghur activists today paint it with bold black and white strokes as the immediate wellspring of their national aspirations—the state that the Chinese Communist conquerors took away from them—there is much that remains fuzzy and grey about the Ghulja Eastern Turkestan Republic. For one thing, there is ambiguity, as with the first ETR, about whether the Ghulja regime began as an 'Islamic' republic. Also reminiscent of the 1930s is the fact that the events of 1944–9 were not a simple case of Uyghurs struggling for self-determination against

---

76 Benson 1990: 155–66.

occupying Chinese, but rather a more complex situation with Turkic nationalists arrayed along an ideological spectrum and divided on both sides of a political and territorial divide between the Guomindang and the Soviet Union.

Historical accounts of the second ETR have a Rashomon-like quality. Scholars, states and political actors disagree as to who was really behind the initial rebellion and the Yili regime. PRC accounts stress the influence of the Chinese communists on some figures who would later be leaders of the ETR (especially Abdul Kerim Abbas, whom PRC writers lionise for his opposition to the violent anti-Han tendencies of the rebellion). At the same time, they quietly acknowledge the Soviet role: in PRC materials, the 'Three Districts Revolution' is officially treated as part of the Chinese revolution as a whole, an uprising against 'reactionary' Guomindang rule that occurred under the influence of the CCP, with Soviet support.[77] Other historians, in keeping with the initial political interpretation of the event by the Guomindang, have seen it as fomented and managed by the Soviet Union from the beginning, part of an attempt to regain influence in Xinjiang, detach the region from China, or gain leverage in post-Second World War treaty negotiations. These scholars point to Soviet military aid, direct military involvement by Soviet advisers and troops, as well as the political programme of the ETR itself as evidence of Stalin's handiwork.[78] Others, including Uyghur nationalists, depict the ETR as a locally-led struggle for self-determination by the Uyghurs (or the Turkic Muslim peoples of East Turkestan) that was restrained and even undermined by Soviet machinations.[79]

Let us look first at Islam in the ETR. The early leadership of the rebellion apparently intended to create a state with a strong Islamic character. This is evident in its early pronouncements (see the proclamation of November 1944, quoted above); in the top government positions afforded religious scholars Ali Khan Töre and Ashim Bey Khoja as Chair-

[77] Xinjiang shehui kexueyuan lishi yanjiusuo 1980–7: III: 353; also Chen Huisheng: 385–6; Chen Yanqi 1998: 275–6.

[78] David Wang 1999; Zhang Dajun 1980. Forbes 1986 considers the Soviet role and manipulation to have been important, but acknowledges that there was sufficient local cause for rebellion and a desire to be rid of Chinese rule in the region in the 1940s.

[79] Benson 1990; Sadri 1984: 315. For a historiographical survey of primary sources and works on the Ghulja Eastern Turkestan Republic written in Chinese, English and Russian, see David Wang 1999: 3–19.

man and Vice-Chairman (later Ashim Bey and Anwar Musa Bei); the establishment of a religious council as part of the government; and the implementation of an Islamic tithe.[80] On the other hand, other statements of the government's programme imply a more secular orientation. These include the Ghulja Declaration of January 1945 and a handbill circulating in 1944–5 entitled 'Why are We Fighting?'[81] The former lists an eight point programme for the ETR, which had just taken control of the Yili valley. Though there is a strong anti-GMD or anti-Han tone here, there is no reference to religion in the proclamation. 'Why are We Fighting?' calls for an end to Chinese rule; equality for all nationalities, with proportional representation for each in the government and in a national assembly on the basis of their relative size; cultural, linguistic and religious freedom; and restored friendship and trade relations with 'our great, freedom-loving friend and neighbour, the Soviet Union'. Except for one reference to taking an oath in the name of the one God, this document is also free of religious language; the rhetoric is, rather, that of a leftist political manifesto. It attacks the Chinese not as infidels, but as 'fascist Chinese oppressors'. Yet again, another pamphlet collected by the US consulate two years later ('Struggle for the Motherland', 1947) is religious in the tone of its appeal, with many references to God and no Communist jargon (the Chinese here are 'crafty foxes', not fascists).[82]

The second Eastern Turkestan Republic, then, like the first, embodied both Islamising and secular modernising impulses. Moreover, the Ghulja regime manifested these impulses in factional differences. Ali Khan Töre, the movement's first leader, was removed by mid-1946, and the secular faction under Ahmetjan Qasimi (some sources call these men 'progressive', others 'pro-Soviet') took control. Most of this cohort of leaders had been educated in Soviet territory, though as Benson points out, this was not unusual given the limited educational options in Xinjiang and the decades-long history of travel to Russia/the Soviet Union for business and study. The Ahmetjan group took pains to welcome publicly non-Muslim Mongols, Manchus and Russians as citizens in the republic and ministers in the government. As seen above, this ETR regime attempted to improve conditions for the populace and continued to organise Tur-

80 Chen Yanqi 1998: 286.
81 Ghulja Declaration in Forbes 1986: 183; Translation of 'Why are We Fighting', from US consular sources, reprinted in Benson 1990: Appendix E, 200–6.
82 Benson 1990: Appendix F.

kic nationalistic opposition to Chinese rule even after the formation of the coalition government.

One obvious difference between the Kashgar-based ETR of 1933–4 and the Ghulja regime lies in the close relationship of the latter to the Soviet Union. The question of the Soviet role can be divided into four parts. Did the Soviet Union instigate the rebellions of 1944 in northern Xinjiang that led to the creation of the ETR? Did the Soviet Union provide military aid and/or intervene militarily to support the ETR in its war with the GMD forces in 1944–5? Did the Soviet Union pull the strings behind the ETR regime? What were the Soviet aims in involving itself in Xinjiang?

As mentioned above, these are points of contention among specialists of the period, and answers range from downplaying Soviet involvement to implying that without Soviet instigation and orchestration, there would never have been a rebellion or second ETR in northern Xinjiang in the 1940s. Definitive answers may await research in the Soviet and Chinese archives, but the best reading possible at the moment recognises plenty of cause for unrest in Zungharia before November 1944 (including, but not restricted to, the horse 'donations' and Sheng's attempt to disarm the Kazaks), as well as a good deal of local interest in creating an independent Turkic state. This interest arose from over two decades of new-style education, nationalist thinking and communication with expatriate Uyghurs and Kazaks in the Soviet Union. Moreover, Osman Batur's Kazaks and the Muslim rebels at Nilka can be credited with launching the movement that ultimately drove the GMD out of northern Xinjiang. The respect commanded by Ali Khan Töre as a religious figure, and his use of Islam as a rallying cry helped him take control of the rebellion and gather more supporters.

However, there is considerable evidence that the attack on Ghulja in November 1944 was coordinated from both inside and outside the city with prior Soviet knowledge, and that the subsequent campaign against GMD reinforcements converging on the Yili District took advantage of Soviet military training, matériel and both Soviet military advisers and troops. The Soviet Union participated in the formation, training, arming and strategic planning of the Yili National Army, and likewise provided advisers and weapons to Kazak guerrillas under Osman Batur and Delilhan, who ousted the GMD from Tarbaghatai and Ashan districts. There are many reports that Soviet commanders, troops and aircraft took part in the key battles of Wusu and Jinghe. Whiting, Forbes, David Wang and Roostam Sadri all link the timing of these campaigns, and of the armistice reached in September 1945, to Soviet manoeuvring at Yalta and negotiations with Chiang Kai-shek for the Sino-Soviet Treaty to determine the post-war settlement in Manchuria, Mongolia and Xinjiang, in all of which the Soviet Union had strategic, territorial and economic interests. Xinjiang was thus a bargaining chip, and the ETR a 'pawn' in a larger game.[83]

The evidence that Moscow called the shots in the ETR after the peace treaty is less compelling, although it is clear that the Soviet Union pressured the ETR representatives in September 1945 to agree to a ceasefire with the GMD, to drop the name 'Eastern Turkestan Republic', and to enter negotiations that produced the coalition government. After the formation of the coalition government the Soviets withdrew many personnel and weapons from the ETR. From the time of the formation of the coalition, and even after its collapse, Yili representatives and operatives organised politically, exploited ethnic tensions and helped focus opposition in southern Xinjiang to the GMD government, to the continued Chinese dominance of military and security forces, and to the slow implementation or non-compliance with social and cultural reforms called for in the 1946 treaty. While ethnic tension and destabilisation of the GMD regime in southern Xinjiang did not run counter to Soviet interests, had Stalin wished to annex the rest of Xinjiang he could have done so in 1946, when ETR armies were almost at the gates of Urumchi. It seems reasonable that the drive behind ETR political activities from the summer of 1946 till late 1949 emanated primarily from nationalist aspirations of Ahmetjan Qasimi and the Turkic leadership of the ETR itself. Of course this may indicate only that Soviet aims in the region had some limits, and not that the ETR leadership

---

83   Forbes 1986: 193–5; Whiting and Sheng 1958: 98–112. 'Pawn' is borrowed from Whiting's title. David Wang has assembled the evidence for Soviet involvement from GMD and unofficial or lesser-known PRC sources. Although his argument that the Soviet Union orchestrated the Yili rebellion and ETR runs counter to the official PRC line (that the Soviet Union merely provided 'support'), it differs little from what many PRC historians will admit privately (David Wang 1999: especially Chapters 5–7). Roostam Sadri's account (based on Russian, Uyghur and eyewitness sources) details Soviet involvement in the Ghulja rebellion, including Stalin's orders for the ETR forces to cease their advance at the Manas River and retreat from Aqsu in southern Xinjiang. Sadri is sympathetic to the ETR partisans (1984).

enjoyed any real independence of action; it was after all militarily and economically dependent on the Soviet Union. As several historians have noted, the Soviet Union was primarily interested in continued cheap access to Xinjiang's oil, minerals and pastoral products (especially wool), which, with the ETR forces in control of northern Xinjiang as far as the Manas River, they had recovered for the first time since Sheng had cut ties in 1942. This access could be maintained in various ways, and until the outcome of the civil war in China became clear, the Soviet Union could afford to wait and see. In 1945, as long as it remained relatively dis-crete, Soviet influence in northern Xinjiang also strengthened the Soviet hand in the negotiations with the Nationalist Chinese government over the post-war status of Mongolia and more significant Soviet interests in Manchuria and north-east Asia generally. Outright Soviet annexation of the whole of Xinjiang or creation of a satellite such as the Mongolian People's Republic, by contrast, would have violated the terms of the Yalta Agreement and risked greater US involvement in the issue.

To sum up, then: the rebellion in the three districts of northern Xin-jiang in 1944, and the ETR government that followed, arose from local anti-Chinese and Turkic nationalist (not 'Pan-Turkic') sentiment; the movement was aided and arguably enabled and controlled by the Soviet Union, who provided military matériel, training and advisers, while as-sisting with political organisation and exercising its influence on prin-cipal leaders. The Soviet Union supported and exploited nationalistic aspirations among Uyghurs, Kazaks and others in Xinjiang for its own purposes; it also reined them in at the critical moment in September of 1945 for reasons more related to Soviet strategic aims in Asia than to the dreams of East Turkestan nationalists.

Anyone who was alive during the Cold War would be familiar with the argument that a given insurgency—in South-East Asia, say, or Latin America—is a 'Soviet plot'. Although this accusation has generally been intended to delegitimate the movement, astute observers also recognise that the presence of Soviet support does not in and of itself obviate the fact that many such movements, be they anti-colonial or class-based or both, derived from genuine grievances and deeply-held nationalistic feelings. There is a similar tendency in some versions of the events of the late 1940s, particularly those closely following GMD interpretations, to dismiss the 'Moslem rebels' as mere dupes of the Soviets and ignore un-derlying ethnic tensions and wide-spread nationalist sentiment. Likewise, to apply the epithet 'pan–Turkic' or 'pan–Islamic' to early stages of the movement is a red herring, for there is no evidence that the Yili rebels embraced Enver Pasha's goals of forming a grand Central Asian Turkic state, or intended any confederation extending beyond the boundaries of Xinjiang. (If anything, the Uyghur leaders in the Guomindang, Isa Alptekin, Muhammad Emin and Masud Sabri, were more pan–Turkic than the Yili group, for they disputed the categories 'Uyghur', 'Kazak' and so on, arguing instead that Xinjiang's Turkic Muslims were a single people.) That after decades of rule by Chinese regimes the Turkic peoples of northern Xinjiang were by 1944–5 angry enough to massacre Han Chinese is a significant fact, one worth understanding. Simply to call them Soviet tools, Muslim fanatics or pan–Turkists is to avoid questions, rather than answer them. Likewise, to suggest that the movement was merely an extension of the Chinese revolution is equally disingenuous, and hard to reconcile with its strong anti–Chinese thrust.

In fact, what makes the period of the second ETR so complex is that Xinjiang Turkic nationalists joined both Guomindang and Soviet sides, with different ideas of how best to achieve a measure of autonomy for the region and its people, caught as it was between the Soviet Scylla and the Chinese Charibdis. The advent of Zhang Zhizhong, a Chinese provincial chairman who was relatively liberal with regard to the cultural diversity of Xinjiang, led figures like Isa Yusuf Alptekin, Masud Sabri and Mohammad Emin Bughra to follow the Guomindang in the hope that this party would eventually eschew Han chauvinism and denial of ethnic difference in China and revert to the policies espoused by Sun Yat-sen in 1923.[84] Likewise, though we know less about the motivations of the Yili leaders, and what we do know is largely filtered through Soviet and PRC sources, there are indications that they too hoped primarily for autonomy for Turkic peoples, but, unlike their compatriots in the Guomindang camp, saw the Guomindang as a greater immediate threat than the Soviets, with whom they shared a preference for socialist or communist paths of development. That even Ahmetjan Qasimi saw his alliance with the Soviet Union as a means toward an end, and could diverge from Soviet policy, is suggested by the denouement of the second ETR, discussed below.

84 Benson 1991.

THE CCP TAKES CONTROL OF XINJIANG

Burhan's was a caretaker and a compromise administration. Through most of 1949 the Nationalist government and its demoralised military, having suffered massive losses of troops in Manchuria and from subsequent defections, were in full retreat from the Communist armies in south China. Meanwhile, the 12,000 men of the Yili National Army were just north of the Manas River, tying down Xinjiang's 80,000 GMD troops in Xinjiang. The Soviet Union attempted to capitalise on the situation by negotiating with the rump Nationalist government for an arrangement like the one they had concluded with Sheng Shicai (granting the Soviet Union tariff-free trade and exclusive mineral rights in Xinjiang), but the deal fell through.

The 'Peaceful Liberation' of Xinjiang

By the summer of 1949 the Peoples Liberation Army (PLA) First Field Army under Peng Dehuai was assembled in Gansu and Qinghai. Meanwhile, Zhang Zhizhong (who had recently defected to the CCP) opened communications with Burhan and Tao Zhiyue, the garrison commander of GMD forces in Xinjiang. Zhang encouraged them to surrender. Chiang Kai-shek reportedly ordered Tao to fight the Communists until the GMD troops were driven over the Pamirs; some of Tao's own officers also supported resistance, and even wanted to march east to engage the enemy. Around the same time Stalin allegedly urged Tao to declare Xinjiang an independent republic along the lines of Outer Mongolia; the Soviet Union would then see to it that the PLA stayed out of the region, which could later become part of a federal Chinese republic.[85] Faced with these unappetising choices, Tao first allowed those GMD military officers, police and politicians who wished to leave to do so. Isa Alptekin and Muhammad Emin Bughra fled at this time, as did others, including British and US consuls and eventually the US 'man in Urumchi', Douglas MacKiernan.

MacKiernan, a CIA agent monitoring Xinjiang and Soviet aid to the Chinese Communists under the guise of a consular clerk, destroyed documents and worked to close up the Urumchi (Dihua, Tihwa) con-

85 Forbes 1986: 220; Whiting learned of Stalin's proposal from an unnamed 'reliable source' in 1955 (Whiting and Sheng 1958: 117–18).

sulate until it was taken over by Communist Chinese troops on 27 September 1949. That evening, together with Fulbright-sponsored anthropologist Frank Bessac and three white Russians, MacKiernan set out for Osman Batur's camp at Lake Barkol, north of Hami. Though it is doubtful whether he could have provided substantive American aid to Osman, whom he described as 'a friend, fighting for his freedom', and unknown if he even promised any, MacKiernan seems to have encouraged Osman to follow his own inclination to resist Chinese Communist control, just as he had resisted control by Sheng Shicai, the GMD and the ETR. MacKiernan's original brief may have been to urge resistance to the Communists among various Muslim peoples, including Huis in the north-west. In any case, it was time to leave, and in mid-October MacKiernan's small party took off south with a Kazak guide across the Taklamakan, up through the Altyn Tagh into Qinghai, where they spent the winter with Kazaks in a place known to them as Goose Lake. The following March they trekked across the Tibetan plateau en route to Lhasa. MacKiernan had maintained radio contact with Washington so the Dalai Lama's government knew from the US State Department that he was on his way and sent word to grant his party free passage. However, this news had not reached the border guards that MacKiernan and his party encountered, and in a case of suspicion and mistaken identity, MacKiernan and two of the Russians were shot and decapitated at Shigarhung Lung at the end of April 1950. The first nameless star on the CIA's wall of honour at Langley is MacKiernan's.[86]

Tao Zhiyue, meanwhile, had cabled the CCP in late September 1949 to announce his surrender with 80,000 troops, and Burhan followed suit the following day. Mao Zedong and Zhu De wired back congratulations for their correct attitude, and urged Tao to 'maintain nationality unity and local order' until the arrival of PLA forces. In mid-October Wang Zhen led his units of the PLA into Xinjiang, where they took control of the seven southern districts with no resistance. The PLA moved more slowly into northern Xinjiang, taking time to reorganise the Yili army, send work teams out among the nomads, and purge any military and

86   Gup 2000: Chapter 1; Frank Bessac, personal communication 17 June 2002. See also Bessac 1950. According to one Chinese source, a professor at the Xinjiang Communist Party school, MacKiernan was the 'puppetmaster' behind Osman Batur as well as Janim Khan and Yulbars, other holdouts against PRC rule (Zhu Peimin 2000: 237).

political leaders suspected of ethnic separatist sympathies. It was thus easier to liberate that part of Xinjiang under GMD rule than it was those districts that had already undergone 'revolution.'

The Chinese Communists, the Soviet Union, the ETR and a plane crash mystery

The ETR posed a problem for the CCP and *vice versa*. For public political consumption, the Ghulja leadership, like its Soviet backer, treated Mao's incipient government as a fellow member of the socialist fraternity. Though Xinjiang's coalition government was virtually defunct, it still existed on the books; and leaders from the ETR remained on the rosters of Xinjiang government ministers. Though he had not returned to the provincial capital since 1947, Ahmetjan was still technically the Xinjiang provincial Vice-Chairman even while he held the chairmanship of the Ghulja government. Though Stalin had reservations about Mao Zedong (Stalin opposed Mao's homegrown peasant-based revolutionary strategy, preferring those Chinese who had studied in the Soviet Union), the Soviet Union welcomed the success of the Chinese revolution, and the ETR likewise could do little but embrace the upcoming victory of the CCP and consult with its representatives. Ahmetjan Qasimi publicly renounced the former anti-Chinese positions of the Ghulja rebels and even the declaration of an 'independent Eastern Turkestan' as an 'absolutely mistaken, wrong policy'.[87]

In July 1949 Deng Liqun met in Ghulja with Ahmetjan Qasimi, Abdulkerim Abbas and Ishaq Beg (a Kirghiz) to learn about conditions in northern Xinjiang.[88] In August Mao invited a representative delegation from the former ETR to attend the National People's Consultative Conference in Beijing, a meeting intended to bring together representatives of the various non-CCP parties and ethnic groups not actively hostile to the CCP and demonstrate their solidarity with the new government. The five representatives from northern Xinjiang—Ahmetjan, Ishaq Beg, Ab-

---

87 Sadri 1984: 311, citing Ahmetjan Qasimi's collected works from a Russian source.

88 Deng Liqun would later serve as Chairman of the Cultural and Educational Committee of the Xinjiang People's Government (1950–3), editor of *Hongqi* (1960–4) and in the 1980s as a member of the 12th CCP Central Committee. Bartke 1990: 31.

dulkerim Abbas, the Kazak Delilhan and a Chinese, Luo Zhi—travelled overland to Almaty and boarded a plane for Beijing. Nothing further was heard of them for several weeks. The following December (after the PLA had occupied northern Xinjiang) Chinese authorities reported that on 27 August the plane had crashed into a mountainside near Lake Baikal in Siberia, killing all on board. Meanwhile, a new Xinjiang delegation led by Säypidin Äzizi (Saif al-Din 'Aziz, Saifudin) had been appointed and flew to Beijing to participate in the meeting, where its members agreed to abandon all calls for autonomy in either the northern three districts or Xinjiang as a whole.[89]

Needless to say, conspiracy theories abound concerning this alleged plane crash, which neatly eliminated the top leadership of the autonomous regime in the three districts at a moment critical to CCP ambitions for the area. Many have suspected the Chinese Communists of shooting down the plane or otherwise eliminating its passengers. (Askhat Iskhat, Deputy Chairman of Xinjiang provincial government from 1955–66, supposedly stated privately that Ahmetjan Qasimi and the others had been arrested upon arrival in China.[90]) The fulsome eulogies to the Yili leaders as 'revolutionary martyrs' on the official memorial in a Ghulja city park have only fuelled these suspicions.

More recently, however, Uyghur exiles in Central Asia, Russian historians and one former KGB agent have claimed that Stalin was behind the liquidation of the Yili regime he had done much to create. These sources maintain that Ahmetjan had made clear to the Soviets his intention of lobbying in Beijing for the self-determination of the East Turkestan Republic, an outcome Stalin opposed or had already bargained away in dealings with Mao.[91] Both Mao and Stalin had motive, means and opportunity to liquidate Ahmetjan, the ETR leaders and their hopes for Xinjiang autonomy. It is possible too that the plane crashed. The answer may wait in an archive somewhere.

89   Forbes 1986: 221–3; Chen Huisheng 1999: 443.
90   Sadri 1984: 313. Askhat Iskhat was himself executed during the Cultural Revolution.
91   Tursun 2002: 42, citing Antonov A. 'Sterategicheskoe partnerstvo v deystvii' [Strategic cooperation in practice], <http:// www.online.ru/sp/chronicle>, downloaded 1999, and Hashir Wahidi et al., 'Masud äpändi Häqqidä Häqiqät' [The truth about Mr Masud Sabiri], serialised in Yängi Hayat (Alma Ata), 3, 5, 7, 10, 12, 14, 17, 19 and 21 September 1991.

6. In the People's Republic of China

(1950s–1980s)

The Turkic language known as Uyghur or Turki, and its ancestral dialects, have been spoken in one form or another in Xinjiang since the
ninth century. Over this 1200-year period it has also been written in
several forms, and those changes in the script used for Uyghur mark
milestones to the region's history. The earliest Uyghur script, written
along a vertical 'spine', was derived from Soghdian and ultimately from
Aramaic. It was later adopted by the imperial Mongols and then the
Manchus and the Zunghars. From around the year 1000, as Xinjiang
Islamicised, an Arabic-based script similar to that used by Farsi and Urdu
was adopted to write Turkic, and later used for the highly Persianised
literary Turkic known as Chaghatai which was employed in Xinjiang
as well as elsewhere in Central Asia. Modified Arabic was used to write
the forerunners of modern Uyghur for a millennium. Then, in a striking
indication of the accelerated tempo of life in the twentieth century, the
writing system used for Uyghur was reformed or replaced outright four
times between the 1930s and 1980s. In 1937 and 1954 reforms of the
Arabic script made it a better fit for Modern Uyghur, but at the same
time rendered it distinct from other Arabic-based scripts in Central Asia
and the Middle East, further establishing 'Uyghur', as opposed to 'Turkic', as a primary identity of Xinjiang's non-nomadic Muslims. Meanwhile, the Soviet Union had introduced Cyrillic-based scripts for the
languages of Turkic peoples in its territory, including Uzbek (very close
to Uyghur), Uyghur, Kazak and Kirghiz. Chinese authorities followed
suit in Xinjiang in 1956, hoping to reduce the appeal of Islamic texts
and improve access to scientific and educational materials published in
the Soviet Union. Then in 1960, with the rift in Sino-Soviet relations,
Beijing dropped the Cyrillic scripts and introduced new writing systems
for Turkic peoples in Xinjiang. Though these orthographies used the

roman alphabet (with a handful of special characters) it is best thought of not so much as a romanisation as a 'Pinyin-isation'; that is, it followed not the global standards for romanising Turkic languages, but rather the idiosyncratic assignments of letters to sounds employed in *Hanyu pinyin*, the PRC romanisation of Chinese. (For example, while an *x* has traditionally been used by Turkologists to represent the uvular fricative 'kh', in the PRC pinyinisation of Uyghur, it stood for the sound 'sh'; likewise, a *q* stood for a 'ch', not the voiceless uvular stop, or 'back k'). Besides cutting off contact with Soviet Turkic peoples, one goal of this reform was to promote 'fusion and assimilation' of minorities by easing the introduction of Chinese vocabulary into Turkic languages. When one considers that Uyghur school-children had to learn both their own new script and Chinese pinyin, avoiding confusion in this way arguably makes a certain pedagogical sense, though one suspects that political considerations were primary.

In 1984, during a period of political and cultural relaxation after the excesses of the Cultural Revolution, China officially reintroduced a slightly modified Arabic-based script for Uyghur, and disseminated it effectively via educational and publishing channels. The terminology for all these writing systems became confusing: The new Arabic-based script for Uyghur was called the 'old script' (*kona yäziq*), and the former pinyinised Roman script was known as the 'new script' (*yengi yäziq*). A cynic might note that this reinstatement of Arabic-based script corresponded to China's reopening to the west after the Maoist years, and thus deprived Uyghur school-children of a leg-up in learning English and other roman-script based languages just when it would have been handy; however, the Arabic-based script also resonates with Uyghur traditions in a way many Uyghurs find satisfying.

Most recently there have been efforts in the 1990s and 2000s both under official auspices at Xinjiang University and among Uyghurs abroad to create a computer-friendly orthographic standard for Uyghur. The *Uyghur Kompyutär Yäziqi* (*Kompyutér Yéziqi*) system, for example, uses roman letters but assigns consonants in the usual turcological way, and for vowels employs only diacritical marks that can be reproduced on the keyboard with common word-processing and internet-browsing software. It resembles the new romanisation system proposed for Uzbekistan. Romanised Uyghur of one form or another is now used increasingly commonly in Uyghur email and internet documents, and has facilitated communication between Uyghurs in China, former Soviet territory, Europe, Turkey, the Middle East and the United States. Not for the first time, changes in the writing system mark changes in the Uyghurs' place in the world.[1]

The fluctuations in Uyghur orthography under the PRC also tell us something about life in Xinjiang under the Chinese Communist Party during the latter half of the twentieth century. Each official change in script (to Cyrillic in 1956, to Pinyin in 1960, to modified Arabic in 1984) marks a swing in PRC policy regarding Xinjiang and its Turkic peoples. Of course all China was disrupted by the vicissitudes of the Maoist era and recovery under Deng Xiaoping, and Chinese readers had to deal with the promulgation of the new simplified characters that to a degree divide Chinese from their own written tradition and from Chinese abroad. However, Han Chinese did not see their dictionaries and corpus of prior publications rendered obsolete *three times* in thirty-five years, and do not feel that their script changes were imposed by others. This difference is emblematic of the fact that many of China's non-Han peoples have experienced the ups and downs of PRC rule differently than have Han Chinese. All PRC citizens suffered from the effects of unwise policies and power struggles, but many Muslims in Xinjiang, like Tibetans and some other 'minority nationalities' in the PRC, came to feel that the turmoil was visited upon them by outsiders.

ESTABLISHING CONTROL AND IMPLEMENTING SOCIALISM (1949–58)

The PLA First Field Army under Wang Zhen, which entered Xinjiang in September and October of 1949, took on the tasks of governing the region for several years while overseeing the creation of new local administrative and party organs. The CCP had very little experience in Xinjiang or with the non-Han peoples of the region, and faced the additional problem of deep-seated Soviet influence among many non-Han élites. Moreover, the Chinese communist forces faced scattered resistance, some of it armed. In Kazak areas, Osman Batur, Ali Beg Hakim,

1   Hahn 1991: 91–6; McMillen 1979: 116; n.a., 'Til yeziq', <http://www.misiran. com/uyghurlar/til_yeziq/index.htm> (downloaded 17 June 2002); chart of the computer orthographic system at <http://www.misiran.com/uyghurlar/til_yeziq/ uiy_elipbe.htm>.

Janimhan and others led small bands of followers against the Chinese. Osman Batur was apprehended and executed in early 1951 amidst much publicity regarding his US connections, but Kazak 'banditry' continued until 1954.[2] In addition, in the early to mid-1950s incidents of resistance broke out in Khotan and Lop Counties in the southern Tarim led by a man named Abdimit, who was reputedly linked to Muhammad Emin Bughra (see Chapter 5). Abdimit's group, consisting of about three hundred members, at one point attacked a labour reform camp. There were other 'counter-revolutionary riots' in 1954–6 which were either repressed or exposed in the planning stages across southern Xinjiang, in Turfan and in Ghulja. These too are said to have been related to Abdimit's group.[3]

Against the background of this scattered, small-scale resistance the Chinese authorities announced the new 'unified Xinjiang Provincial People's Government' in December 1949, but in fact the PLA and party moved slowly in establishing a new administration, at first operating under the policy of a 'united front' which tolerated the continued existence of non-party organisations and greater class and ideological diversity than would later be the case. The PLA military control committees worked with existing leaders, allowing many to continue in their current positions. The surrendered GMD soldiers of the Xinjiang garrison and the Yili National Army were first absorbed into the PLA and later demobilised or disbanded (see below). Moreover, for the first year the CCP and PLA intervened relatively little in the northern three districts, leaving some 17,000 ETR officials to continue in office despite their Soviet connections.[4]

By the early 1950s the PRC began recruiting non-Han party members and replacing existing leaders with its own personnel, some drawn from those identified as activists during the party's mass mobilisation programmes, some trained in new classes which Wang Zhen called 'fac-

2 Benson and Svanberg 1998: 87.
3 On 1950s resistance to PRC rule, see Li Ze *et al.* 1994; Zhang Yuxi 1994; Ma Dazheng 2003: 32ff. Like his Chinese sources, Dillon 2004: 52–5 makes too much of these events, given that they only involved about three hundred men.
4 Moseley 1966: 26. My basic narrative of the political history of PRC Xinjiang through the mid-1970s relies primarily on McMillen 1979; exceptions are footnoted below.

tories for the production of people's cadres'.[5] The purging of officials during the 'Three Anti-' (*sanfan*, late 1951–2) campaign, and indeed continuing through the various political campaigns of the next two decades, was often violent and eliminated many of the pre-PRC era Turkic leaders, especially those associated with the Eastern Turkestan Republic. For example, several of the former officers of the Yili National Army were executed, others 're-educated', and others transferred out of North Xinjiang and their units reorganised. GMD military personnel, including commander Tao Zhiyue who retained a military position, seem to have fared relatively well by comparison, especially those who ended up in the *Bingtuan* state farms (see below).[6]

Direct military control in Xinjiang gave way in most areas in the early 1950s to 'Chinese People's Political Consultative Conferences' which then held closely controlled elections to create local People's Governments. (In Kazak areas of northern Xinjiang, where PRC control remained tenuous, these elections were postponed until 1958–9). A good many non-Han officials staffed the lower levels of these new government organs. For example, of the new city and county chairmen, forty-five were Uyghur, thirteen Han and the rest belonged to other non-Han groups. However, where non-Han held local chairmanships, Han held the vice-chairmanships, and Han from the First Field Army held most of the top provincial ministerial posts. Burhan continued as Xinjiang Provincial Chairman, though without great influence. (He also served as first President of the Chinese Islamic Association.)[7] Another significant non-Han figure to emerge prominently in this government was Säypidin Äzizi (Sai-fu-din, Saif al-Din 'Aziz), who was both Provincial Vice-Chairman and Chairman of the Xinjiang Nationalities Committee. Säypidin was a Uyghur who had studied law and political science in the Soviet Union, where he joined the Soviet Communist party and transferred his membership to the CCP in 1950. He served as Minister of Education first in the northern Xinjiang ETR in 1944 and then in the coalition government. Following his attendance of the first Chinese People's Consultative Conference in Beijing, he became a member of

5   Zhu Peimin 2000: 241.
6   Sadri 1984: 313, citing A.G. Yakovlev, 1955, *Nasionalno-Osvoboditelnoe Dvizhenie v Sintsiane*, Moscow: Izdatelstvo Akademii Nauk S.S.S.R., pp. 175–7 and ff. Benson and Svanberg 1998: 134.
7   Boorman 1967: I: 3–6.

that body as well as other national committees. He would prove one of the most enduring politicians in Xinjiang, of any ethnicity.[8]

Land reform

One of the means by which the Chinese authorities tried to recruit for the party and local administration in Xinjiang (as in China as a whole) was through its land reform programme. Land reform in the early years of the PRC had several goals, both economic and political. It aimed to undermine local élites, usually so-called landlords, by mobilising poorer peasants against them, and to earn the support of the poorer strata of society for the party by lowering rents and redistributing land. The meetings and trials in which people were encouraged to denounce former oppressors publicly also served to bring the most compliant and articulate participants to the attention of organisers, who could then recruit these 'activists' as party members and government cadres, thus expanding and deepening the state's local reach.

However, land redistribution and displacement of local élites was only a first stage of the PRC agricultural programme, and more equitable free-holding only a temporary result. The ultimate goal was collectivised agriculture, and in the first half of the 1950s, at paces that varied across the country, farmers were encouraged to form mutual aid teams and then to merge these teams by stages into larger cooperatives. Marxist and Stalinist developmental theory held that the greater economies of scale and mechanisation of agriculture realised through collectivisation would create resources that could be collected by the state and channelled into industrial development, the highest goal of China's planners, who hoped to strengthen China in the increasingly competitive Cold War world.

PLA workteams carried out the land reform movement in Xinjiang starting in 1950, travelling to rural areas, taking land, population and irrigation surveys, and staging trials and struggle meetings against 'local despots' and the Islamic institutions that were also major land-owners in Uyghur areas (see 'Islam', below). Uyghur farmers reacted to the programme with a good deal of confusion and resistance, but some welcomed the reforms, which provided the poorest of them with land,

8   Dillon (2004: 79) and McMillen (1979) differ on some details of Säpidin's biography; the former says he was from Tarbaghatai, the latter from Artush; the former says he studied in Moscow, the latter Tashkent.

livestock and other property confiscated from landlords and the religious establishment. By early 1954 over 11,000 hectares (7,370,000 *mu*) had been redistributed to some 650,000 households; by the next year 63 per cent of Xinjiang's farmers were in mutual aid teams and 5 per cent in first-stage cooperatives. This was a slower pace of collectivisation than most places in China.[9]

The nomad economy was a still more difficult target for land reform and collectivisation, due to the weak Chinese presence in north Xinjiang, the basic differences between nomadic pastoral and settled agrarian economies, and the type of social organisation that predominated among Kazaks and other nomads. Among nomads in sparsely populated grasslands and mountains, land-holding was not particularly important; what mattered was herds. Moreover, individual family units (*aul*, or tents) were already accustomed to a communal approach to herding in the context of their clans (*uru*), where much ownership and many tasks were collective. Another reason for the party's caution was the very real possibility, experienced during the traumatic Soviet collectivisation of Kazakstan in the 1930s, that herders forced to collectivise against their will would prefer to kill and eat their livestock rather than hand it over to collective (or state) ownership. Because pastoral products comprised the most important exports to the Soviet Union, and were used to pay for crucial imports of industrial plant and products, this was a serious concern.

Initial attempts by PLA work teams to impose reforms on Kazak clans and depose clan and religious elders met with sharp resistance. Therefore, after 1952 Xinjiang authorities backed off and stopped trying to foment class struggle, divide property, or liquidate 'local despots' (i.e. Kazak clan leaders), tacitly recognising that the 'reform' model did not adequately fit the circumstances of nomadic life, and that in any case the state lacked the means to force it through without sparking rebellion and a kill-off of the livestock. By 1956 only one third of the herders in northern Xinjiang were enrolled in mutual aid teams. Nevertheless, the PRC, like all sedentary states, continued to harbour a deep suspicion of mobile peoples, and sought ultimately to bring them under closer observation and control. The state achieved its first gains in this regard by providing incentives (health care, education, tax exemptions, scientific animal husbandry techniques, monetary grants and loans, even shot-

9 McMillen 1979: 131–6.

guns to take care of wolves) and gradually bringing the fully nomadic herdsmen into a semi-nomadic state, settling them in permanent winter quarters, establishing ranches where previously pastures had been open, and merging nomad co-operatives with collective farms worked by Han, Uyghur and Sibe (Xibo) agriculturalists. By late 1957 46 per cent of herding households had been enrolled in primary-stage cooperatives, and the process accelerated by 1958 during the frenzied collectivisation push of the Great Leap Forward (see below), resulting in 72 per cent co-operative membership. Even then, many of the 'collectives' represented something less than a revolutionary rupture with the past, for they were formed on the basis of the old *uru*, in a pragmatic compromise by the party officials.[10]

'Autonomy' comes to Xinjiang

In establishing control over the sprawling and diverse Tsarist empire, the Soviet Union linked former colonies and countries into a union of 're-publics'. The PRC inherited from the Qing a similar legacy of far-flung territories linguistically and culturally distinct from the core popula-tion of the centre, and borrowed from the Soviet Union the concept of 'nationality' and other ideological approaches to managing ethno-na-tional difference. However, the Chinese communist leadership avoided the federalism implied by the designation 'republic', opting instead for a system of theoretical self-rule or autonomy (*zizhi*) by non-Han peoples at local and regional levels, under over-arching control of the Chinese Communist Party. The party laid out this principle in the People's Politi-cal Consultative Conference of September 1949.

In northern Xinjiang there was at first some confusion and contesta-tion over this departure from the Soviet model. In Yili in March of 1951 an official convention to discuss the issue of local 'nationality' autonomy sought Beijing's approval to establish a Republic of Uyghuristan, obvi-ously in imitation of the Soviet Central Asian republics, and suggested that 'the autonomous republic should enjoy the right to manage its own affairs within the republic.' Although to an outside observer there seems little distinction between this and the official Chinese concept of na-tionality 'self-rule', the party nonetheless worked for years to make sure

10   Benson and Svanberg 1998: 113–16, 134–5; Moseley 1966: 45.

Xinjiang people knew what that difference was: No one should mistake autonomy for independence.[11]

As they consolidated control over parts of Xinjiang, in the spring of 1953 Chinese authorities began establishing 'autonomous' areas, starting at the lowest levels of the administrative hierarchy (*xiang* and *qu*) and gradually moving up to prefectural (*zhou*) level by 1954, when the Yili Kazak Autonomous Prefecture was formed, incorporating the districts of Yili, Tarbaghatai and Altai. In October 1955 the process reached the provincial level and the province was renamed Xinjiang Uyghur Autonomous Region (XUAR; *Xinjiang Weiwuer zizhiqu*). Säypidin took over from Burhan as Chairman of the XUAR People's Council, but real power lay in the hands of Wang Enmao, a Long March veteran who replaced Wang Zhen in the top regional military post as commander of the Xinjiang Military Region, and who also served as First Secretary of the Xinjiang branch of the Chinese Communist Party and as a member of the XUAR People's Council.

The theory behind these autonomous areas is closely related to PRC policy towards non-Han peoples in general. This policy, as developed in the years leading up to and immediately following the PRC achievement of power, endeavoured both to distance the party from the assimilationism of the GMD (see Chapter 5) and to avoid encouraging separatism in key frontier areas. The Chinese People's Political Consultative Conference in September of 1949 (the meeting the ETR leadership died trying to reach) passed a Common Programme that guaranteed the equality of all 'nationalities' (*minzu*) and announced that areas with large concentrations of non-Han peoples would enjoy autonomous status, though their territories would remain inalienable parts of the PRC. Language to the same effect appeared again in the first PRC constitution, adopted by the National Peoples' Congress in 1954. One of the first tasks of the new PRC government was to identify which groups, of China's vast and varied ethnic landscape, would qualify as 'minority nationalities' (*shaoshu minzu*) eligible for special representation in an autonomous area, official and educational use of a non-Chinese language, promotion of special cultural characteristics, and other rights. The selection process involved official ethnographic teams working in the field, applying Stalin's definition of a nation as 'a historically constituted, stable community of people,

11   Zhu Peimin 2000: 335.

Members of a Kazak family in their yurt, after erecting it on summer
pastures in the Tianshan (photo: J. Millward 1990)

formed on the basis of a common language, territory, economic life and
psychological make-up manifested in a common culture'.[12] Of some
five hundred groups that applied for legal status by 1955, the authorities of the Nationalities Affairs Commission (*minzu shiwu weiyuanhui*,
today known as the State Ethnic Affairs Commission) ultimately acknowledged fifty-five 'national minorities', which, with the Han, made
fifty-six official nationalities.[13]

In Xinjiang the nationality-identification process identified thirteen
groups, Uyghur, Han, Kazak, Hui, Kirghiz, Mongol, Sibe, Russian, Tajik,
Uzbek, Tatar, Manchu and Daur (other 'nationalities' have since established a presence). Not surprisingly this list did not disrupt the categories
that had enjoyed legal status under the Soviet-influenced regimes of
Sheng Shicai and the second ETR, and which were already for the
most part recognised by the peoples themselves. (One substantial change

12   J.V. Stalin, 1953, 'Marxism and the National Question' in *Works*, Moscow: Foreign Languages Publishing House, II: 307, quoted in MacKerras 1994: 141.
13   Dreyer 1976: 95–8; MacKerras 1994: 141–3. For general discussions of PRC
minority policy theory and practice, see Harrell 1995 and Gladney 1991.

Kirghiz mother and son at Qaraqul, in the Pamirs (photo: J. Millward 2001)

was the formal incorporation of Yili's 'Taranchis' within the Uyghur category after 1949.)

Of the official nationality groups in Xinjiang, the Kazaks, Kirghiz, Hui (Chinese Muslim), Mongols, Tajiks and Sibe were assigned autonomous counties, districts and/or prefectures. The province as a whole was of course designated a Uyghur Autonomous Region in light of the Uyghur majority. In practice, 'autonomy' in this system means that representatives of the various recognised nationalities serve on local representative bodies (not popularly elected) and as functionaries and officials in government offices. The PRC went to great lengths to train non-Chinese cadres in educational institutions at both regional and national levels. However, the autonomous counties and prefectures in mid-1950s Xinjiang all included multiple nationality groups (the smallest number is six different nationalities, in Chapchal and Tashkurgan), and in only twelve of the twenty-seven autonomous units did the eponymous nationality constitute a majority. Moreover, the power of any one minority group is further limited by the nesting of autonomous counties of one nationality within prefectures of another, the whole arrangement of course lying within the Uyghur autonomous region. In practice too, while the chairmen of each autonomous area were members of the nationality with a demographic plurality in that area, the ranking vice-chairmen were Han party members. Moreover, each 'autonomous' unit remained answerable to central authorities and to the Party, whose Xinjiang department heads were almost all Han. In fact the Xinjiang branch of the Chinese Communist Party, which had been under the Northwestern Bureau in Xi'an, now answered directly to the Central Party offices in Beijing—in this way, supervision after the formation of the XUAR was more centralised than before. Finally, although autonomous areas did form their own police forces, military command lay outside the autonomous area structure, as did the *Bingtuan* state farm and militia system (discussed below). The system of local and regional autonomous areas, then, although it placed members of the various recognised ethnic groups at each level of government in Xinjiang, does not provide what most people would understand to be 'autonomy'.[14]

Islam

Muslims live throughout China: there are sizeable populations in Beijing, along the east and south-east coasts and in almost all large urban areas. In many areas of Ningxia, Gansu and Qinghai there are exclusively Muslim (Hui) villages. Only in Xinjiang, however, did the PRC leaders face a non-sinophone majority Islamic population with strong links abroad and a well-established clerical organisation. As experience in China and the Soviet Union has shown, Islam poses a challenge to Communism, and *vice versa*, because both systems compete for influence in social, legal, ideological and political spheres, not to mention for control of land. The CCP, though by principle atheistic, moved relatively slowly in attempting to bring Islam in Xinjiang under its control during the early 1950s. Islamic education in maktaps and madrasas of the type discussed in Chapter 4, for example, continued until the late 1950s. This gradualism arose both from the state's need for the cooperation of Islamic civic leaders in the first years and from its desire to avoid arousing popular unrest. But as in Central Asia as a whole, Xinjiang's Islam was not a monolith, and the Party would find that those very aspects

14 Dreyer 1976: 104–6; McMillen 1979: 44, 68–9; Benson and Svanberg 1998: 99–100; Bovingdon 2004: 12–17.

of institutional Islam that put it in competition with the Chinese state and Communist Party also made it relatively easy to co-opt compared to more loosely organised Sufi (*ishan*) groups. It is worth remembering that principal resistance to the PRC takeover in Xinjiang came not from Islam, but from Kazak chiefs and, more quietly, from the secular and Soviet-influenced ETR.

Before the Land Reform movement, throughout the Tarim Basin oases there were tens of thousands of mosques and tomb-shrines (*mazars*) at various levels ranging from monumental Id Kah (holiday) mosques, to urban Friday mosques and famous saints' shrines with attendant clergy, to small mosques scattered throughout city neighbourhoods and rural villages, to tiny isolated 'orphan' mosques and shrines in the hills and by-ways. At the time of the Communist takeover 12,918 mosques of various sizes were recorded in Kashgar Prefecture alone; 126 of these were in the Muslim old town of Kashgar. The Islamic institutions and clergy—over 300 imams (*akhunds*), *qazi* and other clerical personnel in Kashgar in the early 1950s—formed an interlocking system and authority, funded by the rents from *waqf* (endowment) landholdings, as well as the tithe and alms tax. Though powerful, Xinjiang's Islamic institutions were accustomed to interactions with the non-Islamic state. The Qing dynasty had patronised key mosques and shrines, ratified some imams and shrine managers in office, and employed graduates of madrasas as judges in the *shari'ah* legal system which it maintained for Xinjiang Uyghurs alongside the Chinese-style legal system for Han. After 1911 Xinjiang's warlord regimes had reached various accommodations with Islam. In the 1930s Sheng Shicai and the GMD government, through the Association for Promoting Uyghur Culture, provided grain and monetary stipends to some 7,500 mid- and low-ranked Islamic clergy in the region, and likewise allowed the *shari'ah* system to function parallel to Chinese law, applying in most civil and minor criminal cases.[15]

The PRC first asserted itself against institutional Islam in 1950–1 by prohibiting tax collection by Islamic institutions. Voluntary contributions continued, and for a time mosques retained control of their *waqf* holdings. The PRC authorities also eliminated the *shari'ah* courts, stripping *qazi* of their privileges and sources of revenue. This struck at

---

15   This section on Islam in Xinjiang in the 1950s summarises several sections of Wang Jianping n.d. Wang's information derives from archival material and from surveys conducted in the 1950s, as presented in research by Wu Dongyao.

the heart of Islamic society in southern Xinjiang by eliminating Islamic jurisprudence and Islamic divorce. The one concession to local custom was to allow slightly lower marriage ages for Uyghurs than for other Chinese citizens under the new PRC Marriage Law. Nevertheless, in the first decades of the PRC the new regime eliminated child brides, scaled down marriage festivities, promoted companionate marriage (a novelty), encouraged consideration of political criteria in choice of marriage partner, and discouraged the serial marriage strategy which had been a common way Uyghur women in southern Xinjiang gained wealth and status.[16]

The main source of Islam's wealth and its tightest connection to the community in southern Xinjiang before the Communist period was land and other endowment property, managed in a system known as *waqfiya*. Some *waqfiya* lands provided revenue for charitable and public works (bridge and canal maintenance, for example); some had already been quasi-nationalised from the 1930s by the Association for the Promotion of Uyghur Culture, but had slipped into the private hands of corrupt officials of that organisation; some was caught up in complex and ambiguous relationships with both private and institutional owners. The bulk of *waqf* lands in Xinjiang in 1950, however, belonged to mosques, *mazars* and madrasas, and the revenues from rent on these lands supported the imams and other personnel attached to these centres, physical maintenance of the buildings and such incidentals as lamp oil and reed mats.

Research by Wu Dongyao and Wang Jianping gives an idea of the extent and nature of *waqfiya* in southern Xinjiang around 1949. Overall, about 2 percent of all arable land in southern Xinjiang was held in *waqfiya* endowments, though in some areas the concentration was higher: in the Kashgar district *waqfiya* lands comprised 2.23 percent of arable land, or 55,575 *mu* (about 3,700 hectares). Of that, 16,750 *mu* (1,116 hectares) belonged to the Khoja Afaq *mazar*. This famous Afaqi complex just east of Kashgar consists of a domed shrine enclosing the saints' graves, decorated in green tiles, with an associated mosque, madrasa, cemetery and pond for making ablutions before entering. (This shrine, which has been associated with the Manchu Qianlong emperor in a Chinese legend, is sometimes erroneously called the tomb of Xiang Fei or the Fragrant Concubine.) The managers of the Afaq Khoja *mazar* distributed the in-

16   Clark 1999: 209–16.

come from its *waqf* lands, mills, shops, orchards and other rental property to provide physical upkeep of the *mazar* itself (11.1 per cent) and of associated structures (11.1 per cent), stipends for eight resident shaykhs (44.5 per cent), and expenses for forty other personnel (33.3 per cent).

Given the economic basis of Islamic institutions, rent reduction and the redistribution, nationalisation and collectivisation of land would clearly undermine the independence of major Islamic institutions in southern Xinjiang, and that is precisely what the Land Reform programme, with its associated Movement to Reduce Land Rents and Oppose Local Despots, accomplished. From 1950–2 much *waqfiya* land was redistributed to poor peasants and the rents reduced on the lands not yet expropriated. As a result, with some mosques unable to afford lamp oil, 'the Muslims always performed prayers in the dark .... Sometimes they bumped their heads against the prayer-hall wall when they prostrated.'[17] Local authorities thereupon assumed the responsibility of providing oil and mats to mosques.

In similar fashion, after stripping away the endowments that had provided their personal stipends, the state paid salaries to clergymen and pressured them to give up any private lands and make donations to public works or to support the War to Resist American Aggression and Aid Korea (the Korean War). Those who cooperated (sometimes only after 'ideological education') and used the pulpit to help propagate party campaigns, often retained their high position in society; the Mullah Akhund Halibat, a former *qazi imam* of Kashgar, for example, was elected a delegate to the Xinjiang People's Congress. Although on average the incomes of Islamic clergy and their households declined during the Land Reform period, in a study of nineteen religious clergy in Yengisar, two actually emerged with a higher annual income in 1954 than before 1949; however, for many others incomes declined greatly. Xinjiang's Islamic clergy were also absorbed into a state-controlled administrative structure known as the Chinese Islamic Association, which had its head offices in Beijing.

Besides the majority Sunni Muslims in southern Xinjiang, there were various other sects, including Isma'ilis among the Tajiks in Tashkurgan, Shi'ites in Yarkand (Twelve Imam sect descendents of seventeenth-century Punjabi immigrants) and various Sufi orders. These orders were

17   Wang Jianping n.d.: 8, citing Wu Dongyao.

collectively known as *Ishan*, from a Persian word meaning 'them' and referring to the orders' hereditary leaders, believed to be descendents of the orders' founders and of the Prophet. (Chapter 3 discussed the introduction of these mystical orders into Xinjiang and the secular power achieved by the Naqshbandiyya in particular.) Despite the wars and political upheavals from the mid-nineteenth through the mid-twentieth century, many *ishan* groups remained active during the first half of the twentieth century.

Ishan orders formed around a revered leader and sometimes had a physical locus in an assembly or prayer hall where rites were held. Initiates practised a series of complex breathing exercises, repeated the *dhikr* ('remembrance of God', consisting of repeated chanting of Allah's name, certain Quranic verses or other texts), and committed themselves to obey a set of rules laid down by the *ishan*. The most dedicated followers could advance to become disciples of the *ishan*, who conveyed esoteric knowledge to this select few. Followers met weekly for prayer rituals involving chanting, dancing and/or the music of drum and *surnai* (a double-reed flute); these ceremonies, which could last for hours, promised mystical communion with God as well as physical exhaustion. (An *Ishan* ecstatic ceremony was described in Chapter 4.)

Another facet of *Ishan* practice in Xinjiang was pilgrimage to and worship at *mazars*, shrines to holy personages. Besides the grand *mazars* like that of Khoja Afaq and a few others in Yarkand and Yengisar, there were smaller shrines outside urban areas, some with mud-brick assembly halls, some consisting of little more than ordinary graves festooned with sticks, flags, strips of cloth, yak- or ox-tails, sheep's skulls and horns, in continuation of ancient Inner Asian practice found also in Mongolia and Tibet (see discussion of Sufism in the Tarim Basin in Chapter 3 and photo of the shrine at Qumartagh in the same chapter). People went to *mazars* at various times of the year, some travelling from as far away as Gansu and Qinghai. Shrines were also the venue for festivals, bazaars, entertainment, adoration, fasting, meditation and supplication for good harvests, good health, good marriage, the birth of sons, wealth, rain, revenge and so forth; visitors made donations of money or food to the shrine caretakers, often themselves holy men or *shaykhs*. *Ishan* congregations also held night-time rites at shrines.

Despite ties to *mazars*, Sufi Islam had always been more of a popular activity, carried out in a variety of places, and not as dependent on real estate as was the regular Sunni clergy (though the groups were not mutu-ally exclusive). Thus, although the Land Reform movement undermined the autonomy of southern Xinjiang's Islamic establishment, including the larger *mazars* that had held *waqfiya* property, *ishan* sects remained energetic and in the early 1950s actually experienced an explosion of popularity both in cities and the countryside around the Tarim Basin, opening prayer halls and initiating new members in large ceremonies. PRC tolerance for this and for continuing Islamic education may simply reflect the limited reach of state and party in Uyghur areas of Xinjiang in the early 1950s, or perhaps a recognition that as a popular religion, Sufism in Xinjiang was not political in nature and posed no immediate threat to the state. In any case, this moderation began to change in the mid-1950s, in the lead-up to the Religious Reform Campaign of 1958, as part of a broad shift to radical leftist policies that would continue for twenty years.[18]

Migration, settlement and Xinjiang's peculiar institution

In one critical regard, PRC policy in Xinjiang was identical to that of Qianlong and later Qing emperors: it endeavoured to settle Chinese in Xinjiang, both to relieve population pressure in eastern provinces and to strengthen security on the frontier. In the 1950s Liu Shaoqi, then one of the top leaders in the Politburo, recalled the Qing model in his 'grand border support plan'. The leading edge of this resettlement, or colonisa-tion, programme was the military state farm, a device with ancient roots in Chinese frontier statecraft. Han, Tang, Qing and other Chinese and non-Chinese dynasties had set their troops along the Mongolian and Xinjiang frontiers to working on farms to supply their own grain. The immediate precedents for the PRC version of this institution date back to the eighteenth century when the Qing elaborated on the old model by including civilian and penal colonies together with military farms in its *tuntian* system (see Chapter 3).

The first of the new colonists in post-1949 Xinjiang were some 103,000 demobilised soldiers, including the 80,000 troops of the former GMD garrison, whom Beijing chose to leave in Xinjiang. From early 1950 these men were deployed in agriculture, stock-raising, civil engi-

18   The above section is based primarily on Wang Jianping n.d.; see also McMillen 1979: 115.

neering, industry and mining. Between 1952 and 1954 they were reorganised into what would be the primary institution for handling migration and resettlement of Chinese in Xinjiang, the Production-Construction Military Corps (*Shengchan jianshe bingtuan*, often abbreviated in English as the PCC). The *Bingtuan*, as it is called for short in Chinese, was designed to combine production with militia duties ('one hand on the gun, one hand on the pickaxe') and to promote land reclamation and permanent settlement. Though primarily a civilian organisation, the *Bingtuan* hierarchy maintained a military nomenclature and other elements of military structure, as well as its ties with the PLA, especially the First Field Army. However, in addition to demobilised soldiers, from the 1950s through to the mid-1970s the *Bingtuan* absorbed hundreds of thousands of Han migrants and, in a continuation of the Qing practice of exiling prisoners to the far west, tens of thousands of convicts were dispatched to Xinjiang. (Originally this number included many political prisoners; however, since 1976 the *Bingtuan* prisons have specialised in warehousing hardened criminals coming from outside Xinjiang to serve long sentences).[19] The *Bingtuan* eventually became a higher-level political entity, not under the direct supervision of the 'autonomous' localities or regional government of Xinjiang but rather answering only to the party and Beijing.

Soon after its founding, the *Bingtuan* began actively recruiting manpower to journey west and 'open the frontier'. The Shanghai area became the single largest source of Chinese migrants to Xinjiang in the first decades of the PRC. This was in part because Shanghai was so crowded, and in part because a blockade of Shanghai's ports by the Nationalist regime in 1949–50 sent Shanghai leaders in search of new energy sources. They persuaded the First Field Army then controlling Gansu and Xinjiang to provide oil from the Yumen fields on the Gansu-Xinjiang border directly to Shanghai, and a special Shanghai-Xinjiang connection was formed. *Bingtuan* recruiters worked with local authorities to persuade Shanghainese technical personnel and patriotic youth to rusticate to Xinjiang. From the 1950s through the 1970s tens of thousands of Shanghainese and natives of other cities and provinces were signed up, given clothes, shoes, food and tickets to Xinjiang (the Lanzhou-Xinjiang

19   McMillen 1979: 56–7; Seymour 2000: 172–5. On Qing-era exile to Xinjiang, see Waley-Cohen 1991; on the PRC gulag in Xinjiang and elsewhere, see Seymour and Anderson 1998: Chapter 3.

railroad reached Hami in 1960 and Urumchi in 1962). Many stayed permanently. As part of its special relationship with Shanghai, Xinjiang also purchased a relatively high percentage of the city's manufactured goods, and strove to market its own products in China's largest and most urbane metropole. Optimistic marketers from the Northwest China Animal Products Company tried convincing Shanghai consumers that Xinjiang yak meat was 'better than beef!'[20]

Most of the Han migrants to Xinjiang in the 1950s-70s were resettled and put to work by the *Bingtuan*. From 1954 to 1957 the *Bingtuan* population grew from 200,000 to 300,000 on the strength of this influx; by 1966 it numbered 500,000 to 600,000. The *Bingtuan* also helped handle the massive influxes of Han during the famine years of the Great Leap Forward in 1959, 1960 (over 800,000 each year) and 1961 (over 600,000), and in 1965–7, when the youth of China hit the road during the Cultural Revolution and 1.6 million more Han came to Xinjiang. A report of 1975 claimed that 450,000 urban youth were settled in Xinjiang, making it one of the largest destinations for the rustication programme of the Maoist years. The new city of Shihezi was built by the *Bingtuan* and became its headquarters.

Although Chinese population in Xinjiang remained concentrated in the east and north, with Uyghurs predominating in the south-west as in Qing times, the *Bingtuan* established Chinese enclaves throughout the entire region, as well as in other strategic areas, such as along the Soviet border. (The issue of more recent Han migration and the relative population of Han to other groups in Xinjiang is taken up in Chapter 7.)[21]

The *Bingtuan* and resettled Han Chinese from the east were, to use a Maoist-era term, the 'shock troops' in the campaign to tame nature and wrest farmland from the wilderness.[22] The demobilised soldiers, under quasi-military organisation, and the former GMD solders among them as in effect quasi-prisoners, were put to the labour-intensive tasks of clearing land, building dams, digging canals and planting crops. These efforts greatly expanded the amount of land under cultivation in Xin-

---

20   White 1979: 487–92.
21   McMillen 1979: 61–6; Seymour 2000: 174–5, 184; Hannum and Yu Xie 1998: 324, table 1; Bernstein 1977: 27, table 4; Wiemer 2004: 168–9. See descriptions of individual *Bingtuan* regions in Zhao Yuzheng 1991: 265–311, and endpaper map.
22   For the militaristic approach to the environment in the Maoist era, see Shapiro 2001.

jiang. Yang Zengxin's government had registered between 648,000 and 701,000 hectares of farmland in the 1910s; in 1949 there were some 1 to 1.2 million hectares under cultivation. By 1961 Xinjiang's overall cultivated area had almost tripled to 3.2 million hectares. A good percentage of this increase was due to the *Bingtuan*, whose own area expanded from 77,183 hectares in 1953 to 820,265 in 1961. In the Tarim Basin oases spread out into the desert; according to maps, the Kashgar oasis doubled in area between 1943 and 1962. Much new farmland was carved out of the steppes north of the Tianshan. Before 1949 some 269,000 hectares of land were registered in the Yili district; by 1961 almost 711,000 hectares in the district had been put under the plough.[23]

TWENTY YEARS OF CULTURAL REVOLUTION (1957–78)

Although energetic in its approach to the basic tasks of repressing armed resistance, establishing party and government organs, reforming landholding, opening new farmland, and taking control of the Islamic establishment, the PRC in the early 1950s avoided policies that struck too close to the cultural differences between Xinjiang's Turkic and other nationalities and the Han Chinese. Policy watchwords were to 'practise democracy' in dealings with non-Han, strive to develop economically, and to avoid mechanical application of policies from eastern China to Xinjiang, giving due attention instead to 'local conditions'.[24] Beginning around 1956, however, shifts in the domestic Chinese political and economic situation and in the Sino-Soviet relationship converged to send China lurching to the left, as 'Maoist' policies replaced the more gradual, developmental model embraced by Liu Shaoqi, Deng Shaoping and others in the Chinese leadership. The era of 'class struggle as the key link' began.

Maoism produced by turns episodes of economic chaos (in the Great Leap Forward) and economic, political and military chaos (in the Great Proletarian Cultural Revolution). In the social and cultural spheres, moreover, these years were marked by a climate of communist puritanism, xenophobia and rejection of cultural artefacts and expression seen as 'feudal' (old) or deviating from the norms that came to define the good socialist citizen. Not surprisingly, with the PRC population and

23 Wiens 1966: 75–7, 81, table 4, 84–5; Zhao Yuzheng 1991: 332.
24 McMillen 1979: 86–8.

leadership dominated by Han, these socialist norms were largely Chinese norms.[25] One result was heightened official intolerance and repression of many aspects of Turkic and other ethnic cultures in Xinjiang. PRC policy in Xinjiang took on an assimilationist edge.

Tension with the Soviet Union

Because of its history of Russian and Soviet incursions, Soviet influence on its non-Han intellectuals and cadres, close economic ties and the long shared border, any changes in the Sino-Soviet relationship had an especially heavy impact on Xinjiang. In the first years after 1949, while relations between Beijing and Moscow remained warm, Xinjiang enjoyed continued close relations with the Soviet Union. The CCP even left the Union for the Defence of Peace and Democracy in Xinjiang (Ahmetjan Qasimi's pro-Soviet party structure) intact for a time, while working to 'de-Sovietise' the ranks of Uyghur, Kazak and other non-Han leadership in the region. After 1949 the Soviet Union remained Xinjiang's principal trading partner, export destination and source of manufactured goods and technology transfer. However, some of the factors that would lead to the 1960 Sino-Soviet split were already evident in Xinjiang from the start. In 1950 a protocol attached to the 'Sino-Soviet Treaty of Friendship, Alliance and Mutual Assistance', signed by Stalin and Mao Zedong in Moscow, created two Sino-Soviet joint stock companies in Xinjiang that allowed the Soviet Union continued special access to Zungharia's oil and non-ferrous metals for a projected thirty years. These were continuations of the type of arrangement Stalin had enjoyed with Sheng Shicai and the Eastern Turkestan Republic. Stalin had demanded these and other concessions (including recognition of the independence of Outer Mongolia and Soviet use of Port Arthur and Dairen in Manchuria) in return for a five-year loan of $300 million which China desperately needed. The joint stock companies rankled Mao enough that he brought them up repeatedly in conversations with Khruschev in 1958, referring to Xinjiang as a Soviet 'semi-colony', the same term he used to describe the concessions of European imperialist powers in China before the revolution. (The Soviet Union sold its stake and pulled out of the companies at the end of 1954; they be-

25 Harrell 1995:'Introduction'; Gladney 1994.

came the Xinjiang Non-Ferrous Metals Company and the Xinjiang Petroleum Company.)[26]

Other causes of Sino–Soviet tension included Khruschev's denunciation of Stalin (February 1956) which embarrassed the Chinese leadership who were given no prior indication of de-Stalinisation and had long praised Stalin as a great communist leader. Furthermore, Mao did not appreciate Soviet criticism of his road to socialism (characterised by more rapid collectivisation of agriculture than in the Soviet model) or Khruschev's support for Defence Minister Peng Dehuai in opposing Mao's utopian Great Leap Forward. Mao's bellicose rhetoric with regard to the capitalist world and insouciance towards nuclear war frightened Khruschev, and led to personal recriminations, the pull-out of Soviet technical advisers, and a deep rift between the two countries by 1960. There were serious military clashes along disputed zones of the 4,150-mile Sino-Soviet border through the 1960s.

These growing tensions had an immediate impact in Xinjiang. Although authorities had introduced the Cyrillic-based Uyghur script only in 1956, with the express purpose of enhancing communication with the Soviet Union, from late 1957 they began systematically replacing Soviet textbooks with Chinese-produced ones.[27] And things grew hot for 'minority' cadres. As will be discussed in detail below, the nationwide campaigns of the late 1950s and early 1960s were accompanied in Xinjiang by sharp attacks on non-Han cadres for pro-Soviet sentiments; in political rhetoric, the crime of 'local nationalism' (a label applied to defences of non-Han ethnic distinctiveness, dissent over economic policies that created famine, and to outright separatist sentiments) was linked to that of 'revisionism', a coded reference to the Soviets. Ethnic nationalism in Xinjiang was thus treated as intrigue by foreign powers. Intense anti-Chinese propaganda from Soviet sources added to these tensions. A series of incidents of unrest in the north, including the flight of tens

---

26 Forbes 1986: 226; McMillen 1979: 34–5; Zubok 2001: 19, 27–8. When Khruschev asked if Mao really considered the Soviets 'red imperialists', Mao sarcastically replied: 'There was a man by the name of Stalin, who took Port Arthur and turned Xinjiang and Manchuria into semi-colonies, and he also created four joint companies. These were all his good deeds.' Khruschev responded, a moment later, 'You defended Stalin. And you criticised me for criticising Stalin. And now—vice versa.' To which Mao replied, 'You criticised [him] for different matters.' (Zubok 2001: 29–30).

27 McMillen 1979: 92.

of thousands of people into Soviet territory in 1962, led to a closure of the border, withdrawal of Soviet Consulates in Xinjiang and on-going border clashes over the next several years.

Campaigns of the late 1950s

As the Sino-Soviet relationship soured, the pace of China's economic development was likewise failing to live up to expectations. Chinese leaders had hoped that land reform and the first stages of collectivisation would produce surpluses that could fuel industrial development, an increasingly urgent concern once it became apparent that Soviet industrial and military help would come at a high price. In an effort to understand the reasons for sluggish economic growth and to seek participation by 'the people', Mao experimented briefly with free speech. In spring of 1956 he initiated a nationwide campaign, known as the Hundred Flowers Movement after the slogan 'let a hundred flowers bloom, let a thousand schools of thought contend'. In this campaign the Chinese leadership solicited public criticism of the party and the government. However, the volume, vehemence and content of the response shocked the leadership, and it then launched the Anti-Rightist Rectification campaign, hard on the heels of the Hundred Flowers, to criticise, purge and punish the very critics it had encouraged a few months earlier.

In Xinjiang, the press reports from both the Hundred Flowers and the Rectification campaigns reveal what people of all nationalities felt were the most severe problems after several years of PRC rule. Of most concern to the CCP authorities was the revelation of wide-spread dissatisfaction among non-Han with nationalities policy and with the actual working out of Xinjiang's promised 'autonomy'. The complaints included the assertion that Han officials, who held real power despite the veneer of non-Han autonomy, were haughty and domineering; that excessive numbers of Han cadres looked on as minorities did the difficult work; that Han functionaries did not understand Uyghur, so could not handle issues raised by Uyghurs; that 'minorities' who raised legitimate criticisms were branded 'local nationalists'; that non-Han cadres were chosen for political reasons, not ability, and acted like 'jackals' serving the Han; that the *Bingtuan* 'Han colonists' were destroying the Xinjiang environment; that non-Han people were being forced to learn Chinese. Critics demanded more real autonomy, with all or a majority of local positions to be filled by non-Han nationalities. Some even called for the expulsion of Chinese settlers and cadres from Xinjiang, and for an independent local communist party, or even a state, established separate from China and perhaps attached to the Soviet Union. This criticism derived even from members of the government: the head of the Xinjiang Culture Department and Chairman of the Literary Union, Zia Samit (Zi-ya Sai-mai-ti), is said to have suggested that 'when considering Xinjiang's fate, the best solution would be independence.'[28]

As in the rest of China, the Anti-Rightist Campaign of 1957 also targeted as 'rightists' Han critics of the party, but by late November the campaign in Xinjiang focused on 'local nationalists'. Säypidin, who co-chaired the rectification committee with Wang Enmao, publicly distanced himself from former ETR colleagues and the Soviet Union, and purged many non-Han cadres who had answered the Hundred Flowers call, especially those with past connections to the Yili group or the Soviets. According to a Chinese party historian, 1,612 cadres were labelled 'local nationalists', of whom ninety-two fled to the Soviet Union. The rest were sent to labour camps for thought reform, where they suffered overwork, famine and other hardships in 1958–61; many were rehabilitated only in 1979.[29]

Although it served as an effective ambush of potential dissenters against the regime, the Hundred Flowers Movement and Anti-Rightist Campaign did little to improve China's economy. Despite the collectivisation of much of the Chinese peasantry into higher-level Agricultural Producers' Cooperatives of 100–300 households in size by the end of first Five-Year Plan (1953–7), agricultural production remained inadequate for the needs of industrial development, and development as a whole was severely imbalanced by region and sector. The outcry unleashed during the Hundred Flowers period convinced Mao that too many 'rightists' remained in positions of authority and that their cautious economic policies were slowing development and diverting China from the revolutionary path. At the same time, the loss of Soviet advisers and aid, and the growing threat of hostilities with the Soviet Union raised concerns about the pace of industrialisation and its concentration in a few areas. Mao opted to correct these problems by means of an up-

28   McMillen 1979: 92–4, 117; Benson and Svanberg 1998: 136; Zhu Peimin 2000: 335.
29   Sabri 1984: 315; Zhu Peimin 2000: 351–2.

by-ones-own-bootstraps development blitz, and thus perpetrated one of the greatest policy errors—some call it a crime against humanity—in history.

Mao launched the Great Leap Forward in an attempt to kick-start China's development by merging agricultural and industrial production, telescoping the stages to communism, mobilising massive levies of labour and relying on sheer will-power rather than technocratic planning and material incentives for producers. Ideology trumped all, as it became better to be 'red' than 'expert'. During the Leap the charged political climate generated by Beijing encouraged provincial and local officials to form, on an accelerated timetable, massive 'People's Communes' of some 30,000 people, fifteen times larger than previous collectives. Commune members moved into barracks and ate in communal dining halls to save cooking time and allow family kitchen utensils to be melted down for small-scale rural steel production, the other 'leg' of the campaign. Peasants on many communes worked their fields, dug canals or moved mountains for the commune by day and tried to make steel in backyard furnaces at night. Because communisation and ideological motivation was supposed to unleash unprecedented productive forces, leaders responding to political signals from Beijing set unrealistic production targets and then claimed not only to meet but to exceed them. The fact that many statisticians, accountants and other intellectual 'experts' with dour assessments of the economy had been purged in the Anti-Rightist Campaign made it hard for the centre to evaluate wildly exaggerated reports from the provinces, and led it to interpret bad harvests as bumper crops. The utopian plan was a formula for disaster, and disaster did indeed result, compounded by fool-hardy central directives in some areas allowing peasants to eat all they liked in the mess halls and not to harvest the entire crop in the mistaken belief that storage granaries were already full beyond capacity. Meanwhile, low-tech, decentralised and inefficient industrial schemes produced staggering waste, as the transit system clogged with criss-crossing shipments of coal and iron and the 'backyard furnaces' turned raw materials into useless scrap. Hundreds of millions of peasants were driven to exhaustion at their combined agricultural, industrial and public works tasks. An estimated 30 million people died from famine in 1959–62, a direct result of Great Leap policies.

In Xinjiang the Great Leap followed the same lines as in the rest of China. Communes were formed (in agrarian areas 5,836 agricultural producers cooperatives merged into 562 people's communes by October 1958, and communisation was complete in pastoral areas by April the following year). Localities proclaimed wild targets (Urumchi city authorities in 1958 announced a plan to eliminate rats, mosquitoes, flies, sparrows and filth within the year), and the goals of the Second Five-Year Plan were repeatedly revised upwards.

The political hysteria likewise produced famine in Xinjiang. According to a recent Chinese account, in 1960 over 5,000 people died of starvation in Bai county, because local officials blamed shortages on 'rightist opportunism' and 'capitalist thinking of wealthy middle peasants' and refused to release 9 million kilos of grain available in county storehouses. A total of at least a thousand starved to death in Xinhe, Kucha and Aqsu counties; at least a thousand convicts starved in the *Bingtuan* labour camps. There were incidents of starvation in counties in the Kashgar area as well. Even the regional capital, Urumchi, was reduced to a three day's supply of grain at the height of the shortages in 1961, and had to be relieved by a shipment of 4,400 truckloads of grain. The Han population of Urumchi in 1960 had been 477,321, and that for Uyghurs, 76,496. By 1962 these figures were down to 363,554 and 52,205 respectively, in large part because of a policy requiring new arrivals in the city to return to their home villages. A major steel plant outside the city lost a third of its workers. During the Leap some people in Urumchi were at times compelled to eat tree bark. Needless to say, non-staple items (vegetables, salt, sugar, soap, tea, fuel) were in short supply and tightly rationed. Water too was severely rationed, and in Urumchi public bathhouses closed down. Students at Xinjiang University were fed one meal a day, and years later one graduate recalled being *yerim toq, yerim ach*—half full, half hungry—from 1958 through 1962. Still, he was better off than the Han beggars straggling into Urumchi and other parts of Xinjiang from further east. The Kazaks' pastoral economy also suffered: analysis of herd size statistics from before and after the Great Leap suggest big losses in 1959–62: average annual rates of herd increase for 1958–65 fell to one quarter their pre-Leap average.[30]

---

30   Zhu Peimin 2000: 280–1, 290, 293–5; Zhu's figures on starvation in Xinjiang during the Leap may be assumed to be conservative estimates. Regarding bark eating: personal communication by a Hui restaurateur, Urumchi, June 1998; 1960 and 1962 population figures from Clark 1999: 77–8, citing *Wulumuqi shizhi*, a city gazetteer produced by the local party history committee in 1994; Clark 1999: 112–13;

Though Xinjiang's experience of the Leap was broadly similar to that in China as a whole, Xinjiang's frontier position and the fact that the majority of its population were 'minorities' gave the episode there a somewhat different significance than in core regions of China. The year 1958 marks a watershed between, on the one hand, the relatively more tolerant, pluralistic approach of the early 1950s, when 'Great Han chauvinism' was officially condemned as often as 'local nationalism', and the aggressive assimilationism of the later Maoist years, on the other. Following the nationalistic criticism of the Hundred Flowers Movement at the onset of the Great Leap, the Party launched a series of anti-Islamic measures linked to the Religious Reform Movement. The press fell silent about Islamic holidays which it had formerly acknowledged—the official silence suggesting a changed official attitude if not a full crackdown. The government also refused permission for Xinjiang Muslims to go on hajj, and raised the legal marriage age in Xinjiang to bring it into conformity with that in the rest of China, withdrawing a concession earlier afforded Xinjiang's Muslims.[31]

The collectivisation drive during the Leap was more aggressive and extensive than that of earlier agrarian campaigns. In pastoral areas of northern Xinjiang in particular enrolment in collectives had been incomplete and often softened by state-private arrangements and accounting tricks that allowed herdsmen to retain *de facto* ownership of livestock; some places had not even carried out land reform. Even where settled Kazaks were formed into cooperatives and early communes up to 1959, these still did not break down the nomads' own social structure, because although they aggregated several *uru*, or clan groups, each was simply treated as its own 'production brigade' and accounting and ownership remained at that level.

However, this changed during the high point of the Great Leap in the winter of 1959–60, when teams of party, PLA and *Bingtuan* workers conducted a mass 'education' campaign among the Kazaks to promote communalism and weed out rightism, bourgeois individualism, local nationalism and other sins. Large communes were formed by merging multiple Kazak production brigades with farming collectives and raising the unit of accounting to the level of the commune as a whole, thus

---

Benson and Svanberg 1998: 117, table 4.2; Moseley 1966: 105. The analysis of herd size is complicated by the PRC failure to release statistics for the Great Leap years.
31 Benson and Svanberg 1998: 136.

undermining the decision-making capacity of the production brigade (*uru*). The new communes tried to feed livestock with feed-grain rather than on pasturage as a means of raising pastoral production, but with the politically-desirable side-effect of keeping both herds and herdsmen settled in one place. The institutions of mandatory mess hall and child-care crèches were likewise effective at sedentarising the nomads. Moreover, the Kazaks were not exempted from the national call to make steel. Many were put to work as industrial labourers, some even building and operating blast furnaces on the steppe. A contemporary *People's Daily* reporter described the new socialist idyll:

Our car travelled along the Ku-nai-su River on the boundless grassland. Flocks of sheep were silently grazing ... like white clouds over the green sea. Having climbed over several snow-capped mountains, we suddenly found in front of us a fiery scene, like that of a battle. A long line of hot-air furnaces and iron-smelting furnaces were emitting dark smoke. Trucks loaded with ore and equipment were moving about like shuttles on looms. The blasting of rocks—part of the mining process—and the sound of machines broke the silence of the grassland. This was the new iron and steel city—Hsinyuan Iron and Steel Works—in the Ili Kazak Autonomous Chou.[32]

The overall impact of communisation on herdsmen, then, was to replace clan-based organisation with closer party control, to sedentarise them and to divert as many as possible from herding to agricultural and industrial labour. Xinjiang officials were quite explicit about the non-economic goals of the Leap in the region, especially those relating to nationality policy. For example, Wang Enmao wrote in February 1960 that 'there is reason to say that with the people of minority nationalities being brought into closer contact and cooperation as a result of the establishment of the people's communes, there will be a greater union which will eventually lead to *the complete blending of all the nationalities*, and this will have a tremendously far-reaching significance for the steady development of socialist and communist construction in Xinjiang' (emphasis mine).[33] Here, clearly stated, is the hopeful theory that socialist development would erode ethnic differences

32 Benson and Svanberg 1998: 135; Moseley 1966: Chapter 7. Quote from 'Iron and Steel City on the Grasslands', *Renmin ribao*, 21 June 1959, translated in Moseley 1966: 96–7.

33 Wang Enmao, 'Long Live the People's Commune', *Renmin ribao*, 5 February 1960, cited in Moseley 1966: 77.

among the 'nationalities' of China; furthermore, this fusion of peoples was not to happen in the distant future but, like everything else in the frenetic mentality of the Great Leap era, rapidly, through abrupt, often wrenching, transitions.

The great flight to the Soviet Union and the Yi-Ta Incident

This facet of the Great Leap era in Xinjiang—the sharpened assimilationist agenda—contributed to a major crisis on the northern frontier. As mentioned above, the Great Leap period corresponded to the Chinese Communist break with the Soviet Union, as well as to an upsurge in Han migration to Xinjiang, with 300,000 rusticated urban youth and at least 890,000 voluntary migrants arriving between 1959–61 (the latter no doubt escaping worse conditions elsewhere). The new rail line linked Lanzhou to Hami by 1960 and Urumchi by 1962, promising further waves of Chinese arrivals. Many of the new migrants settled along the railway line between Hami and Urumchi while others entered the *Bingtuan*, which in 1958 began a massive expansion, especially into the belt of settlements extending north-west from Urumchi. New migrants worked in many new industrial enterprises and on *Bingtuan* farms in northern Xinjiang, where vast areas of pastureland were put to the plough. This influx increased available supplies of labour but also increased the numbers of mouths to feed, and when the wild assumptions underlying the Great Leap failed to materialise, the changing demographic balance in the region contributed to ethnic tensions. Han areas in northern Xinjiang (including Urumchi, the capital) ran a persistent grain deficit, which was made up for by shipments from the Uyghur south. As grain shortages throughout the region grew acute, grain continued to be shipped north to supply the capital, the railway route between Hami and Urumchi and the new settlements in Zungharia. Xinjiang also exported some 30,000 tons of grain to other Chinese provinces between 1960 and 1962.[34]

Some or all of these Great Leap era policies (anti-Sovietism and anti-local nationalism; heightened CCP penetration and control of the former ETR and Kazak lands; surging Chinese in-migration; economic disruption associated with communisation and industrialisation, especially among nomads; pastureland commandeered for agriculture; and

34 McMillen 1979: 122–3, 138–43; Moseley 1966: 105–6; Zhu Peimin 2000: 285, 287, 289.

grain requisitions that seemingly favoured Han over Uyghur areas in a time of famine) produced great disaffection in northern Xinjiang. Soviet propaganda, which made much of the Great Leap disruptions, no doubt helped to agitate people further. In April of 1962 tens of thousands of refugees began to flee from Yili and Tacheng (Tarbaghatai) districts, taking livestock and goods with them; by May some 60,000 (according to some estimates, over 100,000) had entered the Soviet Union. The refugees included Kazak and Uyghur intelligentsia with Soviet ties dating from the days of the ETR (who realised that China's definitive split with the Soviet Union would not bode well for them), as well as many herdsmen. Judging from increases in tallied populations on the Soviet side, the émigrés also included Hui and other groups. Many crossed the border with papers issued by Soviet officials. In May Chinese authorities dispatched five battalions and twenty-one companies of *Bingtuan* militia to work with PLA forces to staunch the flow of people and animals by sealing the border. Near the end of the month, people in Ghulja, frustrated in their attempts to buy outbound tickets, rioted at the bus station. According to one Chinese account, 'a small number of bad people' overcame station guards and fifteen soldiers, while shouting 'now is the time to overthrow the Communist Party and eliminate the problem of the Chinese.' Having grown quite large (a Chinese scholar writes 2,000 people), the crowd then attacked the offices of the People's Committee and Communist Party of Yili Autonomous Zhou, taking documents and damaging property. Troops from the *Bingtuan* Agricultural Fourth Division repressed the riot by firing on the crowd.[35]

The cross-border exodus left several counties all but depopulated. Sixty-eight percent of the population of Tacheng county had fled; of three communes in Huocheng county with a former combined population of 16,000, only 3,000 were left. Only nine households remained at the Progress Commune. Besides the blow to its propaganda war with the Soviet Union, China now faced a security threat along its near vacant north-west border. Once again it was the *Bingtuan* that came to the rescue, moving its people into the area in force to take up the agricultural, pastoral and forestry work of the abandoned communes. Over the next four years the *Bingtuan* took over a ten to thirty kilometre band stretching along the Soviet border in Yili, Bortale, Tarbaghatai and Altai

35 Benson and Svanberg 1998: 104; McMillen 1979: 122–3, 157–62; Moseley 1966: 108–9; Zhao Yuzheng 1991: 212.

districts, its members staffing fifty-three farms at key points along this strip, in effect erecting a quarantine zone between Kazaks in China and those in the richer Kazak SSR.[36]

Once the extent of the Great Leap debacle and its effects on minority relations became clear, in order to restore stability and secure the food supply the PRC leadership was forced to back off from its drive towards radical communisation and impossible production targets in favour of a return to smaller units of accounting and material incentives. The state authorised a limited return to private ownership and rural markets. Personal ability rather than political stridency became relatively more important in the selection and promotion of officials than during the Leap. The party returned temporarily to a posture of measured tolerance for the 'unique characteristics' of Xinjiang's non-Han peoples, and lengthened its projections for the 'blending of the nationalities' to 'after a very long historical period'. Nevertheless, because the official CCP explanation of the 1962 exodus and Yi-Ta Incident placed the blame squarely on Soviet instigators, the party conducted another round of purges of non-Han cadres.[37]

The years of the Leap had seen serious frontier troubles: in addition to the exodus from northern Xinjiang and the rift with the Soviet Union, there had been the Tibetan rebellion and the flight of the Dalai Lama (1959) and the Sino-Indian border clash (1962).[38] In the context of the Soviet threat on this exposed frontier, in the post-Leap period Xinjiang's leadership under Wang Enmao thus focused primarily on returning Xinjiang to political and economic normalcy. This was imperative, as standards of living in the region had in three years collapsed to well below pre-1949 levels.

The Cultural Revolution

After the Great Leap Mao was forced to step down from day-to-day command in China, while others tried to repair the shattered economy. Mao, however, nursed a grievance against his critics and opposed

---

36   Zhao Yuzheng 1991: 212–13; Moseley 1966: 112.
37   McMillen 1979: 48, 96, 149–50.
38   The war with India in northern Kashmir resulted in a Chinese victory and annexation of disputed territory (now a road linking Kashgar to Lhasa runs through this Aksai Chin region).

the moderate economic policies undertaken by Liu Shaoqi and Deng Xiaoping. Consequently, in late 1965, as Mao embarked upon a return to power by using his still-substantial charisma to stir up a popular firestorm, the epoch known as the 'Great Proletarian Cultural Revolution' began. He encouraged China's youth, formed into bands of 'red guards', to launch political and often physical assaults on the organs and personnel of the party and bureaucracy, whom they accused of 'taking the capitalist road' and other evils. The high-ranking officials targeted from early 1966 turned the same hyperbolic rhetoric of class struggle on their attackers and organised their own Red Guard factions, while purging low-level scapegoats from their own ranks in a rear-guard effort to defend their own positions. The extreme tone of the campaigns led to attacks on anything old or foreign or anyone associated with such things, including artists, writers, performers, academics and anyone formerly connected with the GMD or Soviet Union. The unlucky objects of these attacks had their houses ransacked, were demoted, publicly humiliated, thrown into labour camps and often killed. Children whose parents had been sent away were left to fend for themselves in the streets. Rival Red Guard factions, joined by workers and soldiers, engaged in pitched battles. When by early 1967 the fratricidal chaos threatened to spin entirely out of control, Mao called in the PLA, which restored a semblance of order. Ultimately 'revolutionary committees', consisting of representatives of military, party and 'the masses', took control of production and administrative units where the party organisation had been shattered. The Red Guards were dissolved and millions of urban youth were sent down to work in the countryside for long years.

Meanwhile, Mao had achieved the demotion and disgrace of his rivals, including that of Deng Xiaoping, Zhu De, Bo Yibo and of his erstwhile chosen successor Liu Shaoqi. A new group rode to power on Mao's coat-tails, including the general Lin Biao (who later tried to overthrow Mao), Mao's wife and other members of the radical Gang of Four, who parlayed their proximity to the Chairman into a grip on power that held until just after his death in 1976, when the Cultural Revolution era finally ended.

Although the Cultural Revolution followed the same general trajectory throughout China, its specifics differed with locality; this was especially so in Xinjiang, where the region's 'peaceful liberation' in 1949 had left a legacy of entrenched control by former First Field Army officers of key offices in the party, local administration and the *Bingtuan*.[39] Wang Enmao, a veteran of the same army, had held the top regional positions since 1954, and the network of First Field Army personnel largely supported him, as did the core of the *Bingtuan* veterans under Tao Zhiyue. When radical red guards began arriving from Beijing and elsewhere to the east late in the summer of 1966, they naturally made 'local emperor' Wang the target of their agitation. They formed a faction that became known as the Red Second Headquarters (*hong er si*). Wang in turn indirectly organised a rival red guard faction (Red First Headquarters) and attempted to contain the disruption, concerned about unrest among the region's Turkic peoples and the possibility of Soviet intervention. His emphasis on the 'special characteristics' of minority nationalities came under fire as a 'bourgeois reactionary line', and posters in Urumchi and Beijing singled out 'nationalist, religious' and 'counter-revolutionary elements' in Xinjiang for obstructing the progress of the Revolution.[40]

The struggle also involved the *Bingtuan*, the destination of many easily politicised youths from Shanghai and other cities. A *Bingtuan* radical faction under Ding Sheng joined the Red Second Headquarters to take on the corps' leader Zhang Zhonghan, whom Ding accused of having perpetuated the capitalist legacy of the *Bingtuan's* largely ex-GMD membership ('they'd do anything but open a brothel', he said of the corps' ambitious roster of economic enterprises). Ding's challenge of Zhang Zhonghan's leadership led to the 'January 26 Incident' (1967) in Shihezi, in which dozens[41] of the radicals were killed by the *Bingtuan* armed forces who fired bullets and grenades into a factory the radicals had occupied.

This first armed conflict and Ding Sheng's subsequent outcry gained the attention of the central authorities in Beijing. On 7 February Mao Zedong said, 'there are some problems that are being handled too slowly.

---

39   McMillen 1979 gives a detailed narrative of the Cultural Revolution in Xinjiang, focusing primarily on Han areas; the account below substantially follows his, except where noted otherwise.

40   McMillen 1979: 185–6; Dreyer 1976: 214. The final quote in this paragraph is from Dreyer, citing Belgrade Radio; the rest are taken from McMillen.

41   Seymour 2000: 177. Dreyer 1976: 214 gives 100 dead and 500 injured; Zhu Peimin 2000: 312 has twenty-six dead and seventy-four injured, but his total figures for casualties in Xinjiang's Cultural Revolution large-scale armed conflicts (700 killed, 5,000 wounded) seem generally low (p. 316; p. 321 for Ding Sheng and the 'brothel' comment).

The Xinjiang problem ought to be resolved a bit more quickly.' Whether they interpreted the Chairman's delphic utterance correctly or not, Zhou Enlai and others, in consultation with Xinjiang authorities, determined that the conditions were not ripe for a seizure of power by 'mass organisations' in Xinjiang and issued a directive calling on the 'Xinjiang Military Region Production Construction Corps [to] promote the Great Proletarian Cultural Revolution under military control'. The military thus took over the *Bingtuan*, as well as the Xinjiang Regional media, administrative and economic organs. In effect the army was to work with Xinjiang's party and government offices to contain the Red Second Headquarters, and a degree of calm prevailed for a while.

Unfortunately Beijing then sent more mixed signals. For example, Premier Zhou Enlai publicly criticised Xinjiang authorities for excluding the Red Second Headquarters and other 'rebel' factions from a public rally in mid-March 1967. Central support for 'rebels' intensified as Jiang Qing and her 'Cultural Revolution Group' gained influence in Beijing. For a month that summer Xinhua, the Chinese national news service, reported favourably on the activities of the Red Second Headquarters. In this climate the PLA itself split, and Unit 7335 of the Ninth Air Force allied with the Red Second Headquarters. Ding Sheng took control of the *Bingtuan*, 2,000 members of which were executed and 7,000 sent to labour camps as 'reactionaries'.[42]

Both the major factions were armed and engaged in some 600 violent clashes in 1967, and 700 in 1968. For example, in July of 1967 Ding Sheng dispatched 6,000 *Bingtuan* permanent troops together with 50,000 *Bingtuan* workers against Urumchi, attacking the Tianshan Foodstuffs Factory, the People's Square, the No. One Normal College, Xinjiang Medical College and thirty other work units. These fights were deadly affairs, destructive enough that people in the streets could be injured by concrete falling from buildings under attack; hospitals crammed with the injured were forced to let some gunshot victims die for lack of blood.[43]

Cultural Revolution politics impinged on all aspects of life, even for those trying to stay clear of the fray. One evening in 1967 two recent college graduates, Tayir and Rena, were holding a wedding party when a gang of young men from Tayir's work unit showed up intent on disrupting the party and preventing the match. The problem was that Tayir's

42   Seymour 2000: 175–9; Zhu Peimin 2000: 310–13.
43   Clark 1999: 79.

work unit, a publishing house, supported Wang Enmao, and the high school where Rena taught belonged to the rebel faction. Though no blood was shed and the couple married after all, the incident demonstrates how factional hostility penetrated down to the level of personal relations even among people with little stake in the politics involved.[44]

The bloodiest battles of Xinjiang's Cultural Revolution took place in Shihezi, Yili Prefecture and Hami, with long-running armed conflicts also embroiling Kashgar and Khotan. Along the railway line between Hami and Urumchi PLA ground troops fought Unit 7335, and striking rail workers and red guards joined the fray, blockading the railway and besieging Hami. Since this conflict threatened to cut the entire Xinjiang region off from the rest of the country—as had happened during the warlord period, with results Chinese central leaders found undesirable— Zhou Enlai repeatedly, but with only modest effect, ordered combatants to lay down their arms. Hami lies not that far overland from 'Base 21', the nuclear weapons testing facility at Lop Nor, where China had just exploded its first hydrogen bomb in June 1967. There were even reports in Hong Kong papers that Wang Enmao had threatened to occupy the nuclear base if Mao did not extend him support to restrain the radical red guards, and that this explains the February 1967 central directive putting the military in charge.[45]

Xinjiang was one of the last places in China to emerge from military chaos. Only in August and September of 1968, when 'revolutionary committees' reasserted some control, did armed conflict die down. Wang Enmao lost his pre-eminent position in the region as the new committees, on which he had no loyal supporters, took over production and administrative units throughout the region. Wang's First Field Army connections had, moreover, became a liability, as his former superior officers Peng Zhen and He Long had been attacked elsewhere in China, and as the star of Lin Biao (of the Fourth Field Army) ascended. Long Shujin, Chairman of the new Xinjiang Revolutionary Committee, was Lin's man. Lin had also infiltrated personally-loyal Fourth Field Army personnel into the Xinjiang PLA, and by November Wang lost his position as commander of the Xinjiang Military Region to Long Shujin. Though subjected to thinly-veiled vilification in the Xinjiang press, Wang Enmao

---

44   Clark 1999: 219–20.
45   McMillen 1979: 215–16; Clark 1999: 79; Zhu Peimin 2000: 316. On the nuclear facilties at Lop Nor, see Shichor 2004: 146–7.

enjoyed a soft-landing: he retained his membership as an alternate on the CCP Central Committee and continued to appear at official functions in Beijing until May 1969. The party would find uses for him again.

Long Shujin promoted the radical economic, political and cultural agendas of Mao and Lin Biao, favouring ideological over material incentives, forbidding private land or livestock ownership, and promoting the campaign to wipe out the 'four olds', a policy with an especially strong impact on Xinjiang's non-Han population. Long himself was purged after Lin Biao's failed coup attempt against Mao. For the next several years the joint leadership of Säypidin and Yang Yong, following Beijing's lead, took a more moderate economic position and backed off from some of the excesses of the height of the Cultural Revolution.

One major change in these years concerned the *Bingtuan*. Taking advantage of the Cultural Revolution disruptions and of Mao's call for young people to travel the country in a 'great linking up', many young Chinese headed back east, resulting in a loss of *Bingtuan* man-power. A Maoist restructuring of the corps effected during the early years of the Cultural Revolution compounded the built-in inefficiencies of this military-governmental-productive organisation, which by 1969 was in any case left in tatters. The zeal with which its militia and workers neglected production to throw themselves into military conflict with the PLA and the Red Guards also worried some leaders, who became reluctant to invest further funds in the organisation. Its population declined steeply as urban youth continued to abandon the militaristic discipline and impoverished conditions of the state farms and factories for their natal homes in Shanghai and other eastern cities; in 1974–5 alone the *Bingtuan* lost over half a million labourers, and its output fell in tandem to an annual 356 million *yuan* from 705 million in 1971. Due to all these problems, the *Bingtuan*, meant to be the spear-head of development in the region, had become a drain on its finances. In October 1975 the central government dissolved the Production Construction Corps, passing jurisdiction over its state farms and other enterprises to prefectural and Xinjiang regional authorities under the rubric of the new 'Xinjiang Reclamation Bureau'.[46]

The central involvement of the *Bingtuan* in the chaos may be one reason why the economic impact of the Cultural Revolution in Xinjiang

46 Seymour 2000: 176, 179–81; Wiemer 2004: 169–70.

was relatively heavier than in other provinces. Whereas over the period of the Third Five-Year Plan (1966–70) combined industrial and agricultural production increased by a modest 9.95 per cent nationally, Xinjiang's increased only 2.98 per cent; during the Fourth Five-Year Plan (1971–5), the national increase was 7.76 per cent versus Xinjiang's 1.98 per cent. In the words of Zhu Peimin of the Xinjiang Party School, 'the "Great Proletarian Cultural Revolution" brought Xinjiang's economy to the brink of collapse.' Agriculture, especially grain, was hit particularly hard, with only a 2.2 per cent increase during a decade in which Xinjiang's population grew 41.5 per cent, a decline of almost 30 per cent in grain production per capita. Xinjiang thus went from being a grain-surplus to a grain-deficit province, and the stated policy goal of economic self-sufficiency for the region (since Qing times an unfulfilled dream of Beijing planners) slipped far out of reach.[47]

The other Cultural Revolution in Xinjiang

It appears from Chinese and Western sources that the most acute factional conflicts of the Cultural Revolution period took place in eastern Xinjiang, among the Han population. Indeed, the first book published in the PRC to survey the post-1949 history of Xinjiang, though it devotes a chapter to the Cultural Revolution, alludes only briefly to the issue of minority policy or the region's non-Han peoples during this period.[48] But there was another face to the Cultural Revolution in Xinjiang. Like the Great Leap Forward, the significance of the events of the Revolution era was different in a region populated mainly by non-Han groups.

Maoist campaigns in China were accompanied by chauvinistic attacks on non-Hans as traitors and on non-Chinese culture as backward, feudal, bourgeois and local-nationalist. Until the 1960s in addition to 'local nationalism' the CCP had tended also to criticise 'Great Hanism', linking it to such failings as 'bureaucratism', 'commandism' and 'isolation from the masses'. Moreover, although real power always remained in Han hands, the party had worked to recruit and train growing numbers of non-Han cadres for lower positions in Xinjiang. This began to change around 1958, and from 1965, when concern over nationality or ethnic difference was subsumed by 'class struggle', total numbers of non-Han

47 Zhu Peimin 2000: 314, 316.
48 Zhu Peimin 2000: 323.

holding Xinjiang government posts fell off, from 111,500 (42,000 of whom were party members) in 1962 to 80,000 by 1975. The new radical policies attacked the concept of accommodation and local 'autonomy' in areas with high concentrations of 'minority nationalities', a principle which had been enshrined in the 1954 constitution. Instead, in Revolution era constitutions it was replaced with Maoist language arguing that 'national struggle is in the final analysis a question of class struggle.'[49]

During the Cultural Revolution, as during the Great Leap Forward, the border with the Soviet Union grew tense and the historical connections of Xinjiang's non-Han political élites with the ETR and the Soviet Union were invoked against them. Most of Xinjiang's non-Han cadres, including Iminov (Uyghur Regional Vice-Chairman) and Burhan (Tatar former Governor of Xinjiang Province), were accused of treason and purged. Burhan was labelled 'the main root of Xinjiang's Three Black Lines' of capitalism, Soviet modern revisionism and local nationalism.[50] One historian reports that 'several ... former veterans of the Eastern Turkestan Revolution ... including Iminov, Askhat Iskhak (Aisihaiti) and Anwar Saljan ... were tortured and secretly executed' during the Cultural Revolution.[51] Even Säypidin's house was ransacked by high-schoolers. When the Xinjiang Revolutionary Committee took control in 1968 only two of its nine vice-chairmen were non-Han: Säypidin and Zia, an obscure Kazak herder who had been promoted during the Cultural Revolution. Later they were joined by Ruzi Turdi and then in 1973 by Tomur Dawamät, both Uyghurs. Nevertheless, military men with no prior experience in Xinjiang continued to dominate the Xinjiang Revolutionary Committee.

Although the attacks on Turkic peoples and non-Han cadres as Soviet fifth columnists and lackeys of the 'revisionists' were no doubt exaggerated, there was indeed reason to fear Soviet intentions in the late 1960s and early 1970s. Soviet troops, including a force called the 'Xinjiang Minority Refugee Army', were massing and engaging in manoeuvres on the frontier, and nearly continuous skirmishes, incursions and some serious clashes took place on the border. The PLA built an unpaved road

---

49 Figures from Benson 2004: 211, citing Xinhua; McMillen 1979: 298, 294–5 table, and MacKerras 1994: 152 make the same point.
50 Dreyer 1976: 216, quoting Urumchi Radio, 5 September 1968; Zhu Peimin 2000: 315.
51 Sadri 1984: 317.

along the banks of the seasonal Khotan River, running south across the entire Taklamakan Desert, to provide an escape route to Tibet should the Soviet Union invade in force. Constant press calls for 'unity' in northern Xinjiang, and warnings of efforts to 'sow disorder' and undermine 'the great alliance' suggest, moreover, that there was anti-Chinese resistance among non-Han nationalities, though little is publicly known about this. One unconfirmed report from early 1969 described an uprising of 4,000 Uyghurs in Ghulja, allegedly with Soviet support.[52] Among the sparse information published concerning Xinjiang's Kazaks during the Cultural Revolution, Linda Benson and Ingvar Svanberg note a one-third decline in livestock population in Yili-Kazak Autonomous Zhou in 1969. As during the Great Leap, this indicates severe disruptions leading to the death or killing-off of herds, which might have included armed conflict, meteorological catastrophes or flight to Kazakstan.[53]

Amid the high-pitched agitation and loss of central control during the early Cultural Revolution years, it would be surprising if Xinjiang's Turkic peoples remained aloof from political movements. However, it appears that of the Beijing leadership, Premier Zhou Enlai at least was anxious to keep Xinjiang's 'minority nationalities' from becoming politicised or embroiled in the factional fighting. In May 1968 a radical group affiliated with the Red Second Headquarters, led by one Aidan (Ai-yi-dan, apparently not a Han name), planned a massive 'Rally to Bring down Wang Enmao's Great Hanism' with projected attendance by several tens of thousands of non-Han participants. This rally seems to reflect an effort by a sub-faction to win the support of Turkic peoples to its side; to accuse Wang Enmao of Great Hanism in and of itself makes little sense. Upon hearing of these plans, Zhou Enlai ordered the Xinjiang Military District, the *Bingtuan* and Unit 3773 of the PLA (supporters of the Red Second Headquarters) to pressure the group into cancelling the meeting, which they ultimately managed to do.[54]

There also seems to have been at least one attempt by Turkic groups to organise for themselves. An internal Chinese publication dating from the early 1990s asserts that the most serious 'counter-revolutionary sepa-

52 McMillen 1979: 206, 241 (citing *Hong Kong Star*, 20 January 1969), 255–6; Sadri 1984: 316–17. In 1992 I had occasion to drive this sandy road across the Taklamakan as part of an academic conference.
53 Benson and Svanberg 1998: 139–40.
54 Zhu Peimin 2000: 323.

ratist conspiracy' since 1949 was the East Turkestan People's Revolutionary Party, which operated in Xinjiang for two years from February 1968. According to the brief account, this party organisation's central and branch offices issued some fifty publications, including a party charter and newspapers entitled *The Torch, Independence* and *Tianshan Guerrilla*. The group allegedly sought creation in Xinjiang of an independent ETR that was secular, communist and pro-Soviet in orientation. It sent delegations to the Soviet Union and Mongolia requesting arms and advisers, but according to Uyghur veterans of the movement now living in Kazakstan, the Soviets never provided the promised aid.[55]

Pigs in the Mosques

Open insurrection and movements aimed at East Turkestan independence probably directly involved only a small percentage of Xinjiang's Turkic peoples during the Cultural Revolution. Others found opportunities in the strident politicisation of the time to further their own careers, again as in China as a whole. The rest, like most Chinese, simply kept their heads down, trying to get through the political storms and confusing ideological about-faces without loss of life, liberty or livelihood.

Just getting by was difficult for many Uyghurs for whom private trading in the bazaars—forbidden under communism—was a way of life as old as Xinjiang's cities themselves. Uyghur music and dance, a central element of marriages, circumcision parties and other ritual celebrations, were forbidden, and Uyghur musical instruments were themselves condemned as 'feudal' (although it was still okay to play accordion and enjoy ballroom dancing on special occasions).[56] The ethnic factor gave the Cultural Revolution decade in Xinjiang a particular cast, as local autonomy, the recognition of Xinjiang's special circumstances, pluralism with regard to its non-Han cultures, and condemnation of Han chauvinism became politically untenable positions. After all, Mao's wife and radical culture maven Jiang Qing considered minority nationalities 'foreign invaders and aliens' with 'outlandish' songs and dances. 'What is special about your tiny Xinjiang? I despise you', she was quoted as saying.[57]

55 Li Ze *et al.* 1994: 209–10. For more on this movement, see Dillon 2004: 57–8, which cites an internal Chinese source.
56 Clark 1999: 220.
57 McMillen 1979: 298.

Thus if the acute military and political struggles of the Cultural Revolution seem to have involved primarily the Han, the cultural agenda of the Cultural Revolution in Xinjiang was aimed squarely at 'minority' customs, resulting in insults and abuses of human rights over a longer period. Han who had lived in Xinjiang for some time had a certain familiarity with Uyghurs, Kazaks and other groups, and Han leaders had before 1958 interfered relatively little with non-Chinese local culture *per se*, even while seeing to it that the party controlled religious, arts, educational and other cultural institutions. Red Guards just off the train from Beijing, on the other hand, knew and thought little of traditional Uyghur culture (or of traditional Chinese culture, for that matter). It seems likely that just as in Tibet and throughout China the Red Guards were responsible for much of the persecution of non-Hans and open destruction and desecration of cultural artefacts in Xinjiang. There are many reports of Qur'ans burnt; mosques, *mazars*, madrasas and Muslim cemeteries shut down and desecrated; non-Han intellectuals and religious elders humiliated in parades and struggle meetings; native dress prohibited; long hair on young women cut off in the street. However, attacks on Islam and non-Han culture continued even after the Red Guards had been dispersed. And of course, powers in Beijing and Urumchi acquiesced to such activities, for the authorities formally cancelled religious holidays, detained non-Han cultural and political leaders in reform camps, and controlled the media from which flowed anti-Islamic and anti-Turkic propaganda.

Since the 1980s Han Chinese have published numerous moving accounts of their and their family's sufferings during the insanity of the Cultural Revolution. Non-Han participants have released fewer such stories, but they tell of similarly atrocious events. One of the earliest memories of one Uyghur man from a village in Yengisar county, near Kashgar, concerns the first time he saw a pig, probably around 1970 or 1971.

Several white and black pigs were kept in a building people called 'mosque'. There was a small window on the wall. I was too short to be able to see the pigs from the window, so my older sister put me on her shoulder. When I grew older I found out that almost all the mosques in our region were turned into pig houses. Even Uyghur songs were written in praise of pigs.[58]

58 Personal communication, 'Erkin', March 2002.

During the Cultural Revolution religious buildings throughout China were converted to other uses: schools, museums of secularism and probably pigsties as well. Statues of gods were commonly desecrated. In the mid-1980s I saw the skeleton of a brontosaurus-type dinosaur assembled in the main hall of a temple in Guangdong, a none-too-subtle symbol of the Party's attitude towards religion. However, bad as it is to house pigs in a Buddhist or Taoist temple, it is worse to do so in a mosque given the strength of Islam's taboo against the consumption of pork. This story is thus representative of the different significance in Xinjiang of common Cultural Revolution practices.

REFORM, RECOVERY—AND RECONCILIATION?
(1978–80s)

Mao Zedong died in 1976; soon thereafter his wife and the other Gang of Four members fell from power. Mao's immediate successor, Hua Guofeng, was in effect a caretaker, holding top positions for a few years until the second rehabilitation and return to power of Deng Xiaoping. At the Third Plenum of the Eleventh Central Committee, held in Beijing at the end of 1978, Deng emerged fully in control, and under his leadership the party and government embarked upon a reform programme that stressed political stability, economic growth and a pragmatic rather than ideological approach to policy-making.

Return to moderation?

Even before Deng Xiaoping consolidated his power, the party under Hua Guofeng realised that the assimilationist policies of the Maoist years had severely damaged support for the Communist Party among non-Han people in Xinjiang. Hua began urging party and government cadres in 'minority nationality' areas to learn local languages—a directive which was not new, and never bore linguistic fruit, but which reflected a changed outlook in Beijing. From 1977 official sources began criticising Cultural Revolution era policies, including official intolerance of non-Han customs, erosion of minority rights and the dismantling of the 'autonomous regions' system. These abuses, like other aspects of the Cultural Revolution, were generally blamed on Lin Biao and the Gang of Four.

Once back in power Deng pressed the return to the non-assimilationist official minority policies of the early 1950s, which a series of formal actions and announcements re-established as official line. In 1978 the central government department concerned with China's non-Han peoples, the Nationalities Affairs Commission (dissolved following Red Guard attacks), was restored. In 1980 the Xinjiang Islamic Association was re-established, and the party posthumously published a 1957 speech by Zhou Enlai that focused on the need to oppose Han chauvinism and 'local nationalism'. These sentiments were echoed by other leaders, including the Mongolian Ulanhu (a Politburo member and the highest-ranking non-Han in the CCP) who renewed the call for real autonomy in non-Han areas and decried assimilationist policies. A party document composed in 1980 (later discovered in the Xinjiang Regional Archives) candidly laid out the party's thinking on minority issues, including autonomy, after seventeen years of 'extreme leftist' policies. Decrying prevalent Han chauvinism, it argued that 'nationality regional autonomy and the right to self-rule is not given to a region (*diqu*) but to the national people (*minzu renmin*) who carry out self-rule.' It also criticised the dominance of Han cadres in Xinjiang's leadership, and argued that since Xinjiang was a Uyghur autonomous region, the proportion of Uyghur cadres region-wide should be no less than 45 per cent, 60 per cent in the mainly Uyghur south. Other nationalities in the region should be represented by at least 15 per cent. This, it added, would be 'fulfilling self-rule'.[59]

When Deng Xiaoping restored Wang Enmao to the position of First Party Secretary in Xinjiang in 1981, Wang's early remarks reflected this backswing of the pendulum in the party's policy on minority areas. Wang simultaneously criticised both Han chauvinism and 'local nationalism'. The party had now returned to the theoretical position that since 'fusion of the nationalities' would occur only in the very long term, continued accommodation to the conditions and characteristics of 'minority' areas and peoples was necessary. The State Constitution of 1982 repeated this provision, and restored much of the language devoted to minority equality, rights, customs and political and fiscal autonomy in earlier constitutions that had been dropped during the Cultural Revolution era. This translated into a temporary loosening of restrictions on Islam in Xin-

59 Ma Dazheng 2003: 184–6.

jiang, with mosques reopening, new mosques built, and easier travel to Islamic countries for the region's Muslims. A 1982 communiqué on the party's basic policy towards religion stated that party members (and thus most officials) must be Marxists and thus atheists, but allowed for flexible application of this rule in areas like Xinjiang where religion was a basic element of social life. (Muslim cadres in Xinjiang told Colin MacKerras that although the rule technically forbade them from attending Friday prayers and praying five times daily, it was only loosely enforced through the mid-1990s.) Finally, in the massive reconsideration of the cases of Xinjiang officials and cultural figures who had been purged for political reasons since 1957, many of Xinjiang's non-Han cadres once labelled 'local nationalist' were rehabilitated, along with tens of thousands of erstwhile 'poisonous weeds', 'ox demons and snake spirits' and 'anti-party black gang' members.[60]

An important event in the CCP reform efforts in non-Han areas was the visit by CCP General Secretary (and Deng protégé) Hu Yaobang to Tibet in May 1980. Hu's shock at the poverty and destruction evident there led him to call for educational, cultural and fiscal reforms based on local conditions and culture in minority areas, under the rubric of 'autonomy' with greatly increased numbers of non-Han cadres.

Deng Xiaoping himself was keen on restoring and strengthening the 'local autonomy' model for handling non-Han regions, emphasising this in a major speech on reform in August 1980. During a ten-day tour of Xinjiang the following year, he spoke against separatism and the idea of a republic in Xinjiang, but again stressed that the principle of local self-rule in 'minority nationality' areas should be enshrined in a special law. The National People's Congress passed such a law in May 1984, which strengthened local autonomy provisions already in the constitution, allowing local and regional authorities to consider local conditions in applying central government laws to their areas. It also called for the training and employment of more minority cadres (article 26), encouraged promotion of non-Han culture and publishing in non-Han languages (article 38), and stipulated that the relevant non-Han language could be designated the primary administrative language of an autonomous region or district (article 21).[61]

60 Dillon 1995: 18; MacKerras 1994: 113, 154–5, 202; Clark 1999: 82–3; McMillen 1979: 298, 303; Zhu Peimin 2000: 350–2.
61 Zhu Peimin 2000: 336–7; MacKerras 1994: 155–6. Text of the law is in *Zhong-*

In economic matters the practical Dengist policies were notably successful in Xinjiang, at least on the macroeconomic level. Perhaps because the province was starting from such a low level, the growth in Xinjiang's per capita production and provincial income on a per capita basis surpassed national averages in the 1980s. Xinjiang's ranking in these measures rose from near the bottom to tenth and twelfth respectively out of China's twenty-seven provinces and autonomous regions. Xinjiang emerged from its subsistence crisis; production of grain, vegetable oil crops and cotton increased markedly; and the region began transferring large cotton surpluses to eastern China for processing. Xinjiang's labour productivity in the early 1980s compared favourably with that of other regions, almost equalling that of workers in Guangzhou.[62]

During the 1980s, then, leaders in Beijing and Urumchi decided that some concessions to the idea of autonomy, at least, were necessary, along with the economic reforms. Ultimate control, of course, remained in the hands of Han figures in the party, but representation by non-Hans in government organs and non-Han cultural expression increased to some extent. Deng Xiaoping, Hu Yaobang and others articulated the view that raising standards of living for 'minority nationalities' in Xinjiang and other frontier regions was an important check on separatism, and believed that liberalisation of economic policies would raise standards of living. Like other Dengist policies, these represented a moderate position and a marked change from what had preceded it.

'Khitays go home!'

However, despite the reforms, the excesses of the Cultural Revolution left a number of problems that lingered through the 1980s. One was the question of the remaining Han youths from Shanghai, Beijing and elsewhere, most of whom had done their bit toiling on the desert frontier for the good of the motherland and wanted to go home. Life in Xinjiang had been difficult for these young Han from the east; besides the coarse food, lack of medical care and primitive dwellings, many simply felt abandoned in *Bingtuan* villages under the control of ignorant of-

---

hua renmin gongheguo falü huibian, 1979–1984, Beijing: Renmin chubanshe (1985); the 2001 revision of this law may be viewed at <http://www.people.com.cn/GB/paper464/2813/396689.html> (*Renmin ribao* online, downloaded 1 August 2002).
62 Zhu Peimin 2000: 343–4.

ficials. They shared a ditty concerning the fate of those who had been packed into trains from Shanghai to rusticate in Xinjiang: *Shanghai wazi guagua jiao, shang le huoche bu yao piao, xia le huoche mei ren yao!* (Shanghai baby always cries/take the train, it's a free ride/get off the train and you're despised!)[63]

For those 'educated youth' who had not already fled Xinjiang in 1974–5, Shanghai city authorities had no jobs and did not welcome them back; nor were Xinjiang authorities keen to lose their labour. In 1979 and 1980 the educated youth began agitating publicly, especially in southern Xinjiang. In the largest mass action in Xinjiang at any time from the end of the Cultural Revolution to the end of the twentieth century, 5,000 to 6,000 'educated youth' originally from Shanghai and other cities gathered in Aqsu and occupied the local party committee administrative offices for over fifty days. (This was larger and of longer duration than later Uyghur demonstrations.[64]) The leaders of the Shanghai educated youth (by then no longer so young) used Uyghur translators to broadcast their case in Uyghur from the local committee headquarters loudspeakers. Since Aqsu local officials and even the police had gone into hiding, the Shanghai youth even handled such local business as punishing pickpockets and filling out marriage licenses for Uyghur couples. They had effectively taken over a major city.[65]

In November 1979 some five hundred Shanghainese, later joined by an additional 1,000, staged a hundred-day hunger strike in the wide intersection outside the Aqsu local committee headquarters. With sashes reading 'hunger strike' tied around their chests, they settled into the intersection under quilts, surrounded by their supporters and in the shadow of three coffins set up there for effect. A few weeks later authorities agreed to issue Shanghai residence permits to the educated youth assembled in Aqsu and those living in other *Bingtuans*. However, soon after the Shanghainese had left the administration building, teams of armed police arrested the movement leaders in a 2 a.m. raid and for the time being revoked the permits and other documents already issued. The main spokesman for the movement, Ouyang Lian, was imprisoned until 1984.[66]

63 Ouyang Lian 2004: 455.
64 Zhu Peimin (2000) gives a figure of 8,000; Ouyang Lian (2004) 5,000–6,000.
65 Ouyang Lian 2004: 473.
66 Ouyang Lian 2004: 488, 496.

Authorities ultimately recognised that youths who had suffered food shortages and worked under lazy, imperious local officials for years had a legitimate grievance. Ultimately a high-level meeting of Xinjiang and Shanghai authorities in Beijing in early 1981, at which Zhao Ziyang delivered the keynote address, drew up a staggered schedule by which youth meeting certain criteria could be transferred back to Shanghai. Others were to remain in Xinjiang.[67]

According to available information, authorities were less accommodating to direct Uyghur expressions of grievance in the post-Cultural Revolution period. Certainly the 1980s saw the emergence of signs of unrest, some with a sharp ethnic and religious cast. Those that we know about fall into three categories: First, demonstrations or street fights arising from minor incidents (police brutality or in one case a fire in a mosque) that turned ugly, with rioters shouting anti-Chinese and some Islamic slogans. Second, both internal and published Chinese sources tell of 'national separatist organisations', one of which is held responsible for an outbreak of 'armed turmoil' outside Kashgar (see Chapter 7), and others of which are said to have been stockpiling weapons. Curiously, the alleged organisers of two of these latter groups were teenaged high-school students.

The third category involves university students, who demonstrated on several occasions to complain about campus living conditions and racist graffiti, or to join their cohort of students nationwide in the late 1980s in a call for democratisation. Some students' slogans at these demonstrations aired the highly sensitive issues of nuclear testing in Lop Nor (and its alleged effects on the health of Xinjiang inhabitants), Han migration into Xinjiang and the extension to minorities of policies limiting family size. Students also took up the official slogan of 'equality between the nationalities', implying in this way that the actual situation was one of inequality. When conjoined with these issues, calls for 'freedom' and 'democracy', though heard frequently on campuses throughout China in the late 1980s, took on a distinct nationalist flavour in Xinjiang.

As noted in Chapter 5, movements for rights or independence in twentieth-century Xinjiang do not fit the commonly held notion of 'Islamic jihad'. The proclamations of the stillborn Eastern Turkestan Republic of 1933–4 sounded both moderate Islamic and liberal democratic

67 Zhu Peimin 2000: 354–6 is a general account of this incident.

notes; in the 1940s the predominant force organising for Turkic autonomy or independence from China was pro-Soviet and secularist. In the
1950s the Xinjiang Islamic establishment accepted nationalisation of its
property and oversight by the CCP with little open resistance. And judging from Chinese rhetoric in the anti-Local Nationalist campaign and
Cultural Revolution, the main perceived threat to 'unity' in Xinjiang derived from Soviet connections, not Islam. Islam and its practitioners were
persecuted during the Cultural Revolution, but though denounced as
'feudal superstition', religious belief itself was not the rationale for high
level political purges.

Why, therefore, some Uyghur movements began to stress Islam as a
cause, with calls for an Islamic republic, and denunciations of Chinese as
'infidels' in the late 1980s, especially in southern Xinjiang, is not entirely
clear. One explanation may be that the Cultural Revolution era attack
on Islam led to increased Uyghur concern with their religion as a core
element of their culture, and thus the greater position of the religion as
a rallying point for the disaffected. The increase in numbers of mosques
and madrasas between 1979 and 1990 suggests a revival of Islam in Xinjiang during this period, or at least an expression of interest pent-up over
the many years when new mosque construction was forbidden. Through
the 1980s, moreover, Yarkand apparently partly regained its traditional
position as a regional centre of Islamic education, and the number of
religious students studying in the city's madrasas increased from 150 in
1979 to 722 ten years later, more than half of them from elsewhere in
Xinjiang.[68] (Over the same period in Tibet monasteries became centres
of anti-Chinese resistance.)

However, not all incidents of ethnic unrest in the 1980s should be
characterised as 'Islamic' in either motivation or expression. In particular,
students in Urumchi concerned themselves first with democracy, the
environment, Chinese population influx and birth control policy. These
issues reflect not religious concerns *per se*, but rather concerns about the
treatment and survival of Uyghurs as a nation.

The narrative in this chapter has focused on political events, many of
them tumultuous, during the first four decades of PRC rule in Xinjiang.

---

68   Ma Dazheng 2003: 13–14.

Livestock section of the Kashgar Sunday Bazaar. Compare architecture with that in photo of old Kashgar *c.* 1926 in Chapter 4 (photo: J. Millward, 2001)

Official Chinese publications, on the other hand, insofar as they discuss this period 'after the founding of New China' at all, prefer to accentuate the record of economic development and improved standards of living in the region. They do this with some justification. As in other parts of China, this period overall saw notable achievements in education, health care, infrastructural construction, women's rights and per capita incomes.[69] The Swedish diplomat Gunnar Jarring, returning to Kashgar in 1978 after having lived in the city fifty years earlier, was struck by the modernisation the city had undergone.[70] Still, to a visitor in 1990, much of Xinjiang retained a traditional, almost sleepy atmosphere. The villages and small cities in southern Xinjiang appeared little changed from those captured in photos decades before. Beyond their new, Maoist central

[69] The economic record is assessed and statistics provided by Wiemer 2004. See also annual *Xinjiang nianjian* (Xinjiang yearbook) volumes for the period. For the official Chinese viewpoint, see People's Republic of China State Council Information Office 2003: 20–5 or Wang Shuanqian 2003.
[70] Jarring 1986.

squares, even cities like Turfan, Kashgar, Khotan or Aqsu largely retained the feel of traditional Central Asian cities, with packed earth roads, winding neighbourhood lanes under dusty shade-trees, dense bazaars and animal-powered transportation. In Kashgar in 1990 the jingle of horsebells remained more common than the roar of motorcycle engines or blare of taxi horns. Indeed this atmosphere was a major reason for the boom in tourism Xinjiang enjoyed following its opening in the 1980s. Even in the regional capital of Urumchi one might still see sheep on the streets (in the days before Qurban festival), and the few new high-rise constructions shared space with mud-brick houses and a few stately Soviet-era buildings waning gracefully, like their counterparts across Central Asia, behind neo-classical façades in fading mustard-yellow.

Not so in 2000. Although Xinjiang was politically more calm, during the period from 1990 into the new millennium many places in the region changed beyond recognition. The revitalisation of Xinjiang's economy, reshaping of its commercial and political relations with its neighbours, wholesale remaking of urban landscapes, and internationalisation of its separatist problem are the subject of the next chapter.

7. Between China and the World

(1990s–2000s)

In the summer of 2001, while walking through an underpass below one of Urumchi's clamorous intersections, I came upon an old Han man kneeling on a scrap of plastic at one end of the tunnel, begging. He was shabbily dressed, as you would expect, in filthy cotton clothes. Frail, bony elbows poked through holes in his jacket. His few teeth were stumpy and yellow. I tossed a small bill into his bowl and walked on. Then, thinking he might have some interesting stories to tell about the old days in Xinjiang, I turned back and started talking with him. '*Lao xiansheng*', I asked, 'How long have you been in Xinjiang?'

'Since last month', he answered. It turned out he came from Hunan province in central China. Recently his son had fallen seriously ill, and although the family had exhausted its meagre savings to buy medicine, the young man had died anyway. With no savings and no child to provide for him, the old man was reduced to begging. 'But why did you come out here to Xinjiang?' I asked. 'Oh!' he replied brightly, flashing me a gappy smile. 'We're developing the great North-west, aren't we!'

The old beggar was not alone in scenting opportunity on the winds off the Tianshan. According to the most recent census, the population of Han Chinese in Xinjiang increased by 32 per cent, to 7.49 million, between 1990 and 2000. Much of this increase was due to migration, not natural increase (Han in Xinjiang have lower rates of natural increase than Uyghurs, but Han population in Xinjiang grew more rapidly over the decade between 1990 and 2000 than did the Uyghur population). Moreover, something like an additional three quarters of a million people officially registered in other Chinese provinces were residing temporarily in Xinjiang (see Fig. 1).[1]

1 Department of Population 2003: vol. 1, table 1–2, pp. 4–26; Gilley 2001; Becquelin 2004: 369.

Urumchi skyline from Hongshan, 1990. Note Boghda Mt on left, and Holiday Inn hotel under construction at right margin (photo: J. Millward)

The changes of the 1990s and 2000s are dramatically illustrated by two snapshots I took from Hongshan, the rocky outcropping that overlooks Urumchi, in 1990 and 2004 respectively. To the far right side of the earlier photo, the Holiday Inn hotel is visible, still under construction in the spring of 1990. Then one of only a handful of tall buildings in the city, it is by the mid-2000s dwarfed by a forest of skyscrapers. New immigrants swelled the ranks of the construction workers erecting these high-rises, the occupants of the new apartments, employees of the new businesses, restaurateurs who feed them, truckers who supply them, shopkeepers who clothe them, and karaoke girls who entertain them. This same story has been repeated in Xinjiang's other cities, even those of the south, on a smaller scale. As elsewhere in China, many old neighbourhoods and even the central bazaars of Tarim Basin cities have been swept aside by waves of urban renewal, to be replaced by new shopping centres and blocks of flats. Rural communities too, especially the *Bingtuan* settlements, have expanded since the 1990s, as labourers from the east come to harvest cotton and other cash crops.[2] The *Bingtuan* farms

2 Wang Lequan, Xinjiang First Party Secretary and Politburo member told re-

Urumchi skyline from Hongshan, 2004. Camera angle and focal length
are roughly the same as for 1990 photo. Former Holiday Inn (see top-sto-
rey circular lounge) is visible on right, now dwarfed by other skyscrapers
(photo: J. Millward)

now grow a phenomenal number of tomatoes, making the Xinjiang
Production Construction Corps responsible for a quarter of the world's
trade in tomato paste.[3]

Xinjiang's international profile has risen along with the skyline. Once
little known outside of China, Xinjiang and the Uyghurs now figure
frequently in world press reports, as issues of human rights, religious
freedom, terrorism, energy and China's position in Central Asia bring
the region if not into the headlines, then at least onto the internet and
inside pages of print media.

A combination of international and domestic developments produced
this accelerated change in the 1990s, causing PRC leaders to reassess

porters in 2004 that a million labourers come to Xinjiang from other provinces
each year for the tomato and cotton harvest, and that some decide to stay. Johnson
2004.
3 'Tomato Paste Exports Hit New High', *China Daily*, 15 July 2005, via <www.
chinaview.cn> (accessed 17 July 2005).

Xinjiang's situation and adopt policies to hasten its integration with the rest of China and with the world. The most significant of these developments was the disintegration of the Soviet Union in 1991, which eliminated the massive rival just over the Xinjiang border that had posed a threat to Chinese rule in the region since the nineteenth century. At the same time, continuing Sino-US tension has increased the strategic significance of Xinjiang's and other Central Asian reserves of oil and gas. The explosive economic growth sparked by China's experiments with market socialism since the 1980s, combined with the emergence of new Central Asian states, opened new niches for Uyghur entrepreneurs to trade Chinese goods in Xinjiang, exchange currency all across China, and extend operations across the borders to Turkic partners in the new Central Asian states.

Meanwhile, following the relative relaxation of state controls and rise of democracy activism throughout China in the 1980s, there were demonstrations, unrest and even armed resistance by Muslim ethnic groups in Xinjiang, especially Uyghurs. These continued in the 1990s and included large-scale demonstrations and violent incidents that gained international attention. Diasporic Uyghurs in Central Asia, Turkey, Europe and America organised, lobbied politicians, and employed the internet to publicise effectively their grievances to a global audience. As a result, in the twenty-first century the Xinjiang region, though still not the 'pivot of Asia' Owen Lattimore predicted, nonetheless looms larger in Chinese, regional and international affairs than it has for centuries.

SILK ROADS AND EURASIAN BRIDGES

The Soviet Union dissolved rapidly in August 1991 following the failed coup in Moscow in which Communist generals and politicians attempted to overthrow Mikhail Gorbachev and roll back the reforms he had ushered in. Some observers in the early 1990s predicted a re-emergence of pan-Turkism in Central Asia, or at least a resurgence of nationalism focused on Central Asian identities. Yet the Central Asian republics were the last of the territories to leave the Soviet Union, and did so only when no other option remained to their leaders.

Although the independence of former-Soviet Central Asia was not driven by centrifugal nationalism, the emergence of states named after other Central Asian peoples (Uzbekistan, Kazakstan, Kyrgyzstan,

Tajikistan and Turkmenistan) did resound symbolically in Xinjiang, where by the early 1990s many Uyghurs were saying that there should be an independent 'Uyghuristan' to match.[4] However, despite predictions of a reprise of pan-Turkic ideology or pan-Islamic ethno-nationalist movements across the region, it was the Chinese state that was best positioned to take advantage of the changed international environment, and it did so quickly. Xinjiang had been relegated to a status of strategic buffer zone and economic *cul-de-sac* since the rise of Sino-Soviet tensions in the late 1950s and 1960s. In the new international context Chinese leaders moved simultaneously both to open the region as a conduit to the rest of Eurasia and to integrate it more tightly with the rest of China.

Already during the 1980s Xinjiang's direct foreign trade had increased fifteen times, from $31 million to $439 million, thanks to liberalised foreign trade regulations and the establishment of Xinjiang regional government and *Bingtuan* foreign trade entities. The upgraded Urumchi airport began to service international flights. Even in northern Xinjiang, where in 1990 the announcements of the few daily flights to Ghulja (Yining) could be readily accommodated on a chalkboard near the airstrip, a new spirit was evident: not far from that same blackboard, an enormous mural greeted arriving passengers with a depiction of people of all races in their native dress happily disembarking from an airliner at the foot of a range of snow-capped peaks.

Most goods, of course, went by land, accommodated by four land ports newly reopened in the late 1980s. The most important of these for international trade was at Horgos in the Yili valley, the truck route between northern Xinjiang and Almaty in Kazakstan (reopened 1983; projected to be a full-fledged free-trade zone by the mid-2000s). The other new border crossings were the Karakoram Highway between southwestern Xinjiang and Pakistan (1987); the Torugart Pass, linking Kashgar to Bishkek in Kyrgyzstan; and the rail line between Urumchi and Almaty via the Alatau Pass (Alashan kou), whose completion in 1990 was grandly hailed as the opening of the Eurasian Continental Rail Bridge. Most of these were old routes for which new road or rail construction had begun decades earlier but stalled for political reasons. Almaty itself began as a Russian outpost astride the China trade route.[5]

4   Roberts 2004: 229.
5   Wiemer 2004: 170–2; Roberts 2004: 218–20.

After 1991 Xinjiang's foreign trade with Central Asia expanded rapidly, as China began providing consumer goods no longer supplied by the Soviet economy, and in return importing steel, other metals, oil and other raw materials. The relationship that had characterised Xinjiang's economic relationship with Russia and the USSR from the mid-nineteenth through the mid-twentieth century was thus now neatly reversed. Deng Xiaoping's famous 'southern tour' early in 1992 announced to the world the Party's intent to promote economic development beyond the already well-industrialised and commercialised parts of China. In keeping with this, his 'three along's policy' (along rivers, along roads and along frontiers) likewise promised to extend benefits of economic reform to remote and non-Han areas. Accordingly, Xinjiang authorities declared Urumchi, Ghulja, Tacheng and Bole to be 'frontier open cities', and Prime Minister Li Peng personally inaugurated the first Urumchi Border and Local Trade Fair. The fair became an annual convention promoting Xinjiang's foreign commerce.[6]

By 1996 there were over three hundred companies engaged in this border trade, compared with only five in 1991. However, almost a third of these belonged to the massive *Bingtuan* conglomerate, whose branches now went by a number of names, including the Xinjiang New Construction Company (*Xinjiang xinjian gongsi*). By the end of the decade, half of all Xinjiang's imports and exports (reported at an overall value of $2.3 billion in 2000) were controlled either by the regional government under the Xinjiang Foreign Trade Group and another *Bingtuan* avatar, Bingtuan Chalkis. Most of the remainder was handled by various other state or *Bingtuan*-owned entities. Moreover, unlike in the eastern provinces, where foreign investment financed the rapid export-led growth, in the 1990s and 2000s there was little foreign investment in Xinjiang.[7] Hence Xinjiang's foreign trade, like its economy in general, has been highly centralised and state managed.[8]

However, there was another side to economic liberalisation and the expansion of Xinjiang's foreign trade. Not all the trade was in state hands: a great many 'suitcase' or shuttle traders also took advantage of the new

6 Zhu Peimin 2000: 343; Dillon 2004: 45.
7 Wiemer 2004: 187.
8 Wiemer 2004: 172, 185–6; Information Office of the State Council of the PRC 2003: 24. In her survey of Xinjiang's economy, Wiemer stresses that it is still largely a command economy, predominantly state-owned, run and financed at a loss.

border crossings and liberalised rules. Uyghurs went abroad or to eastern China to do business, and Pakistanis, Russians and Central Asians came to Xinjiang for the same purpose, as their compatriots had from the eighteenth until the mid-twentieth centuries.

Much of this private trade was small-scale and unreported, relying on personal networks to repatriate profits between inconvertible Central Asian and Chinese currencies. But it was no less lucrative for all that. From manufacturing centres in eastern China, Han and Uyghur merchants brought housewares, clothing items such as track suits, pirated global brands and virtually anything with English printed on it, and sold it in Xinjiang, especially Ghulja, which is close to the Kazakstan border. From there, some Uyghur merchants travelled to Almaty, where they were well represented in the large suburban Barakholka bazaar; others worked in Ghulja's own wholesale bazaar selling to the Uzbek, Kazak and Russian merchants arriving on short term visas. Many of these Uyghur merchants had relatives who since the mass flight of 1962 or before had been living in Kazakstan, Kyrgyzstan or Uzbekistan; these contacts helped make sojourning in the Central Asian republics easier. This may also be a reason why many Uyghurs in Ghulja readily learned Russian, still the *lingua franca* of post-Soviet Central Asia. Multi-lingual Uyghurs in Ghulja filled the essential niche of translator and broker between Han sellers and foreign buyers, coming to be known as *yangpungchi*, a name constructed by adding a Turkic suffix to the Chinese word for the 'sample goods' (*yangpin*) they presented their Russian-speaking clients.

Yangpungchi could make far more money than wage labourers or small urban peddlers. Indeed, trading with the 'Soviets' (as Chinese still called all the Central Asian and Russian traders, much as 'Bukharan' or 'Andijani' were used as catch-all terms in the eighteenth and nineteenth centuries) could be profitable for all concerned. The anthropologist Jay Dautcher, based on fieldwork in Ghulja in the mid-1990s, reports that one Uyghur trader made enough money in a deal selling 4,500 pairs of socks to support a household for three months. More highly capitalised merchants helped everyone bypass the problem of inconvertible currencies. These 'bosses' would bulk the Kazak currency (*tengge*) earned by many smaller Uyghur merchants selling clothes in Almaty, and use it to buy up large lots of steel and other commodities in Kazakstan. They would then officially import the steel to China, receive payment in

Chinese yuan, and repay the small traders while taking substantial profits for themselves.[9]

Though Ghulja was the most important conduit for Xinjiang's foreign trade in the late 1980s and 1990s, other cities benefited as well. For example, Kashgar was the main focus for Pakistani merchants entering via the Kunjerab pass. Kashgar's main bazaar, besides providing entertainment for tourists and locals with needed supplies, also became an international marketplace. Thus, besides the ethnic crafts, livestock pens and vegetable sellers at this colourful market, one could find stall after stall selling shoes, clothes, housewares and other consumer goods with a ready market in Pakistan.

By relaxing restrictions on domestic travel and temporary residence, the economic reforms also encouraged Uyghur traders to travel within China. Uyghurs from the countryside could stay in Urumchi or other cities legally if they purchased an inexpensive temporary permit.[10] Others went further afield. Uyghurs sojourned in Beijing, Shanghai, Guangdong and other large cities where they bought goods to ship to markets in Xinjiang or Central Asia; some sold spiced mutton kebabs skewered on bicycle spokes and cooked over charcoal, a tasty street snack that spawned many Han imitations; others joined a large and shadowy network of Uyghur currency traders, allegedly linked to other underworld ventures. These *koymochi* (from Chinese *kuai* and *mao*, literally 'dollar and dime-ists') were a common sight in newly commercialised Chinese cityscapes during those years that the government still maintained separate domestic and foreign exchange currencies. Until 1994 average Chinese could not easily obtain dollars or foreign exchange certificates (FEC, *waihuijuan*); Uyghur *koymochi* traded in these instruments when the banks would not, and also bought dollars or FEC at a better rate than banks. Sometimes they cut their deals on the front steps of those same banks.

It is fair to say, then, that following the implementation of China's economic reforms and the opening of cross-border trade with post-Soviet Central Asia many Uyghurs became national and transnational

9 Dautcher 1999: Chapter 4.2. Dautcher's ethnography is a fascinating and entertaining look not just at commerce but at many aspects of Ghulja Uyghur society. Sean Roberts provides a history and ethnography of Uyghurs living and working across the border based on his own fieldwork in Almaty (2003).

10   Clark 1999: 86.

entrepreneurs, albeit most on a relatively small-scale. Indeed, a common joke turned on the ubiquity of Uyghur traders in China and Central Asia: When Neil Armstrong lands on the moon he finds two young Uyghurs already there, eager to sell him a grilled kabob.[11]

One result of the new economy and international context was that Uyghur and other non-Han families engaging in commerce began to join the small ranks of Uyghur professionals, political cadres and intellectuals who had comprised the Uyghur middle class in Xinjiang before the reforms. Centred on Urumchi, but likewise present in Ghulja and other cities, this growing middle class partook of the consumer society evident in any larger Chinese city, developing similar globalised tastes in entertainment and fashion—known here as *yengi mädäbiyät*, or new culture. They had fewer children, often educated in Chinese-language schools, and generally cultivated a more secular outlook than rural Uyghurs. They valued education as well as commerce and proved increasingly willing and able to pay tuition for higher education in universities or vocational schools. While thus converging in many ways with the growing Han middle class, they maintained a strong sense of distinctly Uyghur identity expressed through enjoyment of Uyghur music and dance, increasingly lavish celebrations of marriages, circumcisions and other life-cycle events, maintenance of Uyghur language, and fascination with Uyghur history.[12]

DEVELOPMENT

Kazak herdsman Sayram Bek … said to the General Secretary, 'our village used to pasture livestock up in the mountains. Four years ago we finally moved down here to live permanently. Now I'm farming 50 *mu*, making 10,000 yuan a year, and I raise 80 head of sheep and a few cattle. Life is much better than before.'

Secretary Jiang Zemin listened intently, occasionally nodding his head, and replied, 'You've moved down from the mountains? Excellent! The land is good here, and all you need is some effort and you can be prosperous.' Then he asked, 'Do you still rely on horses to get around?'

11 Zhonggong Xinjiang Weiwuer zizhiqu weiyuanhui dangshi yanjiushi 2002: 264; cf Dautcher 1999: 281.
12 The anthropologist William Clark (1999) conducted fieldwork in Urumchi in the 1990s, focusing on changes in the Uyghur family system in this rapidly changing urban setting.

Sayram Bek shook his head. 'We don't ride horses. We ride motorcycles.'

General Secretary Jiang was very happy. 'Ah, you ride motorcycles! Is filling up convenient?'

'Very convenient.'

General Secretary Jiang spoke with a satisfied air. 'When I see your lives getting better day by day, and see you, the masses of every ethnic group, so united with each other, I'm extremely happy. In an ethnic concentration region, as long as we handle the unity of the nationalities well, there's a foundation for the road to prosperity. You here are good examples of this.'

Amidst a chorus of friendly laughter, General Secretary Jiang donned a Kazak hat, and together with the ethnic brothers who had come so far to see him, posed for a picture.[13]

Such scenes have great ritual significance in Chinese political culture. They have been played out by every Communist political leader since Mao, just as they have featured in tales of exemplary officials in imperial times. In the photographs documenting these episodes, the beaming representative of the common people or 'minority nationality' gratefully grasps the party leader's hand with both of his own while the politician smiles kindly, looking silly in the ethnic hat. These encounters project the magnanimous concern of the leader for the masses and the warm affection of the masses for the leader. To be cynical about such obvious propaganda is easy, especially when, as in this example, it appears in an official publication of the Communist Party History Office. Yet such episodes underscore the basic commitment on which the party's legitimacy now depends: the party is supposed to improve the people's lives. With each repetition of the scene above, by trumpeting its success in this task, the party at the same time implicitly repeats its promise and risks highlighting its failings to any reader who knows better.

Development, then, is critical to the public image of the CCP. In an 'ethnic concentration region' (*minzu juju qu*)—a place such as Xinjiang where the non-Han 'minorities' are actually a majority or plurality—the issue of development is still more highly politically charged. Here the question of whether China is truly a multi-national or multi-ethnic (*duo minzu*) state, rather than a nation-state of and for the Han,

13 Zhonggong Xinjiang Weiwuer zizhiqu weiyuanhui dangshi yanjiushi 2002: 340–1.

'Unity of the Nationalities': Uyghur and Han tradesmen in the Urumchi
Erdaoqiao Bazaar (photo: J. Millward, 1990)

hangs in large measure on whether ethnic groups feel they are fairly
treated in the allocation of resources and implementation of development
programmes nationwide.

Xinjiang as a late developer

This, of course, is why there has been heightened official concern over
development in frontier areas since Hu Yaobang's 1980 visit to Tibet and
discovery of the abysmal conditions there and in other minority areas
(see Chapter 6). The initial state response to the non-Han expressions
of dissatisfaction and separatistism in Xinjiang and Tibet in the 1980s
and 1990s was, on the one hand, to crack down and tighten controls
(discussed below); however, on the other hand the state promised increased development efforts, frequently and publicly predicting that with
economic development, ethno-nationalist separatism would disappear.
Thus in 1996, following a flurry of demonstrations and a wave of arrests
of Uyghur separatists as well as bomb attacks and assassination attempts
in Tibet, one top party official, writing in the influential journal *Qiushi*
(Seeking Truth), proclaimed that 'only a strong economy and improved

material and cultural living standards can show the advantages of socialism ... and promote the unification of all peoples towards the Communist Party.'[14] This line was both a pledge to actively develop Xinjiang and
other non-Han majority areas and a tacit admission that minority areas
remained mired in poverty after decades of PRC rule.

Several years later, in a 2003 white paper, the PRC government could
indeed demonstrate its role in creating sustained and rapid growth in
Xinjiang, at least on a gross statistical level. From 1950 to 2001 the state
invested over 500 billion yuan in fixed assets in Xinjiang, transferred
hundreds of thousands of educated personnel into the region, and furnished huge annual budget subsidies. Over the same period (1952–2001)
Xinjiang's GDP increased forty-three times. Per capita GDP in 2001 was
almost 8,000 yuan, compared with 166 yuan in 1952.[15] However, these
and similar figures mask the fact that most of this growth occurred after
1978, with a sharp acceleration in the late 1980s and 1990s. Why was
Xinjiang, despite its strategic importance, developed so late?

The first Beijing ruler to promote Xinjiang development was in fact
neither Jiang Zemin, Deng Xiaoping nor Mao Zedong but Hongli, the
Qianlong emperor. As discussed in Chapter 3, in the mid-eighteenth
century he used his dragon throne as bully pulpit to argue for developing and settling large parts of the 'New Dominion' to the west, rather
than leaving it as a buffer under autonomous rule of local élites. At that
time he was countering the sentiment in certain Chinese official and
literati circles that Xinjiang was too remote, strategically vulnerable and
environmentally and culturally unlike China proper to be worth major
investment. As we have seen in earlier chapters, that debate re-emerged
in various forms in the nineteenth and early twentieth centuries as authorities based in China proper pondered the dilemmas of controlling
the region given unrest in Xinjiang, foreign aggression just over Xinjiang's borders and pressing commitments closer to home.

In the PRC period, although the official position that Xinjiang is an
ancient, inalienable part of China has not wavered, actual policy in the

---

14 'Economic Improvement Only Antidote to Separatism: Chinese Official', AFP,
2 October 1996. The official was Liu Mingzu, Party Secretary of Inner Mongolia.
15 Information Office of the State Council of the PRC 2003: 20, 49. Chinese
and English versions of the white paper are available at <http://news.xinhuanet.
com/zhengfu/2002-11/22/content_638035.htm>. Wang Shuanqian 2003 is an
expanded presentation of the arguments of this white paper.

face of Xinjiang's strategic challenges has reflected a less firm commit-ment. Yitzhak Shicor has written a detailed analysis of the PRC deploy-ment of military forces in Xinjiang. His work reveals that the PRC deployment of troops and matériel in Xinjiang remained modest, despite the conflict with India in Aksai-Chin in 1962 and the still more serious on-going tensions with the Soviet Union. The Soviet Union doubled its forces along the 2,700 kilometre Xinjiang border in the 1960s, intrud-ed many times into Chinese territory in Xinjiang and the north-east, clashed repeatedly with Chinese troops, and supported exile Uyghur forces. Nevertheless, the strength of Chinese force in Xinjiang remained well below what would have been necessary to repel a Soviet invasion, and Chinese leaders were well aware of this. Although the threat of So-viet attack did not wane until the advent of Gorbachev and the warming of Sino-Soviet relations in the 1980s, China's north-western military command remained based far from the border, in Lanzhou, and planners viewed Xinjiang primarily as 'strategic depth' to slow a Soviet assault and stretch out its supply lines, rather than as a piece of the motherland to be held at all costs.[16]

The Chinese planners' view of Xinjiang as a tactically expendable, if strategically useful, buffer explains the delayed development of the region, and, conversely, its accelerated growth in the 1990s. The region's late-blooming communications infrastructure is a case in point. The ports of entry, discussed above, remained closed until the late 1980s, despite their historic importance for trade. The rail link from eastern China reached as far as Urumchi by 1962, and a branch line extended to Korla by 1984. But not till 1990 was northern Xinjiang linked to the rail system (with the completion of the line to Alatau Pass), and not till 1999 was Kashgar and the western Tarim Basin linked to the national rail network. Perhaps more significant, the Lanzhou–Urumchi line itself was just a single track till as late as 1994, causing long delays and limiting freight capacity to one third of what is now carried along the double track. The network of improved roads likewise expanded greatly in the 1990s, financed in part by World Bank loans. The most notable new road was the trans-

16 Shichor 2004. This is the principal conclusion of Shichor's remarkable chapter, which contains a wealth of other information regarding Xinjiang security mat-ters, including the Lop Nor nuclear installation, joint CIA-PLA Xinjiang listening posts, and a US programme to aid the anti-Soviet Afghan resistance by supplying Xinjiang mules to the Mujahidin.

Taklamakan Desert Highway from Luntai to Minfeng which for the first time allowed direct travel by standard motor vehicles from the northern to the southern rim of the Tarim Basin, cutting out the lengthy circumambulation via either eastern or western rims of the desert. (Before the Desert Highway only camels and off-road vehicles could cross the centre of the desert, and that only late in the year along the dry bed of the Khotan River. A sand road, originally intended for retreat to Qinghai or Tibet in the event of a Soviet invasion, ran through the tamarisks and willows along the riverbank from Aqsu south to Khotan.)[17]

State campaigns and the 'one white, one black' strategy

In the 1990s the Chinese state organised its efforts to develop Xinjiang under the rubric of high-profile campaigns: the first, the 1992 programme to 'Open up the North-west' was followed by the March 2000 inauguration of a broader 'Great Development of the West' (*Xibu da kaifa*), which targets Xinjiang and several other western provinces and regions that together comprise 60 per cent of China's territory, inhabited by 25 per cent of its population. (Interestingly, the terminology and concept echo the 'Come to the North-west' [*dao xibei lai*] programme promoted by the Guomindang in the 1930s, and more generally, Qing efforts in the eighteenth and nineteenth centuries to encourage Han settlement and land reclamation in parts of Xinjiang.) The 'Great Development' programme is the fulfilment of a promise China's planners made explicitly at the beginning of the Deng reforms, namely, that the priority given to economic development of the coastal areas in the 1980s would be followed by stepped up investment in poorer inland areas. It also aims to mobilise the considerable natural resources of these regions to more efficient exploitation by the dynamic industries of eastern China. The campaign involves both direct state investments and incentives to encourage investment by Chinese and foreign firms in the underdevel-

17 For data on recent communications improvements, see Zhonggong Xinjiang Weiwuer zizhiqu weiyuanhui dangshi yanjiushi 2002: 22–3, or Wang Shuanqian 2003: 110–14. I had the good fortune to travel the Khotan River route in 1992 along with representatives of the Sven Hedin Foundation and a group of Chinese scholars on a trip organised by the Zhongguo bianjiang shidi yanjiu zhongxin. The team of scholars was accompanied across the desert by two ewes, which were consumed en route.

oped regions. These material measures are accompanied by ample rations of boosterism.[18]

Xinjiang's share of 'Great Development' funds comes to over 900 billion yuan, most earmarked for major projects, including a rail-link from Kashgar to Kyrgyzstan, regional highway construction, telecommunications, water conservancy, environmental rehabilitation, agricultural expansion and especially the exploration, extraction, processing and delivery of energy resources.

One of the catchphrases of the Xinjiang development overall has been 'one white and one black', referring to cotton and oil, seen as the twin pillars of Xinjiang's economy. As Xinjiang became self-sufficient in grain in the 1980s a growing proportion of the land was devoted to cotton. In 1978 Xinjiang produced 55,000 metric tons of cotton; twenty years later the harvest reached 1.5 million tons. Between 1990 and 1997 alone acreage planted in cotton doubled. Many of the water conservancy projects under the development campaigns since the 1990s have related directly or indirectly to cotton production, either by supporting reclamation of land for cotton or, especially in the recent Great Development programme, by attempting to alleviate environmental damage caused by earlier reclamation efforts. Xinjiang became the single largest cotton producer in China in the early 1990s, and by 2001 was responsible for 25 per cent of national cotton cultivation. In 2005 Xinjiang's 1.75-million-ton cotton harvest accounted for 40 per cent of rural income, or as much as 70 per cent in some parts of the region. While cotton's key role seems assured for the immediate future, the slogan 'one white' is no longer entirely accurate, for in 2004 Xinjiang also produced 16 per cent of the world's total crop of so-called 'naturally coloured' cotton—cotton genetically modified to grow in hues other than white.[19] According to unconfirmed rumours, in places where GM and normal cotton are grown too close together, the 'natural colours' are occasionally cross-pollinated, resulting in white cotton with red flecks and other

18 For a general account of the *Xibu da kaifa* programme, see Lai 2002. See also Becquelin 2004: 358–64. Lu Zongyi and Li Zhouwei 2001 is an official compilation of articles on aspects of the Xibu da kaifa economic strategy as it relates to Xinjiang.

19 Becquelin 2000: 81; Information Office of the State Council of the PRC 2003: 21; Zhang Jianjiang 2001; 'China Xinjiang Cotton Crop at 1.75 Mln T 2004', *Xinjiang News*, <www.xjnews.com.cn> (25 January 2005, via China News Digest).

unpredictable blends—an apt metaphor for the Chinese economy under market socialism.

Some 40 per cent of Xinjiang's cotton is grown on *Bingtuan* farms, and not always profitably. At the end of the twentieth century, during an international cotton glut, Xinjiang cotton remained more expensive than that imported by eastern Chinese mills from abroad. Consequently large stocks piled up. Uyghur and Han farmers alike complained that they were forced to grow the crop at a loss. As during the Qing dynasty, state-requisitioned cotton is the lynchpin of today's land reclamation and settlement policies in Xinjiang, and serves political as well as economic purposes.[20]

Xinjiang's oil too is a commodity with a history. Chinese records from the mid-seventh century report a river of crude oil emerging from a mountain north-west of Kucha (Qiuci). Hopeful Kucheans used the smelly ooze as a rejuvenating salve. By late Qing times many surface seeps were known and exploited for lamp-oil by locals. Russian explorers and Xinjiang-based consuls began to investigate these sites from the 1890s. Partly to keep foreigners at bay, and in an early example of the state-private partnership that still characterises Xinjiang (and much of Chinese) industry, the Qing government and private Chinese merchants formed a jointly-operated company to purchase Russian equipment and drill the first mechanised well in Dushanzi in northern Xinjiang in 1909. They struck oil 20 metres down, unleashing an impressive gusher, but the firm folded not long after when the Qing Governor Yuan Dahua pulled the funds and reallocated them to military use. In the late 1920s a Chinese geologist with the Sven Hedin's Sino-Swedish expedition discovered reserves in the Tarim and Turfan Basins and through the 1930s the British, Japanese, Americans (Sinclair Oil) and Germans (Siemens) all sent teams to survey Xinjiang oil possibilities. Extraction began in earnest during the Sheng Shicai era, when Soviet technicians opened the oil fields at Dushanzi, near Wusu, and worked them on-and-off through the 1940s. Soviet exploitation of north Xinjiang oil continued under the new guise of the Sino-Soviet joint stock companies after the PRC takeover, until the Soviets finally sold out in 1954.[21]

20 See Becquelin 2000: 80–3 for an argument that cotton production benefits the state but not growers, and is primarily intended as a vehicle for increasing Han migration to Xinjiang.
21 Deng Shaohui 1992: 52–4; see also Chapter 4 of this volume.

China has controlled the continued development of Xinjiang's oil industry, albeit with some continued investment by foreign oil companies. The main Xinjiang field at Karamay ('black oil') was opened in 1955, and the city of that name has grown into Xinjiang's petrochemical refining centre. Although most extraction of oil and natural gas has so far been in northern Xinjiang, Chinese (and, since 1994, foreign) firms have focused their exploration efforts on the Tarim Basin, despite the formidable obstacles to drilling in the Taklamakan Desert. Claims of new finds are published frequently and Chinese estimates of Xinjiang's petrochemical reserves climb ever higher. In early 2005, for example, after twenty years of exploration, the state-owned oil company Sinopec proclaimed its discovery of a field containing over a billion tons of crude oil and 59 billion metres of natural gas in the Tarim Basin, which if proven true, would increase China's overall known reserves by one third.[22]

Xinjiang figures prominently in China's quest for energy security, an increasingly important concern since China became a net energy importer in 1993. With its high rates of economic growth China's energy imports have accelerated rapidly (oil imports increased by 31 per cent in the 2002–3 period alone). Xinjiang's production of some 20 million tons annually makes it the fourth largest oil producing region in China, and some expect that it will become the foremost producer during the next century. Xinjiang also produces billions of cubic metres of natural gas per year. Xinjiang is, moreover, the conduit for Kazak oil. Construction began in September 2004 on a pipeline ('a bridge of friendship between two peoples') from Atasu in north-western Kazakstan to the Alatau pass (Alashankou) in Xinjiang; completed in May 2006, the pipeline began to replace rail shipments of Kazak oil, with plans for imports of up to 20 million tons annually by 2011. Some foreign analysts considered this pipeline 'economically dubious', but both Xinjiang domestic and Central Asian imports of energy are strategically important, given China's high reliance on Middle Eastern oil. In 2004 some two thirds of China's oil imports, those from the Middle East and Africa, had to pass through the Straits of Malacca, where they were vulnerable to piracy, terrorism or US blockade. Chinese leaders thus urgently want to develop more secure continental sources of energy.[23]

---

[22] Dillon 2004: 39–40; 'Sinopec Oil Discovery Could Lift China Reserves by Third', *Oilvoice*, 4 January 2005 (<www.oilvoice.com>, accessed 4 January 2005).
[23] Becquelin 2004: 365; N.J. Watson, 'Central Asia; China's Looming Presence,'

The same political calculus evidently applied to the flagship project of the 'Great Development of the West' campaign. In September 2004 the 4,200 kilometre West-to-East Pipeline began delivering natural gas from Xinjiang to Shanghai. Much touted in official 'Great Development' literature, and at one time China's single largest foreign-invested project, the 140 billion yuan pipeline was considered too expensive by the energy companies who initially planned to invest in it. Exxon-Mobil, Royal Dutch Shell, Russia's Gazprom and even the Chinese firm Sinopec withdrew from the planned partnership at the last minute, leaving as sole owner PetroChina (majority owned by the Chinese government). The problem was again its economic rationale—or lack thereof. The natural gas shipped from Xinjiang, expected to reach 12 billion cubic metres per year by 2007, cost 45 per cent more than international imports, making natural-gas fuelled power plants in Shanghai lose money. One Chinese analyst criticised the pipeline as 'a commercial project with characteristics of the command economy', aimed primarily at stimulating growth in the far west, without consideration for cost.[24]

This same critique could be applied more generally to the state-led efforts to develop Xinjiang. Several years into the 'Great Development of the West' campaign Xinjiang was only just beginning to attract sizeable investment from other Chinese provinces and regions: over 26 billion yuan in 2004—but this was a jump of 42 per cent over the previous year. Foreign direct investment in Xinjiang remained low into the 2000s (only 358 million yuan in 2002).[25] In fact Xinjiang's economy was much more tightly linked to the central government than was that of other provinces or regions of China. At the turn of the millennium a high percentage of its industry (approximately 80 per cent in 2004) remained state owned; a similarly high proportion of investment in capital construction (almost 60 per cent in 2000) came from the central government. Despite oil and

---

Petroleum Economist, 11 October 2004, p. 18; 'Head of China Oil Co. Hails Project Launch', Associated Press, 29 September 2004.

24 The analyst was Li Fuyong, writing in China Business Daily, cited in Pamela Pun, 'High Prices Fuel Row at 140b Yuan Gas Pipeline', The Standard, 6 October 2004, via Global News Wire; Gladys Tang, 'Pipeline Defections Put Heat on Sinopec', Hong Kong Standard, On-line edition, 1 September 2004.

25 'Development of Western Region Brings Xinjiang Ample Business Opportunities', People's Daily Online, 28 October 2004. This is based on figures released by the Economic Cooperation Office of the Xinjiang Uyghur Autonomous Region; Becquelin 2004: 362.

gas revenues (which make up half of the regions' fiscal revenues), Xin-jiang runs huge annual deficits, its expenditures routinely exceeding its GDP by between 12 and 19 billion yuan. These deficits are covered by price subsidies, poverty alleviation plans, special allocations to Xinjiang's state-owned enterprises and other mechanisms as well as by an annual fiscal subsidy from the central government to the Xinjiang region. Calla Wiemer has calculated the gap between GDP and expenditures—the net resource inflow into Xinjiang—for 1981–2000 as averaging over 20 billion yuan annually, or around 20 per cent of Xinjiang's GDP. While the net inflow did appear to decline towards the end of the period, her calculation does not include the hundreds of billions of yuan recently invested in the region for the 'Great Development' campaign. Although Xinjiang is one of the richest of the inland provinces and regions, and its growth rate in recent years has been exceeded only by the coastal provinces, the region's effective subsidy remains on a par with those of Yunnan and Guizhou, the poorest parts of China.[26]

All of this demonstrates, once again, an uncanny similarity to the state of affairs in the eighteenth and nineteenth centuries, when the Qing imperial government shipped annual subsidies of millions of silver ounces westward to sustain its government, military and state farm op-erations in Xinjiang (see Chapter 3). Xinjiang's energy industry and the prominent economic role of the highly unprofitable *Bingtuan* partly ex-plain the centralised and subsidised nature of the region's economy. But why Xinjiang remains so commandist despite the phenomenal success of privatisation and liberalisation elsewhere in China ultimately comes down to political decisions by China's leadership, which has consistently chosen centralised control and state-driven development over economic efficiency in this frontier region.

This section on development began with the question of how the party has improved the people's lives in an 'ethnic concentration region', as Xinjiang is now commonly called. In fact the 2003 white paper on Xinjiang mobilises battalions of statistics to make the case that the PRC has measurably improved the lives of people in the region. One such measure involves consumption. In rural areas, according to official fig-

26 Wiemer 2004: 173–6. See also Becquelin 2004: 362 for the same argument. Both scholars provide ample statistical evidence of the centralised and state-domi-nated Xinjiang economy. Sautman 2000 makes the same point about subsidies to argue that Xinjiang is not an 'internal colony' of China.

ures, people in 2001 devoted 10 per cent less of their income to food than they did in 1978. Although they still spent half of their money to feed themselves, on average they enjoyed enough discretionary income for every household to have a bicycle—alas, unlike Sayram Bek, not yet a motorcycle. Almost every rural home likewise had a television, and washing machines and tape recorders graced some village homes. Xinjiang's city dwellers were on average nearly as blessed with the *sine qua nons* of modern life (colour TVs, refrigerators, hi-fis, VCD players, mobile phones) as their counterparts in Beijing, or for that matter in London or Washington. In all categories, rates of ownership of these consumer durables have increased many-fold since 1985.[27]

However, other measures of development success are possible. In his talk with the Kazak herdsmen, General Secretary Jiang evoked 'unity of the nationalities' (*minzu tuanjie*), the common slogan and coded reference to separatist sentiments and ethnic unrest in the region. In his words, and in those of the official party line in the final decades of the twentieth century, prosperity in Xinjiang rested upon a foundation of ethnic harmony. But as noted above, the party in those same years also explicitly pegged its hopes for improved ethnic harmony in Xinjiang on its economic development, describing the latter as foundation for the former. By this measure it remains unclear to what extent Xinjiang development had succeeded by the end of the millennium.

According to an attitude survey conducted in 2000 by a scholar from Hong Kong University, some 47 per cent of Uyghurs sampled in Urumchi believed their standard of living under the reforms had risen as fast as that of the Han, and 38 per cent thought it had increased more slowly. (The perception among Han was almost a mirror image, with half thinking they were on a par with Uyghurs and 38 per cent believing Uyghurs had advanced more quickly.)[28] This study no doubt reflects the creation of a relatively well-off Uyghur urban middle class.

However, scrutiny of the official figures themselves reveals a different region-wide pattern. Although the PRC does not break down statistics on income in Xinjiang by ethnic group, Wiemer regressed county-level figures on GDP per capita and ethnic make-up to discover a strong correlation between ethnicity and income: the greater the Turkic population of a given area, the lower the GDP per capita for that area. Or,

27   Information Office of the State Council of the PRC 2003: 30–1.
28   Yee 2003: 443.

as Nicolas Becquelin puts it, southern Xinjiang, with 95 per cent non-Han population, has an average per capita income half that of Xinjiang as a whole.[29]

Han Chinese are concentrated in cities of northern and north-eastern Xinjiang, including Urumchi; they work disproportionately in higher-paying professional and government jobs. Uyghurs in Xinjiang told foreign visitors that they felt shut out of new jobs created by large-scale projects, especially those in the energy sector. Uyghurs also commonly complain that they have no chance to work at the construction sites now ubiquitous even in southern Xinjiang cities. My own observations from the summers of 2001 and 2004 confirm that the labourers erecting new buildings around Id Kah mosque, paving the road through the Uyghur neighbourhoods in old Kashgar, demolishing the old bazaar in Khotan and working on a major renovation of Khotan's central downtown intersection were all Han, as they were even in remote Tashkurghan (on the road to Pakistan). Those workers I talked to, moreover, said they came from provinces east of Xinjiang. Wang Lequan, Xinjiang First Party Secretary and Politburo member, expressed a commonly heard explanation for this when he told foreign journalists that 'many Xinjiang minorities don't want the "dirty, hard and tiring work".' The comments of a labourer from Sichuan to a Western reporter suggests a more nuanced reason:

'We cannot communicate with them. We don't know their language', said Zhang Bizhong, a construction worker from Sichuan province. 'We Sichuanese prefer to eat rice and pork, and dishes with strong flavours. The local minorities don't eat pork. They don't like rice.'[30]

Most Uyghurs actually do like rice: *polu*, rice pilaf cooked with mutton, carrots and onions, is a favourite celebratory meal across Central Asia. But if Mr Zhang could not communicate with local Uyghurs enough to realise this, neither could the labour bosses who hired him. One suspects contractors have deemed it simpler to bring in migrant workers from their own provinces rather than work with local society. This is of course a common problem with development projects in many places: Wash-

29 Wiemer 2004: 177–8; Becquelin 2004: 372.
30 Tim Johnson, 'Throngs of Migrants Flooding China's Silk Road Cities', *Kansas City Star Online* (KansasCity.com, Knight Ridder Newspapers), 22 September 2004.

ington, DC has passed laws forcing contractors from the neighbouring states of Virginia and Maryland to hire local labour if they wish to take on large municipal projects.

'THE PEACOCK FLIES WEST': MIGRATION TO XINJIANG

Han migration to Xinjiang is not new. Based on our best available figures and estimates, at the start of the nineteenth century, forty years after the Qing conquest, there were something like 155,000 Han and Hui in Xinjiang, and something over twice that number of Uyghurs.[31] Han population dropped precipitously in the mid-nineteenth-century wars, and climbed gradually thereafter until the mid-twentieth century. In 1947, on the eve of the PRC takeover, there were some 222,000 Han in Xinjiang, comprising around 5 per cent of the population, compared to over three million Uyghurs, who made up 75 per cent. In 2000 Xin-

31 A 1787 census of Han and Hui settlers in the two Xinjiang prefectures of Zhenxi and Dihua (Urumchi) counted 114,348 individuals in these parts of the region most intensively settled by Chinese (Le-bao memorial, QL53.2.9, in *Gongzhong dang Qianlong chao zouzhe*, vol. 67, p. 264). The modern scholar Wang Xilong, working with gazetteer data from 1803, estimated 'over 155,000' Chinese reclaiming land in the 'Northern Route' (*Beilu*), an area comprising northern and north-eastern Xinjiang (Wang 1990: 179). At that time, Han and Hui were not permitted to settle permanently in the Tarim Basin cities, and there were only a few hundred Chinese merchants sojourning in the south. Wang's figure thus provides a reasonable estimate of the total population of Chinese in Xinjiang, and is in line with the 1787 figure. A Qing census of the Uyghur population published in 1818 (but conducted earlier) counted 63,767 Uyghur households in Yili, the Tarim Basin oases and suburban villages. Assuming an average household size of five, this yields some 320,000 Uyghurs. As there were then few Uyghurs in Urumchi and the new settlements of the north, we may take 320,000 as a rough minimum estimate of the Uyghur population of Xinjiang in the early nineteenth century.

These censuses are no doubt undercounts, as they were taken for tax purposes. Moreover, neither Han, Hui nor Uyghur populations of Turfan and Hami are included in either figure. On the other hand, the estimated Uyghur household size of five may be inaccurate: a 1761 Qing census counted both Uyghur households (59,581) and individuals (208,390), indicating an average household size of only 3.5 persons, not 5 as used above [*Da Qing huidian*, cited in Chia 1991: 134]. Nevertheless, the figures give us a rough guide to the relative populations of these groups at the height of the Qing period in Xinjiang. For a fuller discussion of this estimate, with full citation of Qing archival and published sources, see Millward 1998: 33 n., 271 n. 21, and Millward 2000. See also Yuan Xin 1994: 1–2.

jiang's 7.49 million Han represented 40.6 per cent of Xinjiang's total population of 18.5 million, or 43 per cent if the officially acknowledged 'floating population' of 790,000 non-registered migrants is included in the Han total. Although the Uyghur population (7.19 million in 1990, about 8.35 million in 2000) has also increased markedly since 1949, Han population has grown much faster and by 2000 equalled that of Uyghurs region-wide when the floating population is taken into account, and exceeded it if military personnel stationed in Xinjiang are included. Figure 1 represents population changes in Xinjiang from 1947 to 2000.

Although the Urumchi environs—northern cities like Tacheng and even Korla and Aqsu—has had large Han populations for some time, one of the most obvious changes in Xinjiang in the 1990s–2000s was

Fig.1 Population of various Xinjiang ethnic groups, 1947–2000 (millions)

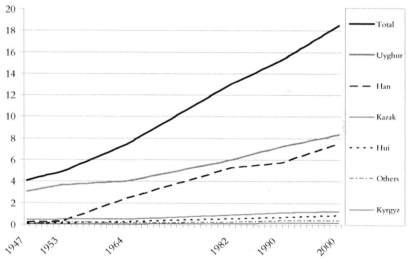

Note: Trend lines are interpolated from figures taken for the years shown.

Sources: 1947 figures are from compilations made by Su-bei-hai while working with the research department of the Xinjiang jingbei silingbu, cited in Liu Weixin *et al.* 1995: 880, '1947 nian Xinjiang gezu renkou tongji biao'. I have combined Uyghur and Taranchi figures from Liu's table to produce the Uyghur figure here. 1953–90 figures are PRC census results, cited in Toops 2004: 246, table 9.3; and Department of Population 2003: vol. 1, table 1–2, pp. 4–26.

the increased numbers of Han Chinese in southern Xinjiang towns. This was evident not only in the faces of the people one encountered, but in the changing cityscapes themselves. For example, after the rail-line reached Kashgar in 1999, neighbourhoods of shiny, new, white-tiled buildings inhabited primarily by Han sprung up between the old town and the train station 11 kilometres away, much like settlements of Han merchants once filled the space between the old town and the new forts constructed by the Qing military in the eighteenth and nineteenth centuries. A night market on Youmulake Xiehaier (Yumulaq Shähär) Road near the intersection with Renmin Road, on the border of the old and newer parts of town, reflected the same reality noted by the construction worker Zhang Bizhong: in 2001 this market was ethnically segregated, with Han carts on one side selling liquor, pork dishes and such snacks as chicken feet; a few feet away on the other side Uyghur carts sold mutton kebabs, noodles and *polu*.

The urban changes proceeding at such a startling pace in southern Xinjiang in the 1990s and 2000s—the demolition of old housing and the growth of apartment blocks, the remodelling of city centres, the commercialisation and privatisation of former public spaces, the replacement of old-style covered bazaars with pedestrian malls and shopping centres—had as much to do with Chinese and global patterns of modernisation as with Han migration. Certainly, many criticised how these projects were conceived and implemented. As happens everywhere, developers often entered into cosy deals with city leaders and the desires of local residents and shopkeepers were ignored.[32] But it is the nature of cities to change.

Still, by the early 2000s expatriate Uyghur dissidents, foreign observers and at least some Uyghurs in Xinjiang came to suspect that one goal of the Great Development of the West campaign was precisely to promote Han migration to Xinjiang. Nicolas Becquelin argues that by the late 1990s PRC leaders had determined that economic development alone could not eliminate ethnic dissent and separatist tensions in Xinjiang. Instead, it opted for a policy of accelerated integration of the region by means of Han migration in order to increase security. (As discussed in Chapter 3, the Qing dynasty revised its policy to allow Han settlement

---

32 This conclusion is based on my conversations with city residents in Kashgar and Khotan in the summer of 2004. On privatisation of public space in Xinjiang, including even sidewalks, see Dautcher 1999: 234.

in southern Xinjiang for precisely the same reason in 1831.) Becquelin points to a 2000 article by Li Dezhu, head of the State Ethnic Affairs Commission, which links Han migration to Xinjiang ('The Peacock Flying West'; *kongque xibu fei*) with the Great Development of the West campaign. In the article Li suggested that directing more policy attention and financial investment to the west would induce a westward flow of population to match the south-eastward flow to the coast that had occurred after the onset of Deng's economic reforms. While population movement is a natural accompaniment to economic development, Li argued, it would result in a decline in the relative population of non-Han groups in western cities and thus could cause ethnic 'contradictions' and 'friction'. Nonetheless, western development would help turn the entire country into 'one big unified market' and that, in turn, would increase the 'centripetal force and cohesive force' (*xiangxinli he ningjuli*) of each nationality towards the greater 'Chinese' nation (*zhonghua minzu*). [33]

From the 1950s through the 1970s the PRC officially resettled millions of Han Chinese from eastern provinces to Xinjiang using the *Bingtuan* to accommodate and employ them. Although many of the young Shanghainese and others sent to Xinjiang during the Cultural Revolution eventually returned home, such forced population transfers were the main reason for the rapid growth of Han population in Xinjiang. In the 1990s–2000s the state no longer directly mandated the resettlement of large numbers of people to Xinjiang, nor could it effectively do so: In 1992 the *China Daily* reported a plan to relocate to Kashgar up to 470,000 people destined to be flooded out of their villages and towns by the Yangzi Three Gorges Dam, then just beginning construction in Central China. After demonstrations by effected villagers, complaints by *Bingtuan* and Xinjiang officials and an international outcry Beijing officials dropped the idea. [34] Nevertheless, official encouragement and recruit-

---

33 Li Dezhu 2000: 24; Becquelin 2004: 373–4. Becquelin reads Li's point as 'explicitly' calling for dilution of non-Han ethnic population through Han in-migration, and translates the term *ningjuhua* as 'homogenisation'. However, far from being explicit, Li dances around this delicate issue: he refers to changes in relative numbers of ethnic groups in western cities as a side effect rather than a goal, and emphasises that the absolute populations of ethnic groups will continue to increase. Li refers to the *ningjuli*—better translated 'cohesion'—of ethnic groups to the *Zhonghua minzu*, not their homogenisation. Still, this is admittedly a fine distinction.

34 Robert Barnett, 'Outrage at Resettlement in Xinjiang', *South China Morning Post*, 9 December 1992; Human Rights Watch 2000; 'China Says Huge Dam Worth

ment—via, for example, public offerings of southern Xinjiang land to Han migrants willing to take out responsibility contracts—continued.[35]

During his 1990 tour of Xinjiang Jiang Zemin offered a wordplay on Mao Zedong's famous line about the Great Wall. Jiang's new version of the epigram became '*Bu dao Xinjiang, bu hao Han!*' (if you haven't been to Xinjiang, you're not a good Han!).[36] '*Hao Han*' has a general meaning akin to 'a real *mensch*', but in the ethnically politicised environment of Xinjiang, it takes on a more literal sense. As the optimism of our Urumchi beggar shows, even without direct state incentives Xinjiang's boomtown atmosphere since 1991 and the call to 'Develop the West' proved a strong draw to hundreds of thousands of 'hao Hans' from the east.

'A DRY AND SEMI-DRY REGION': XINJIANG'S ENVIRONMENT

Xinjiang has its share of baleful environmental stories. Radiation lingers from the nuclear testing grounds of the Lop Nor area, producing, some have claimed, clusters of birth defects. The Tarim Basin's near monoculture of cotton renders Xinjiang's agrarian economy vulnerable to pests. Extinction threatens the region's indigenous species, including the wild Bactrian camel, the Yili pika, the Tibetan antelope and the snow leopard.[37] Fires raging deep underground in over thirty coal fields have so far consumed over three billion tons of coal (the recently extinguished Liuhuanggou fire had been burning for 130 years). One third of China's underground coal mine fires, which together reportedly emit a volume of carbon dioxide equivalent to that produced by all the automobiles in the United States in a year, are in

---

the Price', UPI, 19 August 1996. Human Rights Watch suggested in this report that some dam refugees were ultimately resettled in Xinjiang by the *Bingtuan* starting in 1999.

35   Becquelin 2000: 76–7.

36   Zhonggong Xinjiang Weiwuer zizhiqu weiyuanhui dangshi yanjiushi 2002: 337.

37   Chinese and international efforts to protect the wild camel include the creation in 1999 of the 65,000 sq. km. Arjin Shan Lop Nur Nature Reserve in south-east Xinjiang. See Hare 1998 and <www.wildcamels.com>. In 2002 China formed the Hoh Xil (Tibetan Antelope) Nature Reserve in Qinghai, after a popular movie dramatised the beast's threat from poachers. Wang Ying, 'Plight of Antelope Tied Web of Survival' [*sic*], 29 October 2004. 'Ili Pikas on NW Mountains Endangered', *Xinhua*, 14 February 2005.

Xinjiang.[38] However, the crux of Xinjiang's human and natural ecology, as in Loulan's heyday, turns on the relationship between numbers of people and supplies of water.

If continued Han in-migration has become a prominent feature of Xinjiang's post-1991 history, it is not the only source of population growth. Numbers of 'minority nationalities' also increased by 1.5 million between 1990 and 2000. In fact, from a broader perspective, the story of Xinjiang's demography throughout the modern period is one of faster population growth than for China as a whole. From the time of the Qing conquest until the mid-nineteenth century, Xinjiang's population increased six fold—compared to an increase of four and a half times for China over the whole Qing dynastic period (1644–1911). Likewise, during 1990–2000 Xinjiang's annual growth rate was 1.67 per cent *versus* 1.07 per cent for China overall, and in 1999 Xinjiang's natural growth rate (crude birth rate minus crude death rate) was 1.28 per cent, compared with 0.88 per cent for China as a whole.[39] A projection made in 2000 predicted that Xinjiang's population would continue these high rates of growth, reaching 23.47 million by the year 2015.[40] In the early twenty-first century, then, Xinjiang continued to look demographically like a frontier region, filling up with people due both to in-migration and high natural growth rates among Uyghurs and other non-Han groups.

Because of Xinjiang's extreme aridity human life in the region has always been sensitive to the natural environment, and *vice versa*. The fact that the inhabitants of northern Xinjiang were until modern times primarily nomadic pastoralists is a reminder of how geography has shaped

---

[38] 'China's Biggest Cotton Zone Hit by Pests', *People's Daily*, 13 September 2001; 'Xinjiang Vows to Quell Underground Coal Fires', *Xinhuanet*, 3 November 2004, via <www.chinaview.cn>. Researchers speaking at the 2003 annual meeting at the American Association for the Advancement of Science (in Denver) said that 'putting out the fires in China alone would cut carbon dioxide emissions equivalent to the volume produced by all US automobiles in a year.' 'China Extinguishes 130-year-old Fire', *The World News* (web-based news from Special Broadcasting Service [Australian public broadcasting]), 11 June 2004, <http://www9.sbs.com.au/theworldnews/region.php?id=98319&region=2> (accessed 9 November 2004).

[39] Toops 2004: 247–8; Natural Bureau of Statistics, Peoples Republic of China, 'Major Figures of the 2000 Population Census (no. 1)', from <www.sfpc.gov.cn>, 28 March 2002 (accessed 28 February 2005).

[40] 'Xinjiang Sees Annual Population Growth of 340,000', *People's Daily Online*, 9 June 2000.

socio-economic patterns in Central Asia. The ancient cities now buried in the Taklamakan similarly testify to the key role of the environment and especially water in supporting human settlement in the Tarim Basin.

Against this background, the population growth and land reclamation that accompanied Xinjiang's development in the second half of the twentieth century is, on the one hand, broadly understandable as a continuation of earlier patterns of settlement and environmental exploitation, particularly since the eighteenth century. On the other hand, the past fifty years stand out for the sheer scale of human modifications to the environment.

Water, and its exploitation, is the key to modern human–environmental interaction in Xinjiang. Immediately after the conquest of Xinjiang, Qing officials eager to resolve the formidable logistical difficulties of the occupation set about improving water supplies for roads throughout the region and widely expanding irrigation to support increased agriculture, the harvest from which provided grain to the Qing troops. Till the early nineteenth century state farms and associated hydrological projects were concentrated in northern and eastern parts of the region, but from the 1830s imperial authorities turned more attention to the south as well. During his three years of exile in Xinjiang in the early 1840s, Lin Zexu alone charted out 800,000 *mu* of new irrigated land, two thirds of it in the Tarim Basin. He supervised the digging of everything from *karez* wells to major canals.[41] In fact, the impact of ex-Commissioner Lin's hydrological works in Xinjiang are arguably as profound as his famous destruction of British opium, for he inaugurated the intensive agricultural exploitation of the Tarim Basin, and his surveys formed the template for later agricultural reclamation. Scholars estimate that from the Qing conquest to the late nineteenth century the area under cultivation in Xinjiang increased over ten-fold, to 11,480,190 *mu* (approximately 766,000 hectares) in 1887.

In his plans to reconstruct the region after provincehood, Zuo Zongtang was greatly influenced by the apparent success of this earlier reclamation programme, as he was by a famous essay written by the statecraft scholar Gong Zizhen, which stated confidently that investment in agriculture in Xinjiang and increased settlement by Han Chinese would make the region self-sufficient and stable (discussed in Chapter 4).

41   Yan Shaoda 1989: 182.

Nonetheless, the lands abandoned in the mid-nineteenth-century re-bellions proved hard to recover from the sands; moreover, neither Zuo nor successive Han governors in Xinjiang through the early twentieth century had the funds for a major investment. By the 1910s cultivated land was just over 700,000 hectares, not yet back to its peak level during the Qing. Nevertheless, Gong Zizhen's essay and the Qing record in Xinjiang suggested powerfully to later officials and farmers that popular effort guided by official planning could make even arid Xinjiang bloom and support large numbers of new settlers. By the 1930s cultivated area had reached some 995,000 hectares and was at 1 to 1.2 million hectares in 1949.[42]

After that, the *Bingtuan*, collective farms and more recently individuals contracting land followed the same philosophy, which easily dovetailed with the Maoist vision of nature as an enemy to be conquered by the party and the masses in the drive to build socialism—or, after Deng Xiaoping, the drive to create prosperity.[43] Despite the excesses and en-vironmental damage of the Great Leap Forward, the *Bingtuan* continued to settle new migrants and open new land. The reform policies since the late 1970s too encouraged expansion of arable area. The result was a total of 3,404,120 hectares under cultivation in 2001—an area the size of the Netherlands. Figure 2 shows just how dramatic the expansion was in the second half of the twentieth century.

This rapid expansion of farmland occurred in a region with minimal precipitation. Thus it depended almost exclusively upon channelling ir-rigation water from the streams flowing out of the mountains ringing Xinjiang's basins. Rivers fed by run-off from snowpack and glaciers sup-port settlement and grain fields in the fertile Yili valley and other parts of the north, as well as the Urumchi area, the Turfan Basin and the cot-ton-growing oases of southern Xinjiang.

However, the most acute environmental changes of the past half cen-tury have occurred in the Tarim Basin. After passing through and being tapped in the oases, run-off water in the Tarim system historically either emptied straight into the desert or joined the extensive river system consisting of the Khotan, Yarkand, Aqsu and other rivers whose conflu-ence formed the 1,300 kilometre-long Tarim (see Map 1). Fed by these

42   Hua Li 1994: 262–3; cf. Fang Yingkai 1989: II: 757; Wiens 1966: 75–7, 81, table 4, 84–5; Zhao Yuzheng 1991: 332; Kataoka, 1991: 189–94.
43   See Shapiro 2001.

Fig. 2 Cultivated area in Xinjiang, 1760–2001 (sq. km.)

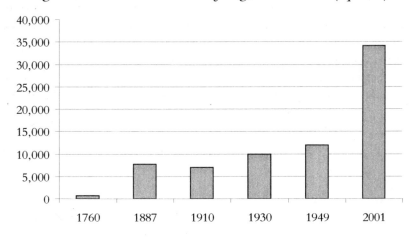

and smaller tributaries, the Tarim meanders from west to east along the northern rim of the basin. It has always been prone to course changes, but no water escaped the vast depression that is the Taklamakan, and the river always terminated in one or another of three lake basins in the south-east corner of the desert: Lop Nor, Kara-Koshun or Taitema. Most of the run-off water joining the Tarim system flows seasonally, with between 60 per cent and 95 per cent of the annual discharge flowing between June and September.

Despite vast infusions of new capital, labour and modern machinery, there was no way agriculture in the Tarim Basin in the second half of the twentieth century could transcend this basic hydrological framework. Agriculture enjoyed no new sources of water; even groundwater sources are linked to run-off discharges which annually replenish the oasis aquifers. The growth in population and expansion of cultivated land area, then, has simply drawn off more of the water flowing through the same Tarim system than had been done in the past. Reclamation engineers and farmers, many with the *Bingtuan*, were able to intensify exploitation of the Tarim system by constructing hundreds of dikes, hundreds of kilometres of canals and *karez* and hundreds of deep tube wells in oases and all along the reaches of the rivers. Ultimately this intensified agricultural and urban use, along with evaporation from uncovered irrigation channels and flooded fields, came to exhaust most of the water before it reached the lower reaches of the Tarim. Lop Nor, once a wetland of reed forests home to fish, birds, wild pigs and tigers, was reduced by 1964 to a thickly crusted salt flat. Lake Taitema, the terminal lake of the combined Tarim and Kongque rivers from 1952 to 1972, likewise dried up in 1972 when a dam was built on the lower Tarim to create the Daxihaizi reservoir.

Besides desiccation of the terminal lakes, intensified upstream use of the Tarim Basin's rivers produced a range of unanticipated consequences. By the 1970s so much water was diverted upstream that little or none reached the lower 300 kilometres of the Tarim's bed. This lowered the water table across this vast area from 3–5 m in the 1950s to 11–13 m below the surface in the 1980s. Not only did this undermine farming in the area's state farms but it shrunk grass coverage by 75 per cent and reduced the poplar forest from 54,000 to 13,000 hectares. What was once called a 'green corridor' in the Taklamakan became largely desert as two thirds of its former farmland filled up with sand.[44]

Population growth and increased land and water use had similar effects along each of the rivers and in each oasis of the Tarim Basin. Diversion and use of water upstream reduced water available to farmers downstream, lowered water tables and shrunk open bodies of water. Moreover, because of high evaporation rates and the common practice of flooding fields to irrigate them, mineral concentrations in downstream water increased markedly. This increased salinification of fields at the outskirts of oases, leading to degradation and abandonment of land. Abandoned land, with neither crops nor original natural vegetation to stabilise it, was easily eroded and covered by wind-blown desert sands. A study of the Cele oasis based on remote sensing data reveals that from the 1970s to the 1990s 8 to 9 per cent of good farmland along the outskirts of the oasis gave way to mixed bands of desert or moderately arable land. The area of bodies of water in the oasis shrunk by over half. This happened even as tree-plantings successfully maintained the overall area of the oasis against an advancing sand dune.[45] At Cele and elsewhere desertification on the peripheries of the oases was exacerbated by the cutting of trees and scrub for use as lumber and fuel by oasis dwellers. Particularly damaging was the extirpation of tamarisk roots, which eliminated a tenacious stabiliser of the desert surface. The availability of tractors to pull out the massive

---

44 Lu Xin *et al.* 2001: 101; Cui Yongjian and Zhong Wei 2001: 206. Lu Xin *et al.* give the current extent of the lower Tarim poplar forest as 16,400 hectares.
45 Ding Jianli *et al.* 2001 and Ya-li-kun Ta-shi and Tashpolat Tiyip 2001.

root clusters and carry them into the oases made this practice possible and economical in a way it had never been before modernisation.

Human changes to the environment were not restricted to southern Xinjiang. To the east increasing numbers of Turfan's ancient *karez* canals ran dry over the latter half of the twentieth century, with only 617 out of 1,784 still functioning in 2004; these remaining *karez* were granted official protected status in 2005, but continued lowering of the water table caused by mechanised deep wells throughout the Turfan Basin was projected to dry out the last *karez* by 2030.[46] In the north the drive to boost Xinjiang's grain harvest led to a rapid conversion of pastures to farmland. In Bortala Prefecture, in the north-west corner of Xinjiang, from 1950 to 1977 the area of Ebinor (Lake Aibi) shrunk by half as the population in its drainage area shot up from 67,800 to 550,500 and farmed area and water use expanded accordingly. Ebinor's area continues to shrink by 23 square kilometres annually. Loss of vegetative cover around the lake led to wind erosion and dust storms: in the 1960s this area experienced high levels of airborne dust only one day in every couple of years. In the 1990s there were a month and half of such days annually.

Encroachment of farmland throughout the region, especially in northern Xinjiang, led to a loss of some 240,000 hectares of rangeland from the 1960s to the end of the century. However, from 1949 to 1998 the livestock population quadrupled from 10.4 million to 42.2 million head. Overgrazing, upstream water diversion and other factors have led an estimated 75 per cent of the available pasture to decline in productivity; the thinner cover of grass can now support fewer sheep per unit of land. Some 1,000 square kilometres of grassland desertified.[47]

Xinjiang's forests likewise retreated, due both to excessive cutting and falling water tables. Besides the 84 per cent reduction of the poplar forest in the lower Tarim drainage, willow (*hongliu*) scrub on the fringes of the Taklamakan has been reduced by 65 to 90 per cent. The slopes of the eastern Tianshan have been virtually denuded, and treeline elsewhere in the range, at an altitude of between 1,200–1,400m in the 1950s, has receded to above 1,700 metres. Nearly 70 per cent of the sacsaoul trees of the Zungharian Basin were cut between 1958 and 1982, and the poplar

46 '2,000-year-old Irrigation System in Xinjiang May Disappear in 25 Years', *Xinhua*, 20 December 2004.
47 Lu Xin *et al.* 2001: 100, 102; 'Traffic Flows Where River Once Did', *South China Morning Post*, 19 July 2002, cited in Becquelin 2004: 370 n. 70.

forests of the southern rim of the basin are gone. Reduced tree cover contributes to flooding, erosion and lower atmospheric humidity.[48]

In the war with the desert, the desert is winning. Of Xinjiang's eighty-seven counties and municipal districts, fifty-three have suffered desertification. Annual economic losses from desertification were estimated in 2001 at 2.5 billion yuan. Of the 33,317 square kilometres reclaimed through state and private efforts from the 1960s to the end of the century, one fifth (an area larger than the state of Delaware) has been abandoned again due to soil exhaustion, loss of water supply, salinification or encroachment by desert sands. Despite a massive programme of tree-planting intended to create greenbelts and windbreaks, in 2001 the Taklamakan desert was estimated to be expanding by 172 square kilometres per year; in 2004 the head of Xinjiang's Forestry Ministry announced that the desert was growing by 400 square kilometres annually. Over 47 per cent of Xinjiang is defined as 'wasteland'.[49]

Moreover, it appears that this human-assisted desiccation took place during a period when levels of water entering the Tarim system and other Xinjiang watersheds were actually on the rise. Average annual temperatures in this region, as elsewhere, have risen to unprecedented levels over the course of the twentieth century. Evidence of global warming is clear in oxygen isotope studies of Kunlun Mountain glacial ice cores.[50] Higher average annual temperatures reduce overall precipitation in Xinjiang even while increasing it in the rest of China (Xinjiang lies outside the monsoonal system that determines eastern China's weather). But unprecedented warming seems to have speeded the melting of the snowcap and glaciers in the Tianshan and Kunlun ranges over the past few decades, so that the average annual Tarim river discharge was some 10 per cent higher in 1976–86 than it was in the decade 1954–64.[51] Xinjiang's twentieth-century development has, therefore, drawn upon water reserves banked in the past: the most recent major deposits occurred during 1400–1900, when temperatures were markedly cooler than today, and especially during the global and local climatic minimums

48   Lu Xin *et al.* 2001: 101.
49   Lu Xin *et al.* 2001: 101–2; 'Xinjiang shamohua tudi meinian yi 400 pingfang gongli sudu kuozhang' [Xinjiang's desertified land expanding at an annual rate of 400 kilometres], *Xinhuagang*, 9 January 2004.
50   Thompson 1995, fig. 27.19; Yao Tandong *et al.* 1997.
51   Cui Jianyong and Zhong Wei 2001: 207.

of that era, from 1420 to 1520, 1570 to 1690, and 1770 to 1890, when precipitation in the mountains peaked.[52]

Recent studies suggest that the benefit from increased glacial run-off cannot continue for long. An international team led by China's pre-eminent glaciologist, Yao Tandong, concluded in 2004 that the glaciers of the high Tibetan massif, which includes the Kunlun range, are melting at a rate 'equivalent to all the water in the Yellow River … every year.' Those in the Tianshan are likewise imperilled. In fact China's glaciers will be two-thirds gone by 2050, and may disappear entirely by the end of the twenty-first century. Since the major tributaries that form the Tarim derive between 41 per cent and 58 per cent of their volume from glacial melt-water, Xinjiang could face a major reduction of its water supplies in a matter of decades.[53] On the other hand, in 2003 the Chinese Geological Survey Bureau announced the discovery of a massive underground reservoir beneath the Taklamakan Desert. Should their initial survey of its size bear out—they estimated its capacity at 36 billion cubic metres, the size of the lake behind the Yangzi Three Gorges Dam—and the obstacles to extracting this deep-lying water be overcome, this aquifer could help alleviate Xinjiang's water crisis. But as fossil groundwater, its exploitation too is ultimately limited.[54]

One side-effect of the ecological changes in Xinjiang over the past half-century has been more *qara buran*, or sandstorms, blackening the sky, damaging property and crops and harming livestock. There were 105 major 'wind disasters' in the region in the 1980s, compared to only sixteen in the 1950s.[55] Desiccation and desertification across north China has produced similar phenomena, and Beijing itself suffered debilitating sandstorms in the spring of 2000. The clouds of red dust enshrouding the capital spurred China's leadership to greater efforts at environmental protection and rehabilitation. Indeed, one of the six publicly promulgated tenets of the Great Development of the West campaign was 'ecological and environmental protection and building'. Although China's environ-

52   Yao Tandong *et al.* 1997; Thompson 1995; Grove 1989: 227–8.
53   'Glaciers Fading Away in Xinjiang', *Xinhuanet*, 9 November 2004; 'China Warns of "Ecological Catastrophe" from Tibet's Melting Glaciers', AFP, 5 October 2004; Cui Jianyong and Zhong Wei 2001: 207.
54   'China Finds Three Gorges-Sized Reservoir in Xinjiang Desert', *Xinhua*, 8 February 2003.
55   Lu Xin *et al.* 2001: 102.

mental protection agency, SEPA, was not included among the twenty-two government agencies leading the campaign, the Great Development plan included measures to continue planting shelter-belt forests, to strengthen protections against logging, and to return farmland to forests and pastures. However, most salient among the environmental programmes in the Great Development and concurrent five-year plan was a major infrastructural project to restore the Tarim River watershed.[56]

Chinese leaders have always displayed a predilection for monumental hydrological works. Throughout history rulers and ministers in China have concerned themselves with water control. One inspiration for this is Yu the Great, a legendary emperor who 'regulated the waters' and founded the Xia Dynasty (2205–1766 BCE), ushering in a period of luxuriant fertility and popular prosperity. Modern leaders, hoping to serve the people and leave their mark on Chinese history, still feel the pull of tradition; they have also been swayed by the high modernist impulses of Communism and grandiose tendencies of Soviet planners. Sun Yat-sen planned but never succeeded in damming the Yangzi. Mao Zedong, fascinated by the old saying that 'when a great leader emerges, the Yellow River will run clear', approved the construction of the enormous Sanmenxia dam on its main channel, designed—disastrously—to prevent the Yellow's river's copious sediment from flowing downstream. More recently Premier Li Peng pushed through plans for the enormous Three Gorges Dam on the Yangzi in the face of domestic opposition and international concerns over its economic feasibility and environmental and social impact.[57]

It is not surprising, then, that as PRC leaders came to understand the severity of water scarcity in north-west China, the first solutions proposed in the 1990s were massive water transfer schemes. One plan envisioned channelling water from the Three Gorges Reservoir to the dry north via an elevated canal; another involved diverting it from the headwaters of several major rivers on the Tibetan plateau, including the Yangzi, Yellow and Yarlung Zangbo, towards Lanzhou or Xinjiang. One version of this scheme proposed an annual transfer of 40 billion cubic metres of water from a Yarlung Zangbo tributary to the upper Yellow

56   Economy 2002: 1, 6; 'Forest Belt Built at Junggar Basin', *Xinhua News Agency*, 12 January 2001; 'China Curbs Expansion of Deserts in Xinjiang', *Xinhua News Agency*, 10 July 2002.
57   Shapiro 2001: 23, 48–51.

River for use in the north-west. The project would have dug a 30 kilometre underground tunnel and built a hydropower dam three times the
size of that at the Three Gorges. 'Experts' promised the project would
'turn green' the barren plateau of the upper Yellow River while at the
same time preventing annual floods in India and Bangladesh.

But it was He Zuoxiu, a retired vice-chief of the Institute of Phys-
ics at the Chinese Academy of Sciences who had helped build China's
first atomic bomb, and Gong Yuzhi, Vice-President of the Central Party
School, who shared the grandest vision. At a national session of the Chinese People's Political Consultative Conference in 1996 they proposed
using nuclear blasts to dig an 800 kilometre underground canal from
the Yarlung Zangbo river, under the Tibetan plateau and through the
Kunlun mountains to the Taklamakan Desert. (The Yarlung Zangbo or
Bhramaputra River flows through southern Tibet, past the main Tibetan
cities of Shigatse and Lhasa, before turning south into India.) Gong and
He reassured their audience that according to Russian scientists over
200 peaceful underground nuclear detonations in the Soviet Union had
produced no pollution. Their project was thus safe, though it would take
fifty years to complete.[58]

China has in fact embarked upon a three stage north-south water diversion project, the final stage of which will move water from the Yangzi
headwaters in Tibet to the upper Yellow River. So far neither nuclear nor
non-nuclear options to transfer water directly from the southern Tibetan
mountains to the Xinjiang desert are in the offing. Nevertheless, PRC
planners have implemented other large water diversion projects in an
attempt to ameliorate environmental damage and alleviate water shortage in Xinjiang. Between 2000 and 2004 engineers with the Ministry of
Water Resources diverted to the Tarim six 'infusions' of water from the
Kongque River and from Lake Baghrash (Bohu or Lake Bositeng). In
2004 they transferred some 300 million cubic metres from the lake.

In northern Xinjiang a canal completed in 2001 drew off some 10 per
cent of the water from the Irtysh to the oil drilling and processing centre
of Karamay. A new canal under construction in 2004 will channel more
water from the Irtysh to developing areas 300 kilometres to the south.
According to the Chinese ambassador to Kazakstan, Zhou Xiaopei, this

---

58   Lai 2002: 453; 'Chinese Experts Propose Diverting Tibetan River to Arid Regions', AFP, 18 April 1997; 'Nuclear Blasts Proposed for China's Greenery Project',
Kyodo News Service (Japan Economic Newswire), 20 April 1996.

new canal will raise the amount of Irtysh water exploited by China to 40 per cent of the total flow. The issue is of great concern in Kazakstan, as the Irtysh fills Lake Zaysan, serves a major hydropower plant, factories and agriculture in central and northern parts of the country, and provides the drinking water for the capital, Astana. The Irtysh also flows into Russia, where its waters are crucial to a large industrial centre. Similarly, the Yili River originates in Xinjiang and empties into Kazakstan's massive Lake Balkash. Increased use of Yili water on the PRC side has started to shrink this lake, and both the Kazakstan parliament and the United Nations Development Programme have expressed concern that without changes in how Kazakstan and China use the Yili waters, Lake Balkash could go the way of the Aral Sea, which lost 60 per cent of its volume during the Soviet Era, causing one of the worst ecological disasters of the last century.[59]

By the mid-2000s both officials and public in Xinjiang were much more aware of environmental issues than they had been fifteen years earlier. Billboards trumpeting such slogans as 'Protect our Xinjiang's Natural Environment' stood in downtown Urumchi, not far from those advertising Xinjiang's genetically modified cotton. Chinese geographers, hydrologists, ecologists and commentators were publishing alarming articles on the state of the Xinjiang environment, even delicately pointing out the tension between continued population growth and sustainable development in the region.[60] Impassioned discussion of Xinjiang's environment buzzed over internet bulletin-boards. Tree-planting campaigns and programmes to modernise irrigation with water-efficient (anti-evaporative) equipment have earned commendation from the United Nations. Yet the public pronouncements of the PRC's news service-cum-propaganda organ, *Xinhua*, retained the old militaristic language ('attacks' by the desert on oases; 'walling off the sand to build fields' and allow 'oases to advance upon the desert'; use forests as 'green screens on the front lines') and triumphalist accounts of renewed reclamation ef-

59 'China Gives Go-Ahead to Kazakh Transborder River Survey', Kazakhstan Commercial Television report, 26 June 2001, via BBC World Monitoring; Antoine Blua, 'Central Asia: China's Mounting Influence, Part 3: Xinjiang's Thirst Threatens Kazakh Water Resources', *Radio Free Europe/Radio Liberty*, 18 November 2004, at <http://www.rferl.org/featuresarticle/2004/11/78161e31-612b-4f88-8acf-b46fcfd088c2.html>.

60 Lu Xin *et al.* 2001.

forts.[61] Such public pronouncements portray the deserts as autonomous, antagonistic invaders to be repelled by Great Walls of trees; they remain silent on the emerging connection between upstream water use (some of it for the new trees in shelter-belts) and downstream desertification. Although they acknowledge the contribution of irrational development policies of the past towards the current problems, these reports have little to say about the continuing—perhaps accelerating—damage done by state entities or corporations and individuals operating in the looser economic and political climate of recent years. In particular, Chinese official publications do not acknowledge the fundamental contradiction between the pro-migration thrust of the Great Development of the West campaign and the environmental constraints on Xinjiang's carrying capacity that will only tighten as the glaciers melt away.

DISSENT AND SEPARATISM

In the 1990s through the 2000s one could read more about Uyghur unrest and separatism in English-language sources than at any period earlier in the twentieth century. The reasons for this are complex. Certainly factors discussed above (the Soviet collapse, economic and political reforms in China, increased travel to and from Central Asia, waves of Han in-migration, rapid economic growth, the reshaping of Xinjiang cities) as well as a limited religious revival may have engendered resentments and stimulated or facilitated expression of dissent by word or deed. Between 1990 and 1997, moreover, several major violent incidents gained international attention and seemingly justified the attachment of such sobriquets as 'powder-keg' and 'simmering cauldron' to the name Xinjiang.

However, something else lies behind the raised profile of Uyghur separatist sentiment. Since the 1980s foreign journalists have enjoyed unprecedented (if far from unfettered) access to Xinjiang as well as to countries in Central Asia with Uyghur diasporas. The advent of the internet further facilitated the collection and broadcast of information about

61 For example, Gao Feng, 'Xinjiang Takelamagan shamo: "weisha zaotian" de shiyanchang' [Xinjiang's Taklamakan desert: experimental field for 'walling off sand to build fields'], *Xinhua*, 17 June 2004; and 'Xinjiang shamohua tudi meinian yi 400 pingfang gongli sudu kuozhang' [Xinjiang's desertified land expanding at an annual rate of 400 kilometres], *Xinhuagang*, 9 January 2004.

Xinjiang while providing a platform for Uyghur dissidents in exile to publicise their cause; more recently the PRC government has begun using the same medium to counter dissident narratives. Meanwhile, events in Palestine and Chechnya and the terrorist tactics of al Qaeda and other groups focused attention on the role of Islam in post-Cold War conflicts. Samuel Huntington famously argued that globalisation was engendering a 'clash of civilisations', and his notion of 'Islam's bloody borders' gained prevalence. Thus for many Western journalists and analysts, just at the time that access and information about Xinjiang improved, Uyghur separatist tensions became the main storyline to pursue with regard to Xinjiang, and this separatism was generally assumed to arise from the Islamic faith embraced by most Uyghurs. A sampling of phrases used in headlines of English-language newspaper stories on Xinjiang from 1985 to 2000 reveals the flavour of much of this reporting: '"Holy warriors" of Xinjiang'; 'flare up ... turmoil'; 'China's danger zone'; 'Muslim separatists wage bloody war'; 'pressure rises'; 'restive'; 'war on terror'; 'uneasy bedfellows'; 'uneasy coexistence'; 'enemy within'; 'climate of fear'.[62] One scholar has referred to 'the region's slide into conflict and violence' and 'a separatist and Islamist fifth column within the party'.[63] Meanwhile, Chinese reports over this period alternated between glowing assurances of Xinjiang's investment prospects and dire warnings of what they called 'Pan-Turkism/Pan-Islamism' and, in the early 2000s, of an 'East Turkistan terrorist organisation' with connections to al Qaeda.

Political violence is a serious concern, and there were times in the 1990s when security in Xinjiang seemed likely to worsen and the type of rhetoric just quoted may have seemed justified. Chinese authorities and some other governments understandably harboured grave apprehensions about Uyghur separatism. But as we seek historical perspective on the period a few points are worth remembering. First, there was more access to, and more reporting about events in Xinjiang after the

62 Compiled from a Lexis-Nexis search selecting the categories 'general news', 'major newspapers' with the word 'Xinjiang' in headline only. Of the 180 hits yielded by this search (conducted 7 March 2005), including some duplicates, seventy-three stories concerned Uyghur separatism, terrorism or concerns thereof. The other most frequent topics were Xinjiang development, business affairs and earthquakes. Of course, as many stories dealing with Xinjiang do not use the region's name in the headline, this is a limited sampling.

63 Dillon 2004: 86, 99. Dillon's book provides detailed accounts of violent events in the 1980s and 1990s as related mainly from Chinese sources.

late 1980s than at any earlier time. We know relatively little about ethnic relations or incidents of unrest before then (see Chapter 6), so the
sense of a gathering crisis in the 1990s and 2000s may have been partly
a function of the greater availability of information. Second, despite increased reporting, information remained limited, and most data about
recent ethnic relations, anti-Chinese dissent and separatist violence derived from either Chinese government or Uyghur exile sources. Both of
these sources have reason to shape the record in their own way. Finally,
perspective is required when assessing the levels of violence associated
with Uyghur separatism. The white paper on terrorism released by the
PRC State Council in 2002 claimed that 162 people were killed and
440 injured by terrorist acts in the 1990s.[64] Of the fifty-seven killings
that the document specifically enumerates, most occurred in small-scale
events involving one or two victims. While the violence is deplorable,
this hardly makes Xinjiang comparable to Northern Ireland, Rwanda,
Palestine, Chechnya, Bosnia, Iraq or other areas where separatism and
ethno-nationalism fuelled conflict in the late twentieth and early twenty-first centuries. Furthermore it is worth remembering that while journalists were writing of 'Xinjiang's holy warriors' 'waging bloody war' in
the region, Xinjiang's per capita GDP was growing between 1990 and
2000 at an average of 7.8 per cent per year, only one point below that
of China as a whole.[65]

Violence

One result of political liberalisation in the 1980s was a modest revival
of Islam, evident from the opening of new neighbourhood mosques
and Quranic schools. According to an early-1990 survey, Xinjiang had
938 Islamic schools with over ten thousand students. Two hundred and
fifty of these were in northern Xinjiang, the rest mainly in Kashgar
(350 schools) with smaller numbers in Khotan, Aqsu, Yarkand and the
Kizilsu Kyrgyz Autonomous Prefecture. Yarkand had only thirty-three
schools, but two thirds of their 722 students came from elsewhere in the
region—perhaps indicating that Yarkand had retained its old reputation

---

64   People's Republic of China State Council Information Office 2002.
65   Wiemer 2004: 164; Becquelin 2000: 68. The difference between Xinjiang and
Chinese growth rates is primarily due to Xinjiang's higher population growth lowering the per capita figure.

as a centre for Islamic learning. The Communist Party worried about these schools, the unemployed or independently employed young men who studied there and the idea that Islam might be taught as an ideology competing with Marxism. As discussed in the last chapter, protestors had referred to Islam in their slogans during a few street demonstrations in the early 1980s. In particular the popularity of Yarkand religious institutions raised the possibility that graduates from these schools, returning home throughout the region, would form a region-wide network. (This is precisely the role played by the Kashgar new schools early in the twentieth century.)

The party also grew concerned about participation by cadres and party members, especially those at the village level, in what the party defined as 'religious activity'. Exactly what this term means is unclear: while it certainly includes prayer and mosque attendance, it may also include fasting during Ramadan and attendance at such ritual events as weddings, circumcision parties and wakes conducted a month after a death. These celebrations grew more elaborate as people gained wealth, and they remain deeply engrained in Uyghur culture, especially in the countryside.[66] In any case, by 1990 the party was retreating from the more liberal and flexible position it had assumed a decade earlier with regard to religion in a 'minority nationality autonomy area' like Xinjiang.

In January of 1990 authorities closed down the privately-run Quranic schools in Yarkand (and presumably other Xinjiang cities as well) and ordered students from outside the city to return home. According to Chinese accounts, several hundred madrasa students (*talip*) in Yarkand demonstrated in response, shouting 'study and protect Islam' and 'down with the infidels' as they marched. The event was dubbed 'the Talip Incident'.

Much more serious—indeed the episode which did the most to sound Chinese alarms and perk up journalistic ears regarding Islam-inspired separatism in Xinjiang—was the Baren incident of April 1990, known in Chinese as the Baren County Counter-Revolutionary Armed Rebellion. Baren county, Akto township (about 10 km south of Kashgar), had been named an 'Ethnic Unity Model Town' in 1984. This designation proved ironic six years later, when evidence of an armed uprising against Chinese rule emerged. As told in 'internal' Chinese

---

66 Ma Dazheng 2003: 13–15. On Uyghur celebrations and their 1990s revival, see Clark 1999.

sources,[67] a group led by Zeydin Yusup and known by the name of East
Turkestan Islamic Party planned a series of synchronised attacks on government buildings in the Akto and Kashgar area. Starting in March 1990
planners are said to have been raising money and issuing a call to arms
through mosques and cassette tapes. According to one report, they were
also buying up horses on local markets, causing prices to sky-rocket, and
telling people in Kashgar to close their businesses on 5 April. Learning that something was afoot, Chinese authorities sent investigators to
Baren, forcing the group to act. A Chinese source says that the group
then dispatched men to Turfan to blow up the railway (they were apprehended before making any attempt to do so). On the morning of 5
April some two hundred demonstrators shouting Islamic slogans surrounded the compound containing government and security offices for
Akto county and Baren township. Later that afternoon the confrontation
grew more aggressive, with some three hundred men surrounding the
compound. Five policemen who had been sent to arrest Zeydin Yusup
were themselves seized and their guns and other equipment taken. At
a nearby bridge men ambushed two cars from the Baren armed police,
killed their six occupants with axes and knives, and seized a few guns
before torching the vehicles.

    In the middle of the night, according to Chinese accounts, Yusup's
group issued an ultimatum threatening to attack if those barricaded
in the compound did not hand over any arms stored within. Shooting broke out as the rebels reportedly tossed homemade grenades into
the compound. During this exchange Zeydin Yusup was shot and the
besiegers fled. Four battalions of infantry and artillery troops from the
southern Xinjiang military district cordoned off the entire area, scattered the men holding the bridge, and pursued sixteen rebels who fled
into the mountains. An Englishman then living in Kashgar with his Uyghur wife (he was selling hashish to make ends meet) saw tanks, jet

---

67 Although the volume edited by Yang Faren, in which Li Ze and Zhang Yuxi's
accounts occur, and Ma Dazheng's 2003 collection are labelled 'internal circulation', nevertheless they circulate widely outside China. Ma's book has an ISBN
number. Moreover, a popular, publicly available account tells essentially the same
stories of most violent events, as does '"East Turkistan" Terrorist Forces Cannot Get
Away with Impunity' (Liu Hantai and Du Xingfu 2003; People's Republic of China
State Council Information Office 2002). These 'internal' sources should therefore
be treated more as approved official versions than as secret internal government
reports.

fighters and helicopter gunships in the Kashgar area for some time after these events.[68]

One Chinese source reports that 16 rebels were killed in fighting, 508 detained for questioning, 124 arrested, 40 convicted, 3 executed and 378 released after 'education'. These numbers may be questioned; news media subsequently reported a wave of arrests across southern Xinjiang, and Amnesty International has published claims from unofficial sources that up to fifty people were killed by security forces, including some killed by mortars and gunfire from helicopters.[69]

Possibly more revealing than casualty figures is the list, published in the same Chinese source, of weapons confiscated by authorities from Baren participants: 16 guns (including 15 taken from police in the course of events on 5 April), 470 bullets of various types, 243 earthenware (homemade) hand grenades, 53 kilos of blasting powder, 512 blasting caps, 180 knives of all sizes, three motorcycles and five horses. While demonstrating signs of prior planning and organisation, and relatively well-outfitted with explosives (said to be easily accessible in China due to loose control over construction materials), the 'East Turkestan Islamic Party' apparently launched its attack on the PRC government with few if any firearms. This much is revealed in the official account of Baren events, which mentions little shooting. Perhaps they were hoping to spark spontaneous mass rebellion in Kashgar and elsewhere, though that did not occur. Another interpretation suggests the convergence around the government offices began as a demonstration, only turning violent as the standoff progressed.[70]

Chinese sources are silent on grievances underlying the Baren unrest, implying that they arose solely from Islamic belief and East Turkestan separatism. Other reports, and my own conversations in Kashgar a few months after the Baren incident, suggest that one underlying complaint was the application (in 1988) of birth limits to minority families: Uyghurs living in cities were now legally limited to two, and those in the countryside to three children. Someone set fire to the state Planned

68   Li Ze *et al.* 1994: 210–11; Zhang Yuxi 1994: 6–7, 10, 19; Davies 2001: 77–9; Ma Dazheng 2003: 56–9.
69   Casualty figures in Ma Dazheng 2003: 62; a few pages later the same source says 377 members of the 'East Turkestan Islamic Party' were apprehended in 1990 in connection with the Baren events. Amnesty International 1999: 64.
70   Ma Dazheng 2003: 59; Amnesty International 1999: 41–3.

Birth office in a county near Khotan at the end of March 1990, shortly before the Baren events.[71]

In 1991 and 1992 another small group was responsible for three explosions and two attempted bombings of civilian targets. According to Chinese reports, Ablimit Talip and several others bombed a bus station video lounge in Kucha on 28 February 1991, killing one and wounding thirteen. A year later, on 5 February 1992, they exploded two bombs on public buses in Urumchi during Spring Festival. One bomb blew up at the terminus where the bus had emptied and no one was hurt, but another killed three and wounded fifteen. On the same day, authorities report, timed devices were planted in an Urumchi cinema and residential area but failed to explode. Ten men alleged to be conspirators in these attacks were apprehended later in 1992, and two were killed in the process. Five men convicted in the case were executed in June 1995.[72] There were other, unrelated, bombings in Kashgar between February 1992 and September 1993, including an explosion in an agricultural equipment company on 17 June 1993 that killed two and injured six, and a bomb in a wing of the Seman Hotel (or a building next door) where no one was hurt.[73]

From 1990 to 1995 security forces reportedly rounded up over one hundred 'separatist counter-revolutionary organisations, illegal organisations and reactionary gangs', arresting 1,831 people.[74] Despite this abundance of enemies, however, the next major outbreak of unrest was not until July 1995, and involved the townspeople of Khotan. Chinese authorities had recently arrested two imams of the Baytulla Mosque in that city for discussing current events in their sermons, and replaced them with a young and charismatic imam named Abdul Kayum. When Kayum began in his own lectures to advocate improving women's rights, he too was arrested for raising proscribed topical issues. Some days later, on 7 July, a crowd converged on a party and government office compound near the mosque, demanding information about the imam's wherea-

71   Clark 1999: 131; Ma Dazheng 2003: 15.
72   PRC State Council Information Office 2002: section headed 'Explosions'; Catherine Sampson, 'Bombers Raise Chinese Fears', *The Times* (London), 22 February 1992; Ma Dazheng 2003: 59–62.
73   PRC State Council Information Office 2002: section headed 'Explosions'; Dillon 1995: 24–5; Ma Dazheng 2003: 11.
74   Ma Dazheng 2003: 62–3.

bouts. The confrontation turned violent and the government called in large numbers of riot police who trapped the demonstrators in the compound, deployed tear-gas, and arrested and beat many of them. Official reports mention injuries to sixty-six officials and police, but supply no figures regarding demonstrator casualties.[75] If the Amnesty International report on this event is correct, it is ironic that Abdul Kayum was detained for *promoting* women's rights—especially in light of the common assumption that Uyghur unrest arises from Islamic fundamentalism.

Another large demonstration took place on 14 August 1995 in Ghulja in northern Xinjiang. Approximately 700 to 800 people marched along a main city street as police and paramilitary units responded with barricades, snipers and armed patrols; the standoff was ultimately defused without violence.[76]

Underlying this demonstration, and the more serious Ghulja (Yining) Incident two years later (see below), was an important social movement among Ghulja Uyghurs and the state's reaction to it. Starting in 1994 Uyghurs in Ghulja and surrounding villages began organising a type of social club known as *mäshräp*. Traditional *mäshräp* as once practised in many parts of Xinjiang refers to a social gathering involving musical performance, comedy or recitations of some kind. The revived form was a grass-roots response to the gathering crisis of unemployment, alcoholism and drug abuse besetting Uyghur youth, one fuelled by frequent all-night drinking parties that had become institutionalised as a primary form of male socialising. Adopting strict rules of personal conduct inspired by Islam, the new *mäshräp* clubs substituted other activities for

75 Amnesty International 2002: 13–17.
76 Dautcher 2004: 286–7. Dillon's account (2004: 68–9) of events in the Ghulja area in April 1995 seems exaggerated: he claims 50,000 demonstrators, strikes of 100,000 workers, armed convoys of rebels in forty vehicles ransacking a government store, and hundreds of casualties. Were these stories true, this would have been by far the largest and most serious insurrection in Xinjiang since 1949, yet it appears only in one Hong Kong source. The 2002 State Council document on terrorism makes no mention of this incident. Ma Dazheng 2003: 62 refers in passing to the 'illegal demonstration' in Ghulja in August 1995, but not to anything in April. It is hard to imagine an event as large as Dillon describes remaining unreported, especially one occurring so close to Kazakstan. Nor is it clear why PRC authorities would publicise Baren and the 1997 Ghulja incident while attempting to completely cover up violent activity in the Ghulja environs in 1995. Anthropologist Jay Dautcher was in Ghulja in 1995–6 and was not aware of any event of the scale Dillon describes.

drinking and meted out humorous ritual punishments (soakings with water and other mild humiliations) for young men who had gone off the wagon since the last assembly. As they grew in popularity, *mäshräp* in and around Ghulja staged a successful boycott of local liquor stores. This drew the attention of government authorities, who banned the *mäshräp* in July 1995: the Communist Party does not tolerate popular organisations outside its purview. Unfazed, the *mäshräps* went on to organise a city-wide soccer tournament, again in order to provide young men with a healthy outlet for their energies. Days before the opening games of the tournament that summer, the city cancelled it, commandeering the playing field for military exercises. To make the point perfectly clear, soldiers confiscated the goals and parked tanks on the pitch. This precipitated the August 1995 peaceful demonstration.[77]

During the first half of 1996 there were three assassinations of, or assassination attempts on Uyghur cadres in the government or the Chinese Islamic Association. One man, who was killed with three family members in his home in Kucha county, had held various village and township party positions and had served as representative at the Sixth National People's Consultative Conference. The most infamous assassination attempt occurred in Kashgar, when three men with cleavers attacked the senior imam, Aronghan Haji, and his son one evening while the imam was on his way to preside over prayers at the Id Kah Mosque. Aronghan, who survived the attack with cuts on his head, hands, back and legs, was Vice-Chairman of the Xinjiang Region Consultative Conference and head of the Kashgar District Islamic Association. Also during this period, police engaged in six shootouts with Uyghur suspects throughout the region.[78]

Besides this violence, there was apparently a good deal of popular unrest in Xinjiang in 1996. Though the accounts are vague and unconfirmed, the foreign press indicated a spike in protests, as well as tightened official repression in the spring of that year. One exiled Uyghur leader in Almaty, Yusupbek Mukhlisi, issued press releases taking credit for bombings, claiming to run a network of underground cells in Xinjiang and alleging that as many as 18,000 people had been arrested and hundreds

---

77 Dautcher 2004: 284–7. On the *mäshräp*, see also Roberts 1998 and Dautcher 1999: Chapter 5.
78 Ma Dazheng 2003: 69–74; PRC State Council Information Office 2002, '"East Turkistan" Terrorist Forces', section headed 'Assassinations'.

injured in clashes in 1996. However, Mukhlisi was prone to exaggeration, and the PRC white paper on terrorism makes no mention of him or his group.[79]

Possibly related to increased unrest in 1996 were three major political developments. The first was the release by the Standing Committee of the CCP Politburo on 19 March of a secret directive (CCP Central Committee Document No. 7) warning of illegal religious activities and foreign influence in Xinjiang.[80] The second was the signing of a mutual tension-reducing and security treaty by China, Russia, Kazakstan, Kyrgyzstan and Tajikistan, the so-called 'Shanghai Five', on 26 April (later expanded to include Uzbekistan and known as the Shanghai Cooperation Organisation). The third was the announcement of the first 'Strike Hard' anti-crime and anti-separatist campaign later that same month. (These are discussed in more detail below.) The high numbers of 'suspected terrorists, separatists and criminals' arrested, initially given by PRC sources as 1,700 and later raised to 'several thousand', may thus be the result not of any upsurge in separatist activity or ethnic unrest at this time, but rather of the 'Strike Hard' campaign itself, which placed a political premium on speed and quantity of arrests and convictions.[81]

The second-largest protest in Xinjiang's recent history (since the demonstration and hunger-strike of thousands of Han 'educated youth' in Aqsu in 1979–80), and the most severe street violence since the Cultural Revolution, occurred in Ghulja in early February 1997. Starkly different accounts of this event emanate from official Chinese sources on the one hand, and foreign press, rights organisations and Uyghur groups on the other. After denying that it had happened at all, initial PRC reports called the incident a case of 'beating, smashing and looting' by 'drug addicts, looters and "social garbage"'.[82] A source dated December 1997 describes organised rioting by several hundred to over a thousand 'thugs' (*baotu*)

79   On Yusup Mukhlisi, see Millward 2004a: 25.
80   Published, in English translation, by the Committee Against Chinese Communist Propaganda (CACCP) and Uyghur exile sources on <www.caccp.org/conf/doc7.html>.
81   PRC State Council Information Office 2002, section headed 'Assassinations'; 'Beijing Alert over Frontier Uprisings', AFP, 19 May 1996; 'China Defends Crackdown on Separatists', UPI, 19 August 1996; Andre Grabot, 'The Uighurs—Sacrificed on Central Asia's Chessboard', AFP, 25 April 1996.
82   Dautcher 2002: 248, citing *Ming Pao*, 11 February 1997, p. A6, as excerpted in BBC Survey of World Broadcasts.

and disturbers of the peace (*naoshi fenzi*). In an internal speech in 1999 Xinjiang Regional Party Secretary Wang Lequan likewise referred to the 'Yili February fifth beating, smashing, looting disturbance incident'. In 2002 the PRC white paper on terrorism went a step further and called the incident a 'serious riot ... perpetrated [by] the East Turkistan Islamic Party of Allah and some other terrorist organisations', claiming that from 5 to 8 February terrorists shouted Islamic slogans, killed seven innocent people, injured 200, destroyed thirty vehicles and burned two houses.[83]

Not surprisingly, accounts by Amnesty International and Uyghur dissident groups operating outside China differ from the PRC version in many respects. In these accounts, people in Ghulja took to the streets on 5 February out of accumulated frustration following the banning of *mäshräp* in 1995 (some of which continued to operate underground), and waves of arrests during the 'Strike Hard' Campaign, the principal targets of which included religious students, some imams and members of 'illegal organisations', including *mäshräp*. According to testimony gathered by Amnesty International, the police presence in Ghulja had been heavy early in the year. Not long before 5 February, still during the month of Ramadan, police had converged on a mosque to arrest two Uyghur religious students, touching off a scuffle as other people at the mosque intervened. Many were arrested. Several hundred Uyghurs then marched on the morning of 5 February to protest these arrests and other examples of what they saw as repression. They carried banners and shouted religious slogans. Armed police confronted the demonstrators; some demonstrators were killed or injured, either by shots the police fired into the crowd or from ricocheting bullets fired into the ground in front of the crowd. Hundreds of demonstrators were arrested. That afternoon more protestors took to the streets, including family and friends of those detained earlier. Police broke up this latest wave with clubs and tear gas, and again detained many people. Amnesty International's informants say many children were injured in this second demonstration. Protests and riots continued and spread to suburban districts over the next few days, with thousands of people in the streets, met by a strengthened police and military presence. Some of the rioters threw stones at

---

83 PRC State Council Information Office 2002: section headed 'Organising disturbances and riots and creating an atmosphere of terror'; Ma Dazheng 2003: 93. This article compiled in Ma Dazheng 2003 is dated December 1997; Wang Lequan 1999: 8.

police, attacked Han Chinese, ransacked shops, and destroyed vehicles. Videotape shown on Xinjiang television includes scenes both of orderly marches and of clashes between rock-throwing youths and police with shields and truncheons. Other Chinese police or soldiers shown in the video carry machine guns. Amnesty cites unofficial claims that security forces fired on protestors, but there are no firm estimates of how many protestors where killed. By 8 February soldiers had restored order and imposed a curfew on Ghulja; the city's rail, air and road links to the rest of the region were sealed off for two weeks.[84]

Only seventeen days after the conclusion of the worst recent street clashes came the single worst terrorist act in PRC Xinjiang. On 25 February 1997 three bombs exploded on Urumchi public buses, killing nine and seriously injuring twenty-eight others. Devices left on two other buses at the same time failed to explode. The date of the bombings was chosen with political intent: official memorial ceremonies for Deng Xiaoping were being held that day in Beijing.[85] Press accounts around this time commonly associated the Urumchi bus bombings with a 7 March explosion on a bus in central Beijing. Although this allegation continues to be recycled by later Western press accounts and academic articles, XUAR Chairman Abdulahat Abdurishit denied in May 1997 that the Beijing bombing was connected to those in Urumchi or perpetrated by Uyghur separatists, and the 2002 PRC document on 'East Turkistan terrorists' does not mention the Beijing incident.[86]

---

84 Amnesty International 1999: 17–19, 64–5; Amnesty International 2005. The video was circulated by the Eastern Turkestan National Research Center (New York) with a new soundtrack sympathetic to the Uyghur demonstrators. However, position of the camera and focus on Han Chinese casualties suggest that the original was shot by government sources in the PRC.

85 PRC State Information Council 2002: section headed 'Explosions'.

86 Reports on the bombing were initially carried by Deutsch Presse-Agenteur and Reuters on 9 March 1997. In August 1997 a Hong Kong newspaper published a report alleging that Uyghur separatists funded by the CIA were responsible for the Beijing bus bombing ('China Reportedly Links CIA, Xinjiang Separatists to Bombing', *Ming Pao*, 10 August 1997, via BBC Summary of World Broadcasts, 13 August 1997). Examples of recycling of the error regarding the Beijing bomb attacks include John Pomfret, 'Separatists Defy Chinese Crackdown; Persistent Islamic Movement May Have Help from Abroad', *Washington Post*, 25 January 2000; Forney 2002; and Rudelson and Jankowiak 2004: 317. Abdurishit's denial is in 'China: Xinjiang "Separatists" Said Not Behind Beijing Bombing', AFP (Hong Kong), 11 May 1997, via FBIS-TOT-97-131.

Amnesty International's informants report thousands of arrests and incommunicado detentions over the weeks and months following the Ghulja riots and Urumchi bombings, enough to result in a severe overcrowding of facilities. There were many alleged cases of abuse or torture of prisoners, including beatings, hosings with water in outside detention areas in the February weather and other techniques. The region-wide crackdown following the events of February 1997 became almost a permanent feature of life throughout Xinjiang. Security certainly remained extremely high until after the 1 July return of Hong Kong to PRC governance—an event which, it was widely rumoured, would be accompanied by some sort of protest or violent act in Xinjiang. Human rights organisations claim that the sweeps resulted in hundreds of arbitrary arrests; 'illegal religious organisations', religious schools and political dissenters were special targets. There were at least 190 executions by April of 1999, many after cursory legal proceedings: in the case of eight Uyghur men accused of the February bus bombings in Urumchi, Amnesty International calculates on the basis of published *Xinhua* reports that 'the sentencing hearing by the court of first instance, the appeal and review process, and the executions all took place within 13 days, between 16 and 29 May 1997.' Convictions were often followed by public sentencing rallies, and another clash between Ghulja residents and police occurred in April 1997 when a small crowd of bystanders, whom PRC sources say were attempting a rescue, approached prisoners on parade after such a rally. Guards shooting into the crowd killed more people.[87]

State response: international aspects

The crackdown in Xinjiang continued into the new century. It was, from one point of view, successful: between 1997 and 2005 there were no further large-scale acts of political violence in Xinjiang—nor, for that matter, any large demonstrations. The white paper on terrorism does mention twelve further deaths of Uyghur cadres and police deaths between February 1997 and January 2002, as well as sabotage of economic targets. Chinese sources claim that security forces continued to smash

[87] Amnesty International 1999: 23–5ff., 44–50, 54–64, quote from p. 55; 'Beijing Police on Alert for Xinjiang Separatists', AFP, 3 October 1997; 'Separatists Kill At Least 22 in China Attacks', AFP, 9 October 1997. See also Human Rights Watch 2000.

terrorist cells and illegal organisations and uncover weapons factories during this period, but it also interdicted attempts to smuggle arms from Central Asia. The main focus of Chinese concern thus shifted beyond its borders.

There are several ways in which the Uyghur separatist issue became 'internationalised' in the 1990s. Chinese sources had long warned of 'foreign forces' lurking behind the separatists in Xinjiang. Specifically they pointed to Uyghur exile groups and especially the activities of Isa Yusuf Alptekin (former Xinjiang member of the Guomindang Legislative Yuan) and his son Erken, who were active in Turkey and Germany; the PRC also indirectly, and sometimes directly, accused the United States of supporting the separatists. For example, when Wang Fang, Minister of Public Security, toured Xinjiang in August 1989 he announced, 'the root cause of [separatist] instability [in Xinjiang] lies in the attempt by the USA and other countries to split and subvert our country.'[88] Given their long historical memories, we may perhaps understand why Chinese leaders think the US is intent on detaching Qing-era acquisitions from modern China: they remember staunch US support for Taiwan, the CIA's infiltration of Khampa guerrillas into Tibet, and CIA agent Douglas MacKiernan's meetings with Osman Batur in 1949 just before Osman and his Kazaks launched their armed resistance to Communist Chinese takeover in Xinjiang (see Chapter 5).

However, of more immediate official Chinese concern was the increased international attention to human rights in Xinjiang that accompanied the greater openness of the region. Amnesty International, Human Rights Watch and the US State Department's Human Rights Report all began tracking the Xinjiang crackdown. From the 1990s the issue of Xinjiang separatism along with that of Uyghur rights took on an international dimension.

Besides these political issues, real security threats were brewing outside Xinjiang. Though the actual details and scale remain unclear, Uyghur groups were engaged in political organisation and some military training abroad. Chinese sources claim that till 1994 there had been secret training camps in southern Xinjiang, which later, under Chinese pressure, moved abroad. It seems likely that at one time or another in the 1990s some sort of weapons training went on in Kazakstan, Kyrgyzstan

---

88 Quoted in Dillon 2004: 61–2.

and Afghanistan. China was also concerned about activities of Uyghurs in Pakistan.[89]

The Chinese response to these threats was a new diplomatic initiative, which, combined with China's rising economic clout, vastly increased its influence in Central Asia. In 1996 officials representing China, Russia, Kazakstan, Kyrgyzstan and Tajikistan met in Shanghai and announced the formation of the 'Shanghai Five', a loose alliance meant to resolve border disputes lingering from the Soviet era, address mutual security questions, and facilitate economic cooperation. The border issues were quickly resolved, and with concerns mounting over Islamic extremism in the region and possible influence from the Taliban regime in Afghanistan, security rose to the top of the agenda. In 1999 a series of bombs in Tashkent targeted Uzbek President Islam Karimov, and in 2001 Uzbekistan, though not bordering directly on China, joined the organisation, which was then renamed the Shanghai Cooperation Organisation (SCO). The SCO thereafter devoted itself primarily to military coordination and anti-terrorism efforts, while providing a symbolic political counter-weight to the influence of the United States, then actively promoting NATO expansion to include Baltic countries once under Soviet control. President Jiang Zemin pointedly referred to the SCO as the 'Shanghai Pact' in what was most likely a conscious echo of 'Warsaw Pact', the Cold War era Soviet counterpart to NATO in Europe.

Under the auspices of the SCO, China established a joint anti-terrorism centre in Bishkek, provided military aid to Kyrgyzstan, and engaged in joint military exercises with SCO partners. As a multi-lateral security organisation the SCO is a departure from earlier Chinese foreign policy approaches, but it has channelled and amplified Chinese influence in Central Asia, at the expense even of Russia, and is now seemingly taking on broader regional, even global significance. Mongolia received observer status in the organisation and in 2005 India, Pakistan and Iran

---

89   In 2003 I was told by Rozi Muhammad, head of the Uyghur cultural association Ittipaq in Bishkek, that some Uyghur youths had formed military groups and engaged in some weapons training in the mountains in Kyrgyzstan around 1995. They were later arrested. The US government implicitly confirmed Chinese stories of Uyghurs training with the Taliban or Al Qaeda (though not in the large numbers Chinese sources assert) by holding twenty-two Uyghurs prisoner in its facility in Guantanamo Bay, Cuba. The US government released five of the Uyghurs in May 2006 to Albania, after searching for years for a country other than China willing to take them.

were each pursuing membership. The United States by 2005 still would not deal directly with the organisation, but had taken notice. The SCO, together with the commercial ventures of mostly Chinese state firms, thus represented the greatest extension of Chinese power into Central Asia beyond the Pamirs since the Tang period. However, China's first goal for the SCO had not been to project power into Central Asia, but to deal with Uyghur dissidents and potential militants abroad.[90]

From Beijing's point of view, the SCO succeeded brilliantly at this task. SCO membership presented the rulers of Central Asia's new states with a choice; some commentators called this 'playing the Uyghur card'. In return for good relations with the PRC, security cooperation, aid and, for Kazakstan, lucrative oil deals Central Asian governments sharply narrowed the scope of Uyghur activities in their countries. Such Uyghur militant training as had gone on in Kazakstan and Kyrgyzstan apparently ended by the mid-1990s; Central Asian governments also curtailed the rights of political assembly and fair legal process for both their long-term Uyghur minority citizens and recent immigrants and sojourners. From the mid-1990s Kazakstan and Kyrgyzstan began extraditing Uyghur suspects to China on Beijing's behest. By the early 2000s only Uyghur 'cultural organisations' could legally operate in Central Asian countries, and then only under close government scrutiny. Uyghur political organisations were banned. In short, whereas during Soviet times Moscow determined that a certain level of support and official sympathy for Uyghurs in the Soviet Union was politically in its interest, in the post-Soviet era Almaty, Bishkek and Tashkent responded to a new calculus.

Though Pakistan is not a member of the SCO, China was likewise able to pressure Islamabad in the 1990s to close a market where Uyghur businessmen operated and to drive Uyghur students out of religious schools; unfortunately the students followed other graduates of Pakistan madrasas to Afghanistan, where some (hundreds in some accounts, 2,000–3,000 according to Chinese claims) wound up as soldiers for the Taliban. Chinese ambassador to Pakistan, Lu Shulin, met with Taliban leader Mullah Muhammad Omar in Kandahar in December 2000, seeking guarantees that Uyghurs would not receive military training. Mu-

---

90 John Daly, '"Shanghai Five" Expands to Combat Islamic Radicals', *Janes Terrorism and Security Monitor*, 19 July 2001, accessed from <http://www.janes.com/security/international_security/news/jtsm/jtsm010719_1_n.shtml>; Martin Sieff, 'Analysis: China Boosts Presence in Central Asia', UPI, 24 September 2004.

hammad Omar's price for such an assurance was Chinese opposition to UN sanctions on the Taliban government in Afghanistan, and because China was not willing to block these sanctions, which stemmed from the 1998 al Qaeda bombings of US embassies in Africa, the Sino-Afghan talks yielded no results. Some Uyghurs fought with the Taliban against the Afghan Northern Alliance; others reportedly joined the Islamic Movement of Uzbekistan, a group connected with al Qaeda.[91]

The 9/11 al Qaeda attacks on Washington and New York changed the ground underlying both anti-terrorism policies and China's new diplomatic position in the region. The US response presented China with a dilemma, and in the first weeks after 9/11 China considered the new situation carefully. While on the one hand the US-led war in Afghanistan would eliminate the Taliban and presumably shut down any camps training Uyghurs in Afghanistan, it would also place the US military squarely in China's backyard. In fact, ignoring the SCO entirely, in preparing for its invasion of Afghanistan the United States concluded separate agreements with Central Asian countries for bases and landing rights extending indefinitely into the future—a strategic disaster from China's point of view. (By 2006 US forces had left the Uzbekistan base on Tashkent's request, and faced pressure from Bishkek to quit Kyrgyzstan as well.)

In the end, in responding to 9/11, Chinese leaders played their own Uyghur card, taking the opportunity to turn the official, public PRC position on Xinjiang separatism on its head. The earliest PRC approach to separatist tension in Xinjiang had been to minimise it by keeping most information under wraps and blaming only small core groups of vicious separatists backed by shadowy 'foreign forces', while at the same time turning out stories and images of beaming minorities thankful for the improvements in their lives made possible by the party. In the late 1990s Xinjiang authorities began discussing the violence in Xinjiang more openly. In March of 1999, for example, Xinjiang Uyghur Autonomous Region (XUAR) Governor Abdulahat Abdurishit claimed that there had been 'thousands' of explosions, assassinations and other incidents in the 1990s.[92] However, officials moderated their statements in the

91 David Murphy and Susan V. Lawrence, 'Beijing Hopes to Gain from US Raids on Afghanistan: a US-led Assault Could Cure a Headache for China', *Far Eastern Economic Review*, 4 October 2001, p. 18.
92 Becquelin 2000: 87; AFP (Hong Kong) 11 March 1999. FBIS-CHI-1999-0311 'Governor Says Xinjiang Suffering Separatist Violence', 11 March 1999. This

early 2000s, perhaps concerned about the impact of such publicity on Xinjiang's development under the Great Development campaign. Thus in welcoming Chinese and international business representatives to the Urumchi trade fair on 2 September 2001, Xinjiang Party Secretary Wang Lequan together with Abdulahat Abdurishit proclaimed that the situation in Xinjiang was 'better than ever in history'. While mentioning separatism, they stressed that 'society is stable and people are living and working in peace and contentment.' Xinjiang's nightlife, Wang enthused, continues until 2 or 3 a.m.! (Because Xinjiang officials set their watches to Beijing time, this is really the equivalent of 12 or 1 a.m.)[93]

Nine days later the September 11 attacks and US response required a revised rhetorical approach to Xinjiang separatism. The new paradigm became apparent by the end of 2001, and was codified in a document released by the PRC State Council Information Office in late January 2002, entitled '"East Turkistan" Terrorist Forces Cannot Get Away with Impunity' ('"Dongtu" kongbu shili nantuo zuize'). The paper outlines a history of resistance to Chinese rule in Xinjiang, tracing the ideological origins of the 'East Turkistan' idea to the machinations of the 'old colonialists with the aim of dismembering China'. It then catalogues violent acts of the 1990s and lists several groups operating inside and outside Xinjiang. The document's wording and argument represent two shifts in the PRC international position with regard to Xinjiang separatism. First, it explicitly links what it now called '"East Turkistan" terrorists' to international Islamist terrorism; the document also refers to Osama bin Laden and al Qaeda several times. However, neither 'East Turkistan' nor 'terrorism' were terms commonly used in earlier writing about separatism in Xinjiang. In internal party documents from 1996 and 1999, for example, the terms 'national separatist' (*minzu fenliezhuyi fenzi*) and 'enemy' were standard; but 'terrorist' or 'terrorism' did not appear.[94] The name 'East Turkistan' had been taboo except in carefully vetted historical contexts; only after 2002 did official sources begin using it in scare

---

number obviously disagrees with those in the PRC State Council Information Office document on terrorism (2002).

93 Bao Lisheng, 'Chinese Officials Say Not Much Terrorism in Xinjiang', *Da Gong Bao*, 2 September 2001 (English translation published via Uyghur-L internet listserv).

94 This is the case both in the Document No. 7 (Zhonggong zhongyang 1996), and in several speeches delivered by Xinjiang regional leaders at a meeting concerning stability in Khotan in September 1999.

quotes. Second, through frequent use of generic terminology ('"East Turkistan" forces') the document suggests that all of the 200 terrorist acts and 162 deaths of the 1990s it lists were the work of a single, unified terrorist organisation, though a close reading of the document reveals this not to be the case.[95]

Despite a measure of scepticism in the international press, the document's account of Xinjiang's terrorist problem made for a simple and dramatic story: a single Uyghur terrorist organisation, linked to al Qaeda, opposing both China and the United States. The US government inadvertently amplified this impression when in August 2002 a State Department spokesman at the US embassy in Beijing announced the US designation of the East Turkestan Islamic Movement (ETIM) as an international terrorist organisation associated with al Qaeda and threatening US interests. ETIM is one of the groups listed in the 2002 document, but is not blamed there for any specific violent acts. Unnamed US government sources claimed that the US designation of ETIM was based on interrogations at Guantanamo of Uyghurs taken prisoner by US forces in Afghanistan. According to this intelligence, ETIM was plotting to blow up the US embassy in Kyrgyzstan. However, despite this independent corroboration of Chinese claims, in the public announcement the US spokesman adopted the language of the 2002 PRC document and *specifically* accused ETIM of 200 acts of terrorism, 162 deaths and 440 injuries in the 1990s. The PRC document itself stresses ETIM's al Qaeda ties but does not mention it in connection with any specific acts in Xinjiang. Although US officials privately acknowledged the spokesman's mistake, the State Department chose not to correct it publicly, and PRC press reports subsequent to the US announcement capitalised on the US error by proclaiming that the United States had designated the 'East Turkestan movement' *in toto* to be a terrorist organisation.[96]

A more nuanced assessment of the record of political violence in Xinjiang in the 1990s would not describe a unified movement, let alone blame a single organisation. Rather, as the above survey shows, there were a series of incidents and attacks through the decade, a few of them clearly terroristic in the sense that they hit random people, irrespective of status, job or ethnicity; others not random, but rather carefully

95 PRC State Council Information Office 2002.
96 Philip P. Pan, 'US Warns of Plot by Group in W. China', *The Washington Post*, 29 August 2002, p. A27.

targeted political murders; and still others more in the nature of protests that turned violent rather than planned attacks. In the 2000s no Uyghur organisation publicly acknowledged militant or violent acts in Xinjiang or Central Asia.[97] Finally, although it is difficult to judge on the basis of limited information, violence in Xinjiang seems to have tapered off from 1997 to 2005.[98]

State response: domestic policy shifts

The other side of the PRC response to both the new international environment and outbreaks of unrest in Xinjiang from 1990 was a broad shift in domestic policy and popular attitudes regarding non-Han ethnic groups, particularly the Uyghurs. This shift was comparable in some ways to earlier pendulum swings in the 1940s, late 1950s–1970s and early 1980s, and involved reforms or reinterpretations of official policies towards religion, education, cultural expression and the ethnic make-up of Xinjiang's government and party cadres, in addition to the encouragement of Han migration to Xinjiang discussed above. It thus entailed a rethinking of the foundations of the nationalities system in place since the 1950s, accompanied by subtle but portentous redefinitions of such key terms as *zizhi* (self-rule, autonomy) and *minzu* (nationality, ethnicity) upon which that system hung. While they were far less extreme than the chauvinistic attacks on Uyghur culture of the Cultural Revolution era, the overall thrust of these changes was nonetheless integrationist and even assimilationist, comprising a reversal of the relative liberality and tolerance of diversity of the early 1980s.

Hints of this new direction are evident in a document issued by the CCP Central Committee in 1996, a month before the first 'Strike Hard'

97 Earlier two groups had announced plans to engage in armed struggle with China. These were Yusup Mukhlisi's United Revolutionary Front of East Turkestan (URFET), which enjoyed Soviet support in the 1970s and issued a flurry of bellicose and unsubstantiated press releases in the 1990s, but was defunct by the decade's end; and the Uyghur Liberation Organisation (ULO), which may have been responsible for the kidnapping of a Chinese businessman and attack on a Chinese delegation in Kyrgyzstan in the spring of 2000. The ULO leader, Hashir Wahidi, was attacked by unidentified assailants in his home in 1998 and died months later at the age of seventy-eight. On these groups and other alleged Uyghur extremism in Central Asia, see Millward 2004a: 22–8.
98 For a fuller examination of this point, see Millward 2004a.

campaign began. Known as 'Document No. 7', it comprises a set of rec-ommendations on Xinjiang security from the Politburo Standing Com-mittee in the face of threats from what it called 'national separatism' and 'illegal religious activity' aided by 'international counter-revolutionary forces led by the United States of America'. While blaming the troubles on the standard 'very small number of national separatists and criminals', the document nevertheless focuses more generally on religion in Xin-jiang as an urgent problem. It advocates strict controls on mosque con-struction and religious students and, in particular, on the religious belief and practices of basic branch level cadres, party members and students. The document refers to 'village level organisations which have fallen into the hands of religious powers' and warns that 'Communist Party members and cadres are Marxist materialists and, therefore, should not be allowed to believe in and practise religion.' In the peculiar parlance of the Chinese constitution, citizens have two religious freedoms—the right to believe and the right not to believe in religion. In the 1990s party propaganda made the Orwellian point that party members and students enjoyed only one freedom: the freedom *not* to believe in religion. This reversed the 1982 policy allowing a flexible interpretation of rules on party atheism in parts of China where religion was an important part of social life (see Chapter 6).[99]

That the party suspected village cadres is further confirmed by an-other recommendation in the document: in addition to training more minority cadres dedicated to unity of the motherland, it orders 'party members and soldiers' from the PLA and the *Bingtuan* to be assigned to the county and township-level to 'improve the structure of cadres'—in other words, to increase the percentage of Han cadres at the lower levels in Xinjiang. Likewise, Document No. 7 recommends training 'a large number of Han cadres who love Xinjiang' and 'then relocating them to Xinjiang'. Indeed, it established a policy to 'continuously import tal-ented people' to Xinjiang. This was a response to a brain-drain problem among educated Han cadres and technical personnel in Xinjiang already acknowledged internally by the 1980s: from 1980 to 1990 nearly 10,000 cadres, 93 per cent of them Han, had left Xinjiang for the east where they expected easier living, more security, better pay and better educa-tion for their children.[100]

99   Zhonggong zhongyang 1996; Bovingdon 2002a: Chapter 2.
100   Zhonggong zhongyang 1996; Ma Dazheng 2003: 18–21.

Document No. 7 also expressed the Party's apprehension about education in Xinjiang. In order to eliminate illiteracy, since the 1950s the national minority policies had permitted, even encouraged, education in autonomous regions in major non-Chinese languages. Uyghur-language education was available from primary through university levels in Xinjiang. However, directives in Document No. 7 to 'investigate and organise schools' and warnings about teachers and textbooks 'which inspire national separatism and publicise religious ideas' suggest that party leaders felt they had insufficient control over the Uyghur-language education system. The document also dictated tight limits on foreign cultural exchanges and instruction by visiting foreign teachers, and made attitude and political background the prime considerations in permitting Uyghur students to study abroad, even with their own money. It is of course ironic that even while promoting Xinjiang as the hub of the Silk Road and of the new Eurasian Land Bridge, the state would restrict foreign contacts and educational exchange for Xinjiang's youth.

In addition to intensified efforts to apprehend criminals and separatist groups under 'Strike Hard', then, the 1996 Central Committee document codified a general tightening in the cultural arena among Xinjiang's minorities in the 1990s. This tightening was especially evident in religious and educational matters. Religious personnel and teachers underwent courses of 'patriotic re-education' and inspections by party work teams, and the state restricted the number of permits granted people applying to go on hajj. There were reports of new rules governing prayer: loudspeakers could not be used in giving the call to prayer; prayer before 9 a.m. was prohibited; and praying was restricted to those people who could fit within the mosque structures themselves—thus prohibiting the traditional practice of worshipers spilling over into squares outside mosques at prayer time on festival days. Regulations forbidding minors from participating in religious activities were strictly enforced in Xinjiang (though not in other parts of China); signs declaring no admittance to anyone under eighteen appeared above the doorways of Xinjiang mosques. University students were told that prayer, fasting for Ramadan, or, for women, wearing a head scarf, were inconsistent with communism and that they would be expelled if they continued the practice.[101]

---

101 Matthew Forney, 'Xinjiang: One Nation—Divided', *TIMEasia.com*, 25 March 2002.

The state also began more vigorous policing of Xinjiang history. The decade began with the banning of historical works by the writer Turghun Almas, who was criticised in a public campaign and put under house arrest in 1991. Almas' works, published in the more relaxed 1980s, famously propounded a version of the past that placed Uyghurs in Xinjiang in ancient times, before the first Han dynasty colonies, and thus ran counter to official historical interpretations that embedded Xinjiang and the Uyghurs as a part of Chinese history and denied Uyghurs' claims to be Xinjiang indigenes. While the works and ideas of Almas and other Uyghur scholars and historical novelists continued to circulate privately, major state-sponsored historiographical projects through the decade turned out a stream of new pedagogical, popular and scholarly historical works publicising the official line of Xinjiang's primordial Chineseness.[102] The state symbolically demonstrated its intention to further ratchet up its enforcement of history in the spring of 2002, when the *Kashgar Daily* newspaper published a list of 330 banned books. These included Turghun Almas' works, but also many other titles, including one on Uyghur craftsmanship that had been published years earlier with government approval. Thousands of volumes of these condemned works were collected and publicly burned in Kashgar.[103]

Even tourist sites reflected the intensification of the historical message: a monument was built in Kashgar commemorating the Han Dynasty general Ban Chao—who in the first century CE had conquered the city by killing its king after inviting him to a banquet (see Chapter 1). In Turfan, the Su Gong Ta (Sulaiman Mosque) received a makeover. The Qianlong Emperor had built this graceful Samanid style minaret and mosque in the eighteenth century to commemorate the collaboration of the local ruler Amin Khoja with the Qing conquest of Xinjiang. The mosque once stood alone on a small rise amid grape arbours and mud-brick houses; by 2004 a large parking lot and garden had been added, and tourists approached the mosque by walking past a large modern statue of Amin Khoja. His hands and eyes are raised in an attitude of supplication as he receives the Chinese emperor's edict. In the 1990s and

102 See the excellent discussion of Xinjiang historiography in Bovingdon and Tursun 2004: esp. 361–8; see also Rudelson 1997: 157–9 on Turghun Almas.
103 'Uyghur America Association Statement on Book Burning', released via internet on 5 June 2002; Cindy Sui, 'China Orders End to Instruction in Uighur at Top Xinjiang University', AFP, 28 May 2002.

2000s Uyghur students and travel guides frequently commented on the pressure they felt to conform to the official version of history, even while doubting it themselves.

The most potentially significant change in Xinjiang cultural policy in the early 2000s was a reform of the multi-lingual education system to increase levels of Chinese fluency and literacy for all students. Like affirmative action for minorities (also implemented in Xinjiang), education in languages other than Chinese (in Xinjiang, including Uyghur and on a smaller scale Kazak, Mongolian, Sibo, Kyrgyz and Russian) posed dilemmas even as it afforded benefits to non-Chinese speaking students. While arguably helping non-Han students in their primary school years and promoting the culture of the nationality, lack of early immersion in Chinese could handicap students who later wished to go on to higher education and seek professional careers in Xinjiang or elsewhere in China.[104] Xinjiang University, the top university in the region, had long maintained two faculties, one for Chinese-language and one for Uyghur-language instruction. In 2002 the government ordered that from the following year all classes except Uyghur literature would be taught in Chinese, and professors accustomed to lecturing in Uyghur were given a year to brush up their Mandarin. Around the same time it was reported that Uyghur schools in Hami (Qumul) were to be merged with Chinese-language schools. Uyghur groups abroad have presented these reforms as an effort to eradicate the Uyghur language, and certainly Xinjiang Party Secretary Wang Lequan's own comments at the time displayed a dismissive attitude toward languages other than Chinese: the shift to Chinese-language education was necessary, he said, to 'improve the quality of ethnic minorities' because 'the languages of the minority nationalities have very small capacities and do not contain many of the expressions in modern science and technology which makes education in these concepts impossible. This is out of step with the twenty-first century.'[105] In fact the introduction into Uyghur and other Turkic languages of scientific terms from Russian from the late

104 For a discussion of the difficult choices faced by parents and the *minkaohan* (ethnics taking exams in Chinese) phenomenon, see Benson 2004 and Smith 2000.
105 Cindy Sui, 'China Orders End to Instruction in Uighur at Top Xinjiang University', AFP, 28 May 2002; 'China Imposes Chinese Language on Uyghur Schools', *Radio Free Asia*, 16 March 2004; Wang Lequan quoted in *Wen wei po* (Wenhui bao) (Hong Kong), 2 August 2002, in FBIS-CHI-2002-0307, 3 August 2002.

nineteenth through the middle of the twentieth century has afforded
them a Latinate technical vocabulary very close to English—and thus to
international scientific terminology.

Nevertheless, solid knowledge of Chinese is important for all PRC
citizens, and official reports from China suggest that the goal of the Xinjiang education reform was not to eliminate Uyghur, as dissidents claim,
but to turn the system of Uyghur-language primary school instruction
into a bilingual education system through increased use of Chinese from
earlier grades. A Uyghur professional with a prestigious government job
described to me the educational reforms as they affected her own young
child. In her characterisation, the new system resembled bilingual schools
in the United States, amounting to a replacement of mono-language
Uyghur instruction with bilingual Chinese-Uyghur instruction, and to
her this was a positive development. Towards this end, in 2004 Xinjiang authorities announced plans to train 55,000 bilingual teachers.[106]
Whatever the motivation and extent of these educational reforms, they
betoken a change from the second half of the twentieth century when
large numbers of non-Han in Xinjiang had little grasp of Chinese.

As with development projects, then, the thrust of both official historiography and these educational reforms was to integrate Xinjiang
more closely to the rest of China. Indeed, there is reason to believe that
by the early twenty-first century Chinese leaders and ideologues had
grown uneasy with the policy towards non-Chinese peoples and regions
implemented half a century earlier. As discussed in Chapter 6, when
inaugurated in the 1950s this system had identified fifty-five official 'minority nationalities' (minzu) and created 'autonomous' units at township,
district, prefectural and regional levels in areas where these peoples were
concentrated. State cultural organs reinforced the definitions of each
nationality through linguistic, literary and historical publications in its
language, codification and promotion of its particular music and dance
forms in arts schools and similar means.

The system had served a propagandistic purpose in the 1950s by casting the Chinese Communist Party as more sympathetic to minority
concerns than the assimilationist Guomindang. Gerrymandering of nationality enclaves and maintenance of real power in the hands of party
officials guaranteed that the Xinjiang Uyghur Autonomous Region did

---

106 'Xinjiang to Train 55,000 Bilingual Teachers in 8 Years', *Xinhuanet*, 12 September 2004.

not deviate far from central directives. Nevertheless, the fruitful ambiguity of 'national autonomy' had defined Xinjiang as a non-Han cultural space and at times—the early 1950s or early 1980s in particular—even justified flexible implementation of central policies and official support for non-Han peoples against 'Han chauvinism'.

Although it was not nationalism *per se* that led to the secession of the Central Asian republics from the Soviet Union, the latter did break up along the same national lines defined by Stalin. The Chinese constitution, unlike the Soviet, never granted the right to secession to Chinese 'nationality autonomous regions'; nevertheless, PRC *minzu* policy over fifty years had highlighted, rather than erased, the seams in China's patchwork national fabric. The US-led NATO intervention in Kosovo in 1999 in the name of human rights and self-determination for a Muslim minority sent a chill through Chinese leaders concerned about the strategic implications of Xinjiang instability. In 2000 Ma Dazheng, head of a research institute dedicated to frontier matters and a prolific writer on Xinjiang, responded to internal debate over *minzu* policy with an interesting reinterpretation of the notion of *zizhi* (the term translated as 'autonomy'). Whenever discussion turned to the implementation of *minzu* policy or Xinjiang autonomy, Ma wrote, many people, especially minority comrades, immediately raised the issue of the representation: the fact that non-Hans hold fewer government positions proportional to their numbers in the Xinjiang population than do Han cadres. Debate over these percentages in Xinjiang was an old problem—indeed, although Ma does not mention this, it goes back to the era of Guomindang rule in the 1940s. 'Nativisation' of Xinjiang leadership was promised in the 1950s; critics raised the issue again in the early 1980s, in the reform era following the Cultural Revolution.[107] However, Ma argued,

107 Bovingdon 2002b: Chapter 2. A party document from 1980 that Ma discovered in the Urumchi archives and of which he is highly critical suggested that in southern Xinjiang 60 per cent of the cadres should be Uyghur, and another 15 per cent should belong to other minority nationalities (Ma Dazheng 2003: 184–6). This, in 1980, was proposed as an ideal to work towards by increasing minority representation. In his speech to the Khotan stability work group in 1999, on the other hand, Wang Lequan set out a guideline of one third Han cadres and two thirds *minzu* cadres for the township level in the Khotan area, and likewise indicated it was a goal 'not to be achieved overnight' (Wang Lequan 1999: 7–8). The text does not specify the proportion of Han to *minzu* cadres at the time of Wang's speech, but implies non-Hans did not yet comprise two thirds.

the phrase 'nationality regional autonomy' (*minzu quyu zizhi*) should not be understood to mean ruling power in the hands of a single nationality, but rather *collective* rule by all nationalities in the region (*quyu nei ge minzu gongzhi*). Autonomy by a single nationality is only a stage on the way to such collective nationality rule. Exclusive focus on one's own group, in a diverse region like Xinjiang, is excessive and divisive. Thus while sounding very reasonable, Ma upturns the premises of fifty years of *minzu* theory.[108]

Ma presents his argument as a personal opinion, and it is unclear what influence it had on the leadership. However, in the early 2000s party theorists were already revising basic concepts of the *minzu* system in a similar direction. One indication of this was a change in the official English translation of the term *minzu*: In place of the old translation, 'nationality', which reflected Stalinist nationalities theory and policy, official PRC materials adopted the term 'ethnic'. For example, the Nationalities Affairs Commission became the Ethnic Affairs Commission, and a white paper released in February 2005 bore the title 'Regional Autonomy for Ethnic Minorities in China'.[109] This departure from the defunct Stalinist nationalities policy turned China at a stroke from an ideologically cumbersome 'multi-national state' into a 'multi-ethnic country' like the United States. Moreover, although the original Chinese terminology remained unchanged, the new English translation effectively downgraded Uyghurs, Tibetans and others from the status of 'nationality' (which in English might imply rights to self-determination and perhaps a nation-state) to that of an ethnic (and hence sub-national) group. In the aftermath of the violent incidents of the 1990s reinterpretations of *zizhi* and *minzu* demonstrated the PRC's new integrationist approach to Xinjiang as clearly as the extension of the railway line to Kashgar.

Inter-ethnic relations and subtle dissent

If the sporadic violent episodes of the 1990s seemed to have tapered off by the 2000s, personal relations between ethnic groups, particularly between Uyghur and Han, were if anything more tense than at the start of the decade. This tension emerged more often in mundane ways than in open acts of protest or oppression, but it remained palpable nonetheless.

108　Ma Dazheng 2003: 187–8.
109　Becquelin 2004: 359 n. 3.

Indications of less than harmonious relations between *minzu* were readily apparent in the 1990s–2000s. Many Han Chinese in Xinjiang, particularly recent arrivals, often harboured fearful, derogatory or stereotyped images of Uyghurs and other minorities, and there were few taboos about openly expressing these views. For example, visitors from abroad were cautioned that Uyghurs carry knives and rob the unwary. At the same time, they learned that Uyghurs 'excel at song and dance' (*nengge shanwu*). Once in 1990 on a visit to Heaven Lake (Tianchi, Tengri köl) I astounded a group of Han tourists by photographing some Kazak children who were mugging for my camera. The tourists asked, 'Why are you taking their picture? Those are Kazak kids!' (*Tamen shi Hazu wawa*). On another excursion, I rode a bus where the Han bus driver had retained the services of a Kazak teenager, evidently in return for free passage to Urumchi. When the Kazak youth made a small mistake while helping the driver, one Han college student rolled his eyes and loudly groaned 'Kazaks!' (*Ha-zu!*) for the benefit of his friends and other riders.

Because of the language difference inter-ethnic friction is often apparent in the educational arena: One Han first grade teacher at Xinjiang University's Chinese-language track primary school expressed dismay when she discovered that half of her students for the new year would be minorities. 'They have their own class', she said. 'Why can't they go there?'[110] Slurs may be unconscious: I have heard well-intentioned Han Chinese praise professional Uyghurs for 'speaking Chinese very well, for a Uyghur'. Nevertheless, intended or not, such comments—and examples could be multiplied manyfold—suggest pervasive Han prejudice regarding Xinjiang's minorities. This prejudice is reinforced by state policies, the practice, widely-resented by Han, of admitting Xinjiang minorities to university with lower exam scores than Han; and the rhetoric of development, which stresses the benefits afforded poor, backward Xinjiang by the centre. In the 1950s propaganda regularly referred to Han as the 'big brother' and minorities as 'little brother' *minzu*.[111] Although these terms are no longer publicly used, their patronising message still permeates private and official discourse, as in the encounter between Jiang Zemin and the Kazak herdsman quoted above. Wang Lequan's recent comments that Chinese-language education was necessary to 'improve

110   Clark 1999: 153.
111   Bovingdon 2002b: Chapter 3.

the quality of ethnic minorities' and bring them 'in step with the twen-ty-first century' are similar examples.[112]

Faced with an 'autonomy' system that leaves real power in the hands of Han party secretaries, rapid economic development that seemingly benefits Han migrants more than Uyghur residents, a strenuous crack-down on anything resembling political organisation or criticism of the government, tightening state restrictions on religion, muscular enforce-ment of a Sino-centric historical narrative, a widespread sense that the government and judicial system favour Han, and pervasive chauvinism on the part of Han neighbours, Uyghurs have responded in a variety of ways. The open protests detailed above have been relatively rare; more common are quiet forms of everyday resistance or dissent. These too can take the form of ethnic slurs, this time directed at the Han. For example, I've been told by Uyghur informants that Han are calculating, dirty and promiscuous; they like to live with pigs and strew garbage all over their own neighbourhoods. Uyghurs will privately refer to Han as *Khitay*, a word centuries old. It originally referred to the Khitan people, is the source of the Russian word for China and the word 'Cathay' in other European languages and is the standard term for China in Cen-tral Asian Turkic languages today. Nevertheless, Chinese authorities per-ceive it as derogatory and ban it—thereby assuring its continued use by, among others, Uyghur school-children. While investigating the situation in Khotan in the late 1990s a 'stability work group' was chagrined to discover that Mao Zedong's portrait had been torn out of 3,722 lower school textbooks in the area—a literally separatist act! Worse still was the explanation one student gave: it's a Khitay head, so he ripped it out of his new textbook, same as he'd done four years in a row.[113] To this Uyghur schoolboy, Chairman Mao was just another Chinaman.

One scholar from Hong Kong has attempted to quantify the state of Han-Uyghur relations in Xinjiang. Despite evident reluctance of Uy-ghur respondents to answer sensitive questions candidly, his surveys of almost four hundred Hans and Uyghurs in Urumchi in the year 2000

---

112 Wang Lequan quoted in *Wen wei po* (Wenhui bao) (Hong Kong), 2 August 2002, in FBIS-CHI-2002-0307, 3 August 2002.
113 Wang Lequan 1999: 8, 10. See also a joke quoted in Bovingdon 2002b: Chap-ter 3, in which Uyghur students misidentify the portraits of the communist pan-theon in their classroom in humorous ways. The punch line comes when they are asked who the portrait of Mao depicts and respond, 'A Han!'

reveal a fairly deep rift between the two communities. Although half of the Uyghurs in the sample spoke good Chinese, only 32 per cent believed Han and Uyghurs should marry. (Indeed, actual rates of intermarriage are much lower than this, and Han and Uyghur socialise little together.[114]) A higher percentage of Uyghur respondents expressed pride in being a Uyghur national (91%) and Xinjiang resident (95%) than in being a Chinese citizen (88%); only 43 per cent of Uyghurs (vs 72 per cent of Han) said they 'strongly believed' that Xinjiang has been part of China since ancient times. Although half of Han and Uyghur respondents agreed that the open door reforms had raised standards of living for both groups 'about the same', nearly 40 per cent of Uyghurs believed that Uyghur standards of living had risen slower than those of Hans, and a majority of Uyghurs thought that there was a significant disparity of income between Han and Uyghur. On a major point of PRC propaganda, 53 per cent of Uyghurs either disagreed or found it 'hard to tell' whether national separatism was the 'main danger to Xinjiang stability'. Not surprisingly, 81 per cent of the Han respondents agreed with this statement. Finally, fairly large percentages of each community believed their own ethnic group to be cleverer and more hygienic than the other.[115]

Other scholars working in Xinjiang have examined Uyghur contemporary culture to uncover a variety of ways in which Uyghurs express dissent through alternative versions of history, political jokes, folk-sayings and allegorical songs. In one joke told in Xinjiang in the mid-1990s, Jiang Zemin meets with Zhao Ziyang (the Chinese leader disgraced for supporting the students on Tiananmen Square in May–June 1989). Jiang offers to rehabilitate Zhao by giving him a position as a vice-chairman. Zhao angrily shouts back, 'I'm not a Uyghur!' The joke turns on the common knowledge that Uyghurs in the 'Xinjiang Uyghur Autonomous Region' never occupy principal positions, but rather fill the number-two seats.[116]

---

114 Clark 1999 makes this point. In 2002 a journalist attended the Uyghur wedding party of a modern, educated and affluent Uyghur couple deeply embedded in the government system. The groom, a politics teacher at a military academy, and the bride, a worker at the Bureau of State Security, had invited 150 guests, most from these two government work units. None was Han (Forney 2002).
115 Yee 2003: 437–44.
116 Bovingdon 2002b: Chapter 3. See also Bovingdon 2002a.

Uyghur singers have used carefully chosen metaphors in their lyrics to make powerful political statements while eluding censorship. For
example, the Uyghur folk-singer Ömärjan Alim has sung about a guest
overstaying his welcome, and about barren chickens occupying the roost
and getting the grain while the fertile hens have to scratch for subsistence outside. Multiple interpretations of such songs are possible; in one
reading, the Han with their strict limits on childbirth are the barren hens
who have displaced the fecund Uyghurs. Such songs were very popular, circulating widely through cheaply reproduced cassette tapes. Some
veiled political expression is critical not of the Han or the government
but of Uyghurs themselves and aspects of Uyghur culture. For example,
the saying 'the axe-handle is always made of wood' slyly points out that
PRC rule in Xinjiang has always relied on a Uyghur support staff.[117]

Perhaps the simplest but most ubiquitous assertion of private independence in Xinjiang consists of setting one's watch to Xinjiang time,
two hours behind that of Beijing. Despite its vast west-east girth, China
has only one time zone—an echo of the imperial era when Chinese
emperors assumed ritual authority over matters calendrical and chronological. The official world and most Han in the Xinjiang, as throughout
China, follow Beijing time. However, non-Han residents in the region
have maintained a *de facto* Xinjiang time zone in the face of official uni-
formity. This is an act of defiance, but also arguably one of convenience,
for by so doing Xinjiang residents can get up at 6 or 7 a.m. (instead of 8
or 9 a.m.), have their lunch (*chüshlük tamaq* = 'noon meal') around noon
(not 2–4 p.m.) and so on.[118]

CHINESE TURKESTAN IN THE EARLY
TWENTY-FIRST CENTURY

As an emblem of globalisation, fast-food chains are now a soggy cliché.
Nevertheless, their advent in a new corner of the world is noteworthy, not so much as a harbinger of globalisation, but as an indicator of
how integrated a place has already become. The *Kendeji–Kentakiy–KFC*
outlet in Urumchi was Xinjiang's first international fast-food franchise.
Before the KFC parent company, Yum Brands, could plant its flag in

117 Smith 2003: 4–5; Dautcher 2002: 286.
118 See Bovingdon 2002b: Chapter 7 for a fascinating examination of the politics
of time zones.

Vendor of sheep lungs and entrails in Urumchi's former Erdaoqiao Bazaar, lunchtime, May 1990 (photo: J. Millward)

Xinjiang, problems of licensing, supply, demand, labour management, accounting standards, quality control and so forth all had to be resolved to its satisfaction. Besides these prerequisites, the arrival of KFC marked still other changes on the local level. The new Grand Bazaar pedestrian mall, of which KFC became an anchor tenant, replaced the old Erdaoqiao Bazaar, until recently the heart of the Uyghur quarter, the commercial centre of the city and a favourite place for lunch. While vibrant, Erdaoqiao bazaar had also been a noisy, messy firetrap.

The Kentuky-isation of Urumchi underscores a central fact about turn-of-the-century Xinjiang: integration with the world and with China were parallel, largely inextricable processes. For good or ill, at the turn of the century Xinjiang was in the throes of both.

This chapter has attempted to encapsulate many still-unfolding events and trends of the decades spanning the turn of the twenty-first century. This is somewhat like trying to sketch, from a stance hard by the tracks, the train hurtling past on its way to Kashgar.

However, the broad lines of the picture are clear enough. In some respects the changes in Xinjiang since the mid-1980s have followed directions already defined during the PRC period, some even introduced during the eighteenth and nineteenth centuries by the Qing authorities. The pace of change has, however, accelerated. Xinjiang's economy has expanded, although governance of the region from Beijing continues to require expensive subsidies. The region's population has grown rapidly, largely through migration, though this migration has been voluntary, not the mandated population transfers of the past. Exploitation of Xinjiang's resources proceeds at an ever faster rate as land is reclaimed, water channelled, oil and gas extracted.

In some ways many developments of the 1990s and 2000s are new. First, Xinjiang's environment may have reached carrying capacity. Although more efficient use of available water will permit some ecological rehabilitation and even some further growth, and there may still be fossil water in untapped aquifers, development in the region cannot continue in the unbridled fashion of the past fifty years. Xinjiang inhabitants may have to cope with steep reductions in water supplies as glacial sources disappear.

Second, China's hold on Xinjiang is now more secure than ever. The disappearance of the Soviet Union and reduced circumstances of Russia eliminated a long-term imperial rival in Central Asia, one once both willing and able to dabble in Xinjiang affairs for economic or political gain. New US bases in Central Asia notwithstanding, there is no new counterpole just across the Pamirs from Xinjiang. In fact China is the emergent economic and diplomatic leader throughout the Central Asian region. A Chinese pipeline spans Kazakstan; Chinese goods fill Central Asian bazaars; one can even find Chinese-language software on computers in Almaty internet cafés.

Third, in tandem with changes in the international context, Xinjiang's own situation vis-à-vis China, the region and the world has changed. Over the long term historically, the region has been more often a crossroads than a cul-de-sac. Though relatively remote for much of the latter half of the last millennium, and particularly during the decades of frosty Sino-Soviet relations, the region is a backwater no longer. The Soviet break-up gave Chinese planners a green light for intensified integration of Xinjiang with China through investment in infrastructure. Reform policies and improved communications likewise opened the region to easier contacts with foreign countries. Moreover, these contacts were not limited to trade: despite state efforts to monitor and control the flow of information in and out of Xinjiang, people there entered into increasingly robust communications with people elsewhere in Central Asia and the world. Expatriate dissidents, international media and human rights groups began to receive and publish regular reports from Xinjiang. Information from these sources on such events as the Ghulja Incident successfully challenges the official PRC versions.

The resentment and resistance of some non-Han groups to Chinese rule during this period was not in itself new. But official approaches to it did present some novel developments. It remains to be seen to what extent Uyghur separatism is linked with groups espousing terrorist methods and a radical Islamist agenda, as Chinese propaganda argues and US acquiescence to it implies. But the new representation of Xinjiang as a battleground in the 'global war on terror' was a departure from previous PRC practice, as was the correspondence of a crackdown in Xinjiang with modest expansion of free expression elsewhere in China. Likewise, early in the twenty-first century Chinese leaders seemed to be departing from the *minzu* autonomy system as the CCP had erected it in the early 1950s. Though this 'autonomy' had always been closely hedged, in the early 2000s the party seemed to be questioning its own earlier theory and the premises underlying special status for non-Han groups and ethnic-majority regions in the PRC. The start of the new century thus saw Xinjiang occupying a new position both in China and in the world.

Conclusion: Balancing Acts

Over the past 4,000 years many people have dwelt in or passed through Xinjiang's oases, steppes and mountains. Some of the more famous ones have crossed the pages of this book. The roster of eminent Xinjiang personages would begin with the mummified Beauty of Loulan from the second millennium BCE, a herding woman buried with a basket of grain. It might also include that later beauty, known as Xiang Fei or Iparhan, whose marriage to the Qing emperor came to symbolise both ethnic harmony and national resistance.

Adventurers Zhang Qian, Marco Polo and Bento de Goes would figure on our list, as would the widely-travelled religious masters Faxian, Kumarajiva, Xuan Zang, Jamâl ad-Dîn, Khoja Ishaq Wali and Afaq Khoja, who translated and spread their beliefs in Xinjiang and beyond. Honourable mention should also go to the many merchants, though they remain nameless, who traded in more tangible goods—especially the ubiquitous Soghdians, who though largely unsung left a deep mark on Central Asian and North Chinese culture.

The victorious first century Han generals Li Guangli and Ban Chao would make the list for their long-distance campaigns, as would later conquerors, such as the Tang era Korean Ko Sŏnji and Qing era Manchu Zhao Hui. So would the Türk khans, Uyghur idiquts, Qarakhanid khaghans, Qara Khitay gurkhans and the Chaghatayid and Oirat khans, who deployed ethnically complex alliances of nomad tribes to control the farming cities of the Tarim Basin, cities whose own élites and inhabitants comprised still other ethnic and religious communities.

Some rulers mobilised religion to help them rule: ancient Tarim monarchs reigned over flourishing Hinayana and Mahayana city-states, medieval Uyghur élites patronised Manichaeism, Buddhism and Nestorian Christianity, and the Qarakhanid Satuq Bughra Khan and Moghul Tughluq Temür famously converted to Islam, bringing many subjects with them.

356

Of the region's scholars, Mahmud Kashghari stands out for his Turkic-Arabic dictionary (written in Seljuk Baghdad) as does Yusuf Khass Hajib, whose work drew upon the Iranian-Islamic tradition to enlighten Turkic monarchs in the Qarakhanid state. Medieval Qocho Uyghur literati like Tatar Tongga and Körgüz lent an urban sophistication to tribal courts as teachers and administrators, educating Naiman and Mongol princes and providing the Mongol empire with an efficient script. Much later, the Musabayov brothers, themselves entrepreneurs and industrialists, borrowed models from Tsarist Central Asia, Ottoman Turkey and Europe to launch a modern education movement in Xinjiang. The new ideas taught in these schools inspired some of the region's nationalists, including the founders of the stillborn East Turkestan Republic in Kashgar. A decade later Ahmetjan Qasimi used socialism to balance a north Xinjiang Turkic state precariously and briefly between the Soviet Union, the Guomindang and the Chinese Communist Party.

These figures, like Xinjiang itself, are culturally complex. They either bridged distances and societies by their travels, or married multiple origins, ideologies, faiths, loyalties and languages within themselves. They personify the betweenness, encounter and overlap that feature in the region's history. Xinjiang has been a contact zone for nomad and farmer; for Central Asian, Persian, Turkic and Sinic languages and cultures; for Russian/Soviet and Qing/PRC realms; for Buddhist, Islamic and Communist governing ideologies. At times those contacts have been violent, at times characterised by accommodation.

By way of conclusion, I will end this survey of Xinjiang's long past with three profiles of figures from its present. Each of these eminent Chinese Turkestanis displays characteristics like those of the historical personages listed above; however, the scope of their activities and renown in the twenty-first century surpasses that of their predecessors. Xinjiang at the start of the twenty-first century lies not merely between branches of the Silk Road, or between China and Islam or Russia. The region is linked to the world, and expanded cultural, economic and political connections shape the lives of its people, whatever their native language.

'MOTHER OF ALL UYGHURS': RABIYÄ QADIR

Fashion designer, entrepreneur, self-made millionaire, former member of the Chinese People's Political Consultative Conference, Muslim, philanthropist, anti-drug crusader, celebrated prisoner of conscience, refugee and twice-married mother of eleven, Rabiyä Qadir is not an average woman.

Rabiyä[1] started her business career humbly in Aqsu in southern Xinjiang in the early 1970s, secretly sewing and selling clothes at a time when such entrepreneurship was still illegal. When caught and criticised, she took in laundry—but soon went back into trade, this time selling rabbit and lambskin hats. After the Cultural Revolution Rabiyä made trading trips to eastern Chinese provinces, where she bought such items as silk scarves, shirts and cassette players to smuggle back to Xinjiang for resale, taking advantage of China's poor distribution system. The authorities caught her, confiscated her goods and fined her several times, but a stint selling noodles in Guangdong finally earned her sufficient seed capital to set up as a green grocer and small restaurateur in Urumchi in the early 1980s. She made enough money in the food business to build a market of 140 stalls on a lot in Urumchi, where she sold her own imports—fresh water pearls from Suzhou were then very popular with Uyghur women—and rented out space to other merchants. From then on her businesses mushroomed, and she built a seven-story department store that became an Urumchi landmark. She also remarried, this time to literature professor and critic Sidiq Ruzi (Rozi), whom she had actively wooed while he was in prison for publishing subtle criticisms of the government. Sidiq is an intellectual, and she a business-woman with only five years of education and six kids of her own. But he was taken by her spirit.

When Xinjiang's borders with Central Asia reopened and the Soviet Union fell, Rabiyä was ideally positioned to exploit the new trading opportunities. She followed in the path of Uyghur traders and industrialists of the late nineteenth and early twentieth centuries, expanding her business interests westward, and taking note of what she saw. She established a leather factory in Kazakstan and built a new store in Urumchi.

Many Uyghurs in those years engaged in shuttle trading, moving small lots of Chinese goods to Kazakstan and Kyrgyzstan to sell in the bazaars there. Rabiyä, more highly capitalised than the shuttle traders, was able to resolve their currency conversion troubles while benefiting herself. Central Asian currencies were not readily convertible to Chinese

---

1 In contemporary Uyghur practice, it is conventional to refer to people by their first name.

yuan. Carrying dollars back over the border to China past rapacious border guards was illegal and risky. Rabiyä and other large-scale traders developed another method to repatriate earnings. They consolidated the profits of dozens of small merchants, and made big deals for steel, cotton and copper to import to China, where there was great demand for raw materials (she imported 13,000 metric tons of steel in 1993). Upon selling the imported commodities in China, she would then repay the Uyghur shuttle traders in yuan.[2]

Rabiyä developed business interests throughout Central Asia, in Turkey and even in Britain, while running two department stores in Urumchi and other enterprises here and there. She became a multimillionaire, and featured in Chinese, Uyghur and English language editions of the Chinese press as a poster-child for the benefits of Deng Xiaoping's reforms to minorities. She was made a member of the Chinese People's Consultative Conference, the PRC assembly for non-Party people and groups. In September 1994 she appeared on the front page of the *Wall Street Journal*, and met with Bill Gates and Warren Buffet during their China tour the following year. She served as a delegate to the International Women's Conference sponsored by the UN in Beijing. Rabiyä also committed herself to charitable works. She became a folk hero among Uyghurs in part because of her accessibility and willingness to help out common Uyghurs in financial difficulty. She hired unemployed farmers to decorate her offices in the department stores because 'our people can't find work'. And she became increasingly concerned about social issues, especially drug and alcohol abuse. These were evident close at hand—she could find Uyghur youths abusing substances even in her own building and the stalls of her market place. She launched her own campaign against heroin, complete with slogans lettered in white on red banners—appropriating the government's role and rhetoric. Meanwhile, her husband editorialised in the Uyghur papers on the subject.

Soon thereafter Rabiyä established the Thousand Mothers Association, a group modelled on Mothers Against Drunk Driving, and dedicated to similar social issues. Ever suspicious of extra-governmental organisations, the CCP kept a close eye on these activities. In 1996 Sidiq Ruzi went into exile in the United States, where he began contributing essays to the Uyghur broadcasts of Voice of America and Radio Free Asia, criticising

2 On this method of profit repatriation used by Uyghur merchants, see Dautcher 1999: 287.

Chinese policies and treatment of Uyghurs in Xinjiang. Though asked by the party to publicly repudiate her husband, Rabiyä refused. Rabiyä also donated money to some of the Uyghur victims of the 1997 Ghulja (Yining) Incident. Authorities then banned Rabiyä from foreign travel and dropped her from the People's Political Consultative Conference.

In 1999 a US congressional delegation investigating human rights issues came to Urumchi and requested a meeting with Rabiyä Qadir. However, as she was en route to meet with them, PRC security forces detained her. At the time of her arrest she supposedly had in her possession a list of political prisoners prepared for the US delegation. Authorities later also formally accused Rabiyä of revealing state secrets by sending clippings from local Xinjiang newspapers to her husband in the United States. In March 2000 she was sentenced to eight years in prison.

Ironically, the detention and prosecution of such a prominent figure accelerated the process of 'internationalising' the Xinjiang issue which the party had sought to avoid.[3] The case of a millionaire entrepreneur turned political prisoner gained acclaim that few dissident writers or scholars in China could hope for. International human rights organisations and some governments added Rabiyä Qadir to lists of political prisoners whose cases they tracked and for whose release they lobbied. The US Congress heard testimony and issued resolutions about Rabiyä,[4] and her case generated unprecedented official and popular attention for Xinjiang and the Uyghurs' human rights complaints. In 2004 Rabiyä was awarded Norway's Rafto Memorial Prize. No doubt largely owing to this attention to her case, the PRC released Rabiyä Qadir three years early, on the eve of the arrival of US Secretary of State Condoleeza Rice for talks in Beijing in March 2005. Rabiyä flew immediately to the United States for a reunion with her husband and five of her children.

In the first photos after her arrival in the United States, only a couple days after her release, Rabiyä appeared tired and a bit overwhelmed

3 The 1996 Document No. 7 issued by the CCP Central Committee urges that the party and government '… prevent, by all means, the outside separatist forces from making the so-called "Eastern Turkistan" problem international' (Zhonggong zhongyang 1996).

4 106th Congress, 2nd session, S. Con. Res. 81, 'Expressing the sense of the Congress that the Government of the People's Republic of China should immediately release Rabiyä Kadeer, her secretary and her son, and permit them to move to the United States if they so desire.'

beneath a shock of grey hair, with a subdued, martyrish air about her. Within a few days, however, this look gave way to something entirely different. Her hair once again jet black, Rabiyä looked professional and dynamic in a trim business suit as she charged about Washington, DC doing press interviews, visiting congressmen, and appearing before supporters who had pressed for her release. As she addressed a gathering and Amnesty International and US State Department staffers, surrounded again by her children, Rabiyä was composed despite her tears. She told her audience that she spoke as the 'mother of all Uyghurs', and few there would have challenged her assumption of that title. But the fact remains that she had come to the United States, and eight million Uyghurs live in Xinjiang.[5]

A FAR WESTERN 'FAIRY TALE' SUCCESS: SUN GUANGXIN

The biography of Xinjiang's richest man follows a track broadly similar to that of its richest woman. Both millionaires arose from humble origins, both skilfully turned Xinjiang's geography, the Chinese economic reforms and the fall of the Soviet Union to their advantage, both erected Urumchi landmarks, and both have achieved near mythic status, attracting the attention of the international as well as domestic press. Yet their careers also differ in telling respects.

Sun Guangxin was born in Shandong (some sources say Xinjiang) in 1962. According to some versions of his story, he got his start in business with $400 he had saved during nine years in the PLA. He had graduated from a military college in Anhui and seen action during the Chinese war in Vietnam in 1979 before moving to Xinjiang as an officer in an Urumchi military academy. In another version, Sun's seed capital

---

5 This profile is compiled from the following sources: Dautcher 2004: 289–92; Clark 1999: 191–2; Roberts 2004: 224 and 423 n. 33; Michael Dillon, 'Rebiya Kadeer's Imprisonment Focuses Global Attention on Xinjiang', *Central Asia-Caucasus Institute Analyst*, 13 September 2000. It also draws on these press accounts: Kathy Chen, 'Rags to Riches Story: How Rebiya Kader Made her Fortune—Muslim Chinese Trader Defied Poverty and Convention, Her Husband and Police', *Wall Street Journal*, 21 September 1994, p. A1; 'Xinjiang Women Active in Market Economy', *Xinhua*, 27 May 1995; 'CPPCC Members on China's Development Plan', *Xinhua*, 3 March 1996; Eric Eckholm, 'Prominent Chinese Muslim Secretly Sentenced to 8 Years', *New York Times*, 11 March 2000.

was a $50,000 loan from a Japanese cotton dealer for whom Sun had finessed a hard-to-arrange rail shipment from Xinjiang back to eastern China. In any case, Sun's first big success, like Rabiyä's, was in food services. Sun's restaurant, however, was no hole-in-the-wall noodle shop. His Guangdong Jiujia specialised in fresh seafood flown in daily from the coast 3,000 km away, a true novelty in Urumchi in 1989. Such an up-market establishment seemed quixotic in Xinjiang at the time, but the venture was timed to supply the demand for fresh ocean products that rose with the tide of Han in-migration. Because seafood is so expensive, seafood restaurants are favourites of high-rolling Chinese businessmen and officials. Just as Urumchi's oil and real estate markets picked up, then, Sun created a venue where relationships could be nurtured and deals concluded. By serving them pricey fish dishes, Sun secured his own con-nections among the city's oilmen and bankers. Building on his success as a restaurateur, Sun next racked up a string of additional entertainment firsts: the story goes that he opened the first karaoke bar, disco, swim-ming pool and bowling alley in the Xinjiang region.

As Sun's enterprises grew, he employed many former army officers in top corporate positions. His military connections and contacts from the restaurant came in handy as he moved on to still bigger things in late 1990, importing oil drilling equipment from the former Soviet Union and selling it to Chinese state firms. After a run-in with the authori-ties in 1993, when he was accused of paying bribes, Sun intensified his cultivation of official connections, a practice that would be a hallmark of his future endeavours. He opened a branch of the Chinese Commu-nist Party within his own company and poached a party secretary away from a state-owned firm to lead it. This introduction of the commissariat into a private corporation startled many at first, and the CCP almost expelled the secretary involved. The move proved prescient, however, as collaboration between the party and big capitalists was the wave of the future and would in fact comprise Jiang Zemin's central contribution to Marxism-Leninism (in promulgating his 'Three Represents' theory, Jiang would in 2001 invite businessmen to join the party on the grounds that they comprised society's most productive forces). In any case, Sun's public recognition in 1995 as one of the 'Outstanding Chinese Young People' removed the stain of the earlier bribery accusation.

The next phase of his career saw Sun selling construction materials, especially stone. Joining with a Hong Kong partner to enjoy the tax-

breaks afforded joint ventures, he established the Guanghui Stone Corporation in 1994. (In 2000 Guanghui was listed on the Shanghai Stock
Exchange). From construction materials, it was a logical step into real
estate development, which provided a ready market for the stone he ex-
cavated. Again, Sun's timing was perfect: in the 1990s real estate was one
of the most dynamic sectors of the Xinjiang economy, and Sun seized
the opportunities presented by the restructuring Chinese economy to
turn himself into a major tycoon. He began buying up failing state enterprises, including the Tianshan Shoe Factory, the May First Lumber
Factory, the Xinjiang Specialised Automobile Factory and the Xinjiang
Cooking Utensils plant, financing the deals with bank loans and his
own assets. By the early 2000s Guanghui had acquired more state firms
than any other private enterprise in China. The company portrayed its
purchase of these assets in patriotic terms, as 'joining in the reforms of
government enterprise, ardently repaying society' and 'greatly lighten-
ing the burdens of local government'. When Sun acquired the historic
October Tractor Factory, built in 1950 by the PLA under Wang Zhen's
command and once the largest tractor manufacturer in the north-west,
People's Daily reported that Guanghui would invest 200 million yuan
and 'undertake technical renovations' at the plant.

But Sun had other ideas. He razed the factory, sold off the machinery as scrap, and erected a fancy new apartment compound on the site
dubbed 'Red October Garden'. He did the same with most of the other
factories he acquired, and the city also granted him development rights
to other prime sites. Sun ended up with some thirty-seven housing
complexes and several downtown office towers—amounting to control
of 60 per cent of Urumchi's real estate market. He managed this because
he was relieving the Xinjiang government of its unprofitable firms, and
because he continued to hire local officials. For example, he paid a re-
tainer to the head of the local office that issued demolition permits, of
which he required quite a few.

By the early 2000s Sun Guangxin had accomplished a spectacular
rise. His Guanghui Group was called the '*Xibu shenhua*'–fairy tale of the
west. A mythic aura clung to Sun, who credited the discipline he had
learned as a soldier, and let it be known that he often worked till three
in the morning. Still, he admitted to taking the occasional break to play
basketball, go drinking, or ride his Harley Davidson motorcycle around
the city. Sun Guangxin made the annual Forbes list of China's richest

businessmen each year, placing within the top ten several years running and ranking third nationwide in 2002, when his personal net worth was estimated at 3.6 billion yuan. His Guanghui Group employed over 20,000 people, paid 10 percent of all the taxes in Urumchi, and made three major stock offerings between 2000, when it first went public, and 2003. 'Guanghui functions like a great state-owned enterprise', Sun told a correspondent from the *Washington Post*. 'Our social function in terms of ensuring stability is unparalleled. The big difference is that we make money.'[6]

But Guanghui also engendered what one Chinese reporter called 'social contradictions'.[7] The drawback to Sun's approach was that in buying up state firms at fire-sale prices, Guanghui also acquired the factories' former workforces. Although Guanghui claimed that it absorbed all these workers in its other operations or put them to work as custodians of the housing complexes, many were in fact laid off with small severance payments, and all lost the retirement and health benefits they had expected under their old state jobs. Thousands of these laid-off workers marched in protest several times in late 2001 and 2002, staging what may have been the largest demonstrations in Xinjiang since those in Ghulja in 1997. Moreover, Guanghui's monopoly of the Urumchi real estate market allowed it to force subcontractors to complete projects before receiving payment and to accept ownership of units in the new buildings in lieu of cash as payment for construction services. As a result, cash-strapped subcontractors delayed paying their own workers and some of these unpaid workers took to the streets as well.

Nor is Sun's own financial condition entirely rosy. Guanghui and other developers in Urumchi built much new high-end housing in the city. Some analysts have estimated that in the early to mid-2000s as much as 60 per cent of the units in Guanghui's properties remained unoccupied, largely because Urumchi citizens could not afford to purchase them. A Chinese investigative reporter scoped out the Red October Garden one night in 2003, observing few lights shining in the windows of the compound's multi-storey apartment buildings. The same reporter argues that Guanghui maintained the appearance of robust profitability despite deep liabilities in its real estate holdings by posting exaggerated profits based

6 John Pomfret, 'Chinese Capitalists Gain New Legitimacy; Ties to State Pay Off for Some Ventures', *Washington Post*, 29 September 2002, p. A01.
7 Xie Jiu 2003.

on internal trading among various subsidiaries of the Guanghui Group. For example, Guanghui Stone claimed up to 50 per cent profit on its sales of granite, marble and other materials to the property development wing of the company. Urumchi housing authorities and some bankers are said to be nervous about these low occupancy rates and to question Guanghui's ability to repay its loans.[8]

Whether or not these doubts were justified, Sun Guangxin's ambition remained unchecked. In the early 2000s he leapt into two huge new ventures. The first was an enormous wholesale distribution centre to supply western Chinese and Central Asian markets with construction materials. In this enterprise Guanghui would face off with the Hualing Corporation, itself a giant firm that already dominated the saturated market. The second venture, launched in 2002, was a scheme to ship liquefied natural gas from Xinjiang fields to markets in south-east China. Promising to avoid Shanghai and other areas scheduled to be served by the natural gas pipeline, Sun Guangxin gained high-level acceptance for his plan, despite the fact that private Chinese enterprises had not previously been vouchsafed such a role in the energy sector. In fact Xinjiang First Party Secretary Wang Lequan personally attended the ribbon-cutting, and promised that 'the government's support of Guanghui and this project is unquestioned.' Taxes from Sun's profits, unlike pipeline revenues, would be paid only in Xinjiang, not shared among several provinces. Still, Sun was unable to gain approval for rail shipments and was forced to transport his natural gas by truck, a more expensive option. Its price inflated by high transport costs, his fuel could not compete in Guangdong, Fujian or other coastal markets where Australian LNG remained 30 percent cheaper. By 2005 Guanghui was exploring markets in central and western China. Xinjiang's remoteness remains a factor, even for an entrepreneur of mythic stature.[9]

8   Xie Jiu 2003.
9   This profile of Sun Guangxin is drawn primarily from four news articles: Xie Jiu 2003; Yang Hanting, 'Fubusi fuhao Sun Guangxin Guanghui LNG pengbi waizi, suohui qian gongli' [Forbes millionaire Sun Guangxin's Guanghui LNG bumps against foreign capital, pulls back a thousand kilometres], *Dongfang zaobao*, 15 March 2005, via Sina *Caijing congheng*, <http://finance.sina.com.cn> (accessed 13 April 2005); John Pomfret, 'Chinese Capitalists Gain New Legitimacy; Ties to State Pay Off for Some Ventures', *Washington Post*, 29 September 2002, p. A01; Mark O'Neil, 'The King of Xinjiang: Business Genius or Carpetbagger?', *South China Morning Post*, 17 January 2004, p. 11. I also consulted 'Xinjiang's Richest Man to

PATRIOT ON A TIGHTROPE: ADIL HOSHUR

One of the hallmarks of Chinese nationalities policy has been support and showcasing of the performance traditions of minority peoples in the PRC. Since the 1950s the state has intervened to collect, codify, edit and reproduce the arts of the various Chinese peoples at scholarly centres in Beijing and the regional capitals. At a network of arts conservatories and cultural halls throughout the country non-Han ethnic performers are trained in reworked versions of music and dance traditions that were once taught only through direct teacher-disciple or parent-child relationships. For Xinjiang, dance and the Uyghur classical music suites known as *muqam* have been a particular focus of this process.[10] Costumed, singing and dancing Xinjiang peoples are ubiquitous: in restaurants, in magazines, on food packaging, on television, on websites, at tourist banquets, in Silk Road stage shows, at the opening ceremonies for sporting events, in international arts delegations, in feature films like *Crouching Tiger, Hidden Dragon* and even at the Splendid China theme park a few miles from Florida's Disney World. Such colourful images of China's minorities help represent China for both domestic and international consumption as a multi-nationality state.

Dawaz, or Uyghur acrobatics, has maintained itself more independently of the state cultural apparatus than has music or dance. The preeminent Uyghur acrobats today are still descendants of old acrobatic families; most receive their training from early childhood within the troupes themselves, not at a centralised academy. *Dawaz*, once performed primarily at bazaars and shrine festivals by itinerant performers, has never lost its local flavour. The troupe led by Adil Hoshur, China's top highwire artist who claims multiple Guinness World Records, still tours for months every year, performing two to three shows a day in dusty communes, villages and oasis towns as well as larger cities. They travel together in an in an old bus, a truck piled high with gear rumbling behind.

Ship LNG from Far-west Region to East', *South China Morning Post*, 5 April 2002; 'Sun Guangxin 2003 Rich List Position: no. 8', <http://www.hurun.net/detail_sunguangxin.htm> (accessed 1 July 2004); 'Sun Guangxin', <http://www.forbes.com/global/2002/1111/058.html> (accessed 1 July 2004); and 'Sun Guangxin: gong qi zuiruo' [Sun Guangxin: attack the weakest points], *Zhongguo jingji zhoukan*, 3 August 2004, via Sina *Caijing congheng*, <http://finance.sina.com.cn> (accessed 15 April 2005).
10   On state canonisation of Uyghur music, see Light 1998 and Trebinjac 2000.

Adil (sometimes spelled Ahdili after the Chinese transcription A-di-li Wu-shou-er), like any Chinese hero, endured great hardships to get where he is today. He was born in Yengisar (in the Kashgar district) in 1971 as the sixth generation scion of a family famous for *dawaz*. Despite his father's initial reluctance to let him pursue this dangerous profession, Adil took to the tightrope at the age of five, enduring a regimen of practice so rigorous, we are told, that it impressed permanent grooves into the soles of his feet. He first gained public recognition in 1985, when he performed at the festivities commemorating the thirtieth anniversary of the formation of the Xinjiang Uyghur Autonomous Region. However, according to a profile published on a popular Chinese website, Adil was not content with mere regional acclaim. 'In order to forever nurture his magical art, he decided to surmount the Tianshan, stride through the Jade Gate Pass, and even venture beyond the gates of the Nation.'[11]

Adil's quest to globalise Uyghur *dawaz* suffered a frightening setback a few years later. While he was performing in Shanghai in 1990 the tightrope suddenly snapped. Nineteen-year-old Adil fell twenty-one metres and broke seventeen bones. The injuries crippled his right hand, and when the bones in his right arm reknit, the arm would no longer straighten. Nevertheless, after two months in the hospital and three months of recuperation he once again took to the wire, although he had to adjust his performance routine: no longer able to stand on his hands, he had to master a one-arm handstand.

Working with a Han coach, Adil added new tricks to the *dawaz* repertoire. Besides walking or running forwards, backwards and sideways on the wire, he would ride a unicycle, balance on a chair, take a pretend nap or don a blindfold and walk the high wire with tin tea-trays strapped to his feet. Such stunts helped earn him first prize at a Chinese national acrobatics competition in 1995. He also began touring abroad, visiting Malaysia, Thailand and Japan.

However, that same year Adil's ambitions suffered a blow as painful in its way as the fall in Shanghai. A Canadian tightrope walker, Jay Cochrane, successfully crossed the Three Gorges of the Yangzi River on a high-wire. Adil had long hoped to perform at this famous national landmark, but had lacked funds to stage the event. Now that he had been

11 'A-di-li Wu-shou-er', *Sohu Campus* (Souhu Xiaoyuan), 19 June 2004 at <http://campus.sohu.com/2004/06/19/53/article220615344.shtml> (accessed 16 April 2005).

scooped, however, he vowed to repeat the feat himself, but in a shorter time than Cochrane's fifty-three minutes. This he managed two years later, when he walked the 400 metre-wire over the gorges in just under fourteen minutes. Exulting in his victory over the foreign competition, the Chinese press dubbed Adil 'King of the Sky'.

Over the next few years Adil broke more records and performed at several other significant Chinese sites. He crossed a damp, swinging wire between two mist-shrouded peaks at Hengshan in 2000. In May 2002, in order to break another record held by Jay Cochrane, he lived for twenty-two days on a wire and a small platform above Jinhai Lake in eastern Beijing, braving wind, rain, bloating, blisters and loneliness while performing on the wire an average of five hours a day. His only interpersonal contact during those three weeks came via email exchanged with his wife from a laptop installed in his small covered platform. In August 2003 Adil balanced on his head on a highwire over Tiankeng Canyon in Chongqing municipality. In December of that year he walked a wire 480 metres long strung between two buildings in Shantou, Guangdong, beating the record Cochrane had set in Kaohsiung, Taiwan, a year and a half earlier. Adil also spanned skyscrapers in Shanghai and other cities. He could now command high performance fees—up to 800,000 yuan for one high wire walk. With a million yuan from a Hong Kong donor, Adil established his Ahdili Foundation to support those who challenged the limits of human ability. And he became a delegate to the Tenth Chinese National People's Congress.

Adil plans still more dramatic, patriotic feats. Since 2002 he has talked about crossing a wire strung between two watchtowers of the Great Wall, and he challenged the world's top tightrope performers to compete with him there. As the towers are 2,008 metres apart, the event is designed to promote the 2008 Beijing Olympic Games. He is considering a walk over Niagara falls. But his greatest ambition, he told a reporter in 2004, is to walk across the Taiwan Straits.

If Adil is a Chinese hero, he is a Uyghur superhero: he is even mentioned beside famous literary figures Mahmud Kashghari, Yusuf Khass Hajib and Abdurehim Otkur. Unfortunately, Uyghur celebrity can rest uncomfortably with Chinese celebrity.

In June of 2001 city authorities in Kashgar planned a three-day festival to boost tourism. The event would feature Uyghur traditional wrestling, *muqam* performance, *mäshräp* (here referring to comedy sketches)

Adil Hoshur performing on a tightrope in Xinjiang. (Photo: Deborah Stratman)

as well as *dawaz*. Headlining the event, of course, was to be Kashgar's favourite son, Adil Hoshur, who was to perform in a large public performance in the historic square in front of Id Kah Mosque at the centre of old Kashgar. People from surrounding villages poured into Kashgar by motorbike, horse and donkey cart, but as their numbers swelled to an estimated 100,000, authorities grew alarmed. After the parade and first day's *dawaz* performance the city government cancelled the festival and dispersed the crowds before Adil's Id Kah performance. Though this was a particular disappointment, such cancellations were not uncommon, as Adil commonly drew large Uyghur crowds.[12]

In early 2004 Adil again found himself engaged in a delicate balancing act. Following an invitation from the Canadian Chinese Association, he was touring Canada with a thirteen member acrobatic troupe from Xinjiang. While the troupe was in Toronto seven members of the troupe evaded their minders, went into hiding, and sought political asylum. Adil returned home with the other five acrobats while the Uyghur refugees

12 I learned of this cancellation while in Kashgar myself a few days later; the course of events was confirmed for me by Deborah Stratman, who was travelling with Adil's troupe.

in Canada, who included two women, told of suffering political and religious repression and sexual harassment from the troupe's Han supervisors. The Chinese press, meanwhile, pointed out that the asylum seekers,
despite their relative youth, all held prestigious, lucrative jobs, 'comparable to those of deputy professors of Chinese universities'. Xinjiang
Party Secretary Wang Lequan appealed publicly for the acrobats' return,
alleging that they had been tricked into defecting by overseas separatists.
Wang promised that their 'mistakes' would be forgiven. Adil too delivered a public statement about, and to, the defectors, most of whom he
had known since childhood and performed beside for years. 'Their old
parents, lovely children and gentle and pretty wives are longing for their
return. Xinjiang is the homeland that has nurtured them and the stage
for their professional achievements.'[13]

Xinjiang is the homeland of many peoples and it has been the stage
for much history. Whether different peoples can agree that Xinjiang is
a common homeland for all who live there, as opposed to an exclusive

13   Wang and Adil's quotes from 'China's Xinjiang Head Urges Acrobat Defectors
in Canada to Return', *Zhongguo xinwenshe*, 7 February 2004, via BBC Monitoring
International Reports. Information on the Kashgar Dawaz festival of 22 June 2001
is based on my own conversations in Kashgar where I happened to be a few days
after the event, as well as on 'Kashgar to Hold Dawaz Festival', *Uyghur Information
Service*, 7 May 2001, based on a *Zhongguo xinwenshe* report. Besides these, my profile
of Adil Hoshur in general is based on the following sources: 'China Adventurers Scale New Heights', *China Daily*, 7 October 2005; 'Tightrope Walk in Beijing
Breaks Guinness World Record', *China Daily*, 8 May 2002; Sun Ming, 'Daredevil
Issues Challenge to World's Tightrope Elite', *Beijing Today*, vol. 55, 31 May 2002,
via <www.ynet.com> (accessed 23 July 2003); Wang Lei, 'Ahdili: The Prince of
Tightrope Walking', *China Pictorial*, August 2002, via <www.china-pictorial.com>
(accessed 17 April 2005); 'Tightrope Walker Breaks Record in Shantou', *Shenzhen
Daily*, 19 December 2003, via *People's Daily Online*, <http://english.peopledaily.
com.cnl> (accessed 15 April 2005); Daniel Kwan, 'Defectors Urged to Return to
Xinjiang', *South China Morning Post*, 8 February 2004, p. 6; Nicholas Keung, 'We
Had No Rights: Acrobats', *Toronto Star*, 8 February 2004; 'More on the Acrobat
Defectors', *Radio Free Asia*, 24 February 2004; 'A-di-li Wu-shou-er', *Sohu Campus*
(Souhu Xiaoyuan), 19 June 2004, <http://campus.sohu.com/2004/06/19/53/
article220615344.shtml> (accessed 16 April 2005). In addition, I have consulted
Deborah Stratman's film about Adil Hoshur, *Kings of the Sky* (Stratman 2004). I am
grateful for personal communications with Stratman, who toured with Adiljan's
troupe for four months.

stage for one group or another, will depend on how they choose to understand and use the region's history. It will depend still more on how they grasp the present and future, and how they choose to treat each other and the environment of Xinjiang. Future heroes can span the distances between Xinjiang, China and the world as well as the divides between peoples. But to do so they will have to maintain a sense of balance.

Appendix: Xinjiang Historical Timeline

	Southern Xinjiang (Tarim and Turfan Basins; Pamir and Kunlun Mountains)	Northern Xinjiang (Zungharian Basin; Tianshan and Altai Mountains)	Nearby regions
Paleolithic: c. 3 million to 20,000 BP	Possible paleolithic stone cores, flakes, evidence of fire use; period poorly known		
20,000–15,000 BP	More humid environment. Hunter-gatherers; simple chipped stone tools		
10,000–4,000 BP	Well-made stone tools: arrowheads, blades; coloured pottery; food cultivation, processed grains; evidence of fixed habitations		Extent of links to neighbouring neolithic cultures unknown.
2000–1200 BCE	Inhabitants probably Indo-European speakers (Tokharian, Iranian). Wheat, sheep, camels of western provenance. Small bronzes, textiles, ceramics, ornaments, agricultural implements		Central Eurasian steppe pastoralists migrating east with iron; agrarian technologies from Ferghana, Afghanistan
1200–500 BCE	Pastoral nomadic migrations from west; horse herding. Complex interactions between pastoralists and farmers. Iron implements, mines, smelting; animal style ornaments; 'Phrygian caps'. 'Beauty of Loulan' (btw. c. 1800 and c. 1000 BCE) and other mummies. Sakas (Sai) in north from 650 BCE		Iron earlier in Xinjiang than in North China

	Southern Xinjiang (Tarim and Turfan Basins; Pamir and Kunlun Mountains)	Northern Xinjiang (Zungharian Basin; Tianshan and Altai Mountains)	Nearby regions
6th through 2nd c. BCE	Possible Tokharian speakers in Tarim oasis cities Taklamakan mummies	Wusun Yuezhi (Tokharians?) Proto-Xiongnu, Xiongnu in Altai	Chinese empire formed on north China plain under Qin, followed by Han dynasty
3rd c. through mid-1st c. BCE	Xiongnu commandery by Lake Baghrash (from 162 BCE) Xiongnu and Han contest control over Turfan and Tarim Basin oases (from 120 BCE) 103–102 BCE: Li Guangli expedition to Ferghana for horses	Wusun Xiongnu	Xiongnu ascendant in Mongolia; attack and drive Yuezhi from Yili (162 BCE) to Amu River, where they form Kushan empire
mid-1st c. BCE	Han establishes protectorate general and *tuntian*	Wusun Zungharia and Mongolia: Xiongnu split into northern and southern confederations; southern Xiongnu ally with Han	
1st–mid-2nd c. CE	8–60s: Autonomous and warring city-states; Xiongnu influence over Tokharian- and Iranian-speakers in oasis towns 70s–102: Han offensives and control under Ban Chao 107–25: Northern Xiongnu control 127–50: Han controls oases under Ban Yong	Wusun Northern Xiongnu	Han interregnum 8–25 followed by Latter or Eastern Han Dynasty (25–221)

150 to late 3rd c.	Influence of Kushan empire over southern Tarim Basin Indic-language Kharoshthi-script official documents, coins Entry of Buddhism into Tarim Basin, Buddhist text translation	Wusun Xiongnu	Kushan empire based in Bactria promoted Buddhism and its dissemination from northern India into Tarim Basin
3rd c. to mid-5th c.	Gaochang culturally Chinese, generally under control or influence of north China-based state; later falls to Ruanruan 3rd–4th c.: Continued Chinese influence, *tuntian* in Lop Nor region Chinese embassies and occasional military expeditions Oasis city-states generally independently ruled by local élites. Indic-language documents. Residents of oases speaking Indo-European languages Thriving Buddhism. Kumarajiva (343–413), Qizil caves Soghdian commercial networks	Wusun	After fall of Han dynasty, north China controlled by a series of smaller dynasties, some of Inner Asian origin; many promoted Buddhism From mid-4th century, Ruanruan rise in Mongolia
mid-5th to mid-6th c.	Hephthalites rule Tarim Basin oases as far as Turfan Soghdian commercial networks expand		Hephthalites based in Soghdiana and Bactria (old Kushan lands), 450–560

	Southern Xinjiang (Tarim and Turfan Basins; Pamir and Kunlun Mountains)	Northern Xinjiang (Zungharian Basin; Tianshan and Altai Mountains)	Nearby regions
mid-6th to 7th c.	560: Kök Türk Khaghanate destroy Hephthalites	560: Türk Khaghanate replace Ruanruan 583: Türks divide into Eastern and Western Khaghanates Western Türk Khaghanate controls Zungharia (from 583)	Sui Dynasty (581–618) reunifies China
7th century	630: Tang advance into Tarim with Eastern Türk allies; est. Anxi Protectorate General in Turfan then in Kucha Soghdians managing Silk Road trade 651–57: Western Türk control Tarim 657: Tang take control of Western Türk empire, est. garrisons as far as Central Asia, Afghanistan and NE Iran 670–693: Tibetan empire drives Tang from Tarim Basin 690s–730s: Rivalry among Tang, Tibet and Turkic tribes for control of Tarim	Türks and Tang	Tang Dynasty (618–906) At greatest extent (657–62) Tang holds garrisons in Transoxiana, Afghanistan and NE Iran In 8th century Arabs advancing into Bactria, Ferghana, Soghdiana Tibetan–Arab rivalry for Pamirs

8th century	Tang regains control (from 730) 744–51: Ko Sŏnji campaigns in Pamirs and Ferghana 751: Battle of Talas River: Tang loses to coalition of Arabs and Turkic tribes 755: Tang retreat	Tang regains control, extending power to Issyk Kul 755: Tang retreat	744: Uyghurs establish khaghanate in Orkhon Valley, Mongolia. Soghdian middlemen, advisers important to new state 755–63: An Lushan Rebellion, Soghdian involvement 762–3: Uyghur khaghan converts to Manichaeism
9th–12th centuries	840: Uyghur state established in Qocho/Beshbaliq; lasts to 14th c. Tibetan empire crumbling; Khotan independence 9th c.: Qarakhanids take control of western Tarim Basin (Kashgaria) Qarakhanids convert to Islam (from c. 960) c. 1000: Qarakhanid conquest of Khotan	Qarluqs, Kirghiz Qarakhanids	840: Uyghur Orkhon state destroyed by Kirghiz Rise of Tangut state in Gansu, Qinghai; absorbs southern Uyghur state (from 930) 1000: Qarakhanids destroy Samanids, take Transoxiana 1125: Jurchen Jin destroy Khitan Liao in north China
12th century	Qara Khitay control territory of former Uyghur and Qarakhanid empires (from 1142)		Qara Khitay control Xinjiang, Northern Afghanistan, Transoxiana
early 13th century	1209: Qocho Uyghur state submits to Chinggis Khan of the Mongols 1211: Küchlük usurps control of Qara Khitay empire 1216–18: Mongols conquer Xinjiang 1227–51: Chaghatayids in alegiance with Ögedeid great khans control northern and southern Xinjiang		1227: Death of Chinggis; division of empire into four khanates Ögedei is great khan (r. 1229–41) Great Khan Güyük (r. 1246–8)

	Southern Xinjiang (Tarim and Turfan Basins; Pamir and Kunlun Mountains)	Northern Xinjiang (Zungharian Basin; Tianshan and Altai Mountains)	Nearby regions
latter half 13th century	1251–9: Xinjiang under control of great khan Möngke 1260–71: Mongolia-based and China-based khans struggle for control 1271: Qaydu (Ögedeid) controls Xinjiang and Transoxiana through puppet Chaghatayid khans		Great Khan Möngke (r. 1251–9) Great Khan Khubilai (r. 1260–94)
14th century	1301: Qaydu dies; series of Chaghatayid khans rule thereafter c. 1340: Chaghatayid khanate splits into Transoxiana and Moghulistan Dughlats rule Moghulistan and Tarim Basin through puppet Chaghatayids (from 1340s) c. 1350: Tughluq Temür converts to Islam 1390s: Khizr conquers Uyghuristan (Turfan Basin), putting it under Chaghatayid rule Chaghatayid khans, Dughlat emirs		From 1330s western Chaghatayid khanate Islamicised Ming Dynasty (1368–1644) Tamerlane (r. 1370–1405)
15th century	Chaghatayid khans, Dughlat emirs Yunus Khan (r. 1462–81) reunites Moghulistan and Turfan region	Oirats (NE Zungharia) Yunus Khan (Moghulistan = Turfan to western Zungharia and Lake Balkash) Kirghiz in Tianshan, Issyk Kul, Pamir	1408: Turfani embassy to Ming led by Buddhist priests; more embassies and trade follow Timurids in Transoxiana Naqshbandi order gaining strength in Transoxiana
16th century	Chaghatayid khans, Dughlat emirs Sa'id Khan (r. 1514–33) in Kashgaria reaches rapprochment with brother Mansur (r. 1503–43) ruling Turfan and Moghulistan.	Oirats, Kazaks Kirghiz in Tianshan	1500–99: Uzbek (Shibanid) dynasty Makhdum-i A'zam (1461–1542) in Transoxiana

16th century (cont.)	Greater unity in Altishahr (Tarim Basin) and Moghulistan (Zungharia) Khoja Ishaq (d. 1599) preaching in Tarim Basin, est. Ishaqiyya		
17th to mid-18th c.	Khojas come to power in Altishahr 1603: Bento de Goes travels from India to Yarkand and then Gansu Khoja Yusuf (d. 1653) and Khoja Afaq (d. 1694) est. Afaqiyya Afaqi-Ishaqi rivalry 1678–80: Zunghars conquer Tarim and Turfan Basins	Zunghars (Oirats) Galdan is Zunghar khan (r. 1671–97) Tsewang Rabdan (r. 1697–1727) Galdan Tseren (r. 1727–45) 1745: Zunghar internecine strife	Dalai Lama V (1617–82) 1640: Mongol-Zunghar *Quriltai* 1688: Zunghars invade Outer Mongolia 1691: Khalkha Mongols join Qing 1717: Zunghars intervene in Tibet; Qing invade Tibet 1723: Zunghars invade Transoxiana
mid-18th through mid-19th c.	1750s: Qing conquer Xinjiang 1765: Ush Rebellion 1771: Return of the Torghuts 1826: Jahangir invasion of Kashgaria 1830: Khoqandi invasion under Yusuf 1831: Qing permits permanent Han settlement in Tarim Basin 1832: Qing agreement allows Khoqand extraterritoriality, tariff collection rights in Kashgar 1847, 1852, 1855, 1857: Khoja raids		Rise of Khoqand in Ferghana 1850–64: Taiping Rebellion in central and south China 1862: Tunggan rebellion in Gansu 1860s: Russia advancing into western Turkestan

	Southern Xinjiang (Tarim and Turfan Basins; Pamir and Kunlun Mountains)	Northern Xinjiang (Zungharian Basin; Tianshan and Altai Mountains)	Nearby regions
latter half 19th c.	1864: Tunggan (Hui) and Uyghur rebellion 1865–71: Ya'qub Beg conquers Tarim Basin and Urumchi 1873–4: British embassy to Yarkand, Kashgar 1876–8: Hunan Army under Zuo Zongtang and Liu Jintang reconquers S. Xinjiang 1884: Xinjiang province created, Liu Jintang first governor 1885: Hüsäyin Musa Bay opens primary school in Artush	1851: Sino–Russian Treaty of Ghulja 1864: Yili valley under Taranchi khan 1871: Russia invades Yili Valley 1879: Treaty of Livadia (unratified) 1881: Treaty of St Petersburg; China recovers most of Yili valley, makes commercial concessions to Russia	1884–5: Sino–French war over Annam
early 20th c.	1912: Yang Zengxin takes power 1924: Trade treaty opens six Russian consulates in Xinjiang 1928: Yang Zengxin assassinated; Jin Shuren becomes governor 1931: Hami Rebellion 1932–3: Rebellion in Turfan and throughout province 1933: Sheng Shicai takes command in Urumchi 1933–4: Eastern Turkestan Republic proclaimed in Kashgar (November–February)		1900: Boxer Rebellion in north China 1904: Completion of Trans-Siberian Railroad 1911: Fall of Qing dynasty 1917–22: Russian Revolution and civil war 1928: Northern Expedition, GMD control in China

early 20th c. (cont.)	1944: GMD remove Sheng Shicai from power 1944: Three Districts Revolution; Eastern Turkestan Republic proclaimed in north Xinjiang 1946: Coalition government announced 1949: CCP takes control in Xinjiang	1929: Completion of Turkestan-Siberian Railroad 1937–45: Japan occupies much of China 1945–9: Chinese civil war
latter half 20th c.	1952–4: Production Construction Military Corps (*Bingtuan*) organised from demobilised GMD troops 1955: Proclamation of Xinjiang Uyghur Autonomous Region 1962: Yi–Ta Incident, North Xinjiang 1966–8: Armed factional conflict in Xinjiang during Cultural Revolution 1968 (September): 'Revolutionary Committees' restore order in Xinjiang; Wang Enmao displaced 1979–80: Aqsu Incident: 5,000–8,000 Han educated youth seize control of Aqsu party offices 1990: Baren Incident 1997: Ghulja (Yining) Incident; Urumchi bus bombings 2000: Great Development of the West (Xibu da kaifa) programme inaugurated	1950: PLA enters Tibet 1951–2: Three–anti (*sanfan*) campaign in PRC 1956: Hundred Flowers movement followed by Anti-Rightist Rectification 1958–62: Great Leap Forward in PRC 1966–76: Great Proletarian Cultural Revolution 1978: Deng Xiaoping in full control 1980: Hu Yaobang's trip to Tibet 1991: Collapse of Soviet Union 1996: Formation of Shanghai Five; 2001 renamed SCO

General bibliography

Abduqadir Haji, 1986, '1933–1937-yilighichä Qäshqär, Khotan, Aqsularda Bolup otkän wäqälär [Events during 1931–1937 in Kashgar, Khotan and Aqsu], *Shinjang tarix materiyalliri*, no. 17.

A-la-teng-ou-qi-er (Altan Ochir), 1996, *Qingdai Yili jiangjun lungao* [On the Yili Generals during the Qing], Beijing: Minzu chuban.

Allsen, Thomas T., 1983, 'The Yüan Dynasty and the Uighurs of Turfan in the 13th Century' in Morris Rossabi (ed.), *China Among Equals: The Middle Kingdom and its Neighbors, 10th–14th Centuries*, Berkeley, CA: University of California Press, pp. 243–80.

———, 1993, 'Mahmud Yalavač (?–1254), Mas'ud Beg (?–1289), 'Ali Beg (?–1280); Bujir (*fl.* 1206–1260)' in Igor de Rachewiltz, Hok-lam Chan, Hsiao Ch'i-ch'ing and Peter W. Geier (eds), *In the Service of the Khan: Eminent Personalities of the Early Mongol-Yüan Period (1200–1300)*, Wiesbaden: Harrassowitz, pp. 122–34.

Alptekin, Erkin, 1987, 'The Uyghurs', *Journal of the Institute of Muslim Minority Affairs*, 8, no. 2 (July): 302–10.

Amnesty International, 1999, *People's Republic of China: Gross Violations of Human Rights in the Xinjiang Uighur Autonomous Region*, London: Amnesty International.

———, 2002, *People's Republic of China: China's Anti-Terrorism Legislation and Repression in the Xinjiang Uighur Autonomous Region*, London: Amnesty International.

———, 2005, 'China: Remembering the Victims of Police Brutality in Gulja, Xinjiang on 5–6 February 1997', Public Statement, 4 February 2005.

An Jiayao, 2004, 'The Art of Glass along the Silk Road' in James C.Y. Watt (ed.), *China: Dawn of a Golden Age, 200–750 AD*, New York: Metropolitan Museum of Art and New Haven, CT: Yale University Press, pp. 57–66.

Atwood, Christopher, 1991, 'Life in Third–Fourth Century Cadh'otha: A Survey of Information Gathered from the Prakrit Documents found North of Minfeng (Niyä)', *Central Asiatic Journal*, 35, nos 3–4: 161–99.

Bagchi, Prabodh Chandra, 1981, *India and China: A Thousand Years of Cultural Relations*, reprint, based on second revised edition, Calcutta: Saraswat.

Bai Zhensheng and Koibuchi Shinichi (eds), 1992, *Xinjiang xiandai zhengzhi shehui shilue* [Brief History of Contemporary Xinjiang Political and Social History], Beijing: Zhonguo shehui kexue yuan chubanshe.

Bailey, H.W., 1970, 'Saka Studies: The Ancient Kingdom of Khotan', *Iran. Journal of the British Institute of Persian Studies*, 8 (1970): 65–72.

——, 1971, 'The Kingdom of Khotan', *Papers on Far Eastern History*, 4 (1971): 1–16.

Bao-er-han (Burhan Shahidi), 1984, *Xinjiang wushi nian* [Fifty Years of Xinjiang], Beijing: Wenshi ziliao chubanshe.

Barber, Elizabeth Wayland, 1999, *The Mummies of Ürümchi*, New York and London: Norton.

Barfield, Thomas J., 1989, *The Perilous Frontier: Nomadic Empires and China*, Oxford and Cambridge, MA: Basil Blackwell.

Barthold, V.V. [W. Barthold], 1956–62, *Four Studies on the History of Central Asia*, trans. Vladimir and Tatiana Minorsky, Leiden: E.J. Brill, vol. 1 (contains 'A Short History of Turkestan' and 'History of Semirechyé').

Barthold, W., 1968 [1900], *Turkestan Down to the Mongol Invasion*, trans. Tatiana Minorsky, 3rd edn, E.J.W. Gibb Memorial series, London: Luzac.

Bartke, Wolfgang, 1990, *Biographical Dictionary and Analysis of China's Party Leadership, 1922–88*, Munich, London and New York: K.G. Saur.

Beckwith, Christopher I., 1987, *The Tibetan Empire in Central Asia: A History of the Struggle for Great Power among Tibetans, Turks, Arabs and Chinese during the Early Middle Ages*, Princeton University Press.

Becquelin, Nicolas, 2000, 'Xinjiang in the Nineties', *China Journal*, 44 (July): 65–90.

——, 2004, 'Staged Development in Xinjiang', *The China Quarterly*, 178 (June 2004): 358–78, special issue: 'China's Campaign to "Open Up the West": National, Provincial and Local Perspectives'.

Bellér-Hann, Ildikó, 2000, 'The Written and the Spoken: Literacy and Oral Transmission Among the Uyghur', *Anor*, 8.

Bellew, H.W., 1875, *Kashmir and Kashghar: A Narrative of the Journey of the Embassy to Kashghar in 1873–74*, London: Trubner.

Bello, David, 2000, 'Opium in Xinjiang and Beyond' in Timothy Brook and Bob Tadashi (eds), *Opium Regimes: China, Britain and Japan, 1839–1952*, Berkeley, CA: University of California Press, pp. 127–51.

Chouban yiwu shimo (Xianfeng chao) [Complete Record of the Management of Barbarian Affairs, Xianfeng reign] *1851–61*, 1979 [1930, based on Qing court manuscript edition], reprint edition, 8 vols, Beijing: Zhonghua shuju.

Christian, David, 2000, 'Silk Roads or Steppe Roads? The Silk Roads in World History', *Journal of World History*, 11, no. 1: 1–26.

Chu Wen-djang, 1966, *The Moslem Rebellion in Northwest China, 1867–1878: A Study of Government Minority Policy*, The Hague: Mouton.

Chung, Chien-Peng, 2002, 'China's "War on Terror": September 11 and Uyghur Separatism', *Foreign Affairs* (July–August 2002).

Clark, Willam C., 1999, 'Convergence or Divergence: Uighur Family Change in Urumqi', Ph.D. dissertation, University of Washington.

Clubb, O. Edmund, 1971, *China and Russia: The Great Game*, New York: Columbia University Press.

Courant, Maurice, 1912, *L'Asie centrale aux XVIIe et XVIIIe siècles: Empire kalmouk ou empire mantchou?*, Lyon: Annales de l'université de Lyon, N.S., fasc. 26.

Crossley, Pamela K., 1990, 'Thinking about Ethnicity in Early Modern China', *Late Imperial China*, 11, no. 1 (June): 1–31.

Cui Jianyong and Zhong Wei, 2001, 'Talimuhe liuyu renlei huodong yu huanjing xiaoying' [Human Activity and Environmental Effects in the Tarim River Watershed] in Xiong Heigang (ed.), *Xinjiang ziyuan huanjing yu kechixu fazhan* [Resources Environment and Sustainable Development in Xinjiang], Urumchi: Xinjiang daxue chubanshe, pp. 205–11.

Dabbs, Jack Autrey, 1963, *History of the Discovery and Exploration of Chinese Turkestan*, The Hague: Mouton.

Dautcher, Jay Todd, 1999, 'Folklore and Identity in a Uighur Community in Xinjiang China', Ph.D. dissertation, University of California at Berkeley.

——, 2002, 'Reading out of Print: Popular Culture and Protest on China's Western Frontier' in Timothy Weston and Lionel Jensen (eds), *China Beyond the Headlines*, New York: Rowman and Littlefield.

——, 2004, 'Public Health and Social Pathologies in Xinjiang' in S. Frederick Starr (ed.), *Xinjiang: China's Muslim Borderland*, Armonk, NY and London: M.E. Sharpe, pp. 276–95.

Davies, Robert, 2001, *Perfection She Dances: A True Story of Love, Drugs and Jail in Modern China*, Edinburgh: Mainstream Publishers (republished in 2002 as *Prisoner 13498: A True Story of Love, Drugs and Jail in Modern China*).

De La Vaissière, Étienne, 2003, 'Soghdians in China: A Short History and Some New Discoveries', *The Silk Road* (publication of the Silk Road Foundation, available at <www.silkroadfoundation.org>) 1, no. 2 (December 2003): 23–7.

——, 2004, *Histoire des marchands Sogdiens*, Bibliothèque de l'Institut des Hautes Études Chinoises, vol. 32, Paris: Collège France, Institut des Hautes Études Chinoises.

Debaine-Francfort, C., 1988–9, 'Archéologie du Xinjiang, des origines aux Han', part I, *Paléorient*, 14, no. 1 (1988): 5–27; part II, *Paléorient*, 15, no. 1 (1989): 183–213.

Deng Shaohui, 1992, 'Jindai Xinjiang shiyou gongye shulue' [Brief History of Modern Xinjiang's Oil Industry], *Xinjiang daxue xuebao, zhexue shehui kexue ban* [Bulletin of Xinjiang University, Philosophy and Social Sciences Edition], 20, no. 2 (1992): 52–8, 71.

Department of Population, Social, Science [*sic*] and Technology Statistics of the National Bureau of Statistics of China (Guojia tongjiju renkou he shehui keji tongji si) and Department of Economic Development of the State Ethnic Affairs Commission of China (Guojia minzu shiwu weiyuanhui jingji fazhan si) (eds), 2003, *Tabulation on Nationalities of 2000 Population Census of China (2000 nian renkou pucha zhongguo minzu renkou ziliao)*, 2 vols, Beijing: Minzu chuban she.

DeWeese, Devin, 1994, *Islamization and Native Religion in the Golden Horde: Baba Tükles and Conversion to Islam in Historical and Epic Tradition*, University Park, PA: Pennsylvania State University Press.

Di Cosmo, Nicola, 1996, 'Ancient Xinjiang between Central Asia and China' in F. Hiebert and Nicola Di Cosmo (eds), *Between Lapis and Jade*, special issue of *Anthropology and Archaeology of Eurasia*, 34, no. 4 (spring 1996): 87–101.

——, 1999a, 'China on the Eve of the Historical Period' in Michael Loewe and Edward Shaughnessy (eds), *The Cambridge History of Ancient China: From the Origins of Civilization to 221 B.C.*, Cambridge University Press.

——, 1999b, 'State Formation and Periodization in Inner Asian History', *Journal of World History*, 10, no. 1: 1–40.

——, 2002, *Ancient China and its Enemies: The Rise of Nomadic Power in East Asian History*, Cambridge University Press.

Dillon, Michael, 1995, 'Xinjiang: Ethnicity, Separatism and Control in Chinese Central Asia', *Durham East Asian Papers*, 1, Dept. of East Asian Studies, University of Durham.

——, 2004, *Xinjiang: China's Muslim Far Northwest*, London: Routledge Curzon.

Ding Jianli, Tashpolat Tiyip and Liu Chuansheng, 2001, 'Ji yu yaogan de Cele lüzhou tudi fugai dongtai bianhua yanjiu' [Research on Dynamic Changes in Ground Cover in the Cele Oasis Based on Remote Sensing) in Xiong Heigang (ed.), *Xinjiang ziyuan huanjing yu ke chixu fazhan* [Resources Environment and Sustainable Development in Xinjiang], Urumchi: Xinjiang daxue chubanshe, pp. 180–8.

Document No. 7, 1996, Chinese Communist Party Central Committee Document Number 7, Record of the Meeting of the Standing Committee of the Political Bureau of the Chinese Communist Party, 19 March 1996. Circulated via internet by Committee Against Chinese Communist Propaganda (<www.caccp.org>) and other dissident groups.

Dreyer, June Teufel, 1976, *China's Forty Millions: Minority Nationalities and National Integration in the People's Republic of China*, Cambridge, MA: Harvard University Press.

Dunnell, Ruth W., 1996, *The Great State of White and High: Buddhism and State Formation in Eleventh Century Xia*, Honolulu, HI: University of Hawai'i Press.

Economy, Elizabeth, 2002, 'China's Go West Campaign: Ecological Construction or Ecological Exploitation', *China Environment Series* (Woodrow Wilson International Center for Scholars), no. 5: 1–12.

Edney, Matthew H., 1997, *Mapping an Empire: The Geographical Construction of British India, 1765–1843*, University of Chicago Press.

Emmerick, R.E., 1979, *A Guide to the Literature of Khotan*, Tokyo: The Reiyukai Library.

Enoki, K., G.A. Koshelenko and Z. Haidary, 1994, 'The Yueh-chih and their Migrations' in János Harmatta (ed.), *History of Civilizations of Central Asia*, vol. II, *The Development of Sedentary and Nomadic Civilizations: 700 B.C. to A.D. 250*, Paris: Unesco, pp. 171–89.

Everest-Phillips, Max, 1990, 'The Suburban King of Tartary', *Asian Affairs* (Royal Society for Asian Affairs), 21, no. 3: 324.

Fairbank, John King, Edwin O. Reischauer and Albert Craig, 1978, *East Asia Tradition and Transformation*, Boston, MA: Houghton Mifflin.

Fan Hua (ed.), 1961, *Ershiliu shi* [The Twenty-six Histories], Taipei: Qiming shuju.

Fang Yingkai, 1989, *Xinjiang tunken shi* [History of Agricultural Reclamation in Xinjiang], 2 vols, Urumchi: Xinjiang qingshaonian chubanshe.

Feng Jiasheng, Cheng Suluo and Mu Guangwen (eds), 1981, *Weiwuer zu shiliao jianbian* [Concise Compilation of Historical Materials Relating to the Uyghur Nationality], 2 vols, Beijing: Minzu chubanshe.

Fields, Lanny, 1978, *Tso Tsung-t'ang and the Muslims: Statecraft in Northwest China, 1868–1880*, Kingston, ON: The Limestone Press.

Fleming, Peter, 1983 [1936], *News from Tartary: A Journey from Peking to Kashmir*, reprint edition, London: Futura [1936, London: Jonathan Cape].

Fletcher, Joseph F., 1968, 'China and Central Asia, 1368–1884' in John King Fairbank (ed.), *The Chinese World Order: Traditional China's Foreign Relations*, Cambridge, MA: Harvard University Press.

———, 1978a, 'Ch'ing Inner Asia *c.* 1800' in John King Fairbank (ed.), *The Cambridge History of China*, vol. 10, *Late Ch'ing, 1800–1911, part 1*, Cambridge University Press, pp. 35–106.

———, 1978b, 'Sino-Russian Relations, 1800–62' in John King Fairbank (ed.), *The Cambridge History of China*, vol. 10, *Late Ch'ing, 1800–1911, part 1*, Cambridge University Press, pp. 318–50.

———, 1978c, 'The Heyday of the Ch'ing Order in Mongolia, Sinkiang and Tibet' in John King Fairbank (ed.), *The Cambridge History of China*, vol. 10, *Late Ch'ing, 1800–1911, part 1*, Cambridge University Press, pp. 351–408.

———, 1986, 'The Mongols: Ecological and Social Perspectives', *Harvard Journal of Asiatic Studies*, 46: 11–50.

———, 1995 [1976], 'Confrontations between Muslim Missionaries and Nomad Unbelievers in the Late Sixteenth Century: Notes on Four Passages from the 'Diyâ' al-qulûb' in Joseph F. Fletcher, *Studies on Chinese and Islamic Central Asia*, Variorum Collected Studies Series, Aldershot: Variorum (V), pp. 167–74 (originally published in Walter Heissig [ed.], 1976, *Tractata Altaica*, Wiesbaden: Harrassowitz).

———, 1995a, 'The Naqshbandiyya in Northwest China' in Joseph F. Fletcher, *Studies on Chinese and Islamic Central Asia*, Variorum Collected Studies Series, Aldershot: Variorum (XI), pp. 1–4.

———, 1995b, 'Integrative History: Parallels and Interconnections in the Early Modern Period, 1500–1800' in Joseph F. Fletcher, *Studies on Chinese and Islamic Central Asia*, Variorum Collected Studies Series, Aldershot: Variorum (X) (reformatted and repaginated from the *Journal of Turkish Studies*, 9 [1985]).

Foltz, Richard C., 1999, *Religions of the Silk Road: Overland Trade and Cultural Exchange from Antiquity to the Fifteenth Century*, New York: St Martin's Press.

Forbes, Andrew D.W., 1986, *Warlords and Muslims in Chinese Central Asia: a Political History of Republican Xinjiang, 1911–1949*, Cambridge University Press.

Forney, Matthew, 2002, 'Xinjiang: One Nation—Divided', *Time*, 159, no. 11 (25 March 2002).

Forsyth, Sir T.D., 1875, *Report of a Mission to Yarkund in 1873, Under Command of Sir T.D. Forsyth, K.C.S.I., C.B., Bengal Civil Service, with Historical and Geographic Information Regarding the Possessions of the Ameer of Yarkund*, Calcutta: The Government Press.

Foust, Clifford M., 1992, *Rhubarb: the Wondrous Drug*, Princeton University Press.

Frank, Andre Gunder, 1998, *ReOrient: Global Economy in the Asian Age*, Berkeley and Los Angeles, CA: University of California Press.

Gabain, Annemarie von, 1961, *Das uigurische Königreich von Chotscho, 850–1250*, Berlin: Akademie-Verlag.

——, 1973, *Das Leben im uigurischen Königreich von Qočo, 850–1250*, Wiesbaden: Harrassowitz.

Giles, H.A. (trans.), 1981 [1923], *The Travels of Fa-hsien (399–414 A.D.) or Record of the Buddhistic Kingdoms*, reprint edition, Westport, CT: Greenwood Press [1923, Cambridge University Press].

Gilley, Bruce, 2001, '"Uighurs Need Not Apply": Beijing's "Go West" Development Campaign is Unlikely to Benefit most Uighurs', *Far Eastern Economic Review*, 23 August 2001.

Gladney, Dru C., 1991, *Muslim Chinese: Ethnic Nationalism in the People's Republic*, Cambridge, MA: Council on East Asian Studies, Harvard University; distributed by Harvard University Press.

——, 1994, 'Representing Nationality in China: Refiguring Majority/Minority Identities', *Journal of Asian Studies*, 53, no. 1 (February): 92–123.

——, 2004, 'Responses to Chinese Rule: Patterns of Cooperation and Opposition' in S. Frederick Starr (ed.), *Xinjiang: China's Muslim Borderland*, Armonk, NY and London: M.E. Sharpe, pp. 375–96.

Golden, Peter B., 1990, 'The Karakhanids and Early Islam' in Dennis Sinor (ed.), *The Cambridge History of Early Inner Asia*, Cambridge University Press, pp. 343–70.

——, 1992, *An Introduction to the History of the Turkic Peoples*, Wiesbaden: Harrassowitz.

Grenard, Fernand (ed.), 1897–8, J. L. Dutreuil de Rhins, Mission scientifique dans la Haute Asie, 3 vols (vols 2–3 ed. Grenard), Paris: E. Leroux.

——, 1900, 'La légend de Satok Boghra Khan et l'histoire', Journal Asiatique (Paris), January–February 1900: 5–79.

Grousset, René, 1997 [1970], The Empire of the Steppes: A History of Central Asia, trans. Naomi Walford, reprint edition, New Brunswick, NJ: Rutgers University Press.

Grove, Jean M., 1989, The Little Ice Age, London: Routledge.

Gup, Ted, 2000, Book of Honor: Covert Lives and Classified Deaths at the CIA, New York: Doubleday.

Hafiz Abru (Shihabu'd-Din 'Abdullah bin Lutfullah Al-Khwafi), 1970 [1422], A Persian Embassy to China, Being an Extract from Zubdatu't Tawarikh of Hafiz Abru, trans. K.M. Maitra, reprint edition, New York: Paragon.

Hahn, Reinhard F., 1991, Spoken Uyghur, Seattle, WA and London: University of Washington Press.

Hamada Masami, 1978, 'Supplement: Islamic Saints and their Mausoleums', Acta Asiatica: Bulletin of the Institute of Eastern Culture (Tokyo: Tôhô gakkai), 34: 79–105.

——, 1990, 'La transmission du mouvement nationalists au Turkestan oriental (Xinjiang)', Central Asian Survey, 9, no. 1: 29–48.

Hambis, M. Louis et al., 1977, L'Asie Centrale: histoire et civilization, Paris: l'Imprimerie nationale.

Hannum, Emily and Yu Xie, 1998, 'Occupational Differences between Han Chinese and National Minorities in Xinjiang, 1982–1990', Demography, 35: 323–33.

Hare, John, 1998, The Lost Camels of Tartary: A Quest into Forbidden China, London: Abacus.

Harrell, Stevan (ed.), 1995, Cultural Encounters on China's Ethnic Frontiers, Seattle, WA: University of Washington Press.

Harris, Rachel, 2002, 'Cassettes, Bazaars and Saving the Nation: The Uyghur Music Industry in Xinjiang, China' in Tim Craig and Richard King (eds), Global Goes Local: Popular Culture in Asia, Vancouver, BC and Toronto, ON: University of British Columbia Press, 2002.

Hedin, Sven, 1925, My Life as an Explorer, New York: Boni & Liveright.

——, 1931, Across the Gobi Desert, London: Routledge.

——, 1936, The Flight of 'Big Horse': The Trail of War in Central Asia, trans. F.H. Lyon, New York: E.P. Dutton.

——, 1938, *The Silk Road*, New York, E.P. Dutton.

——, 1940, *The Wandering Lake*, London: Routledge.

Hevia, James L., 1995, *Cherishing Men from Afar: Qing Guest Ritual and the Macartney Embassy of 1793*, Durham, NC: Duke University Press.

——, 2003, *English Lessons: The Pedagogy of Imperialism in Nineteenth-Century China*, Durham, NC: Duke University Press.

Hiebert, F. and Nicola Di Cosmo (eds), 1996, *Between Lapis and Jade: Ancient Cultures of Central Asia*, special issue of *Anthropology and Archaeology of Eurasia*, 34, no. 4 (spring 1996).

Hopkirk, Peter, 1980, *Foreign Devils on the Silk Road: The Search for the Lost Cities and Treasures of Chinese Central Asia*, London: John Murray.

Hostetler, Laura, 2001, *Qing Colonial Enterprise: Ethnography and Cartography in Early Modern China*, University of Chicago Press.

Hoyanagi, Mutsumi, 1975, 'Natural Changes of the Region along the Old Silk Road in the Tarim Basin in Historical Times', *Memoirs of the Research Department of the Tōyō Bunko* (The Oriental Library), 33 (1975): 85–113.

Hsü, Immanuel C.Y., 1965a, 'The Great Policy Debate in China, 1874: Maritime Defense vs. Frontier Defense', *Harvard Journal of Asiatic Studies*, 25 (1965): 212–28.

——, 1965b, *The Ili Crisis: A Study of Sino-Russian Diplomacy, 1871–1881*, Oxford University Press.

——, 1968, 'The Late Ch'ing Reconquest of Sinkiang: A Reappraisal of Tso Tsung-T'ang's Role', *Central Asiatic Journal*, 12, no. 1 (1968): 50–63.

Hua Li, 1994, *Qingdai Xinjiang nongye kaifa shi* [History of the Qing Period Agricultural Opening of Xinjiang], Bianjiang shidi congshu, no. 5, Harbin: Heilongjian jiaoyu chubanshe.

Hulsewé, A.F.P. and M.A.N. Loewe, 1979, *China in Central Asia: The Early Stage: 125 BC–AD 23*, Leiden: E.J. Brill.

Human Rights Watch, 2000, 'Xinjiang, China's Restive Northwest: Press Backgrounder', *Human Rights Watch World Report 2000, China and Tibet*.

Huntington, Ellsworth, 1919, *The Pulse of Asia: A Journey in Central Asia Illustrating the Geographic Basis of History*, Boston: Houghton Mifflin.

Ibn Khaldun, 1969 (1377), *The Muqaddimah: An Introduction to History*, trans. Franz Rosenthal, ed. and abridged N.J. Dawood, Bollingen Series, Princeton University Press.

Ibrahim Niyaz, see Yi-bu-la-xin.

Issar, Arie S. (ed.), 2003, *Climate Changes during the Holocene and Their Impact on Hydrological Systems*, Cambridge University Press.

Jagchid, Sechin, 1989, *Peace, War, and Trade along the Great Wall: Nomadic-Chinese Interaction through Two Millennia*, Bloomington, IN: Indiana University Press.

Jarring, Gunnar, 1951, *Materials to the Knowledge of Eastern Turki: Tales, Poetry, Proverbs, Riddles, Ethnological and Historical Texts from the Southern Parts of Eastern Turkestan, with Translation and Notes*, Lund: Ethnological and Historical Texts from Guma.

——, 1975, 'Gustav Raquette and Qasim Akhun's Letters to Kamil Efendi' in *Ethnological and Folkloristic Materials from Southern Sinkiang*, ed. and trans. with explanatory notes, Lund: CWK Gleerup (Scripta Minora Regiae Societatis Humaniorum Litterarum Lundensis, 1975–6: 1).

——, 1979, *Matters of Ethnological Interest in Swedish Missionary Reports from Southern Sinkiang*, Lund: CWK Gleerup (Scripta Minora Regiae Societatis Humaniorum Litterarum Lundensis, 1979–80: 4).

——, 1986, *Return to Kashgar: Central Asian Memoirs in the Present*, Durham, NC: Duke University Press.

——, 1991, *Prints from Kashgar: The Printing Office of the Swedish Mission in Eastern Turkestan, History and Production with an Attempt at a Bibliography*, Stockholm: Svensca Forskningsinstitutet i Istanbul.

Ji Dachun (ed.), 1997, *Xinjiang lishi baiwen* [100 Questions on Xinjiang History], Urumchi: Xinjiang meishu xieying chubanshe.

Ji Zongan, 1996, *Xiliao shilun, Yelü Dashi yanjiu* [Historical Discussions of the Western Liao, Research on Yelü Dashi], Urumchi: Xinjiang renmin chubanshe.

Johnson, Tim, 2004, 'Throngs of Migrants Flooding China's Silk Road Cities', KansasCity.com (*Kansas City Star* online), 22 September 2004, <http://www.kansascity.com/mld/kansascity/news/world/9732486.htm?1c> (accessed 25 October 2004).

Juvaini, Ata-Malik, 1997 [1958], *Genghis Khan: The History of the World-Conqueror* (*Tâ'ríkh-i Jahân-gushâ* [1260]), trans. and ed. J.A. Boyle, with a new introduction by David O. Morgan, Manchester University Press and Unesco [1958, Manchester University Press].

Kamal, Ahmad, 1940, *Land without Laughter*, New York: Scribners.

Kashgharî, Mahmûd, see Mahmûd al-Kashgharî.

Kataoka Kazutada, 1991, *Shinchô Shinkyô tôji kenkyû* [Researches on Qing Dynasty Rule in Xinjiang], Tokyo: Yû San Kaku.

Khalid, Adeeb, 1998, *The Politics of Muslim Cultural Reform: Jadidism in Central Asia*, Berkeley, CA: University of California Press.

Kim, Hodong, 1986, 'The Muslim Rebellion and the Kashghar Emirate in Chinese Central Asia, 1864–1874', Ph.D. dissertation, Harvard University.

——, 2004, *Holy War in China: The Muslim Rebellion and State in Chinese Central Asia, 1864–1877*, Stanford University Press.

Kuropatkin, A.N. (Aleksei Nikolaevich), 1882, *Kashgaria*, Calcutta: Thacker.

Lai, Hongyi Harry, 2002, 'China's Western Development Program: Its Rationale, Implementation and Prospects', *Modern China*, 28, no. 4 (October): 432–66.

Lattimore, Eleanor Holgate, 1934, *Turkestan Reunion*, New York: John Day Company.

Lattimore, Owen, 1930, *High Tartary*, Boston: Little, Brown and Company.

——, 1950, *Pivot of Asia: Sinkiang and the Inner Asian Frontiers of China and Russia*, Boston: Little, Brown and Company.

——, 1988 [1940], *Inner Asian Frontiers of China*, reprint edition, Hong Kong: Oxford University Press.

Le Coq, Albert von, 1928, *Buried Treasures of Chinese Turkestan: An Account of the Activities and Adventures of the Second and Third German Turfan Expeditions*, trans. Anna Barwell, London: G. Allen & Unwin.

Lei, Shao, Karl Stattegger, Wenhou Li and Bernd J. Haupt, 1999, 'Depositional Style and Subsidence History of the Turpan Basin (NW China)', *Sedimentary Geology*, 128, nos 1–2: 155–69.

Levi, Scott, 1999, 'India, Russia and the Eighteenth-Century Transformation of the Central Asian Caravan Trade', *Journal of the Economic and Social History of the Orient*, 42, no. 4: 519–48.

Li Dezhu, 2000, 'Xibu da kaifa yu minzu wenti' [The Great Opening of the West and the Nationality Question], *Qiushi* [Seeking Truth], no. 11 (1 June 2000): 22–5.

Li Sheng, 1990, 'Xinjiang Eguo maoyiquan yanjiu' [Research on Xinjiang Russian Trade Zones] in Xiyu shi luncong editorial group (ed.), *Xiyu shi luncong* [Collection of Articles on the Western Regions], Urumchi: Xinjiang renmin chubanshe, vol. 3, pp. 420–80.

——, 1993, *Xinjiang dui Su (E) Maoyi shi 1600–1990* [A History of Xinjiang's Trade with the Soviet Union (Russia), 1600–1990], Urumchi: Xinjiang renmin chubanshe.

———, 1995, *Zhong-E Yili jiaoshe* [Sino-Russian Negotiations over Yili], Urumchi: Xinjiang renmin chubanshe.

Li Ze, Liu Tongqi, Li Dongsheng and Liu Yongqian, 1994, 'Xinjiang minzu fenliezhuyi yanjiu' [Research on Separatism among Xinjiang Nationalities] in Yang Faren *et al.* (eds), *Fanyisilanzhuyi, fantujuezhuyi yanjiu* [Research on Pan-Islamism and Pan-Turkism], Urumchi: Xinjiang shehui kexueyuan, pp. 164–239.

Light, Nathan, 1998, 'Slippery Paths: The Performance and Canonization of Turkic Literature and Uyghur Muqam Song in Islam and Modernity', Ph.D. dissertation, Indiana University.

Lin Yongkuang and Wang Xi, 1991, *Qingdai xibei minzu maoyi shi* [History of Commerce among North-western Nationalities in the Qing Period], Beijing: Zhongyang minzu xueyuan chubanshe.

Lipman, Jonathan, 1997, *Familiar Strangers: A Muslim History in China*, Seattle, WA: University of Washington Press.

Liu Hantai and Du Xingfu (eds), 2003, *Zhongguo daji 'dong tu' baogao* [Report on China's Attack on the 'East Turkestan' Movement], Urumchi: Xinjiang renmin chubanshe.

Liu Jintang, 1986 [1898], *Liu xiang le gong zougao* [Memorials of Liu Jintang], reprint edition with introduction by Wu Fengpei, in Zhongguo wenxian shanben chushu series, Beijing (?): Shumu wenxian chubanshe.

Liu, Kwang-ching and Richard Smith, 1980, 'The Military Challenge: The North-west and the Coast' in John K. Fairbank and Kwang-ching Liu (eds), *Cambridge History of China*, vol. 11, *Late Ch'ing, 1800–1911, part 2*, Cambridge University Press, pp. 202–73.

Liu Weixin *et al.*, 1995, *Xinjiang minzu zidian* [Dictionary of Xinjiang Nationalities], Urumchi: Xinjiang renmin chubanshe.

Liu Xiaomeng, 2004, *Zhongguo zhiqing koushu shi* [Oral History of Chinese Educated Youth], Beijing: Zhongguo shehui kexue.

Lu Xin, Zhu Ruijun and Luo Yunqiang, 2001, 'Xinjiang renkou, shui ziyuan, shengtai huanjing yu kechixu fazhan' [Xinjiang Population, Water Resources, Ecological Environment and Sustainable Development] in Xiong Heigang (ed.), *Xinjiang ziyuan huanjing yu kechixu fazhan* [Resources Environment and Sustainable Development in Xinjiang], Urumchi: Xinjiang daxue chubanshe, pp. 100–3.

Liu Xinru, 1988, *Ancient India and Ancient China: Trade and Religious Exchanges, AD 1–600*, Delhi: Oxford University Press.

———, 1996, *Silk and Religion: An Exploration of Material Life and the Thought of People, AD 600–1200*, Delhi: Oxford University Press.

Lopez, Robert Sabatino, 1952, 'China Silk in Europe in the Yuan Period', *Journal of the American Oriental Society*, 72, no. 2 (April–June): 72–6.

Lu Zongyi and Li Zhouwei (eds), 2001, *Xibu da kaifa yu Xinjiang jingji fazhan zhanlüe* [Great Development of the West and Xinjiang's Economic Development Strategy], Urumchi: Xinjiang renmin chubanshe.

Ma Dazheng, 2003, *Guojia liyi gaoyu yiqie: Xinjiang wending wenti de guancha yu sichao* [The National Interest is More Important than All Else: Observation and Reflection on the Xinjiang Stability Question], Urumchi: Xinjiang renmin chubanshe.

Ma Yong and Sun Yutang, 1994, 'The Western Regions under the Hsiungnu and the Han' in János Harmatta (ed.), *History of Civilizations of Central Asia*, vol. II, *The Development of Sedentary and Nomadic Civilizations: 700 BC to AD 250*, Paris: Unesco, pp. 227–46.

Ma Yong and Wang Binghua, 1994, 'The Culture of the Xinjiang Region' in János Harmatta (ed.), *History of Civilizations of Central Asia*, vol. II, *The Development of Sedentary and Nomadic Civilizations, 700 BC to AD 250*, Paris: Unesco.

MacKerras, Colin, 1990, 'The Uighurs' in Dennis Sinor (ed.), *The Cambridge History of Early Inner Asia*, Cambridge University Press, pp. 317–42.

———, 1994, *China's Minorities: Integration and Modernization in the Twentieth Century*, Hong Kong: Oxford University Press.

———, 1995, *China's Minority Cultures: Identities and Integration since 1912*, Melbourne: Longman and New York: St Martin's Press.

Mahler, Jane Gaston, 1959, *The Westerners among the Figurines of the T'ang Dynasty of China*, Rome: Instituto italiano per il Medio ed Estremo Oriente.

Mahmûd al-Kashgharî, 1982–5 [1072–7], *Compendium of the Turkic Dialects* [*Divanu lugat-it-Türk* (Arabic/Turkic)], trans. R. Dankoff and J. Kelly, 3 vols, Cambridge, MA: Harvard University Press, vol. 1, parts 1–3.

Mai-ji-te Aibu-zha-er, 1985, 'Ji yijiuerling nian Wulumuqi chuangban xinxue de pianduan' [Note Recalling the Opening of a New School in Urumchi in 1920] in *Xinjiang wenshi ziliao xuanji*, 13: 78–9, Chinese edition, Urumchi: Xinjiang renmin chubanshe.

Maillard, Monique, 'Essai sur la vie materielle dans l'oasis de Tourfan pendant le haut moyen âge', *Arts Asiatique*, 29 (1973): 3–185.

Maillart, Ella K., 1935, *Turkestan Solo: One Woman's Expedition from the Tien Shan to the Kizil Kum*, trans. John Rodker, New York: Putnam's.

Mallory, J.P. and Victor Mair, 2000, *The Tarim Mummies*, London: Thames and Hudson.

McMillen, Donald H., 1979, *Chinese Communist Power and Policy in Xinjiang, 1949–1977*, Boulder, CO: Westview Press.

Miao Pusheng, 1995, *Boke zhidu* [The Beg System], Urumchi: Xinjiang renmin chubanshe.

Millward, James A., 1992, 'The Qing Trade with the Kazakhs in Yili and Tarbagatai, 1759–1852', *Central and Inner Asian Studies*, VII: 1–41.

——, 1994, 'A Uyghur Muslim in Qianlong's Court: The Meanings of the Fragrant Concubine', *Journal of Asian Studies*, 53, no. 2 (May): 427–58.

——, 1998, *Beyond the Pass: Economy, Ethnicity and Empire in Qing Xinjiang, 1759–1864*, Stanford University Press.

——, 1999, '"Coming onto the Map": "Western Regions" Geography and Cartographic Nomenclature in the Making of Chinese Empire in Xinjiang', *Late Imperial China*, 20, no. 2 (December): 61–98.

——, 2000, 'Historical Perspectives on Contemporary Xinjiang', *Inner Asia*, 2, no. 2: 121–35.

——, 2004a, *Violent Separatism in Xinjiang: A Critical Assessment*, Washington, DC: East-West Center Policy Studies, 6.

——, 2004b, 'Contextualizing the Qing: The Return of the Torghuts and the End of History in Central Eurasia' in Lynn Struve (ed.), *The Qing Formation and World Time*, Berkeley, CA: University of California Press.

——, 2005, 'The Advent of Modern Education on the Sino-Central Asian Frontier: *Xinxue* vs *usul-i jadid*' in B.J. Parker and L. Rodseth (eds), *Untaming the Frontier: Interdisciplinary Perspectives on Frontier Studies*, Tucson, AZ: University of Arizona Press.

—— and Laura Newby, 2006, 'The Qing and Islam on the Western Frontier' in Pamela Kyle Crossley, Helen Siu and Donald Sutton (eds), *Empire at the Margins: Culture, Ethnicity and Frontier in Early Modern China*, Berkeley, CA: University of California Press.

Minorsky, Vladimir (trans.), 1970, *Hudûd al-'Âlam, 'the Regions of the World': A Persian Geography, 372 AH–982 AD*, second edition, ed. C.E. Bosworth, E.J.W. Gibb Memorial series, 11, London: Luzac.

——, 1978, 'Tamim ibn Bahr's Journey to the Uyghurs' in *The Turks, Iran and the Caucasus in the Middle Ages*, London: Variorum Reprints.

Mirza Muhammad Haidar Dughlat, 1972 [1895], *A History of the Moghuls of Central Asia, being the Tarikh-i-Rashidi of Mirza Muhammad Haidar, Dughlat*, ed. N. Elias, trans. E. Denison Ross, New York: Barnes & Noble.

Molla Musa Sairami, 1988 [1903], *Tarixi Äminiyä*, modern Uyghur edition, ed. Mähämät Zunun, Urumchi: Shinjang xälq näshriyati.

Moseley, George, 1966, *A Sino-Soviet Cultural Frontier: The Ili Kazakh Autonomous Chou*, Cambridge, MA: East Asian Research Center, Harvard University.

Muhiti, Ibrahim, see Yi-bu-la-yin Mu-yi-ti

Myrdal, Jan, 1979, *The Silk Road: A Journey from the High Pamirs and Ili through Sinkiang and Kansu*, trans. Ann Henning, New York: Pantheon.

Narain, A.K., 1990, 'Indo-Europeans in Inner Asia' in Dennis Sinor (ed.), *The Cambridge History of Early Inner Asia*, Cambridge University Press, pp. 151–76.

Newby, Laura, 1999, 'The Chinese Literary Conquest of Xinjiang', *Modern China*, 25, no. 4 (October 1999): 451–74.

———, 2005, *The Empire and the Khanate: A Political History of Qing Relations with Khoqand, c. 1760–1860*, Brill's Inner Asian Library, no. 16, Leiden and Boston, MA: Brill.

Newman, Robert P., 1992, *Owen Lattimore and the 'Loss' of China*, Berkeley and Los Angeles, CA: University of California Press.

Niyaz, Ibrahim, see Yi-bu-la-xin.

Nizam oul-Moulk (Nizâm al-Mulk), 1893, *Siasset Namêh, Traité de Gouvernement composé pour le Sultan Melik-Châh par le Vizir Nizâm oul-Moulk*, trans. Charles Schefer, Paris.

Nyman, Lars Eric, 1977, *Great Britain and Chinese, Russian and Japanese Interests in Sinkiang, 1918–1934*, Stockholm: Esselte Studium.

Olcott, Martha Brill, 1987, *The Kazakhs*, Stanford, CA: Hoover Institution Press.

Olsen, John W., 1992, 'Digging beneath the Silk Road', *Natural History*, 101, no. 9 (September): 30.

Ouyang Lian, 2004, 'A-ke-su shijian shimo' [Account of the Aksu Incident] in Liu Xiaomeng (ed.), *Zhongguo zhiqing koushu shi* [Oral History of the Chinese Educated Youth], Beijing: Zhongguo shehui kexue, pp. 445–529.

Paine, S.C.M., 1996, *Imperial Rivals: China, Russia and their Disputed Frontier*, Armonk, NY: M.E. Sharpe.

Pan Zhiping, 1991, *Zhongya Haohan guo yu Qingdai Xinjiang* [The Central Asian State of Khoqand and Qing Xinjiang], Beijing: Zhongguo shehui kexueyuan.

Papas, M. Alexandre, 2004, 'L'Islam en Asie Centrale: etude d'une grande confrerie soufie du Turkestan Oriental, la Naqshbandiyya Âfâqiyya, Ph.D. dissertation, École des Hautes Études en Sciences Sociales, Paris.

Pelliot, Paul, 1930, 'Notes sur le "Turkestan" de M.W. Barthold', *T'oung Pao*, 27 (1930): 12–56.

People's Republic of China State Council Information Office, 2002, '"East Turkistan" Terrorist Forces Cannot Get Away with Impunity', 21 January 2002 (downloaded from <www.china.org.cn> 25 January).

——, 2003, 'History and Development of Xinjiang', Beijing: New Star Publishers. In 2004 this white paper was also available online from the China Internet Information Center <www.china.org.cn> or PRC embassy websites.

Perdue, Peter, 1996, 'Military Mobilization in Seventeenth- and Eighteenth-Century China, Russia and Mongolia', *Modern Asian Studies*, 30, no. 4 (1996): 757–93.

——, 2004, 'The Qing Empire in Eurasian Time and Space: Lessons from the Galdan Campaigns' in Lynn Struve (ed.), *The Qing Formation in World-Historical Time*, Cambridge, MA: East Asia Research Center, Harvard University, pp. 57–91.

——, 2005, *China Marches West: The Qing Conquest of Central Eurasia*, Cambridge, MA: The Belknap Press of Harvard University Press.

Pratt, Mary Louise, 1992, *Imperial Eyes: Travel Writing and Transculturation*, London and New York: Routledge.

Pritsak, O., 'Von den Karluk zu den Karachaniden', *Zeitschrift der Deutschen Morgenländischen Gesellschaft*, 101 (1951): 270–300.

Prokosch, Frederic, 1937, *The Seven who Fled*, New York and London: Harper & Brother.

Rawski, Evelyn S., 1996, 'Re-envisioning the Qing: The Significance of the Qing Period in Chinese History', *Journal of Asian Studies*, 55, no. 4: 829–50.

Reeves, Richard W., Charles F. Hutchinson and John W. Olsen, 1990, 'Agricultural Development in China's Arid West: Variations in Some Familiar Themes' in T.C. Tso (ed.), *Agricultural Reform and Development in China: Achievements, Current Status, and Future Outlook*, Beltsville, MD: Ideals, pp. 339–50.

Richards, Thomas, 1993, *The Imperial Archive: Knowledge and the Fantasy of Empire*, London and New York: Verso.

Roberts, Sean R., 1998, 'Negotiating Locality, Islam, and National Culture in a Changing Borderlands: The Revival of the *Mäshräp* Ritual among Young Uighur Men in the Ili Valley', *Central Asian Survey*, 17, no. 4 (1998): 673–99.

——, 2003, 'Uyghur Neighborhoods and Nationalisms in the Former Sino-Soviet Borderland: An Historical Ethnography of a Stateless Nation on the Margins of Modernity', Ph.D. dissertation, University of Southern California.

——, 2004, 'A "Land of Borderlands": Implications of Xinjiang's Transborder Interactions' in S. Frederick Starr (ed.), *Xinjiang: China's Muslim Borderland*, Armonk, NY and London: M.E. Sharpe, pp. 216–37.

Rossabi, Morris, 1972, 'Ming China and Turfan, 1406–1517', *Central Asiatic Journal*, 16, no. 3: 206–25.

——, 1975, *China and Inner Asia: From 1368 to the Present Day*, London: Thames and Hudson.

——, 1990, 'The "Decline" of the Central Asian Caravan Trade' in James Tracy (ed.), *The Rise of Merchant Empires*, Cambridge University Press, pp. 351–70.

Rowe, William T., 2001, *Saving the World: Chen Hongmou and Elite Consciousness in Eighteenth-Century China*, Stanford University Press.

Rowland, Benjamin, Jr., 1964–5, 'Art along the Silk Roads: A Reappraisal of Central Asian Art', *Harvard Journal of Asiatic Studies*, 25 (1964–5).

Roy, Olivier, 2000, *The New Central Asia: The Creation of Nations*, London: I.B. Tauris.

Rudelson, Justin Jon, 1997, *Oasis Identities: Uyghur Nationalism along China's Silk Road*, New York: Columbia University Press.

—— and William Jankowiak, 2004, 'Acculturation and Resistance: Xinjiang Identities in Flux' in S. Frederick Starr (ed.), *Xinjiang: China's Muslim Borderland*, Armonk, NY: M.E. Sharpe.

Sadri, Roostam, 1984, 'The Islamic Republic of Eastern Turkestan: A Commemorative Review', *Journal (Institute of Muslim Minority Affairs)*, 5, no. 2 (July 1984): 294–319.

Saguchi Tôru, 1963, *18–19 saeki Higashi Torukisutan shakai shi kenkyû* [Researches on the History of Eighteenth- to Nineteenth-Century Eastern Turkestan Society], Tokyo: Yoshikawa Kôbunkan.

Said, Edward W., 1978, *Orientalism*, New York: Pantheon.

Samolin, William, 1964, *East Turkestan to the Twelfth Century*, The Hague: Mouton.

Sautman, Barry, 2000, 'Is Xinjiang an Internal Colony?', *Inner Asia*, 2, no. 2: 239–71.

Schurr, Theodore G., 2001, 'Tracking Genes across the Globe', review of Luigi Luca Cavalli-Sforza, 2000, *Genes, Peoples and Languages*, New York: North Point Press, in *American Scientist Online* (January–February 2001), via <http://www.americanscientist.org> (accessed 2 December 2004).

Schuyler, Eugene, 1877, *Turkistan: Notes of a Journey in Russian Turkistan, Khokand, Bukhara, and Kuldja*, New York: Scribners.

Schwarz, Henry G., 1976, 'The Khwâjas of Eastern Turkestan', *Central Asiatic Journal*, 20, no.4: 266–96.

——, 1992, *An Uyghur-English Dictionary*, Bellingham, WA: Center for East Asian Studies, Western Washington University.

Seth, Vikram, 1983, *From Heaven Lake: Travels through Sinkiang and Tibet*, New York: Vintage Books.

Seyit, Mirähmät, Yalqun Rozi and Ablikim Zordun, 1997, *Mämtili äpändi* [Mr Mämtili], Urumchi: Shinjang Uniwersiteti näshriyati (Xinjiang Daxue chubanshe).

Seymour, James D., 2000, 'Xinjiang's Production and Construction Corps, and the Sinification of Eastern Turkestan', *Inner Asia*, 2, no. 2: 171–93.

—— and Richard Anderson, 1998, *New Ghosts, Old Ghosts: Prisons and Labor Reform Camps in China*, Armonk, NY and London: M.E. Sharpe.

Shapiro, Judith, 2001, *Mao's War against Nature: Politics and the Environment in Revolutionary China*, Cambridge University Press.

Shaw, R.B., 1897, 'The History of the Khojas of Eastern-Turkestan, summarised from the Tazkira-i-khwajagan of Muhammad Sadiq Kashghari', ed. N. Elias, supplement to the *Journal of the Asiatic Society of Bengal*, LXVI, part 1.

Shaw, Robert, 1871, *Visits to High Tartary, Yarkand and Kashgar*, London: John Murray.

Shichor, Yitzhak, 2004, 'The Great Wall of Steel: Military and Strategy in Xinjiang' in S. Frederick Starr (ed.), *Xinjiang: China's Muslim Borderland*, Armonk, NY and London: M.E. Sharpe, pp. 120–60.

Shimazaki Akira, 'On Pei-t'ing (Bisbaliq) and K'o-han Fu-t'u-ch'eng', *Memoirs of the Research Department of the Toyo Bunko*, 32 (1974): 99–114.

Shinmen Yasushi, 1990, 'Shinkyô musurimyu hanran (1931–34 nen) to himitsu soshiki' [The 1931–34 Muslim Rebellion in Xinjiang and Secret Organizations], *Shigaku Zasshi*, 99, no. 12 (December 1990): 1–42.

——, 1994, '"Higashi Torukisutan kyôwakoku" (1933–34 nen) ni kansuru ichi kôsatsu' [An Inquiry into the Eastern Turkestan Republic of 1933–34], *Ajia-Afurika gengo bunka kenkyû*, nos 46–7 (30th anniversary commemorative no. 1), Tokyo gaigokugo daigaku Ajia-Afurika gengo bunka kenkyujo.

Silay, Kemal, 1996, *An Anthology of Turkish Literature*, Indiana University Turkish Studies 15, Bloomington, IN: University of Indiana Press.

Sims-Williams, Nicholas, 1992, 'Sogdian and Turkish Christians in the Turfan and Tun-Huang Manuscripts' in Alfredo Cadonna (ed.), *Turfan and Tun-Huang, The Texts: Encounter of Civilizations on the Silk Route*, Firenze: Leo S. Olschki Editore.

Sinor, Dennis (ed.), 1990, *The Cambridge History of Early Inner Asia*, Cambridge University Press.

——, 1990, 'The Establishment and Dissolution of the Türk Empire' in Dennis Sinor (ed.), *The Cambridge History of Early Inner Asia*, Cambridge University Press, pp. 285–316.

Skrine, C.P., 1926, *Chinese Central Asia*, London: Methuen.

—— and Pamela Nightingale, 1987, *Macartney at Kashgar: New Light on British, Chinese, and Russian Activities in Sinkiang, 1890–1918*, Oxford University Press.

Smith, Joanne, 2000, 'Four Generations of Uyghurs: The Shift towards Ethno-political Ideologies among Xinjiang's Youth', *Inner Asia*, 2 (2000): 195–224.

——, 2003, 'Barren Chickens, Stray Dogs, Fake Immortals and Thieves: Coloniser and Collaborator in Popular Uyghur Song and the Quest for National Unity', paper delivered at the annual meeting of the Association for Asian Studies, New York.

Smithsonian Folkways, 2002, *The Silk Road: a Musical Caravan*, two-CD set, Washington, DC: Smithsonian Folkways.

Songshi [History of the Song], 1975, ed. Tuotuo, reprint edition, Taipei: Hongshi chubanshe.

Soucek, Svat, 2000, *A History of Inner Asia*, Cambridge University Press.

Steensgaard, Niels, 1975, *The Asian Trade Revolution of the 17th Century: The East India Companies and the Decline of the Caravan Trade*, University of Chicago Press.

Stein, Sir M. Aurel, 1904, *Sand-buried Ruins of Khotan: Personal Narrative of a Journey of Archaeological and Geographical Exploration in Chinese Turkestan*, London: Hurst and Blackett.

——, 1933, *On Ancient Central-Asian Tracks: Brief Narrative of Three Expeditions in Innermost Asia and North-western China*, London: Macmillan.

——, 1980 [1928], *Innermost Asia: Detailed Report of Explorations in Central Asia, Kan-su and Eastern Iran*, 4 vols, reprint edition, New Delhi: Cosmo [1928, Oxford: Clarendon Press].

——, 1987 [1912], *Ruins of Desert Cathay*, 2 vols, reprint edition, New York: Dover Publications.

Stevens, Stuart, 1988, *Night Train to Turkistan: Modern Adventures along China's Ancient Silk Road*, New York: Atlantic Monthly.

Stratman, Deborah, 2004, *Kings of the Sky*, 68 min., colour and b&w, digital video, Pythagoras Films (<www.pythagorasfilm.com>).

Su Beihai and Huang Jianhua, 1993, *Hami, Tulufan Weiwuer wang lishi* [History of the Uyghur Kings of Hami and Turfan], Urumchi: Xinjiang Daxue chubanshe.

Sun Yat-sen, 1933, *Sun Yat-sen, his Political and Social Ideals: A Sourcebook*, ed. Leonard Shihlien Hsu, Los Angeles, CA: University of Southern California Press.

Tan Qixiang (ed.), 1982–7, *Zhongguo lishi dituji* [The Historical Atlas of China], vols 1–8, Shanghai: Ditu chubanshe.

Tang Yongcai (ed.), 1994, *Ma Zhongying zai Xinjiang* [Ma Zhongying in Xinjiang], *Xinjiang wenshi ziliao*, no. 26, Urumchi: Xinjiang renmin chubanshe.

Tao Mo, 1987 [1914], *Tao qinsu gong zouyi* [Collected Memorials of Tao Mo], 1914, reprint edition, Wu Fengpei (ed.), Beijing: quanguo tushuguan wenxian suowei fuzhi zhongxin.

Teichman, Eric, 1937, *Journey to Turkestan*, London: Holder and Stoughton. Reprinted with introduction by Peter Hopkirk, 1988, Hong Kong, Oxford and New York: Oxford University Press.

Tekin, Ibrahim Alip (ed.), 2000, *Hüsäyniyä rohi: Täklimakandiki oyghinish* [The Husayni Spirit: Awakening of the Taklamakan], Urumchi: Shinjang xälq näshriyati (Xinjiang renmin chubanshe).

Togan, Isenbike, 1998, 'Inner Asian Muslim Merchants at the Closure of the Silk Routes in the Seventeenth Century' in Vadime Elisseeff (ed.), *The Silk Roads: Highways of Culture and Commerce*, Paris: Unesco.

Thomas, F.W., 1930, 'Tibetan Documents Concerning Chinese Turkistan', *Journal of the Royal Asiatic Society* (1930): 47–97; 251–300.

Thompson, L.G., 1995, 'Ice Core Evidence from Peru and China' in Ramond S. Bradley and Philip D. Jones (eds), *Climate Since A.D. 1500*, revised edition, London and New York: Routledge, pp. 517–48.

Toops, Stanley W., 2004, 'The Demography of Xinjiang' in S. Frederick Starr (ed.), *Xinjiang: China's Muslim Borderland*, Armonk, NY and London: M.E. Sharpe, pp. 241–65.

Trebinjac, Sabine, 1990, 'Musique ouigoure de Chine: de l'authenticité à la folklorisation' in *l'Asie centrale et ses voisins: influences réciproques* (Actes du colloque escas III), Paris: INALCO; Institut des langues et civilisations orientales, pp. 227–38.

——, 2000, *Le pouvoir en chantant, l'art de fabriquer une musique chinoise*, vol. 1, Nanterre: Société d'ethnologie.

Tsai, Tsung-te, 1998, 'The Music and Tradition of Qumul Muqam in Chinese Turkestan', Ph.D. dissertation, University of Maryland.

Tursun, Nabijan, 2002, 'Chinese Control over Xinjiang in Theoretical and Comparative Perspective', paper contributed to the preparation of Frederic Starr (ed.), *Xinjiang: China's Muslim Borderland*, Armonk, NY and London: M.E. Sharpe. While this version was not published, much material from it was included in a chapter written with James A. Millward for the same volume.

Twitchett, Denis (ed.), 1979, *The Cambridge History of China*, vol. 3, *Sui and T'ang China, 589–906, part 1*, Cambridge University Press.

Tyler, Christian, 2004, *Wild West China: The Taming of Xinjiang*, Piscataway, NJ: Rutgers University Press.

Valikhanov, Chokan Chingisovich, 1961, *Sobranie Sochinenii* [Collected Works], ed. A. Kh. Margulan, 5 vols, Alma Ata: Izd-vo Akademii nauk Kazakhskoi SSSR.

Veselovskii, Nikolai Ivanovich, 1898, 'Badaulet Iakub-bek Atalyk kashgarskii', *Zapiski Vostochnogo otdeleniia Imperatorskogo Russkogo arkheologicheskogo obshchestva* [Letters of the Eastern Department of the Imperial Russian Archeological Society], 11.

Waley, Arthur, 1931, *The Travels of an Alchemist, The Journey of the Taoist Ch'ang-ch'un from China to Hindukush at the Summons of Chingiz Khan, Recorded by his Disciple Li Chih-ch'ang*, tr. with an introduction by Arthur Waley, London: Routledge.

Waley-Cohen, Joanna, 1991, *Exile in Mid-Qing China: Banishment to Xinjiang, 1758–1820*, New Haven, CT: Yale University Press.

——, 1996, 'Commemorating War in Eighteenth-Century China', *Modern Asian Studies*, 30: 869–99.

Wang Binghua, 1996, 'A Preliminary Analysis of the Archaeological Cultures of the Bronze Age in the Region of Xinjiang' in F. Hiebert and Nicola Di Cosmo (eds), *Between Lapis and Jade: Ancient Cultures of Central Asia*, special issue of *Anthropology and Archaeology of Eurasia*, 34, no. 4 (spring 1996): 67–86.

Wang, David D., 1999, *Under the Soviet Shadow: The Yining Incident, Ethnic Conflicts and International Rivalry in Xinjiang, 1944–1949*, Hong Kong: The Chinese University Press.

Wang Jianping, n.d., 'Islam in Kashgar in the 1950s', unpublished manuscript.

Wang Lequan, 1999, 'Secretary Wang Lequan's Address to the Khotan District Stability Work Conference' (Wang Lequan shuji zai Hetian diqu wending gongzuo huiyishang de jianghua), *c.* 27 August 1999, circulated outside China via internet.

Wang Shuanqian (ed.), 2003, *Huihuang Xinjiang* [Splendid Xinjiang], Urumchi: Xinjiang renmin chubanshe.

Wang Xilong, 1990, *Qingdai Xibei tuntian yanjiu* [Research on Agricultural Reclamation in the Western Regions in the Qing Dynasty], Lanzhou: Lanzhou Daxue chubanshe.

Watanabe, Hiroshi, 1975, 'An Index of Embassies and Tribute Missions from Islamic Countries to Ming China (1368–1466) as Recorded in the Ming *Shih-lu* Classified According to Geographic Area', *The Memoirs of the Toyo Bunko*, 33: 285–347.

Wei Liangtao, 1994, *Yeerqiang hanguo shigang* [Historical Outline of the Yarkand Khanate], Bianjiang shidi congshu, Harbin: Heilongjiang jiaoyu chubanshe.

Wei Yuan, 1965 [1842], *Sheng wu ji* [Record of Imperial Military Achievements], reprint edition, Jindai Zhongguo shiliao congkan, vol. 102, Taipei: Wenhai.

Wessels, C., 1924, *Early Jesuit Travellers in Central Asia, 1603–1721*, The Hague: Martinus Nijhoff.

White, Lynn T. III, 1979, 'The Road to Urumchi: Approved Institutions in Search of Attainable Goals during Pre-1968 Rustication from Shanghai', *The China Quarterly*, no. 79 (September): 481–510.

Whitfield, Susan, 1999, *Life Along the Silk Road*, Berkeley, CA: University of California Press.

Whiting, Allen S. and Sheng Shih-ts'ai, 1958, *Sinkiang: Pawn or Pivot?*, East Lansing, MI: Michigan State University Press.

Wiemer, Calla, 2004, 'The Economy of Xinjiang' in S. Frederick Starr (ed.), *Xinjiang: China's Muslim Borderland*, Armonk, NY and London: M.E. Sharpe, pp. 163–89.

Wiens, Harold J., 1966, 'Cultivation Development and Expansion in China's Colonial Realm in Central Asia', *Journal of Asian Studies*, 26, no. 1 (November): 67–88.

——, 1969, 'Change in the Ethnography and Land Use of the Ili Valley and Region, Chinese Turkestan', *Annals of the Association of American Geographers*, 59, no. 4 (December 1969): 753–75.

Wills, John E., Jr., 1988, 'Tribute, Defensiveness, and Dependency: Uses and Limits of Some Basic Ideas about Mid-Ch'ing Foreign Relations', *American Neptune*, 48: 225–9.

——, 1995, 'How We Got Obsessed with the "Tribute System" and Why It's Time to Get Over It', paper presented at the panel 'Rethinking Tribute: Concept and Practice', Annual Meeting of the Association for Asian Studies, April 1995.

Wittfogel, Karl A. and Feng Chia-sheng, 1949, 'Appendix V: Qarâ-Khitâi' in *History of Chinese Society: Liao (907–1125)*, transactions of the American Philosophical Society, new series, vol. 36, Philadelphia, PA: American Philosophical Society.

Wood, Francis, 2002, *The Silk Road: Two Thousand Years in the Heart of Asia*, Berkeley and Los Angeles, CA: University of California Press.

Wu, Aitchen (Wu Aizhen), 1984 [1940], *Turkestan Tumult*, reprint edition, Hong Kong: Oxford University Press [1940, London: Methuen].

Wulumuqi Shizhi [Gazetteer of Urumchi], 1994, ed. Wulumuqi dangshi difangzhi bianzuan weiyuanhui, Urumchi: Xinjiang renmin chubanshe.

Xie Bin, 1990 [1925], *Xinjiang youji* [Record of Xinjiang Travels], reprint in *Minguo congshu* (Republican Period collectanea), 2 *bian*, no. 87 (*lishi, dili lei*), Shanghai: Shanghai shudian.

Xie Jiu, 2003, 'Zhongguo sanhao fuhao Sun Guangxin de caifu zhenxiang' [A True Look at the Wealth of China's Third Richest Person, Sun Guangxin], *Xin Caijing*, 2 December 2003, via Sina *Caijing congheng* at <http://finance.sina.com.cn> (accessed 13 April 2005).

Xinjiang shehui kexueyuan lishi yanjiushu (Historical Research Institute, Xinjiang Academy of Social Sciences) (ed.), 1980–7, *Xinjiang jianshi* [Concise History of Xinjiang], 3 vols, Urumchi: Xinjiang renmin chubanshe.

Xinjiang shehui kexueyuan minzu yanjiusuo (Nationalities Research Institute, Xinjiang Academy of Social Sciences) (ed.), 1980–7, *Xinjiang jianshi* [Concise History of Xinjiang], 3 vols, Urumchi: Xinjiang renmin chubanshe.

Xue Zongzheng, Ma Guorong, Tian Weijiang (eds), 1997, *Zhongguo Xinjiang gudai shehui shenghuo shi* [Social History of Ancient Xinjiang], Urumchi: Xinjiang renmin chubanshe.

Ya-li-kun Ta-shi and Tashpolat Tiyip, 2001, 'Liyong zhibei gaidu tuxiang dui lüzhou huanjing zhiliang bianhua de pingjia yanjiu' [Research to Evaluate Changes in Quality of the Oasis Environment Based on Vegetative Cover Imagery] in Xiong Heigang (ed.), *Xinjiang ziyuan huanjing yu kechixu fazhan* [Resources Environment and Sustainable Development in Xinjiang], Urumchi: Xinjiang daxue chubanshe, pp. 177–9.

Yamamoto Tatsuro and Dohi Yoshikazu (eds), 1984–5, *Tun-huang and Turfan Documents Concerning Social and Economic History*, part II: Census Registers, in two volumes A (notes and transcriptions) and B (photo-reproduced texts), Tokyo: Tôyô Bunko.

Yan Shaoda, 1989, 'Lin Zexu he Xinjiang de shuili yu tuntian shiye' [Lin Zexu and Xinjiang Irrigation and Reclamation Efforts] in Gu Bao (ed.), *Lin Zexu zai Xinjiang* [Lin Zexu in Xinjiang], Urumchi: Xinjiang renmin chubanshe, pp. 182–93.

Yang Faren, Li Ze and Dong Sheng (eds), 1994, *Fanyisilanzhuyi, fantujuezhuyi yanjiu* [Research on Pan-Islamism and Pan-Turkism], Urumchi: Xinjiang shehui kexueyuan.

Yang Jianxin (ed.), 1987, *Gu xi xing ji xuanzhu* [Records of Ancient Western Travels, Excerpted and Annotated], Ningxia: Ningxia renmin chubanshe.

Yang, Richard, 1961, 'Sinkiang under the Administration of Yang Tseng-hsin, 1911–1928', *Central Asiatic Journal*, 6, no. 4: 270–316.

Yao Tandong, Yafeng Shi and L.G. Thompson, 1997, 'High Resolution Record of Paleoclimate since the Little Ice Age from the Tibetan Ice Cores', *Quaternary International*, 37 (1997): 19–23.

Yee, Herbert S., 2003, 'Ethnic Relations in Xinjiang: A Survey of Uygur-Han Relations in Urumqi', *Journal of Contemporary China*, 12, no. 36 (August): 431–52.

Yi-bu-la-xin Ni-ya-zi, 1985, 'Atushi xian Yikeshake xiang kaiban jindai xinxue jiaoyu de qingkuang' [Circumstances Surrounding the Institution of Modern New Education in Yikeshake Village, Artush County], *Xin-*

jiang wenshi ziliao xuanji, 13: 80–7, Chinese edition, Urumchi: Xinjiang renmin chubanshe.

Yi-bu-la-yin Mu-yi-ti, 1985, 'Huiyi qimeng yundong de xianquzhe, Mai-he-su-ti Mu-yi-ti' [Remembering a Leader in the Enlightenment Movement, Maqsud Muhiti], *Xinjiang wenshi ziliao xuanji*, 13: 91–100, Chinese edition, Urumchi: Xinjiang renmin chubanshe.

Yu Taishan (ed.), 1996, *Xiyu tongshi* [Survey History of the Western Regions], Zhengzhou: Zhengzhou guji chubanshe.

Yü Ying-shih, 1986, 'Han Foreign Relations' in Denis Twitchett and John K. Fairbank (eds), *The Cambridge History of China*, vol. 1, *The Ch'in and Han Empires, 221 BC—AD 220*, Cambridge University Press, pp. 377–462.

Yuan Dahua (ed.) with Wang Shunan and Wang Xuezeng, 1992 [1910], *Xinjiang tu zhi* [Xinjiang Gazetteer], reprint from 1923 Dongfang xuehui edition, Shanghai: Shanghai guji chubanshe.

Yuan Xin, 1994, 'Weiwuer renkou wenti zonghe yanjiu' [General Research on Problems of Uyghur Population], *Xinjiang daxue xuebao, zhexue shehui kexue ban* [Xinjiang University Bulletin, Philosophy and Social Sciences Edition], 22 (1994), no. 4: 1–19.

Yule, Henry, *Cathay and the Way Thither*, 1913–4, revised edition by Henri Cordier, 4 vols, London: John Murray.

Yûsuf Khâss Hâjib, 1983 [1069], *Wisdom of Royal Glory* (Kutadgu Bilig): *A Turko-Islamic Mirror for Princes*, trans. Robert Dankoff, University of Chicago Press.

Zarcone, Thierry, 1995, 'Sufism from Central Asia among the Tibetans in the 16–17th Centuries', *The Tibet Journal* (Dharamsala, India), 20, no. 3 (1995): 96–114.

——, 1996, 'Soufis d'Asie centrale au Tibet aux XVIe et XVIIe siècles', *Cahiers d'Asie Centrale*, special issue on 'Inde-Asie centrale: Routes du commerce et des idées', Aix-en-Provence: Edisud, 1–2 (1996): 325–44.

Zeng Wenwu, 1986 [1936], *Zhongguo jingying Xiyu shi* [History of China's Management of the Western Regions], reprint edition, Urumchi: Xinjiang Weiwu'er zizhiqu zongbian shi.

Zhang Dajun, 1980, *Xinjiang fengbao qishinian* [70 Years of Turmoil in Xinjiang], 12 vols, Taipei: Lanxi chubanshe.

Zhang Jianjiang, 2001, 'Xinjiang nongye he nongcun jinjgi jiegou tiaozheng de silu' [Thinking about the Adjustment of the Structure of Xinjiang's Agriculture and Village Economy] in Lu Zongyi and Li Zhouwei (eds),

Xibu da kaifa yu Xinjiang jingji fazhan zhanlüe [Great Development of the West and Xinjiang's Economic Development Strategy], Urumchi: Xinjiang renmin chubanshe, pp. 360–7.

Zhang Yuxi, 1994, 'Xinjiang jiefang yilai fandui minzu fenliezhuyi de douzheng ji qi lishi jingyanti' in Yang Faren *et al.* (eds), *Fanyisilanzhuyi, fantujuezhuyi yanjiu* [Research on Pan-Islamism and Pan-Turkism], Urumchi: Xinjiang shehui kexueyuan, pp. 331–63. Published in English as Zhang Yumo [*sic*], 'Anti-separatism Struggle and its Historical Lessons since the Liberation of Xinjiang', English translation and web-publishing by Uyghur America Association at <www.taklamakan.org/erkin/Chinese/transl.htr>.

Zhao Songqiao and Xia Xuncheng, 1984, 'Evolution of the Lop Desert and the Lop Nur', *Geographical Journal*, 150: 311–21.

Zhao Yuzheng, 1991, *Xinjiang tunken* [Xinjiang Land Reclamation], Urumchi: Xinjiang renmin chubanshe.

Zhong Wei, Shu Qiang and Xiong Heigang, 2001, 'Ta-li-mu pendi nanyuan Niya peimian de baofen zuhe ji qi dui lishi shiqi huanjing yanhua de fanying' [Sporo-Pollen Assemblage of a Section from Niya, on the Southern Margin of the Tarim Basin, and What it Reflects Regarding Environmental Change in the Historical Period] in Xiong Heigang (ed.), *Xinjiang ziyuan huanjing yu kechixu fazhan* [Resources Environment and Sustainable Development in Xinjiang], Urumchi: Xinjiang daxue chubanshe, pp. 1–6.

Zhonggong Xinjiang Weiwuer zizhiqu weiyuanhui dangshi yanjiushi [Party Research Department of the Xinjiang Uyghur Autonomous Region Branch Committee of the Chinese Communist Party] (ed.), 2002, *Contemporary Xinjiang's Changeable Situation*, Urumchi: Xinjiang renmin chubanshe.

Zhonggong zhongyang, 1996, 'Guanyu weihu Xinjiang wending de huiyi jiyao, zhongyang zhengzhiju weiyuan hui' [Records of the Meeting of the Standing Committee of the Political Bureau of the CCP: Regarding the Protection of Xinjiang's Stability], Zhonggong zhongyang (1996) 7 hao wenjian [Chinese Communist Party Central Committee, 1996, Document No. 7], 19 March 1996.

Zhou Hongfei, Song Yudong and Hu Shunjun, 1999, 'Irrigated Agriculture and Sustainable Water Management Strategies in the Tarim Basin', proceedings of the workshop 'New Approaches to Water Management in Central Asia', sponsored by United Nations University and the International Center for Agricultural Research in the Dry Areas, Aleppo.

Zhou Jingbao, 1987, *Sichou zhi lu de yinyue wenhua* [Musical Culture of the Silk Road], Urumchi: Xinjiang renmin chubanshe.

Zhu Peimin, 2000, *Ershi shiji Xinjiang shi yanjiu* [Research on Xinjiang's 20th-Century History], Urumchi: Xinjiang renmen chubanshe.

Zhu Yingrong and Han Xiang, 1990, *Qiuci shiku* [The Qizil Grottos], Urumchi: Xinjiang daxue chubanshe.

Zubok, Vladislav M. (ed.), 2001, 'The Khrushchev-Mao Conversations 31 July–3 August 1958 and 2 October 1959', online archive of the Cold War International History Project, Woodrow Wilson International Center For Scholars, CWIHP Dossier No. 2, (downloaded 5 March 2002, from <http://cwihp.si.edu/files/zubok-mao.htm>).

Zuo Zongtang, 1968 [1888–97], *Zuo wen xiang gong quanji* [Complete Collected Works of Zuo Zongtang], Taipei: Wenhai chubanshe.

Index